CLOWNS TO THE LEFT OF ME, JOKERS TO THE RIGHT

ALSO BY MICHAEL A. SMERCONISH

Flying Blind: How Political Correctness Continues to Compromise Airline Safety Post 9/11 (2004)

Muzzled: From T-ball to Terrorism—True Stories That Should Be Fiction (2007)

Murdered by Mumia: A Life Sentence of Loss, Pain, and Injustice, co-authored with Maureen Faulkner (2007)

Instinct: The Man Who Stopped the 20th Hijacker, with Kurt A. Schreyer (2009)

Morning Drive: Things I Wish I Knew before I Started Talking (2009)

Talk: A Novel (2014)

MICHAEL A. SMERCONISH

With a Foreword by **DAVID AXELROD**

TEMPLE UNIVERSITY PRESS
Philadelphia | *Rome* | *Tokyo*

CLOWNS

TO THE LEFT OF ME,

JOKERS

TO THE RIGHT

AMERICAN LIFE IN COLUMNS

TEMPLE UNIVERSITY PRESS
Philadelphia, Pennsylvania 19122
www.temple.edu/tempress

Text design by Kate Nichols

Jacket front and back-flap/title-page photographs: *Philadelphia Daily News,*
Jessica Griffin, staff photographer

Library of Congress Cataloging-in-Publication Data

Names: Smerconish, Michael A., author. | Axelrod, David, 1955– writer of
   foreword.
Title: Clowns to the left of me, jokers to the right : American life in
   columns / Michael A. Smerconish ; with a foreword by David Axelrod.
Description: Philadelphia : Temple University Press, 2018. | Collection of
   the author's columns from the Philadelphia Daily News and Sunday
   Philadelphia Inquirer, 2002–2016.
Identifiers: LCCN 2017051755 (print) | LCCN 2018013014 (ebook) |
   ISBN 9781439916377 (E-book) | ISBN 9781439916353 (cloth : alk. paper)
Classification: LCC PN4874.S54 (ebook) | LCC PN4874.S54 A25 2018 (print) |
   DDC 070.4/4—dc23
LC record available at https://lccn.loc.gov/2017051755

♾ The paper used in this publication meets the requirements of the American
National Standard for Information Sciences—Permanence of Paper for Printed
Library Materials, ANSI Z39.48-1992

Printed in the United States of America

9 8 7 6 5 4 3 2

THE CHILDREN'S CRISIS
TREATMENT CENTER

ONE HUNDRED PERCENT of the author's proceeds from the sale of this book will benefit the Children's Crisis Treatment Center (CCTC), a private, nonprofit agency that provides behavioral health services to children and their families. In 1971, CCTC began at the Franklin Institute in Philadelphia as a small but pioneering federally funded program focused on addressing the needs of young children who had experienced trauma. Since then, CCTC has increasingly diversified and expanded its programs and services targeting the needs of our most vulnerable youth. For over 40 years, CCTC has developed and implemented innovative ways of helping children as young as 18 months old and their families cope with obstacles that interfere with their emotional, social, and cognitive growth. CCTC offers a wide array of services and programs that are provided at the center as well as in the home, community, and schools. Most recently, CCTC expanded its services into Montgomery County, Pennsylvania. CCTC's approach is based on the belief that despite tremendous challenges, children heal from psychological injuries. Through partnerships with families, schools, and communities, CCTC creates the contexts in which this healing may occur.

CCTC serves more than 3,000 children and their families annually. CCTC's success and reputation for excellence have gained the center recognition for expertise in the areas of trauma, school-based services, and early childhood treatment and reflect CCTC's leadership role in the children's mental health services community. Consider "James," a 6-year-old boy from North Philadelphia who came to CCTC when he was 3½ years old after being expelled from preschool. James, who was witnessing domestic violence at home, was admitted into CCTC's Therapeutic Nursery and Trauma Services programs, where staff worked with him and his parents, who are now separated. Today James is attending second grade at his local elementary school, where his teachers report that he is thriving both academically and socially. James's mother is also actively engaged in CCTC's parenting programs.

The author's wife, Lavinia, serves on CCTC's Board of Trustees.

You can learn more at www.cctckids.org.

CONTENTS

2007–2011

2011–2016

2017

FOREWORD

I N AN ERA OF GRINDING DISCORD and withering partisanship, Michael Smerconish offers blessed relief. As the varied works in this collection reveal, Michael can be counted on for consistently informed, insightful commentary and compelling storytelling, whether the topic is politics, personalities, or the ups and downs of sports teams in his beloved Philadelphia.

He plays no favorites and spares little in his contempt for hypocrisy or flouting of facts, for the trampling of people or the fundamental tenets that underpin our democracy. His is the voice of the grizzled idealist, knowledgeable of the real world but unwilling to relinquish the essential belief that we can do better.

For much of 2016, I sat beside Michael on a CNN panel of analysts as we chewed over what was perhaps the most extraordinary—and disturbing—campaign of our times. What I learned is that Michael always resists the knee-jerk reactions so common to instant analysis. Instead, he reaches for the deeper meaning of events, offering observations that defy partisanship and the vapid "who's up and who's down" obsession that too often has gripped the coverage of our elections and government. As a panelist, rather than purveying conventional wisdom, Michael often invoked the experiences of his neighbors in Pennsylvania to help illuminate the tectonic shifts in our politics. When he spoke, I sat up in my chair and listened.

Like Teddy Roosevelt, I admire those men (and women) who have actually been "in the arena." Michael came to journalism from politics, his passion having been fired by Ronald Reagan in the early 1980s. He has run for office and run campaigns, including mayors' races in the City of Brotherly Love (an ironic phrase to anyone who has experienced the brawling politics of Philadelphia). Michael also has served in government, an appointee of the first President Bush. He understands how it works for the people it is meant to serve—and when and why it doesn't. So while he writes in these pages about the journeys of others, Michael's rich and thoughtful insights derive from his own. Whether chatting with Fidel Castro, a family farmer in rural Pennsylvania, or a Philadelphia ward leader, he tells their stories with an equal measure of wit and wisdom. He is a champion to those unsung heroes who deserve one, and he hesitates not one whit to take the haughty down a peg.

This collection of columns from the *Philadelphia Daily News* and Sunday *Philadelphia Inquirer*—with the new Afterwords he has penned—reflects all of that. Here you will find a rich sampling of more than a decade and a half of pieces in which he tackled big stories in a refreshing way and brought obscure but important stories to light.

As millions who have read his work and listened to his daily commentary on radio and TV know, Michael Smerconish always has something worthwhile to say.

Knowing Michael and his investment in his community, I was not surprised to learn that any and all of his proceeds from this book will go to the Children's Crisis Treatment Center in Philadelphia, which passionately serves the emotional needs of children and families at risk beginning in early childhood and where his wife, Lavinia, is a board member. Congratulations to them both for their important work.

—DAVID AXELROD
*Director, Institute of Politics at the University of Chicago
and former senior adviser to President Barack Obama*

INTRODUCTION

FIFTEEN YEARS.

That's how long I have been writing weekly columns for the *Philadelphia Daily News* and the *Philadelphia Inquirer*. By my count, between 2001 and 2016, I authored 1,047 columns ranging in subject matter from the hunt for Osama bin Laden to exploring what the color of your Christmas lights (white versus colored) says about you.

I joined the *Daily News* two months after 9/11, at the invitation of then-editor Zack Stalberg. I was practicing law full time while also hosting a daily radio program in what was the early part of my broadcast career. While there was already a lot on my plate—two careers, four kids, and an equal number of dogs—I viewed the invitation as an additional opportunity to weigh in weekly, with 600–800 words, from a great platform and to do something enjoyable. That Zack is a terrific guy was also part of the draw—he's smart, funny, and centered. I remember my excitement when the *Daily News* announced my association with a series of display ads, which I clipped and still have: "Would You Like That Smerconishized?"; "Gaze on in Utter Smerconishment"; "We're Starting to Look a Little Smerconish"; and "Smerconish . . . The Sound of Opinions Hitting Paper."

I hope that readers of this compilation will find it interesting to note the changes evident in my thinking over fifteen years of American history. There's no doubt that my worldview has shifted in the time period that I've been chronicling local, state, and national events. And while many people's opinions change over time, in my case, these columns provide a weekly timeline capable of being charted. Readers can (and I am sure will) decide whether those changes in my thinking have been for better or worse.

I've enjoyed looking back. In my first piece as a columnist for the *Daily News*, published on November 13, 2001, I made the case for Rudy Giuliani heading the Department of Homeland Security. And for the next decade, I published a column every Thursday. Then, in 2007, I also began writing for the Sunday edition of the *Philadelphia Inquirer*. For the next few years, I was in the unique position of writing for both newspapers. When that workload finally proved too much, in 2011, I became exclusive to the Sunday *Inquirer*. All told, I wrote a total of 449 columns for the *Daily News* and, through the end of 2016, wrote 598 columns for the *Inquirer*. Some stand the test of time and I am eager to republish them here. A few I wish I'd never written.

A couple of notes on how the book was put together: As I read through the archives, I divided the columns into the four broad subject categories of politics, profiles, life, and miscellaneous, in order to ensure that the 100 or so columns selected would equitably cover a variety of topics. The next question was how to organize the columns, and the way that made the most sense was to run them chronologically with a couple of key markers of change. So, sandwiched between the introductory and concluding sections, the main body of the text consists of 2002–2007, which covers my time with just the *Daily News*; 2007–2011, which covers my time writing for the *Daily News* and *Inquirer* simultaneously; and 2011–2016, which covers my time writing for just the Sunday *Inquirer*.

Interestingly, the periods that mark my evolution as a Philadelphia columnist reflect periods of change in American culture, with 2002–2007 comprising the post-9/11 George W. Bush years, 2007–2011 covering Barack Obama's ascension, and 2011–2016 spanning the latter half of the Obama era and the rise of Donald Trump.

For the most part, every column appears here exactly as it appeared in the newspaper, including the original headlines (which, by the way, were all written by editors, not by me). The handful of minor changes made throughout in spelling and punctuation were done to promote clarity and consistency but never to change meaning (though I was tempted!).

I've written an Afterword for each column to provide updates on facts and feelings. Although I am happy to report that I stand by most columns I wrote, there are a few mea culpas sprinkled throughout.

I took the title of this collection from a line in the classic rock song "Stuck in the Middle with You" by Stealers Wheel, which is, fittingly, the theme song to my SiriusXM radio program. A surprise hit upon its release in 1972, the song enjoyed renewed interest after providing the soundtrack for a particularly grisly scene in Quentin Tarantino's 1992 debut film, *Reservoir Dogs*. Should you make it through all these columns, I think you will find a catalogue of views that, on balance, defies labeling toward the left or the right. Words like "liberal" and "conservative" lack the nuance necessary to sum up an outlook like mine that includes approving of airline passenger profiling and legalizing prostitution and mistakenly supporting the Iraq invasion (after appropriately questioning it initially). And while my thought process continues to evolve, the last column included in this collection, actually written in 2017, acknowledges the bubble in which I found myself at the outset of the Trump presidency, and, as I note in that column, it's a bubble I've been seeking to burst.

There is, of course, plenty of politics discussed in these pages, but there are also many columns that serve up slices of life outside that arena. I've enjoyed writing about such disparate subjects as our family dogs, my favorite lunch counter, our kids' yard sales, the tortuous SAT exams, and a special college professor who became a good friend. My favorite columns are those that capture unique scenes from the interesting life I am fortunate to be leading. I met Ronald Reagan as an 18-year-old newly registered voter; worked in the G.H.W. Bush administration when I was 29; had dinner with Fidel Castro; took a foreign leader (Pervez Musharraf) to my local American polling place to watch me vote; hosted the members of YES, the (now) Rock and Roll Hall of Fame inductees, at a backyard barbeque; conducted Barack Obama's first radio interview live from the White House; confronted the living members of Led Zeppelin with a demand that they reunite; heckled Roger Waters from the front row of Madison Square Garden; worked for Pennsylvania's longest-serving U.S. senator, Arlen Specter; brought the "living legend" Bruno Sammartino to my law office; spent the same night with Pete Rose and Ted Nugent; had my portrait painted in front of a live audience, by Nelson Shanks (the portrait artist of choice of Princess Diana and Baroness Margaret Thatcher); shared an uncomfortable train ride with David Duke; drank champagne from the Stanley Cup; and conducted Bill Cosby's only pretrial interview.

My most surprising find during this compilation process was a column I have no memory of having written. It was published as a Guest Opinion in the *Daily News* in 1985, when I was 23 years old and a first-year law student at the University of Pennsylvania, 16 years before I joined the newspaper as a columnist. I thought it appropriate to offer the column as the first in this collection; it's a good baseline to show where I started and where I am now.

—MICHAEL SMERCONISH
June 10, 2017

GUEST OPINION

AMERICA OFFERS OPPORTUNITY
TO THOSE WHO WORK

Philadelphia Daily News, Friday, August 9, 1985

THE UNITED STATES is still the land of opportunity.
What brought a flood of immigrants to this nation at the turn of the century continues to bring them today: the dream of a better life not only for oneself, but also for one's children.

Speak to those who have endured this process, and you will find they are believers in America, in free enterprise, and in an honest wage. They are believers in a system that allows its citizens to enjoy the fruits of their labors. They realize that families of zero wealth built our country, and that these "bootstrappers" should be our role models. Unfortunately, they are not.

Horatio Algers are still the economic backbone of America. They are the easily identifiable men and women willing to work harder than those around them in order to better their lifestyles. In every neighborhood we see these entrepreneurs in every profession. They are restaurateurs, carpenters, and video arcade owners. They are computer salesmen, real estate brokers, fitness experts, and produce merchants. They did not fall for the negative doctrines that emanated from a vocal minority in the 1960s, and they are the economic lifeblood of the United States.

The process our forefathers once endured continues today. Thousands arrive at our shores annually, both penniless and homeless, yet they succeed in large part due to optimistic attitudes. Their outlooks are the same that our ancestors once held; only the names of the homelands have changed. Instead of coming from Irish, Jewish, Polish, or Italian descent, these new upstarts come here from Cuba, Mexico, Vietnam, and other Third World nations.

Few can legitimately argue that they have not had an equitable chance to better themselves in the United States. Surely, a middle-class man who is well educated and was reared in suburbia is going to have advantages in the job market over an uneducated ghetto dweller who is a member of a minority. There is no reason, however, why the ghetto dwellers' children, or at least their grandchildren, cannot one day compete for the same job. This has been the pattern of life since our nation was founded: Success sometimes takes generations.

The formula for success today remains unchanged. Simply stated, it is hard work and perseverance that gets results. Moving up the economic ladder is not easy, but it is easier for one's children, provided the parents have at least attempted to reach the next rung. By settling in America, they have.

I recall my favorite professor at Lehigh University, David Amidon, once telling me it is time for disenchanted Americans to stop envying what the rich have, and time for them to work to get it for themselves. I agree. In taking a critical approach to our system, people only delay their descendants' prosperity.

It is time to reassess our attitudes toward our homeland, for no other nation in the world provides a setting more conducive to success. After all, we never hear of overcrowded, dirty, unsafe boats setting sail in an effort to escape from the United States.

AFTERWORD

As noted in the Introduction, this essay was not part of my weekly Daily News/ Inquirer *column; it was a Special Opinion printed in the* Daily News *in 1985, when I was a first-year student at the University of Pennsylvania Law School. Three decades later, would I still write this? Yes, but with important caveats. I had a tendency to see things in black and white back then, but in the years since, through my writing, I have explored more shades of gray. After discovering this guest column in the newspaper archives while compiling this book, I thought it appropriate to reference it and reconsider its sentiments in my July 3, 2016, Sunday* Inquirer *column, where I wrote:*

> *Today I don't see desire as an absolute. To be sure, as an adult, I've watched many work hard and become financially successful. But now I'm equally aware of those working hard just to remain in place or, worse, falling behind. I suspect that, as I wrote those words back in 1985, the seeds of income inequality were being sewn with technological advances, the start of globalization, the weakening of labor unions, and financial deregulation. Imperceptive to those factors, I instead drew confidence from watching my parents exceed the socioeconomic achievement of my coal-cracker grandparents and was certain in my ability to continue the climb up the ladder of opportunity. Now, with four children of my own, I worry about their futures, regardless of both the education they have been afforded by my wife and me, and their individual abilities.*

2002–2007

HIGH FIDEL-ITY: *DAILY NEWS* COLUMNIST
GETS UP CLOSE AND PERSONAL WITH CASTRO

Philadelphia Daily News, Monday, January 7, 2002

'LL BET THAT every conceivable question has been put to Fidel Castro in his 43 years of power.

Except mine.

"Mr. President," I said to him, in the wee hours of last Friday, "there was a mayor in Philadelphia in the 1970s named Frank Rizzo who once said something that was perhaps inappropriate.

"Mayor Rizzo said that his police force could invade Cuba, and win. I am wondering, Mr. President, whether you were aware that such a claim had been made by Mayor Rizzo?"

Castro paused, stared me in the eye and with a straight face said, "No, I never heard that. But I can tell you that while the first part may be true, the second half is definitely false." His laugh then broke up the room, and the conversation returned to more serious matters.

That was just one of many such exchanges during a six-hour-and-20-minute dinner and conversation with the Cuban president last week in Havana. I was in Cuba at the invitation of U.S. senator Arlen Specter. The setting was Castro's Palacio de la Revolución.

The conversation was spellbinding.

"Mr. President, next week I will write for the *Daily News* and I will tell our readers about our meeting," I told him. "I would like to report that within my earshot, you condemned Osama bin Laden for his role in the attacks on America. Will you do that, sir?"

Castro took the bait and began a 10-minute discourse about the September 11 attacks. Before it ended, he would condemn terrorism and propose that the United States and Cuba enter a bilateral agreement to fight terrorism. But he would not condemn bin Laden.

Later, when asked how close we came to nuclear war during the Cuban missile crisis in 1962, he responded, through an interpreter. "Very close," he said and added, "I can't go into details."

In June 1999, Senator Specter met with Castro and wrote about it in his book *Passion for Truth*. Specter (R., Pa.), reported that the two had a lively exchange. I was enthralled with the thought of the author of the "single-bullet

Engaged in debate with President Fidel Castro in Havana, Cuba, on January 4, 2002.
Photo by Shanin Specter.

conclusion" sparring with a man many think played a role in JFK's demise. I told Specter that if he returned, I wanted to go with him. To my delight, he obliged.

In fact, three Philly trial lawyers were on this trip: Shanin Specter, Senator Specter's son; his law partner, Tom Kline; and I. For the record, we each paid our own way and entered the country legally—in my case, as a journalist. We each had the unbelievable opportunity to cross-examine the 76-year-old Cuban leader.

When Castro said that he did not believe in using nuclear weapons on civilians, Shanin Specter pointedly asked him why, then, he had authorized the use of nukes against the United States during the missile crisis.

"We were not in a position to use them," was the reply.

Castro was vibrant, animated, courteous, fully engaged, and unflinching in his views. He had an agenda and a message to deliver to us. But no subject was off-limits. He was the opposite of today's sound-bite, blow-dried politicians.

Needless to say, this was a unique opportunity for any American.

"Cuba made the first statement against terrorism after September 11," he told me. "We offered Cuban airports for the landing of any aircraft that needed to get on the ground. We offered blood. We offered nurses." He said that America never acknowledged his offers.

Castro said the only difference he has with the Americans on terrorism is the best way to eradicate the problem, adding that it is important to "attack it from a moral and ethical point of view, not the bombing of innocent civilians."

I asked whether he had seen the videotape in which bin Laden acknowledged his role. He had but was in no position to "authenticate" the tape.

"I can't judge a person based upon a video," he said.

Tom Kline brought Castro a gift—one of the New York Fire Department hats that are so popular now in the States. Kline told Castro that the hat was a symbol of America's solidarity against terrorism and a testament to the men and women who lost their lives trying to save others.

Kline asked Castro to put the hat on. Castro obliged, and in front of cameras for the world to see, Castro for at least one moment looked no different from Rudy Giuliani.

The exchanges were priceless. The "D.A. vs. the Dictator" I scratched on a notepad as I listened to Specter and Castro mix it up.

"How long do you have before your next election," Specter asked early in the evening. "I mean against an opponent."

"You would have to tell me what type of election," Castro coyly responded.

Specter told him the kind in which he had run for district attorney. An election where competent candidates campaign and people can vote for whomever they choose. "That's the sort you should have run," he told Castro.

Castro didn't miss a beat. "You mean like you had in Florida?" he said in reference to the 2000 presidential race.

He expounded on everything—the missile crisis, the Cuban elections, the embargo, the Internet, the fall of the Soviet Union, bin Laden, and his recollection of a visit to Philadelphia in 1955.

On democracy: "The presidential system has been a disaster for many Latin American nations. Perhaps if you had more information on our constitution, you would realize that we are more democratic than many that are democratic."

On human rights: "How do you define human rights? Is there any proof of torture in Cuba? We don't have much money, but we will give you all that we have if you can prove anyone has been tortured here in the past 43 years. There are no missing people in Cuba."

On nuclear weapons: Castro said there is no justification for the use of nuclear weapons today, even the self-defense of a country. He stated that the use of a nuclear weapon in World War II would have been more "just" if the targets were two Japanese military bases instead of Hiroshima and Nagasaki.

On the collapse of the Soviet Union: "Today I feel like I should erect a monument to the collapse of the Soviet Union because it made us stronger and made us free. The ideas we sustained are much more noble than the ideas developed over there."

On the imprisonment of captured al Qaeda terrorists at Guantanamo Bay:

"We are willing to cooperate with the Americans on relevant measures." It was the one time during the meeting he pulled out a carefully worded, previously released Cuban government statement and read it verbatim.

There was a great debate about free speech. Specter asked Castro whether people could criticize him. Castro responded that Cubans are perhaps the "world's most opinionated people" and said that he knew the mood of the country.

"In general they are praiseful," Castro said. "Yes, people criticize me and the government.

"Can they attack the Cuban revolution in the media? No."

What an admission. It provided a jolt of reality, and something I went to bed thinking about in room 646 of the Golden Tulip Central Park Hotel.

Tom Kline was in room 346. Shanin Specter was in 746. Was it a coincidence that in a hotel with nine stories and 200 rooms, each of us was in a room that was located in the same stack?

Or was it because listening devices were installed in those rooms? My mind raced. Before I nodded off, I wrote a reminder to ask Senator Specter his room number.

AFTERWORD

When I met Castro and wrote this column, I was a full-time trial attorney also doing some work as a television contributor at the NBC network affiliate in Philadelphia, NBC10. The night of the Castro meeting and dinner, I hoped to obtain some video footage for use on television and confided my desire in advance to Senator Specter. So as soon as we arrived at Palacio de la Revolución, at my urging, Specter asked Castro whether an American camera crew that I had on call nearby could film our meeting for my use on American television. Much to our surprise, Castro readily agreed. Then, just as the formal meeting portion of the evening was about to get under way, two of his aides asked me to step into a hallway, where they proposed an alternative plan: the Cubans would film the discussions and hand me a VHS tape to take away at the end of the night. I was hesitant and objected on the grounds that Castro himself had just given permission for me to summon an NBC film crew. A debate ensued, and every minute that I stood in the hallway with my new Cuban friends, I was missing the dialogue between Specter and Castro. So I relented, went back into the meeting, where I was comforted by the arrival of a Cuban cameraman, who remained present throughout the evening. At the end of the night, one of Castro's aides handed me a VHS tape. Mission accomplished, right? My Havana hotel room had no playback capability, but the next day, when I landed in Miami, I went to my mother's apartment and put the tape in her VCR. From an evening that lasted more than six hours, there was no more than two minutes of recording on the tape!

In August 2016, I returned to Cuba with my family and a swashbuckling travel expert and author named Christopher P. Baker. My wife and I were eager for our four children to see the island while Fidel Castro was alive and before things change in the aftermath of more normalized relations with the United States, begun under President Barack Obama. We had a terrific, week-long trip, and upon my return, I wrote a lengthy essay for the Sunday Inquirer *about what I'd seen, which the* Inquirer *editor Bill Marimow promoted on the front page. I said that I'd found "a nation of great disappointment and contradiction."*

Friendly people live amid spectacular scenery but are nevertheless trapped in a socialist system that never delivered on the promises of the revolution. So often, on the same residential block, I was transfixed by both natural and architectural beauty, while distressed by the sight of squalor and blight. And yet, amid the decay, there are unmistakable signs of initiative and optimism, people who represent hope and the prospect of freedom to come.

Three months later, Fidel Castro died.

A POLITICALLY INCORRECT
EXTRAVAGANZA

Philadelphia Daily News, Thursday, January 24, 2002

THE MOST ANTICIPATED SPORTING EVENT in the recent history of the city needs little hype from me. It's already on everybody's mind. And why not? It's got all the elements.

You could say the appeal lies in the Olympic-like training. Or the massive brawn of the combatants. Perhaps it is all the color and pageantry. Or maybe it's the camaraderie among fans.

Eagles vs. Rams? Hardly.

It's Wing Bowl X, the real granddaddy of Philadelphia sporting events. And it is tomorrow.

Relegated (for one day) to second-tier status are guys named McNabb, Staley, and Reid. Tomorrow's headlines belong to Philadelphia heroes with monikers like Sloth, Magnificent Bastard, Chili Dog, and Tollman Joe.

What I like about Wing Bowl is not only the laughs and giggles that it will provide to thousands at the FU Center, and thousands more in their cars and kitchens, but—dare I say it—I like the social and political ramifications of the great event.

The truth is that this distinctly Philadelphia event has not been invaded by the PC police. PETA has not calculated the number of chickens sacrificed for fun and games. NOW has yet to discover the Wingettes, who serve the wings to the mammoth contestants while wearing thongs. MADD has held no press conferences to criticize the sunrise spectacle of thousands of men guzzling beer for breakfast. And John Street's fitness czar is a guaranteed no-show.

In a society gone crazy with PC notions like avoiding saying "Indian giver" or "welshing" on a bet, where the idea of gay scout leaders draws legitimate debate, where smoke Nazis run the bars and restaurants, where the 10 Commandments have been banished from courthouses, where the swimsuit competition in beauty pageants is barely tolerated, and in which we honor kids' rights not to recite the pledge of allegiance in schools, there is something to be said for a return to some good old-fashioned fun.

Nobody gets hurt. Everybody has a laugh.

And it could only happen here.

Can you imagine 20,000 upstanding citizens of St. Louis, or L.A., or

Tampa packing into a major arena beginning at 5:30 A.M. to cheer on truck-sized men in a chicken-wing-eating competition? I doubt it.

Many will never even make it to work tomorrow, choosing instead to attend one of the many "after parties." This is arguably the only radio-station-created holiday in a major American city and the honors go to WIP and its P. T. Barnum–like ringleader, Tom Bigby.

That must say something about us as a community. Just what I'm not sure we want to know.

What I can tell you is that it began 10 years ago in the lobby of the Wyndam Franklin Plaza when 150 people showed up to watch just two contestants. Carmen "the Beast from the East" Cordero won by eating 100 wings. You want a sign of the city's progress? How about the fact that last year Bill "el Wingador" Simmons took the title by besting a field of 25 and eating 137 wings?

Rumor has it that more beer is sold at this morning event than at any other booking at the First Union Center. Not to mention the 2,000 or so wings that will be downed by the contestants, who have worked hard to get this far.

You can't help but appreciate that Gentleman Gerry ate three pounds of melon and prosciutto in under five minutes. Or that Ali Blobba ate four pounds of tripe in under 20. And Tailgate Russ, who ate a pig's head, including the snout, cheek, and brain, garnished with shrimp and parsley.

Wing Bowl. The Lakers in town. And that other game Sunday afternoon. It doesn't get any better than this.

AFTERWORD

Challenging political correctness was a focus of my columns and books long before Donald Trump used the subject to propel himself into the White House. Two years after I wrote this column I published my first book, Flying Blind: How Political Correctness Continues to Compromise Airline Safety Post 9/11, *and three years after that I published my second book,* Muzzled: From T-ball to Terrorism—True Stories That Should Be Fiction. *Still, the longevity of such a politically incorrect "contest" as Wing Bowl surprises me. You have to think the prospect of an organized protest against 20,000 individuals, mostly men, coming together to celebrate women in thongs is always looming, but perhaps these antics will get a reprieve in the era of Trump. On February 3, 2017, Wing Bowl celebrated its 25th anniversary. Bob "Notorious B.O.B" Shoudt downed 409 wings to win—at age 50! In the preceding two years, he had finished in third place. The victory earned Shoudt a new Hyundai Santa*

Fe and a check for $10,000. Meanwhile, Catherine Clee beat out the other nine finalists to be named Wingette of the Year, earning her $5,000. The wrestling great "Nature Boy" Ric Flair was among the dignitaries on hand in the sold-out Wells Fargo Center. Flair implored the crowd to "get drunk, eat chicken wings, then take your woman home and do your thing."

KOBE? HE'S NOT ONE OF US

Philadelphia Daily News, Thursday, February 14, 2002

L OOKING FOR A SIGN that we've returned to some sense of normalcy in the aftermath of September 11?

One word: Kobe.

After all, which of the following received more of your attention in the past few days: the booing of Kobe Bryant, or the extraordinary terrorism warning issued by the FBI?

The answer, I'm sure, is Kobe. His treatment at the All-Star Game is the talk of the water coolers from West Philly to Wissinoming.

Instead of trying to figure out where Yemen is located, we've become a bunch of shrinks offering our own explanations for the psyche of the Philadelphia fans who delivered the razzing. Well, pull up a sofa, because this Bob Newhart has a different diagnosis to offer.

Kobe's reception had nothing to do with his pledge about the Sixers last spring to "cut their hearts out." You give the boobirds too much credit to think that they universally had that comment in mind.

Ditto for the speculation that we, as a city, still haven't gotten over our thumping by the Lakers. We've moved on, thanks to the Eagles.

And it's not because he took too many shots in the All-Star Game. Seems to me he made most of them.

Kobe got booed because of self-image. Ours, not his. We like people who look like us. We like people who act like us. People with a gritty, urban determination. People with imperfections. People without privilege. People with fannies that freeze in the winter and bake in the summer.

And when we look at Kobe, we don't see ourselves. He's gone Hollywood. And if you're not one of us, we're against you. And we don't keep you in the dark about our feelings.

In a world divided into Apollo Creeds and Rocky Balboas, Kobe is down with Apollo Creed.

Allen Iverson is another story.

AI is a legitimate Rocky figure. An underdog. Humble roots. Small stature. Enormous heart. Truth is, we see more of our collective self in the little guy from Newport News than the homegrown traveler from Lower Merion Township.

Think about it.

Who did you take to your high school prom? Kobe took a pop tart whose name escapes me. (AI recently married his childhood sweetheart.) What do you see when you look in the mirror? Kobe's still got his smooth skin and boyish looks. (AI may not have the celluloid good looks, but he has adopted a style all his own with cornrows and tattoos.)

Philadelphia has always had an underachieving mentality, and we're more comfortable rooting for a man who is a questionable 6-foot-0 supporting 165 pounds on two skinny ankles than a fellow with a legitimate NBA physique at 6-foot-7, 210 pounds.

This is nothing new. There are plenty of other examples.

Think Bobby Clark, not Wayne Gretzky.

John Kruk, not Steve Garvey.

Buddy Ryan/Andy Reid, not Jimmy Johnson.

Kobe might have the local roots, but when push comes to shove, we're each a bit more like AI than Kobe.

And THAT'S why Kobe got booed.

AFTERWORD

One of the first things to hit me when rereading this column was my characterization of Kobe's prom date as a pop tart. Uh oh. I have no idea why I wrote that and have long since forgotten the meaning of the reference. A quick Google search reminded me that Kobe's prom date was the singer-songwriter Brandy, to whom I apologize.

When I think of the sports-related highlights of my life, they are all Philly-centric and the list is short: Joe Frazier defeating Muhammad Ali at the Garden in 1971; the Philadelphia Flyers winning the Stanley Cup in 1973–1974 and again in 1974–1975; the Philadelphia Eagles reaching the Super Bowl in the 1980–1981 season (I know, they got there in the 2004–2005 season, too, but for me it wasn't as special); the Philadelphia Phillies winning the World Series in 2008 (I know, they won in 1980, but it wasn't as personally exciting as 28 years later); and the Philadelphia 76ers reaching the NBA finals against the Los Angeles Lakers in the 2000–2001 season (again, this run was more special to me than even their championship in 1982–1983). All such great memories!

At the time of the 76ers' 2001 run to the NBA finals, our next-door neighbor was Pat Croce, then the president of the 76ers. That season, Pat and I were acquaintances but not yet the close friends we would later become. (Kinda funny, we moved into the house next to Pat after having lived in a place that was two doors down from 76ers coach Larry Brown.) You could fit our house inside Pat's house; in fact, one day I discovered a guy nailing a Christmas wreath to our front door, and when I asked him what he was doing, he said, "Isn't this the Croce pool house?" Anyway, the Sixers' success in 2000–2001 reflected Croce's work ethic and gritty determination. It's hard to describe the mania that swept Philadelphia that basketball season, but everyone would agree that it was due in large part to Pat's getting the city stoked. During the Sixers' conference semifinal series against Toronto, Croce climbed the 265-foot Connelly Containers Water Tower in Manayunk and hung a 20-by-30-foot sign that read, "Go Sixers!" Then during the NBA Finals, he climbed a 640-foot cable to the top of the Walt Whitman Bridge and hung a 5-by-70-foot banner that read, "Go Sixers—Beat L.A."

Everyone in Philadelphia and its suburbs was into basketball. Cars had 76ers flags on them. And at our house, we flew an Allen Iverson flag on our flagpole. The finals had all the elements and high drama. AI versus Kobe. Dikembe Mutombo versus Shaq. The Lakers won in five games, but the excitement of that season, and the heart of Allen Iverson on the court, is something I will never forget. I still get goosebumps when I hear the sound of then–First Union Center announcer Matt Cord introducing a "six-foot guard from Georgetown, No. 3, Alllllllen Ivvversson!"

And while Kobe might have been a better NBA star than Iverson, he would never have been a better Philadelphia 76er.

GAY NUMBERS AND 9/11

Philadelphia Daily News, Thursday, June 13, 2002

I N 1948, ALFRED KINSEY did some research and concluded that 10 percent of the population was gay. Ever since, there has been great debate about that figure. It's not just cocktail chatter.

There is power at stake because gays draw political support from politicians' perception of their numbers. It's all about the votes.

Now, information from the 9/11 tragedy casts doubt on Kinsey's number.

Kenneth R. Feinberg is the special master of the fund created by Congress to compensate the victims of 9/11. He made headlines recently by clearing the way for the compensation of surviving gay partners. Feinberg's decision may enable gay survivors to collect about $1.85 million. That's a big incentive to come out of the closet. The wishes of next of kin will be considered as part of the funding decision.

If we assume Kinsey to be correct, 10 percent or so of the victims of 9/11 would have been gay or lesbian. So, assuming a total of 3,000 victims, that would equate to 300 gay victims.

Now, not all of the 300 could be expected to be in committed relationships. Line up any 300 people who are straight or gay and many will not be in such relationships. So, let's cut it in half and take the number down to 150. In fact, let's be cautious and cut it by another third. Say that 100 of the 300, or a third, were in committed relationships.

Now the rub: There aren't 100 surviving partners seeking compensation—there are only 22 known surviving gay partners!

That suggests that the gay population among the victims of 9/11 was less than 1 percent!

Some may say that we'll never get an accurate picture because of a lingering social stigma that is attached to being gay. I can think of 1.85 million reasons that no surviving partner would remain in the closet.

Others may say gays were underrepresented in the tragedy. I think the victims were a pretty random cross section. Men, women, blacks, whites, Americans, foreigners, cops, firefighters, busboys, brokers, the young, and the old. Obviously none of them volunteered for this fate.

By contrast, Professor Kinsey relied entirely on volunteers. And 25 percent of his survey sample were prisoners, who arguably had a higher proportionate share of individuals who had engaged in homosexual behavior.

So this just might be the most accurate assessment of the percentage of gay population.

But even if the gay population is closer to 1 percent than 10 percent, it should not alter the debate about compensation.

Despite opposing gay marriage, I think we should compensate surviving gay partners as long as there is evidence of a committed relationship. William Randolph and Wesley Mercer are one case: They were together for 26 years until Mercer died on 9/11.

Mercer, who was vice president of corporate security at Morgan Stanley, has been credited with saving all but two of the company's 3,300 employees. Mercer never divorced his wife, so she will be getting his Army pension, Social Security, and worker's compensation. I think Randolph should share in the fund created by Congress.

My conservative friends see the compensation of gay survivors as an example of gay leaders capitalizing on tragedy. I disagree. It's the proper response to the greatest domestic attack on our country. Even if they are only 1 percent.

AFTERWORD

I remember getting some blowback to this column by a few who misinterpreted my aim as somehow being dismissive of gay rights and the size of the gay population. That was never the intent. Instead, I simply thought the tragedy of 9/11 provided a lab experiment of sorts about how many of us are gay—not that there's anything wrong with that! I also wanted to highlight the work of Kenneth Feinberg, whose name to me is synonymous with the word "competence." I later heard Feinberg deliver the Edward B. Shils Lecture at my alma mater, Penn Law, in December 2003 and found him to be brilliant. That Feinberg, a former chief of staff to Senator Ted Kennedy, was tapped to be the special master of the 9/11 fund by the George W. Bush appointee Attorney General John Ashcroft is a testament to the universal recognition of his capabilities. In fact, Congress gave him a blank check to settle thousands of 9/11 cases, such was their trust in him. And after resolving a mountain of litigation in that capacity, Feinberg similarly played Solomon in compensation matters involving the Boston Marathon bombing, General Motors, BP, and Volkswagen. Not long after Feinberg's lecture at Penn Law, I ran into him in New York City on the Avenue of the Americas near 30 Rock. I was glad I got the opportunity to introduce myself and tell him how much I admired his work.

As to the number of Americans who identify as LGBT today—at least via poll—the percentage continues to grow, especially among young adults. The most recent *Gallup Poll* report, released in January 2017, indicates that 4.1 percent of all adults over 18 identify as LGBT. But among Millennials (born between 1980 and 1998), the number is 7.3 percent.

Seth Stephens-Davidowitz, a brilliant Harvard-educated Ph.D. and Internet data explorer, took his own shot at discovering the truth behind the number of gay men in the United States based on an analysis of pornography using Google analytics for his book Everybody Lies: Big Data, New Data, and What the Internet Can Tell Us about Who We Really Are. *Think about it—no leading questions, no judgmental stares, no social pressures, just you and the Google search bar that can answer your deepest questions and concerns. Using data from Google Trends and Google AdWords, he found that among male searches for porn, about 5 percent of those searches are for "gay-male porn." Interestingly, he found that there is parity in those searches between what would be thought of as gay-friendly states and less-tolerant states. For example, among searches for porn by men who live in Mississippi, 4.8 percent of those searches are for gay-male porn, which is fairly close to the 5.2 percent of searches for porn in Rhode Island that are for gay-male porn. Here's his conclusion: "So how many American men are gay? This measure of pornography searches by men—roughly 5 percent are same-sex—seems a reasonable estimate of the true size of the gay population in the United States."*

THE SINS OF THE FATHER . . .
AND MOTHER

Philadelphia Daily News, Monday, July 29, 2002

ARE WE READY for a candid conversation about the circumstances surrounding the Erica Pratt kidnapping?

I seriously doubt it.

I tried on the radio the other night and it only took about 10 minutes until a caller used the R-word to describe me and what I had to say. (Perish the thought that a white guy should offer an opinion on a crime where both victim and perpetrator were black.) The injection of the R-word is usually all it takes for most—but not me—to end the discussion. It also explains why we often don't have the tough talks and why nothing ever changes with race relations.

Maybe you're thinking that there is nothing left to be said. After all, two guys are in jail. Erica is all right. The story has a happy ending.

Me? I say there is more to this than just James Burns and Edward Johnson. Something about what is wrong in America.

First, a gut check. If the last thing you want to remember about the Erica Pratt case is the television image of a happy child reunited with family and friends, then stop reading this column now. But if you're up for some dialogue about what really caused this crime, read on.

Erica has been put in harm's way by those around her. Her relatives have not only put themselves at odds with the system, which is their adult decision, but they have placed this promising young girl in the crosshairs of drug violence, a situation over which she had no control.

They are as much to blame as the men who kidnapped her. There. I said it.

She has one uncle who was found dead last March—shot after being charged with attempted murder in connection with a September 2001 shooting. (A subject for another day is why he was out on the street after being charged with attempted murder.)

Another uncle was acquitted of murder by a jury in 1993. More recently, this gentleman survived a murder attempt outside a Center City hotel during Philadelphia's NBA All-Star week celebration.

Then there is dad. He is reported to be on probation after being arrested on charges of drug possession and intent to distribute.

It gets no better with mom. She reportedly was found guilty of reckless endangerment in January. Apparently she sprayed two women in the face with a dog repellent. And she has a prior arrest for drug possession.

And so the responsibility for raising Erica—as it so often does in urban America—has been left to extended family, not a mother and father. In Erica's case, that task belongs to a 45-year-old grandmother.

I don't know anything about her except her young age for being a grandmother. But I have read that the kidnapping happened about 9:30 P.M., when Erica was outside with a 5-year-old. By my clock, that is about an hour and a half past her bedtime.

This is no environment for a child to grow up. Poverty. Drugs. Despair. And most important, an absence of male role models.

The deck has been stacked against Erica Pratt. Not by race. But by relatives.

AFTERWORD

Shortly after this column was published, I received an e-mail that began as follows: "Michael: Let me briefly introduce myself. My name is Bernie Goldberg. I was a correspondent with CBS News for 28 years, I now work at HBO's Real Sports *and I wrote a book recently called* Bias."

I knew of his work because six months before this column was published, Goldberg's book, full title Bias: A CBS Insider Exposes How the Media Distort the News, *reached No. 1 on the New York Times Best Sellers list for nonfiction. Goldberg benefited from the fact that President George W. Bush was famously photographed holding the book while walking past the camera-ready media to board* Marine One *on a trip to Maine. The New York Times's Eric Alterman referenced the photo in a March 2003 article, stating that Bush carried the book "quite conspicuously" and suggested that the president was giving "the so-called 'liberal media' . . . a presidential thumb in the eye."*

As it turns out, Goldberg was writing me to seek permission to use this column in his next book, Arrogance: Rescuing America from the Media Elite *(2003), which I gladly provided, and so he did.*

THAT APOLOGY?—IT'S BUNK

Philadelphia Daily News, Thursday, September 5, 2002

R EPUBLICAN BOSS BILLY MEEHAN was fond of telling candidates seeking his blessing that he could be for them or against them, whichever would help more.

I was reminded of those words as I debated whether to write in support of *Daily News* editor Zack Stalberg and managing editor Ellen Foley. (I wondered, a la Billy Meehan, if they would be better served by my opposition!)

But I gotta go with my gut on this one.

I think any of the original criticism of the paper for the August 21 cover showing the city's most-wanted fugitives is off base and that the *DN*'s recent apology was unwarranted—and probably counterproductive.

I wish the paper had responded to the criticism of a few with a demand for dialogue about the very real problem highlighted in photos and print that day. Instead, the capitulation of the *DN* does nothing but prove that, as a society, we remain unwilling to broach any subject that involves substantive dialogue about race.

I'm not surprised by this.

I learned my lesson recently by weighing in on slavery reparations. What did I say? First, that there exists a real disparity between the races; second, that slavery played a role in the ori-gin of the disparity; third, that society must do something to level the playing field; and fourth, that a new commitment to minority education was the best answer.

What did it get me? Hate mail.

So I knew when I picked up my copy of the paper at a Wawa down the shore at 6 A.M. that Thursday that there'd be hell to pay for the cov-

The controversial cover of the *Philadelphia Daily News* **on August 21, 2002.** Photo courtesy of the *Daily News*.

er. But not for any reason having to do with the facts. And on this I have been proven correct. Note that nowhere among the criticism is anybody saying the *Daily News* got anything wrong.

To review, the homicide unit identified 56 individuals wanted in the city for murder. The *DN* then profiled 27 of them, which I consider to have been a public service. The cover featured mugs shots of 15 of the fugitives.

None of the 56 individuals identified by homicide is white—and there's the rub. Of course, it's not the DN's fault that 56 nonwhites are being sought for murder, but in the twisted racial world in which we live, this is perceived by a few to be the fault of the newspaper.

So here we go again. Instead of discussing why black-on-black crime threatens the city—minorities in particular—we're caught up in a bogus debate as to whether the paper should have presented the information the way it did.

Meanwhile, the crime continues and energy that should be dedicated to ending it is wasted by debate on the propriety of the *DN* telling it like it is.

Not long ago, the William Penn Foundation funded a study by Public/Private Ventures, which was published in the spring of 2001 and titled *Murder Is No Mystery*. It is an analysis of Philadelphia homicides from 1996 to 1999. Then–police commissioner John Timoney wrote the foreword. The introduction sums up the study this way:

> And the tragedy of all is that murder, in this city at least, is not exactly a mystery. A look at the homicides committed between 1996 and 1999 reveals a pattern: 9 out of 10 victims were men, and over half were young men between 18 and 34 years old. Three victims out of four were African-American. Four victims out of five were shot to death with handguns. Virtually all alleged murderers were the same race as their victims, with over 90 percent of African Americans dying at the hands of another African-American.

Further along, the study reported that whites made up over half of the city's population but represented only 5 percent of its alleged murderers, while African Americans made up less than half the population—but represented over three-quarters of its alleged murderers.

In the August 21 cover, the pictures told the story.

But, Shhhhhhh—don't talk about it.

No wonder nothing ever changes.

AFTERWORD

As I say in my book Muzzled:

> I remember where I was when I first saw that cover. That's how startling it was. As we like to say in Philadelphia, I was "down the shore" in Ocean City, New Jersey, on vacation. On a humid, early-August morning, while en route to a workout with my friend, the fitness guru and former president of the 76ers, Pat Croce, I stopped at Wawa for a newspaper and cup of coffee.
>
> It was a Thursday, the day my own weekly column [ran] in the Daily News, and I was eager to see what headline my editor, Michael Schefer, had put on a column I had filed before going away with my family.

By pure coincidence, the column I'd written for that day's paper also dealt with race, under the headline (which I didn't write): "Reparations: Ending the Guilt Trip." In it I argue that educational opportunities are the only legitimate form of modern redress:

> So much of what ails us is attributable to the lack of strong fathers in African American households. . . .
>
> How do we [fix] that? Through reparations. Not the Farrakhan land giveaway kind. The only way to really repair black America is through unprecedented educational opportunities for black youth. That must be our chief focus on a local, state, and national level.

And in my column a week later (August 29, 2002), I addressed the public reaction to my reparations column from the week before:

> My column got picked up by Newsmax.com, so I got reaction from all across the country. . . . [T]he most disappointing reaction came from a few knuckleheads—some of whom actually showed up at my law office with hateful signs the day after my column appeared—who refused to look beyond the fact that I was a white guy with something to say about reparations. . . . Their virulence is exactly why many whites don't share my willingness to discuss the issue [at] any level deeper than a sound bite.

Until I started compiling this book, I had completely forgotten that the protest of my column extended to the sidewalk in front of my law office!

REBUILD 'EM!

Philadelphia Daily News, Thursday, September 12, 2002

I ATTENDED THE FIRST ANNIVERSARY of the events of September 11 at the former site of the World Trade Center yesterday, and broadcast my radio show while the president stopped by to pay his respects.

It was a scene I will never forget.

I have visited this area often over the years: a job interview. Dinner at Windows on the World. The PATH train.

And, like all Americans, I've watched the televised changes at this location for a solid year. But no matter how many times I've seen the footage, I was not prepared for the enormity and emptiness of the 16-acre hole in the ground.

I'm sure my emotions would be magnified if I had been there before the debris was removed.

But today, the day after the first anniversary, I want to look forward, not back.

Maybe patriotic fervor has clouded my judgment because it is hard not to survey the scene without a numbing of the senses, but I came home believing that the WTC needs to be rebuilt—just as it existed. Both towers should soar at least as high as they were before the attack.

Earlier in the summer, the Lower Manhattan Development Corp. presented six proposals for the rebuilding of the site. I looked them over on the Internet. Each called for replacing the 11 million square feet of office and retail space lost in the Trade Center attack. Each used the word "memorial" in its title.

One would feature eight acres of open space and a free-standing tower. Another would create several triangular parks and triangular building sites. Another would have a six-acre park.

I'm not surprised that people were underwhelmed by what they saw. It's not possible to come up with any replacement plan that will represent a consensus, particularly since you can't help but compare any proposal to the unique architectural feat that they seek to replace. There are just too many divergent opinions, all well-intentioned, and no one wants to offend the victims' families.

Even former mayor Giuliani has recently written that the entire site should be set aside as a memorial, befitting the burial ground that it represents.

And I recognize that there are other reasons not to rebuild what existed pre-9/11: Potential occupancy problems. Security concerns. Insurance woes.

America can overcome them all. And, collectively, the arguments against what I will call the "replica plan" are outweighed by the spectacular opportunity we have to construct the ultimate monument to American resilience. Imagine the message that would send to friends and foes alike. We would be saying that absolutely nothing can deter the American spirit.

That's the same spirit embodied in the actions of the passengers of Flight 93 who fought back. We have them to thank for the failure of the terrorist mission to reach Washington. Why should we let the terrorists succeed in their mission to permanently remove the WTC from America's skyline when we have the ability to deny them their goal?

I'm not the first to make this suggestion. There is a group dedicated to this goal—but the idea of rebuilding what existed isn't getting serious consideration for reasons I don't quite understand.

The group has a website, teamtwintowers.org.

They are correct when they state that "building anything shorter, or smaller, than the Twin Towers is tantamount to kneeling to terrorism."

AFTERWORD

As you can tell, I was in a patriotic, chest-thumping mood when I wrote this on the first anniversary of the 9/11 attacks. On that day, I did my morning radio program from a building adjacent to Ground Zero, where I watched President George W. Bush lay a wreath. Obviously that location was not ultimately rebuilt in the mirror image of the Twin Towers, and I'm fine with the result. Instead, 15 years later, the Freedom Tower was completed on a site that also includes the incredible National September 11 Memorial and Museum, which I have visited several times.

I'm proud of the fact that a Zeta Psi fraternity brother of mine at Lehigh University, the engineer Jim Durkin, was the construction manager for the WTC Transportation Hub, an important part of the overall site development. Coincidentally, his father, Francis "Frank" Durkin, an engineer who graduated from the Citadel, had been a resident engineer for the Port Authority of New York and New Jersey during the construction of the original Twin Towers. As Jim described to me, his father was involved in the construction of the towers "from the foundation stage when they found an old anchor from a schooner to the day that Philippe Petit did his high-wire act between the towers." So a father-son engineering duo was instrumental to both projects. Pretty cool.

WANT RATINGS?
BRING BACK THE BEAUTY

Philadelphia Daily News, Thursday, September 26, 2002

THE FOLKS WHO RUN the Miss America pageant got exactly what they wanted.

A brainiac, but not necessarily a beauty.

"You have a Miss America that absolutely personifies what this program is about and where we're going," said George Bauer, the interim CEO of the pageant, after the crowning. "The walk is matching the talk."

It sure is. And that's too bad for television viewers and the future of the pageant.

Miss Illinois, Erika Harold, is the Harvard law student who won the title Saturday night.

Don't get me wrong, she's an attractive woman, but she is not a "10." Or a 9. Or even an 8. Frankly, she's a good-looking Paula Jones. And I suspect that suits the PC crowd who run the pageant just fine. The last thing they seem to want is a raving beauty whose well-rounded-ness might be overshadowed by good looks.

After all, they've stacked the deck against a "10" winning the thing. Good looks have been minimized, and to acknowledge them is taboo.

Just consider the scoring in the finals:

- Composite attributes: 40 percent.
- Lifestyle and fitness in swimsuit: 10 percent.
- Presence and poise in evening wear: 10 percent.
- Artistic expression in talent: 20 percent.
- Peer respect and leadership: 10 percent.
- Top five knowledge and understanding quiz: 10 percent.

Lifestyle and fitness in swimsuit? Presence and poise in evening wear?

What exactly does that mean? Heaven forbid one of the contestants would have a shapely frame that looks good in both a bikini and a Vera Wang.

Someone has decided that more important are the competitors' platforms on issues, like they were political candidates running for office. And on this score, only the PC need apply. This year's winner intends to promote anti-violence and anti-bullying.

No wonder the TV ratings are in a tailspin.

Left unsaid is that we all love to look at attractive women. The current pageant dismisses the time-honored custom of Americans gathering in living rooms and voting among friends on which of several competing beauties should win. And I'm not just talking about guys. Women love to check out other women. Just think about how they scrutinize one another in social settings.

The scoring system needs to be changed to reflect a woman's ability to turn heads on Walnut Street. There is nothing wrong with requiring that Miss America be a showstopper. Guess what—there are plenty of them who are also fit, poised, artistic, and smart. (Vanessa Williams was all of the above. She just happened to have a few other less-sedate items on her curriculum vitae.)

In other words, I think we can have the best of both worlds. But let's stop the ridiculous trend toward ignoring looks.

If the pageant wants to become a televised Mensa meeting, that's their choice. But I have a hunch America wouldn't mind a little more of an old-fashioned beauty pageant. Bring back the busty baton twirler.

Until then, Bert Parks will continue to roll over in his grave.

AFTERWORD

The subsequent television ratings would seem to support my thesis. In the ensuing years, viewership declined as the pageant bounced between venues and networks. Take a look at the ratings. The total number of viewers (in millions) for the next few years after this column was published were as follows: 2003: ABC (12); 2004: ABC (10.3); 2005: ABC (9.8); 2006: CMT (3.1); 2007: CMT (2.4); 2008: TLC (3.6). Those numbers, by anyone's standards, are not pretty.

CONSPIRACY:
THE OKLAHOMA CITY–SEPTEMBER 11 CONNECTION

Philadelphia Daily News, Thursday, October 3, 2002

'M NOT A CONSPIRACY GUY. I think Oswald killed Kennedy, and that he acted alone. And, like all Americans, I figured that the tragic bombing of the Murrah Building in Oklahoma City was the work of two sick ex-Army guys, Timothy McVeigh and Terry Nichols.

Now I'm not so sure.

Last night, my radio station, the Big Talker 1210, brought three speakers to town for a remarkable presentation: Jayna Davis, a reporter from Oklahoma City; Larry Johnson, ex–deputy director of the State Department's office of counterterrorism; and Patrick Lang, Middle East expert formerly of the Defense Intelligence Agency.

In a spellbinding presentation, they made the case for a connection between Middle Eastern terrorism, the Murrah bombing—and the attacks on the Twin Towers.

Now I know why former CIA director James Woolsey has been quoted as saying that when the full truth is known about these acts of terrorism, the nation will owe Davis "a debt of gratitude."

Why her name is not already a household word is the greatest mystery of all. Just this week, Defense Secretary Donald Rumsfeld said that U.S. intelligence has "bulletproof" evidence of links between al Qaeda and Saddam Hussein. Rumsfeld didn't offer specifics. But here is what we know from the work of Davis.

When the Murrah bombing occurred at 9:02 A.M. on April 19, 1995, Davis was a reporter for the NBC affiliate in Oklahoma City. She was among the first journalists to broadcast that an enormous truck bomb had rocked the heartland, killing 168 and injuring hundreds.

In the immediate aftermath of the explosion, the FBI launched an international pursuit of several Middle Eastern–looking men seen fleeing the Murrah Building in a brown Chevy pickup right before the blast. Without explanation, that all-points bulletin was later canceled. Two days later, Timothy McVeigh was a household name. So was Terry Nichols.

And that's where most of us left the tale. Stunned, but convinced that two Army buddies, homegrown terrorists, acted alone.

Thankfully, Davis didn't close this book as quickly as most of us did. She pursued the APB and set off to track reports of multiple sightings of McVeigh with an elusive dark-haired accomplice. The infamous sketch of John Doe No. 2 was always tucked firmly in her grip.

Davis soon uncovered that several employees at an Oklahoma City property-management company said they had seen a brown Chevy truck like the getaway vehicle aggressively pursued by law enforcement parked outside their office in the days before the bombing. The company's owner was a Palestinian with a rap sheet and suspected ties to the PLO.

Davis learned that, six months before the bombing, the Palestinian hired a handful of ex-Iraqi soldiers to do maintenance at his rental houses. Eyewitnesses told Davis that they celebrated the bombing.

She was also made aware that these same men were absent from work on April 17, 1995, the day McVeigh rented the Ryder truck that carried the bomb.

While pursuing the story of these Middle Eastern men, Davis also became aware of another ex-Iraqi soldier in Oklahoma City named Hussain Hashem Al-Hussaini. She was taken aback to see that Al-Hussaini's picture, when overlaid with the government sketch of John Doe No. 2, was arguably a perfect match. He even sported a tattoo on his upper left arm indicating that he likely had served in Saddam Hussein's Republican Guard.

Davis then set about looking for a connection to McVeigh, Nichols, Al-Hussaini, and other Iraqis. It came when a colleague located two eyewitnesses who claimed to have independently seen Al-Hussaini drinking beer with McVeigh in an Oklahoma City nightclub just four days before the bombing.

This convinced her station to run with the Iraqi-connection story. It was met with some controversy.

The Justice Department responded that the identification of John Doe No. 2 was merely a case of mistaken identity. Al-Hussaini contacted local reporters, claiming to be falsely accused. Davis did not back off because she believed she could repudiate Al-Hussaini's alibi.

And she located two dozen witnesses who identified eight specific Middle Eastern men, the majority of whom were ex–Iraqi soldiers, who were seen with McVeigh and Nichols. Two witnesses named Al-Hussaini as the dark-haired, olive-skinned man they observed one block from the Murrah Building just before daybreak on the day of the blast.

She also uncovered evidence that implicated several of Al-Hussaini's co-workers. One of these men was identified as sitting in the driver's seat of a Chevy pickup at an Oklahoma City apartment complex hours before the truck was abandoned on the lot and towed to the FBI command post. According to police records, the truck had been stripped of its vehicle identification numbers and identifying body molding.

The story gathered steam. Here, it would appear, was the deserted pickup that was the same vehicle that was seen speeding away from the vicinity of the Murrah building with two Arab-looking occupants.

And there was more. Five witnesses independently fingered several of Al-Hussaini's associates as frequent visitors to an Oklahoma City motel in the months, days, and hours leading up to 9:02 A.M. on April 19. On numerous occasions, the subjects were seen in the company of McVeigh, and during a few instances, associating with Nichols—at the same motel!

Davis spoke to the motel owner and a maintenance worker who said the men came within feet of a large Ryder truck parked on the west side of the parking lot at 7:40 A.M. on April 19. An unexplained odor of diesel fuel emanated from the rear carriage. Minutes later, McVeigh entered the motel office and returned the room key. The motel owner then saw McVeigh drive off the lot with a man identified as Al-Hussaini.

To this day, the Justice Department has refused to return the original registration logs for the motel.

Davis has 80 pages of affidavits and 2,000 supporting documents, and they suggest not only an Iraqi connection to the Murrah bombing, but also to the attacks against the Twin Towers.

For example, Nichols was a man of modest means. Yet he traveled frequently to the Philippines. Davis discovered that Nichols was there, in Cebu City in December 1994, at the same time as the convicted mastermind of the first World Trade Center attack, Ramzi Yousef.

She has also found evidence that Islamic terrorists boasted of having recruited two "lily whites" for terrorism.

Al-Hussaini had a very American response to Davis's investigation. He sued for defamation. In a ruling on November 17, 1999, federal judge Timothy Leonard dismissed the case.

In 1995, the federal grand jury proclaimed in the official indictment that McVeigh and Nichols acted with "others unknown." And several members of the Denver juries who convicted the two said publicly that they thought they had help.

Since 1997, Davis has repeatedly tried to interest the FBI in her investigation. She has been rebuffed.

As for Al-Hussaini, after leaving Oklahoma City, he went on to work at Boston's Logan International Airport, the point of origin for several for the 9/11 hijackers, including Mohammad Atta.

One more thing. That motel where McVeigh, Nichols, and Al-Hussaini were seen together was later visited (pre-9/11) by Atta, Zacharias Moussaouy, and Marwan Al-Shehi.

AFTERWORD

As I said, I've never been big on conspiracy theories. I think Lee Harvey Oswald was solely responsible for JFK's assassination, I believe we landed on the moon, and I don't think 9/11 was an inside job. But for a while, I was consumed with this one. I still remember this night well—the event was at the old Adam's Mark Hotel on City Line Avenue in Philadelphia. By the time Jayna Davis had finished presenting her case, the members of the audience (composed of my talk radio listeners) seemed ready to grab their pitchforks and invade Iraq themselves in retaliation for the Oklahoma City bombing. In retrospect, I attribute my own susceptibility to a pervasive lack of evidentiary thinking of the same type that made Americans willing to support the invasion of Iraq on the basis of WMDs. We wanted to hold somebody—anybody—responsible for the nearly 3,000 deaths on 9/11.

Unfortunately, I didn't let my interest in a possible Oklahoma City/Iraq connection end with this column. Instead, I cajoled U.S. senator Arlen Specter into meeting with Jayna Davis and receiving her evidence in his Capitol Hill office, an exchange that I broadcast live on radio on October 10, 2002. Senator Specter then asked the FBI for a formal statement about why the government discounted a link between Oklahoma City and Middle Eastern terrorism. Of course, some radio listeners let me know that they thought Specter was the wrong man for the inquiry, given that he was the author of the Warren Commission's much debated "single-bullet theory" regarding the Kennedy assassination. Ultimately, Specter didn't see any conspiracy with regard to Kennedy, or to Oklahoma City, and today, neither do I.

SUSPENSIONS: A WAKE-UP CALL FOR PARENTS

Philadelphia Daily News, **Thursday, December 19, 2002**

MAYBE IT TAKES ONE to know one.

I am uniquely qualified to comment on the flap over a record number of kindergarten students who've been suspended in the Philadelphia public schools. That's because I was once suspended from school—and I will never forget the experience.

The year was 1976.

Ford was president.

Rizzo was mayor.

The city was celebrating the Bicentennial, and I was an eighth-grade student at Holicong Junior High School out in the suburbs.

This was a relatively new state-of-the-art public school.

In the morning, we had a moment of silence and then some announcements via a closed-circuit television system. The station was student run.

One day, some of the cable geeks came into my gym class to film a commercial for the upcoming gymnastics show. With my buddies watching, I "flicked a moon" on camera. It was good for a laugh—up until the point that Vice Principal Roberts had a private screening. And that was it. I was given a one-day pass.

My father almost had a heart attack. When he got the call, he was told that his son had "exposed himself," generating, I am sure, visions of me dropping my trousers while walking out of the men's room.

Although he's never said so, I suspect he was actually relieved when he figured out what I had really done. Not that he would have told me. Then, he was pissed. And I was afraid to go home.

Although we didn't use such a fancy term, corporal punishment was a part of the drill at my house. So were chores. And getting grounded.

Which is exactly what has changed over the years and why the suspensions in the public schools—even for kindergarten kids—are welcome news.

School discipline was never worrisome in my day. It was what you faced at home that kept you in line. And that is what I suspect is lacking today.

I don't think the 33 5-year-olds who have been suspended this year are the targets of the "zero-tolerance" program. I think it's their parents. Guys like my dad are few and far between these days. Parents today are apt to be lawyers for their kids, not disciplinarians.

The fact that 33 young kids have been suspended this year—compared with just one last year—is very good news.

It says that chief executive Paul Vallas is getting tough and trying to get the attention of parents before it's too late. It's perhaps the only way he can get the attention of the parents while there is still time to save their kids. By middle or high school, it's probably too late.

And I don't buy the argument that suspensions traumatize the kids. I have a 2-, 4- and 6-year-old. They don't remember today what they were punished for yesterday, and I seriously doubt any suspended kindergarten child is going to carry scars for life.

And it's not like anybody is ever going to ask on a job application whether you were suspended from school at such a young age.

Instead, this program may cause parents to come to terms with serious behavioral problems while they can still be modified. Punching a pregnant teacher in the tummy and stabbing a classmate with a pencil are serious incidents. And exposing your genitals to other students is not, well, flicking a moon (which I haven't done since).

AFTERWORD

At the time of my "mooning" incident, the AV department at Holicong Junior High School was run by a young teacher named Linn Brucker. His title was "media specialist." Forty years later, we reconnected after he watched me hosting my own program on CNN and reached out. One day in the summer of 2016, "Mr. Brucker" came over to my house with his wife, Pat. We reminisced about Holicong Junior High, what had become of other students, and, of course, the incident. I asked him what he remembered, and he said:

> *I'm not sure to this day who exposed you. The first I heard about it was when Vice Principal Tom Roberts came to the TV studio and said, "We have a problem that we need to get to the bottom of fast." I'm not sure I ever saw the tape, but I remember your mom had to view the tape in private with Mr. Roberts to identify your rear end. I think the administration covered up the incident for all the right reasons. But can you imagine how it would have played out today with social media? You would have been the butt of a lot of jokes.*

I'd forgotten that my poor mother had to make the ID! When I recently e-mailed her to ask what she recalled, she replied:

I did not blink as it was soooo fast moving.

Love,
Mom

C'MON, MR. PRESIDENT,
SHOW US THE EVIDENCE

Philadelphia Daily News, Thursday, January 2, 2003

WHERE'S THE BEEF?

If I had the ear of the president, that's the question I would ask him about Iraq because I don't think it has yet been answered. In fact, I am terribly disappointed in the Bush administration's public case for the war against Iraq.

And I am not some left-wing loony. I served in the administration of Bush the father. I am a consistent Republican sound bite. I'm a white guy in a blue suit with a red tie who is inclined to support this president.

But the administration needs to show me something before I can buy into the need to risk American lives to take out Saddam now. And if I have my doubts, it says a great deal about the poor public-relations face being put on the impending war.

My analysis is simple: (1) The world is a dangerous place. (2) One reason the world is dangerous is because of evil leaders who wield power capable of human destruction. (3) Saddam is such an individual. (4) We can't take action against all those sick pups in the world; we need to focus on those who pose an imminent risk to our safety. (5) There must be some urgency in taking action against Saddam, now.

My question is why? No one is saying.

For months, I have been waiting for a presentation of the evidence of weapons of mass destruction akin to what Adlai Stevenson showed the U.N. at the height of the Cuban missile crisis. And I think the president owes us that before committing American troops.

On a recent day when Hans Blix and company were given unfettered access to a Saddam palace—an inspection that yielded squat—the president was quoted as saying that things in Iraq are not looking so good.

Huh? I'm left wondering what he's talking about. And no one is asking. It's akin to heresy to raise the question.

Contrast this lack of specifics with the situation in North Korea. On Christmas Eve, the media were filled with stories about North Korea opening a sealed plutonium-reprocessing plant. It could represent a dangerous reviving of the country's nuclear program. Newspapers contained satellite photographs of the storage buildings that contained the pool where spent fuel rods were stored. The *New York Times* showed it to me on page A8.

And that's what I want to see about Iraq. Because absent public evidence, I don't think it's appropriate to ask for an American commitment to war.

Now, don't go lumping me with Sean Penn or anybody else from the Hollywood left. I believe that Saddam is an evil SOB who wishes bad things for my kids. But so do lots of others around the globe.

The question here is not whether he's a bad guy with an agenda. The question, it seems to me when you're contemplating a preemptive strike, is whether there is a viable threat that needs to be dealt with immediately. And that requires a show of evidence.

I'll tell you what's ironic. The president hates trial lawyers. He did them in down in Texas and hopes to do the same in Washington. But he would benefit from having a Philadelphia lawyer around him to stage a presentation of whatever he's got on Saddam.

Where are the blow-ups of military installations that threaten us? How about some affidavits from ex-Iraqi scientists who will attest to a program of weapons of mass destruction? Give me something tangible, anything, that supports the risking of U.S. lives, and I will support the president in military intervention in Iraq.

But until then, forget it.

AFTERWORD

Two and a half months after writing this, I wrote another column in which I supported President Bush's decision to use military intervention in Iraq as a preemptive measure to avoid another 9/11. I wrote: "So now we face a choice. We can do nothing, and risk a repeat of the events that culminated in the horror of Sept. 11, or we can act decisively and rid the world of another Osama bin Laden. The president made the right call."

What changed my mind was Secretary of State Colin Powell's presentation to the United Nations Security Council on February 5, 2003. I wrote in my book Morning Drive:

> *Just before the invasion, I bellied up to the administration bar and drank the Kool-Aid. What changed? Secretary of State Colin Powell unintentionally poured me a tall glass. The speech that he delivered to the United Nations [Security Council] on February 5, 2003, was a turning point in my thinking on Iraq. . . . Powell drew on his enormous credibility in the world community as he painstakingly made the case that preemption was needed to rid the world of another Osama bin Laden in*

the making. The meticulous way in which he outlined the case for war before the world body convinced me that we were doing the right thing.

In hindsight, we all now know the decision to invade Iraq was a mistake, but I don't believe that the president or the secretary of state set out to intentionally deceive U.S. citizens about the presence of WMDs in Iraq.

Still, I wish I'd stuck to my initial skepticism.

TWO GOOD REASONS
TO OPPOSE TORT REFORM

Philadelphia Daily News, Thursday, January 23, 2003

L INDA McDOUGAL'S MISSING BREASTS are two reasons the president's proposed limitation on so-called noneconomic damages in medical malpractice cases is shortsighted and potentially cruel.

McDougal was told in May that she had breast cancer and had to have both breasts removed. She underwent a double mastectomy, thinking she needed the radical surgery to save her life. Forty-eight hours later, she heard some devastating news. She did not have cancer and the surgery was unnecessary.

United Hospital in St. Paul, Minnesota, told McDougal that a "tragic mistake" occurred when her biopsy slides and paperwork were mixed up with another patient's sitting in the same tray.

It's a clear case of malpractice. So what's it worth?

According to the president, $250,000. Under the plan he touted during his Scranton swing last week, McDougal's damages would be capped at that level for this egregious case of malpractice. That's outrageously insufficient. In the year 2003, is the value of a 46-year-old woman's breasts 125G each? But that's all she'd get.

Yes, her medical bills would be a compensable item, but in all probability they would be paid by an insurer which would garnishee that portion of her recovery.

And unless she is an exotic dancer who relies on her breasts for income, she would have no wage claim. Total payout: 250G.

Like the trashing of trial lawyers, caps make for good sound bites. But a limit on pain and suffering awards is terribly unfair to non-wage-earners, mainly the elderly and the poor. And the disfigured, like McDougal, completely get the shaft.

Which is not to say that there isn't a need for change. Insurance for physicians is skyrocketing. But blaming the trial lawyers and capping pain and suffering isn't going to solve the problem. It may help W. beat Senator John Edwards if he wins the Democratic nomination, but it won't fix the flaws in our system.

Here's what will:

First, the core cause, missing from Bush's discussion: physician error. Harvard's Institute of Medicine reported in 1999 that 44,000 to 98,000 people (think a full house at last week's Eagles-Bucs game) die every year due to medical errors. That needs to be reduced.

Second, accountability. The only way a member of the public learns of physician error is if they are the injured party. The usual malpractice settlement contains a confidentiality provision. Only jury verdicts hit the news—and usually, only the aberrant case involving millions makes headlines.

Left unsaid is that doctors win the majority of malpractice cases—even in Philadelphia. Mistakes must be acknowledged by the wrongdoer, as was done with McDougal, and the public should be able to access a data bank that keeps track of the information.

Third, rid the medical community of bad actors. The bulk of malpractice payouts are made for a handful of physicians. Just as there are bad plumbers, deficient carpenters, incompetent housewives, and, yes, lousy lawyers, there are bad doctors.

We're not talking about leaking pipes, burnt dinners, or sloppy wills—bad doctors cause permanent injury. They have to be drummed out of the business.

Fourth, no claim should be allowed to be filed without an affidavit signed by a physician willing to state under oath that the case looks like one involving malpractice. This should cut down on the number of meritless cases. Doctors are correct in saying that many claims amount to no more than a fishing expedition.

Fifth, there needs to be accountability for insurance companies. Several malpractice carriers have gone belly-up due to the bad business practices and outright greed of those who run them. And nobody is talking about that.

It's going to take a little give from everybody—the doctors, the lawyers, and the insurance companies. Otherwise, any "solution" is just window dressing.

AFTERWORD

Everybody hates trial lawyers . . . until they need one. While I've been careful not to exploit my many media platforms to the benefit of my former livelihood, there are certain instances that have compelled me to defend trial lawyers and their work.

Many politicians find it easy to enlist public support for limiting claims for pain and suffering because everyone hears about the cases deemed excessive. The famous McDonald's coffee-scalding case in 1994 fits that bill, because the plaintiff became the national poster child of tort excess. As is true, however, in so many of these types of cases, when you delve into the facts, you find that the award was justified. I'll never forget a radio interview I did with a close relative of Stella Liebeck's (the McDonald's scalding victim) who moved many skeptics in my audience. She told the harrowing tale of how the 79-year-old Liebeck was hospitalized for eight days, underwent multiple skin grafts, and required two years of medical treatment.

I wrote this column because a woman's breasts made it abundantly clear that, although what President George W. Bush was seeking might sound fine on the campaign trail, it was fundamentally unfair in practice.

More recently, I discussed on CNN the incredible backstory concerning the GM ignition imbroglio. In 2014, I told the story of Ken and Beth Melton, who lost their daughter Brooke on her 29th birthday. Three days earlier, her 2005 Chevrolet Cobalt shut off while she was driving. She lost control of the vehicle momentarily but was able to pull over and restart the car. She had it serviced at the local dealership. They returned it, telling Brooke it was fixed. Then on her birthday, she was traveling on Highway 92 in Paulding County, Georgia, on a rainy night. She was wearing her seatbelt and driving 58 miles per hour on the two-lane road with a 55 miles per hour speed limit. According to the accident report, she lost control of the car and it collided with another vehicle. Brooke's car rolled 15 feet down into a creek, and she died.

The Meltons hired a Georgia trial lawyer, Lance Cooper, and he hired experts who were able to determine that the key had slipped from the "on" position to the "accessory" position three seconds before the accident, which would have shut off the power steering and brakes, just like what had happened a few days earlier. Mark Hood, an engineer hired by Cooper, figured out that the original part from Brooke Melton's car did not match store-bought replacements, despite possessing the same identification number. In the discovery phase of the Melton family's lawsuit against GM, it was revealed that the automaker was aware of the problem even before the car was sold to Brooke in 2005. Which begs the question: Why wasn't the problem fixed?

A 2005 memo cited by lawmakers revealed that it wasn't fixed because redesigning the ignition switch would have cost 90 cents per car. We now know this only because of the Meltons' pursuit of justice and their willingness to file a lawsuit.

The bottom line is this: Our civil justice system is often maligned, but it remains a great check on our free-enterprise system, often serving as a more vigilant force than the government itself, whether it's the National Highway Traffic Safety Administration's being slow to force the recall of defective cars, the Securities and Exchange Commission's not reining in the forces of Wall Street that brought about the bank collapses and ensuing Great Recession, the Food and Drug Administration's years of irresponsible oversight for products like Merck's Vioxx, or the Consumer Product Safety Commission's hesitancy to recall defective products like BB guns.

I'LL MISS THE MERRY PRANKSTER

Philadelphia Daily News, Tuesday, April 15, 2003

L IKE MANY, I am going to miss Thacher. And I am thinking about so many stories in which he played a role that I will never forget. Here's a favorite.

Like Thacher, I am a proud member of the Union League. Yes, guys with names like Smerconish now belong. One of the benefits of membership is that you get to use clubs around the globe through a reciprocal membership agreement. They include some great places, like the prestigious Union League of New York.

I have been a member of the Union League since law school and have forged some great friendships there. And while the public perception of members might be one of a little, shall we say, stiffness, the truth in our case is far from it.

Every December, I stay at the Union League of New York while attending a dinner for the storied Pennsylvania Society. This group exists for no other purpose than to meet annually at a formal dinner every year in Manhattan.

The Pennsylvania Society dates from a time when Philadelphia was the center of the universe. Every year, the members would travel from Philadelphia to New York City for a grand dinner. Wives would shop and husbands would do business. Lots of political business. Candidates would get slated in smoke-filled rooms during the gathering. To this day, the Pennsylvania Society lives. It's watered down, of course. Not as many deals get cut as in the old days, and it is now bipartisan.

In the early 1990s—before I was married—some friends from the Philadelphia Union League would go to the society shindig in December, and we would use our reciprocal relationship to stay at the Union League of New York. Like the League in Philadelphia, New York's version is a spectacular facility. It's located on Park Avenue. Dark wood. Deep leather chairs. Cigar smoke. You get the picture.

And so a group of us spent a weekend in Manhattan. This was a particularly raucous time. We'd closed the Oak Room at the Plaza Hotel on a Saturday night before we headed back to the Union League, where the drinking and shenanigans continued.

Suffice it to say things were a bit out of hand. There were some calls from the front desk made to our rooms, and we watched the sun come up on Sunday morning. (Did I mention we are all married now?) Later that day, we headed back to Philly. A good time was had by all. Nobody got hurt.

When we were all back at our jobs, my wheels were turning. One of the guys along for the trip was Dave Singer (now an equally married, respectable real estate investor). Back then, we called him "CCD," a moniker meaning Center City Dave. The New York rooms at the League were in Dave's name—something he would soon regret.

Another of the posse was Robert M. Flood III, or "Floody." (Did I mention that he, too, is now married and respectable?) Floody's dad was then the president of the Union League in Philly. That meant Floody had access to the club's stationery. Soon after the trip to New York, here is what David Singer found in his mailbox on the fancy letterhead of the Union League:

December 26, 1991

Dear Mr. Singer:

The Union League of Philadelphia is extremely proud of its reciprocal relationships with fifty-seven other similarly situated men's clubs world-wide. It is for this reason that we place great value on maintaining these relationships.

In this context, I am sorry to have learned from the Union League of New York of their displeasure with your recent visit to their facility. The President of the Union League of New York has recently corresponded with the President of the Union League of Philadelphia, outlining allegations of conduct unbecoming of a League member.

The Committee on Member Conduct has reviewed this correspondence and would like to provide you with a forum in which to discuss this matter. You should realize that we are contemplating sanctions against you and other League members that may have been with you on this occasion and are therefore considered to have been accessories in your misconduct.

The Committee on Member Conduct will hold its next meeting on Thursday, January 9, 1992, at 5:30 in the Binney Room. Please plan to join us at this meeting. In the event you are unable to do so, please call my office.

Sincerely,
Stanley Orr, Manager

Not bad, eh? And so Union Leagueish.

I'd completely made up the Committee on Member Conduct, but it would not surprise me to learn we actually had one. And better than the text was the way we anticipated his reaction. He was numb. We correctly predicted whom he would call to authenticate the reprimand. So he took this hook, line, and sinker.

But to really pull off this stunt, we knew we needed somebody from the League community in our corner. Somebody with credibility. Somebody with stature. Somebody with a sense of humor. Somebody like Thacher Longstreth.

So I called him in his City Hall offices to invite him to participate in the gag. He took my call and listened to my recap of the events. And then he laughed. And laughed. And laughed.

I could tell I had made his day. Thacher told me he loved the scheme and would do anything to support the sting.

Just think about that. Here was the original Main Line WASP. The prototype of a Union League member. A proud Princeton alumnus. A World War II naval veteran who early in his career was *Life* magazine's top salesman and ended up the president of Philadelphia's Chamber of Commerce. A two-time GOP mayoral candidate who served more than a decade as a member of City Council. And he couldn't wait to help some young guys carry out a schoolboy prank. You have to love that about him. And I did.

At the appointed hour of CCD's appearance before the Committee on Member Conduct, Thacher stood in a foreboding manner on the front steps of the august Union League, pacing like an expectant father as CCD approached from down the block.

He greeted CCD and simply told him, "Whatever you do, be contrite." He then spun on his heels and escorted CCD into the League and toward the meeting room, giving no hint of what was really to come. I followed closely behind.

CCD was nervous about what awaited him behind the big oak door. Thacher then acted like he was administering a secret knock—what a great effect—and opened it wide. But instead of a dozen fuddy-duddies, it was the crew who had attended the Pennsylvania Society and a few add-ons, all with cigars and drinks, applauding and anxious to greet our nervous pal. And nobody laughed harder than Thach.

Boy am I going to miss this guy.

AFTERWORD

Thirteen years after one of the greatest pranks of all time, I went back to CCD and asked him what he most remembered about that day he walked up to the Union League, prepared to meet his fate, only to see the foreboding face of a septuagenarian city councilman standing atop the front steps.

"The way he roared with laughter, at age 75, when it was over," Dave recalled. "He just loved the idea of hanging out with guys in their 20s and being in on the gag. He felt right at home, and we loved having him around—what a rarity."

Then Dave, sounding more like a wise alter cocker than a real estate maven in his 50s, shared another observation: "Do young guys today even pull practical jokes on each other without fear of political incorrectness or getting sued?"

Bob Flood had a similar reflection:

People today, including Millennials, risk offending or bullying someone. The population today lacks tolerance to conduct a prank as you orchestrated in the early '90s. . . . I look at my son, even in college, what he and his friends have to do to avoid upsetting one group or person. From designing a fraternity T-shirt to raise funds for a charity—the wording for the T-shirt has to be approved by the administration. . . . These are 21-year-olds. I could go on about the hypocrisy of colleges.

SUMMER AND SMOKE:
MY GAY EPIPHANY

Philadelphia Daily News, Thursday, August 28, 2003

L AST SUMMER, child abductions grabbed all the headlines. This summer, it's gay rights. Not a week passed without some headline on the topic. Canada sanctioned gay marriage. Senator Rick Santorum got in hot water by equating homosexuality with incest. The Supreme Court threw out the Texas sodomy statute. The Boy Scouts in Philly tried to institute a "don't ask, don't tell" policy.

Episcopalians elevated their first gay bishop. *Queer Eye for the Straight Guy* became a TV rage. And the University of Michigan put a course in the curriculum called "How to Be Gay."

It's a lot to process, and Americans remain conflicted as to how to react. But sitting in my backyard in the middle of summer, smoking a cigar on a hot Sunday afternoon, I think I sorted it out.

I had an epiphany while reading the wedding announcements in the *New York Times*. A photo of two guys caught my attention.

"Gregory Krzyminski, Raymond Konz" was what it said above a picture of two men in tuxes. Nice write-up. There was a mention of their education and ages and a brief description of their commitment ceremony. Turns out "he" is a retired minority recruiter. And the other "he" is a clinical social worker.

But here is what grabbed my eye. It said that Gregory is the son of a steelworker from Chicago, and Raymond is the son of a Milwaukee detective.

Wait a minute.

One guy's father was a leatherneck for U.S. Steel, the other's a cop? That doesn't fit the stereotype. Sounds way too macho an upbringing for a couple of guys with sugar in their pockets.

I was expecting a career in the theater. Or someone working as a hairstylist.

Here's why that's relevant.

If sexual orientation is a part of someone's wiring and not a matter of choice, then there should be no debate as to whether we afford the full protection of the law to homosexuals.

Common decency dictates that if a person is born with some characteristic that separates them from the norm, we must take measures to assist with their assimilation and ensure that whatever separates them from the mainstream is not used to hinder their attainment of a full and prosperous life.

That's why I was interested to learn about the backgrounds of Raymond and Gregory, with both of whom I later spoke.

According to Raymond, they've been together for 23 years and are both Roman Catholics from "strong Polish backgrounds."

Not surprisingly, both men said there was nothing in their upbringing that prompted or promoted a gay lifestyle, and that their sexual orientation, in this view, comes down to their wiring.

"Sending our announcement to the *New York Times* was a choice. Sexual orientation is not," Raymond said.

I think he's right.

It's all about genetics and very little about environment. If we're talking about a set of characteristics over which people have no control, then it's unfair to ostracize them for what separates them from the mainstream.

While I remain uncomfortable in calling a same-sex union a "marriage," my afternoon in the backyard shed some light on the way things should be.

AFTERWORD

First, I'm over it. I no longer feel proprietary about the word and am perfectly fine calling a same-sex union a "marriage."

The Times's *wedding announcement that was the catalyst for my column was among the first published in that paper for same-sex couples. At the time, Greg and Raymond had a big blessing ceremony, a three-day event, in their hometown of Milwaukee. Fourteen years after their marriage blessing, all is well with the Konz-Krzyminskis, the name they adopted in 2007 after what Greg describes as "a particularly harsh and restrictive Wisconsin constitutional marriage amendment which passed with a surprising majority." The law not only limited marriage to that between one man and one woman but also explicitly stated that anything giving the illusion of marriage to same-sex couples "shall not be recognized." That phrase became a rallying cry for some and was used as the title of a photo/biographical essay of Wisconsin same-sex couples. Greg and Raymond were proud to be included.*

Then, in 2011, when New York allowed same-sex marriage, their niece, a long-time Upper West Sider and one of their staunchest supporters, along with her three children and husband, invited and encouraged them to come there and get married. Although they were unable to be married in their beloved Roman Catholic Church, they were fortunate to have their wedding ceremony at Christ and St. Stephen's Episcopal Church on the Upper West Side of Man-hattan. When Raymond told his last surviving aunt about their getting mar-ried in New York City, her response was "Why should you do that? I was at your beautiful wedding in Milwaukee—you are already married in the eyes of God!" He agreed with her but said they were doing this ceremony so he could get Greg on his insurance and they just wanted to be like everybody else; she understood. And she came and danced at the Polish wedding reception they hosted the fol-lowing month in Milwaukee, polka band and all!

After Greg retired from his job as a culinary/restaurant management col-lege instructor, he worked as an airline customer service agent and undertook an overseas assignment in Liverpool, England. He's also an amateur actor and director and now has a TV commercial under his belt. In 2012, he and his ex-wife returned with their daughter to Ethiopia, where they had been Peace Corps volunteers from 1969 to 1972, after a Facebook reunion with one of their most beloved students. Raymond spends most of his time laboring in social work at the VA Medical Center in Milwaukee. Their mutual new "job" is a granddaughter, Eleanor Rose, born June 6, 2014, the day Wisconsin's "shall not be recognized" amendment was struck down as unconstitutional.

Greg reports:

> *I guess the takeaway is that Raymond and I, who are approaching our 34th year together, are the epitome of family values. We've built a last-ing relationship with each other, with our families of origin, friends and our nuclear family, which includes a son, daughter, son-in-law, grand-daughter and an ex-wife.*
>
> *Although Raymond and I have very different personalities, we've become adept at conflict resolution. We do believe we've had a positive impact on one another. We believe our relationship is healthy, comprised of him, me, and us, and people seem to enjoy all three entities.*

ROBBING DR. BARNES'S GRAVE

Philadelphia Daily News, Thursday, September 25, 2003

TO: MONTGOMERY COUNTY ORPHANS' COURT
ATTN.: HON. STANLEY OTT

Dear Judge Ott:

I rolled over in my grave last Saturday when Lincoln University chose not to fight the attempt to move my art from Lower Merion into the city by those now running the foundation I created.

As the fate of my collection now rests in your hands, and as neither of these parties appears to be speaking for me now, I have no alternative but to try to speak for myself.

I don't think I could have been more clear when I wrote my will: "All the paintings shall remain in exactly the places they are at the time of the death of Donor and his said wife."

Apparently, I wasn't clear enough for the likes of Governor Rendell, Attorney General Fisher, the Annenberg Foundation, the Pew Charitable Trusts, and the Lenfest Foundation. Some things never change. This group is the latest version of the same establishment crowd I fought while alive.

These types of people were never my kind. If they were, I would have opened an art gallery and invited them in. Instead, I created an educational institution and clearly stated in my will those who were to benefit:

"It will be incumbent upon the Board of Trustees to make such rules and regulations as will ensure that the plain people, that is, men and women who gain their livelihood by daily toil in shops, factories, schools, stores and similar places, shall have free access to the art gallery."

Please don't let them get away with it. At least not without making them each answer a few questions that have yet to be raised.

Governor Rendell: Why are you willing to raise $100 million if the Barnes collection is moved into town, but unwilling to raise one dime should the same paintings stay in a nearby part of the commonwealth you govern?

Attorney General Fisher: Why all the sudden interest in my art collection? Where were you (and where was the oversight of your office) when the Barnes Foundation was being run into the ground?

The Annenberg Foundation: Be careful what you wish for. Perhaps down the road some group will seek to unravel Walter Annenberg's similarly specific gift of 52 paintings to the Metropolitan Museum. Annenberg himself required that his collection be shown as a group and banned all outside loans.

Here's a solution: Why not re-route those paintings from Manhattan to the Benjamin Franklin Parkway right now?

The Lenfest Foundation: Isn't Gerry Lenfest the same fellow who recently gave a "permanent" art exhibit consisting of 59 Pennsylvania Impressionist paintings and a $3 million endowment to the James Michener Art Museum in Doylestown? Maybe it won't be so permanent after all.

AND the Pew Charitable Trusts: Maybe someone should take a look at whether your meddling in this squabble squares with the intentions of the Pew family members.

I'm tempted to go ask Joe Pew right now what directives he and his family left behind that you think enable your involvement.

It was my fondest hope that a historically black college like Lincoln would have control of my art, and now all of these lily-white do-gooders have instead turned back the clock.

If the real agenda of any of these folks were to "save" the Barnes Foundation, they would have been heard from long before now, and they would be offering to raise money to bolster the endowment regardless of location.

For a quarter of what Governor Rendell is promising to raise for the relocation, they could put the Barnes in clover, forever.

If I had died in Red China, I would have expected my property to be state controlled. But I didn't. And, as far I know, the United States is still a place where you can work hard, accumulate the fruits of your labor, and determine what is to be done with that personal wealth at the time of your death.

Judge Ott, don't let them do this to me. Everyone else wants to ignore the law—the courts are supposed to uphold it.

Sincerely,
Albert C. Barnes

AFTERWORD

On December 15, 2004, Judge Ott ruled that the Barnes Foundation could move from its Merion location to the city of Philadelphia (although litigation continued for years thereafter). It opened its new home on a 4½-acre site on the Benjamin Franklin Parkway on May 19, 2012, where it has had great success. By October 2015, the foundation celebrated its one-millionth visitor to its new location. Tod Williams and Billie Tsien Architects, a New York City–based husband-and-wife team, designed the Barnes's new home. Coincidentally, we were seated together at the 2016 Pritzker Architecture Prize Ceremony, which I attended with my mother at the United Nations Headquarters in New York City on April 4, 2016. I think they did a spectacular job and I told them so. I particularly appreciate that the interior of the building that houses the paintings is a precise replica of the original gallery in Merion. The foundation's website (BarnesFoundation.org) notes that visitors can immerse themselves "in the greatest private collection of impressionist, post-impressionist and early-modern paintings," which consists of "more than 3,000 masterpieces, including 181 Renoirs, 69 Cézannes, 59 Matisses, 46 Picassos, 16 Modiglianis, and 7 Van Goghs, plus textiles, metalwork, decorative objects, African sculpture, Native American ceramics and jewelry, and Pennsylvania German furniture."

And while I recommend visiting the Barnes to all my out-of-town guests, I remain unsettled about the way in which Dr. Barnes's desires were disregarded. For those interested in the backstory regarding the foundation and the move, I recommend a 2009 documentary directed by Don Argott called The Art of the Steal.

MAUREEN FAULKNER,
STILL ON THE JOB

Philadelphia Daily News, Thursday, October 23, 2003

TWENTY-TWO YEARS after a degenerate taxi driver shot her husband, Maureen Faulkner is not only still defending Danny's honor, but she's doing so with a new sense of purpose.

With very little fanfare, Maureen has begun making education grants to students whose parents have been murdered or incapacitated by violent crime.

The money comes from the nationwide outpouring of support that Maureen has received in the face of the Hollywood left's rallying to the aid of the man who was convicted of Danny Faulkner's murder. (You know his name. I will not stain this column by repeating it.)

Many years ago, Maureen Faulkner reached a point where she couldn't take it anymore. More than 100 websites were created in support of the cop killer. Colleges were inviting him to speak via tape at commencement. A cottage industry of lawyers, so-called experts, and liberal apologists were feeding off the sham that was his defense. And there seemed to be an endless supply of funds for their shenanigans.

So she formed Justice for Police Officer Daniel Faulkner to honor the memory of Danny and spread the truth about the manner in which he died. Through a series of fund-raisers—and without ever hiring a single person— she collected the money necessary for the fight.

Soon, Maureen Faulkner was able to fund a website containing the entire 1982 trial transcript [http:// murderpedia.org/male.A/images/abu_jamal_ mumia/justice-police.pdf]. When the likes of Whoopi Goldberg and Ed Asner sponsored a full-page ad in the *New York Times* spreading lies about the case, Maureen was able to respond in kind, publicizing portions of the transcript that the Hollywood left hoped the public would never see.

And in 2000, she quietly formed the Daniel Faulkner Educational Grant Fund as a means of channeling some of the pro-Faulkner money to a charitable purpose. She decided to help educate the kids of crime victims.

Tonight, four more awards, each for $5,000, will be made to these worthy students: Vilika Meade (Art Institute of Philadelphia), Willima Billy Keitt (Kutztown State University), Michael Selby (Frankford School of Nursing), and Edward Fields (University of Pittsburgh).

These four now join Aking Beverly, Justin Frisby, Erma Aponte, Dana

Dutch, and Charles Ritterson, who have previously benefited from Faulkner education grants.

Erma Aponte's personal tragedy is typical. Her father was murdered close to Christmas in 2000 while driving a taxi in North Philadelphia. Before reporting for work the night he was killed, he'd told Erma that he'd try to earn the $50 she needed for an application to computer school. Erma is one of six Aponte kids now fatherless.

Jerry Watkins, who administers the grant program, told me, "I called her to tell her she was the recipient of $5,000 from Maureen Faulkner to continue her education. She told me that very day she had been in court to hear a jury find her father's killer guilty of murder. [She said,] 'It shows my dad is still watching over me.'"

Watkins, one of several Faulkner volunteers, told me that the requirements include a parent having been murdered or incapacitated by violent crime, Philadelphia residency, an educational plan, and financial need.

Tonight's presentation will take place at 6:30 at Geno's Steaks in South Philadelphia. Police Commissioner Sylvester Johnson and ex-commissioner John Timoney are expected to be there.

Why Geno's? Because one of Maureen's biggest boosters has been owner Joe Vento, who three years ago hosted a block party and gave a full-day's gross to the Faulkner cause—$60,000.

Maureen Faulkner's channeling of her energy into educating the children of victims of violence does not mean the fight against Danny's attackers is over. Two weeks ago, Paris named his murderer an honorary citizen, and last week she debated actor Mike Farrell on the *O'Reilly Factor* on Fox News.

With class and conviction, Maureen continues to make Danny proud.

AFTERWORD

In 2007, Maureen and I released the book we'd written together, Murdered by Mumia, *which spent two weeks on the New York Times Best Sellers list. We did a number of well-attended signings in the Philadelphia area, and the response was really extraordinary. The number of people who stood in long lines to meet Maureen and me was richly rewarding for a project that had taken two years to complete and for which I donated all of my author proceeds (roughly $200,000) to her charity.*

One funny memory is from the day we launched the book with a joint appearance on NBC's Today *show, where we were to be interviewed by Matt Lauer. As we sat waiting to begin the segment, Matt was on an adjacent set, but someone had placed his interview notes on a coffee table in front of us. I didn't touch them but snuck a peek at his index cards and saw that he was going to begin by asking Maureen about recently released photographs of the crime scene of her husband's murder that were then being used to peddle yet another conspiracy theory about the case.*

I tried to cover my lapel mic as I whispered to Maureen, "He's going to ask you about the new photos." A look of horror crossed her face as we were set to speak to an audience of millions, and I wasn't sure why. Maureen was a seasoned pro at batting away any conspiracy theory thrown her way.

"What nude photos?" she whispered. I burst out laughing and put her mind at ease. It was a funny moment in an otherwise stressful environment.

ONE VOICE FOR KATZ

Philadelphia Daily News, Thursday, October 30, 2003

I T TOOK THE EDITORIAL PAGE of this newspaper until paragraph 22 of a 25-paragraph endorsement of John Street to say what matters most:

"If he is guilty of anything, it is in unfairly demonizing this federal investigation as a racial and partisan witch-hunt."

This statement should have been the lead, and it alone justifies a vote for Sam Katz. Here's why.

Watching our mayor's race, an out-of-town friend said to me, "Only in Philadelphia could an elected official be identified as a subject of a federal investigation and see his odds of re-election increase."

How true. And how embarrassing.

We like to think that the Philadelphia of the New Millennium is the city that pulled off a national political convention, just christened a National Constitution Center, and has all the hot restaurants, the Kimmel Center, and the gorgeous Pennsylvania Convention Center.

Forget it. In the eyes of the nation, we're headed back to being the city that burned down a neighborhood, pelted Santa with snowballs, and blew the Bicentennial.

Attract business to Philadelphia in this climate? Bring a convention to town against this backdrop? Stop the brain drain? Reverse the suburban exodus? You gotta be kidding. Think laughingstock and national embarrassment instead.

Thankfully, with one day of effort, we can turn that around. But it will take something monumental. It will take the strongest electoral rebuke of our lives.

City government needs a housecleaning. And nothing less than a total rejection of those responsible for returning us to national prominence in the most negative of lights will suffice.

Here is the threshold question voters need to ask: How did it come to this? One answer is that it's the fault of J. Edgar Hoover, Richard Nixon, and John Ashcroft. Good sound bite—but totally lacking in logic.

Here is another answer as to how we got here: The pay-to-play culture in city government has finally caught up with it.

Connecting the dots of the published accounts would lead a reasonable voter to conclude that the feds have been looking for the last two years at the way in which city business gets done—because something stinks in City Hall. If that's the basis of the investigation, then there would be no more logical time to tighten the screws of a probe than in the middle of a campaign.

And remember, nobody cried race or partisanship when any of these investigations first made the newspapers.

Remember too that investigators must have been able to convince a federal judge, someone who has the same job as Governor Rendell's wife, a person immune from politics by virtue of a lifetime appointment, to permit the bugging of the mayor's office. To sign such an order, that judge must have determined that crimes have been or are about to be committed and that there is probable cause to believe the office is being used in connection with those crimes. Common sense would dictate that an even higher level of scrutiny would be applied to the decision to bug a U.S. mayor in a major city than a random citizen.

Why did the mayor tell us his office was bugged? So that in the midst of a lackluster campaign being run on his behalf, he and his supporters could manipulate this discovery to suit their political objectives by appealing to people's worst instincts.

And that is the reason that the rebuke is necessary. It isn't because John Street is under investigation. He is absolutely owed the presumption of innocence. No, John Street deserves to be thrown out of office because as mayor he is playing the race and partisan cards, and in the process, destroying our ability to get along when this election ends.

Voters need to call Mayor Street on the fact that it was he who created the speculation and concern that this is racially motivated, and ever since he has failed to rein in those around him who play the race card. In the final debate, he would not even condemn Ron White's outrageous comment that he was involved in the probe because "I am a black man in America doing what I think needs to be done, and people resent that. They resent that, that black men in America are supposed to be bowing down all the time and not doing nothing but having babies and not taking care of them."

Voters need to reject the playing of the race and partisan cards.

Voters need to reject John Street.

AFTERWORD

Bear in mind, this is me vociferously disagreeing with my own newspaper's editorial endorsement of the reelection of Philadelphia mayor John F. Street. And here's why. On October 7, 2003, about a month before Election Day in a hotly contested mayoral race, a listening device planted by the FBI was discovered in the office of Mayor Street. The race was an election rematch between Street and Republican Sam Katz. The latter, despite an enormous registration edge for Democrats, had come within a whisker of beating Street four years earlier. Now, you'd think that the discovery of a bug and an FBI corruption probe would politically sink the man in whose office the listening device was discovered, right? Not so fast. The Street campaign, relying on the expertise of David Axelrod, who would later guide a certain junior senator from Illinois to the White House, saw this as an opportunity. They spun the bug as evidence of a racist, partisan witch-hunt, initiated by the Bush administration and John Ashcroft's Department of Justice. Well, the strategy worked. Street was reelected as mayor with 58.35 percent of the vote, which was a larger margin than he racked up four years earlier without the probe! Not that it mattered to the electorate, but U.S. Attorney (now Representative) Patrick Meehan was able to deliver nearly two dozen convictions in corruption cases, including the city treasurer, related to the probe that led to the bug. Mayor Street was never accused of wrongdoing. In his 2015 memoir, Believer: My Forty Years in Politics, my now–CNN colleague David Axelrod writes about how it all went down: "I got a call from George Burrell, Street's savvy political deputy at City Hall. 'I think we have a problem.' 'Problem?' I asked warily. 'Yes, it seems we've found a bug in the mayor's office.'"

After learning that the bug belonged to the federal government, Axelrod saw an advantage. "It struck me, as I thought about it," he writes, "that this was our problem but also our opportunity."

> In an overwhelmingly Democratic town, a probe launched by the Republican Justice Department in Washington would surely be greeted with skepticism, perhaps even outrage. I called Burrell back. "We need to hold a press conference on the steps of City Hall and accuse John Ashcroft of trying to steal this election." . . . When Street confronted reporters, frantic over the news, he came armed with a line I had written for him: "I'm happy to speak into a microphone I can see."

As I later wrote for the Sunday Inquirer in February 2015, I wondered whether, in the light of the many convictions that resulted from the probe, Axelrod had any regrets about his role in blaming the GOP? "No," was his emphatic answer. "I don't, Michael, because, as you know, John Street was never indicted for anything," he said. "He was never accused of anything and I felt that to have bugged his office particularly in the midst of a very competitive partisan race was not the right thing to do and would not have happened without the knowledge of the Justice Department at the highest levels."

Meanwhile, the Philadelphia political consultant Frank Keel took umbrage at Axelrod for taking credit for the Street strategy, which Keel said was the "defining moment" of his career. Keel sued Axelrod, alleging false designation of origin under the Lanham Trademark Act and unfair competition. A federal judge dismissed the suit.

Finally, during the 2016 presidential campaign, I spent about a dozen primary and caucus election nights, two full weeks of party conventions, and four debates seated next to Axelrod as a CNN panelist, and I have come to enjoy his wit, insight, and friendship. At no time were those qualities more appreciated than during the nine-hour tour of duty we pulled together on election night, starting at 7 P.M. when the cameras started to roll and ending in a shared cab ride back to our respective hotels close to 5 the next morning.

DREAMING OF A
NON-WHITE CHRISTMAS

Philadelphia Daily News, Thursday, December 4, 2003

THERE'S A BATTLE UNDER WAY between the coloreds and the whites. Nobody wants to talk about it, even though it's got nothing to do with race relations.

It's been brewing for years. The stakes are high. The survival of Christmas as we have known it is at stake.

To protect Christmas past will require nothing short of a rebellion. I want it to start right here, right now.

Let me explain.

With Black Friday behind us, the mad dash toward the holidays is under way.

You know the drill. First comes the shopping. Then the holiday tipping. Next the caroling. Then Midnight Mass. And, finally, the gift-giving. And all along the way, there will be decorating.

And that's what's got my goat. It's those decorations. We've got to stop them.

The white ones. They are everywhere.

It didn't used to be like this. Not when we were growing up. Back then, we looked forward to the Christmas season, and Christmas decorations. All of us. Regardless of religion.

But how did we celebrate that special time of year back then? By putting up lights on our homes and along our Main Streets. Not just any lights.

I'm talkin' big, fat COLORED Christmas lights.

They were red. They were green. They were orange and they were blue. They were bright. They were gaudy and they were everywhere.

And they were beautiful. They were Christmas.

Every year it was the same thing. And life was wonderful.

And then something happened. We got a little more education than our folks.

Our jobs were a rung higher on the ladder than where they had toiled. And we moved into houses that are a little bit larger than the ones in which we had grown up. And once we got there, we somehow decided that we were no longer colored-lights people.

No, now we're white-lights people.

Yeah. White lights. Petite, nonoffensive, uniform white lights. The lights of power and prestige. The lights of suburban panache and urban glamour.

And so the colored lights were banished to the basement, or worse.

Well, I for one have had enough.

This emperor of Christmas present has no clothes and I am prepared to say so.

White lights are boring.

White lights are sedate.

White lights are pretentious.

White lights are for fakers

White lights are un-Christmas.

There—I said it.

And I am prepared to do something about it. I am finished with white lights. I am tired of being a phony. I am returning to my roots. I am going back to colored lights.

I want you to join me.

Go to Kmart. Find the colored lights. The bigger the better. Then pull out a ladder, and put them up. Everywhere.

Colored lights.

The survival of Christmas may depend upon it.

AFTERWORD

This column sprung from an extemporaneous monologue I delivered on radio one year earlier. Coming back from a commercial break, I told the audience that after my program ended, I planned to pick up my wife and kids to go pick out a Christmas tree at our local firehouse as was then our custom on my wife's birthday—December 7. Then I observed that we'd become white-lights people like the rest of the families in our neighborhood. I said that I felt as though I'd abandoned my colored-lights, childhood roots. Well, the phones began ringing off the hook with callers offering similar confessions and observations about how they, too, had grown up in a colored-lights home but had somehow become white-lights people. It was one of the more memorable segments of radio with which I've been associated.

Years later people still approach me to weigh in on this debate, and I wrote a few follow-ups in subsequent holiday seasons, noting continued change with regard to the color of our decorations. For the Sunday Inquirer, *on December 21, 2014, I wrote, "I no longer wanted to be the sort of faker who displayed [white lights]. And for a decade, I walked the walk. My family hung colored lights outside our home and on our tree in the family room. But not this year. . . . The tipping point came when my wife relayed that after driving past our home, a friend, Dr. Martin Snyder, derisively referred to our exterior as 'Whoville.' That was it."*

We went back to white lights.

TOUGH QUESTIONS FROM TOUGH GUY
ON 9/11 COMMISSION

Philadelphia Daily News, Monday, April 12, 2004

JOHN LEHMAN.

If we had nine more like him on the 9/11 Commission, I'd be much more confident that we're really getting to the bottom of what went wrong and ensuring it doesn't happen again, rather than continuing the high-stakes partisan skirmish that seems to have taken shape.

What we've seen of Lehman's public work on the commission thus far, coupled with comments he made to me over the weekend, suggest he is prepared to call them as he sees them, without regard for politics.

Which is precisely what the commission is supposed to do.

Among those comments:

- The public hearings are more to please the public than to uncover crucial information about 9/11.
- The panel is getting plenty of vital information from officials in their private sessions.
- Both administrations share responsibility for allowing terrorists to complete their deadly attacks on September 11, 2001.
- Government agencies have done a bad job sharing information about suspected terrorist activities.
- And, most surprisingly, the Federal Aviation Administration punishes airlines that don't follow a quota system in regard to questioning passengers. "That is why you see so many blue-haired old ladies and people that are clearly not of Middle Eastern extraction being hauled out."

Lehman is Philadelphia's contribution to the commission. Maybe some of his no-BS style can be traced to his Jesuit training at St. Joe's. Or perhaps to his experiences flying combat missions over Vietnam as a Navy reserve officer.

The man has an impeccable resumé. This is an individual who was only 38 years old when Ronald Reagan tapped him to be secretary of the Navy, a post he held from 1981 until 1987, all the while overseeing a massive military buildup.

His importance, and uniqueness among 9/11 commissioners, was on full display last week when Condoleezza Rice testified.

Many played to the cameras. Not Lehman. Maybe that's because he questions the value of the public hearings themselves, one of many subjects he openly discussed with me. He said:

> Really, in a way, these public hearings have been a real distraction from our mission, because all of the people you have seen appear, we have already interviewed in depth.
>
> We had 15 hours, for instance, with [former counterterrorism czar and recent Bush administration critic] Dick Clarke in private before he testified in public, so nobody on the commission learned anything, but it was felt that the public needs to understand and get a view of what was going on.
>
> However, once you put the cameras on everybody, it really becomes theater, so particularly the Democrats are under extreme pressure from the Democratic leadership not to let President Bush off the hook. Unfortunately, that brought a partisan edge to the Clarke hearing and, with several of the commissioners, to the Condi Rice hearing.

Lehman showed in his questioning, however, that the country is after more important things than partisan bickering.

Lehman's focus was the transition between the Clinton and Bush administrations.

He told Rice that he was "struck by the continuity of the policies rather than the differences," and then he proceeded to ask Rice a series of blunt questions as to what she was told in the transition. Among his questions:

> Were you told that there were numerous young Arab males in flight training, had taken flight training, were in flight training?

> Were you aware at the time of the fact that Saudi Arabia had, and were you told that they had in their custody, the CFO and the closest confidant of al Qaeda, of Osama bin Laden, and refused direct access to the United States?

Taken as a whole, Lehman's line of inquiry paints the big picture of the collective failures that enabled 9/11.

But not all of what Lehman asked Rice has received a public airing. This nugget was buried in the proceedings but is worthy of more attention:

Were you aware that it was the policy . . . to fine airlines if they have more than two young Arab males in secondary questioning, because that's discriminatory?

Huh? What was Lehman talking about? This I'd never heard before. Here is what he told me:

We had testimony a couple of months ago from the past president of United and current president of American Airlines that kind of shocked us all. They said under oath that indeed the Department of Transportation continued to fine any airline that was caught having more than two people of the same ethnic persuasion in a secondary line for questioning, including, and especially, two Arabs.

Wait a minute. Was Lehman revealing that if airline security had three Arab guys up to no good they had to let one go because they'd reached a quota? He said:

That is really the source, because of this political correctness that became so entrenched in the 1990s, and continues in the current administration.
    No one approves of racial profiling. That is not the issue. The fact is that Norwegian women are not, and 85-year-old women with aluminum walkers are not, the source of the terrorist threat.
    The fact is that our enemy is the violent Islamic extremism. And the overwhelming number of people that one needs to worry about are young Arab males, and to ask them a couple of extra questions seems to me to be common sense.
    Yet if an airline does that in numbers that are more than proportionate to their number in a particular line, then they get fined, and that is why you see so many blue-haired old ladies and people that are clearly not of Middle Eastern extraction being hauled out in such numbers, because otherwise they get fined.

But Lehman makes clear that he sees more institutional failure than individual failure:

The real problem that enabled this shoestring operation, it cost less than half a million dollars in total, to succeed and penetrate every single one of our defenses was because of a whole series of long-standing dysfunctions in our security systems.

When pressed about the differences between the Clinton and Bush administration responses, Lehman said:

> If you look at the blame game . . . the Democrats are far more vulnerable because the Clinton administration was there eight years and did nothing effective against al Qaeda, while the Bush administration, while they might not have had as much of a sense of urgency, for which they might justifiably be criticized, nevertheless, they were only there for eight months.

Reflecting that both President Bill Clinton and Vice President Al Gore had just completed testimony in front of the commission, Lehman said:

> All of these people feel very deeply that things are not as they should be within government, that things could have been done better, that we've got to make some very running changes, and some have begun, but things are by no means where they need to be.
>
> So they are not playing politics in private. That is why I think the public hearings are a distraction to our work, because we learn nothing. It's theater.
>
> But, we have nothing but full cooperation and seriousness in the private meetings where there are no cameras.

I asked Lehman how he believed the American people would react to the president's daily briefing of August 6, 2001, which has just seen the public light of day. Lehman said:

> It's alarming stuff, and the president was alarmed when he saw it.
>
> It is not a smoking gun. It is a pulling together of intelligence reporting of the prior, especially six months, and it makes it very clear that there is a heightened activity among terrorists, that there are terrorists in the United States, and that Osama bin Laden is determined to attack in the United States.
>
> But nowhere in that daily briefing will you find anything that says Osama bin Laden or al Qaeda is going to hijack airlines and use them as weapons against targets in the United States.

The whole focus was the vulnerability abroad of American embassies and American officials.

The bottom line is that, yes, there is a real threat, and yes, they want to attack in the United States, but we cannot support the more extreme reports that some have sent in.

Then, the bureau points out that they have 70 investigations going on in United States.

So what, then, is to be made of the president's response, or lack thereof, to that daily briefing?

The whole impression from the bureaucracy to president was that we have a serious problem, but we're on top of it.

If not that briefing, then, what is the most damning document as to intelligence failures that he has seen in his work of more than a year as part of the 9/11 Commission?

We have over 2 million classified documents that we and our staff have pored over for over a year.
This administration has given this commission more cooperation and access to sensitive documents and people than any administration in history. . . .
Everybody has been going through this and nobody had found a smoking gun. There is no smoking gun.

So where does it all lead? What can we expect midsummer when the work of the commission is made public?
Lehman rattled off a pretty succinct summation of what his work has revealed and what he thinks we will read in a few months.

What we have is a very clear picture that we had an intelligence community that could not penetrate al Qaeda because of the post-Watergate era dismantling human intelligence and covert actions capabilities.
We had a domestic intelligence community that was unable to penetrate the cells operating here in the United States, and those

pieces of intelligence that they did have, we had no sharing between CIA and FBI of these vital pieces of al Qaeda intelligence.

We have the treating of intelligence within the FBI. Most of the FBI didn't know what the rest of the FBI had because they had a "case" mind-set that anything gathered had to be sealed and protected because it might be used in a prosecution.

We had an FAA that airlines kept totally toothless and ineffective and not carrying out its responsibilities, and we had an INS that Congress wanted to keep weak because they want open borders that illegals can penetrate.

We had a system endorsed and supported by two administrations that allowed cities like Los Angeles, New York, Chicago, and Houston to pass laws prohibiting their police from cooperating in any way with Immigration and Naturalization.

People were saying, and the Clarke testimony implied, that the Bush administration was told everything, when in fact they were told nothing about what the real problems were, and they were the things that really enabled al Qaeda to do what they did.

No wonder John Lehman is anticipating a final report with "very, very far-reaching reforms."

I say hand him the pen, and let him take the first crack.

AFTERWORD

This column stands out as the most consequential (and maybe the longest) I ever wrote for the Philadelphia Daily News. *It propelled the publication of my first book,* Flying Blind: How Political Correctness Continues to Compromise Airline Safety Post 9/11, *although no such book was on my mind when I wrote the column.*

Perhaps the reason I was drawn to the subject of profiling and airline security after 9/11 is that just before I wrote this column, in March 2004, my family of six was heading to Florida for spring break when something odd occurred. At a ticket counter in the Atlantic City airport, my 8-year-old son was singled out for "secondary" or random screening. I thought it was utterly ridiculous, nothing more than window dressing to give comfort to the people standing in line who had more in common with the 19 on 9/11 and were also about to be given a heightened screening.

Then, on April 8, 2004, I saw Secretary of State Condoleezza Rice testify before the 9/11 Commission. And after listening to Secretary Lehman question

Dr. Rice (especially his asking, "Were you aware that it was the policy . . . ?"), I was very eager to have him on my radio program.

We recorded the interview, by phone, two days after the hearing, on the Saturday of Easter weekend, while Lehman was at his home in Bucks County. Maybe that had something to do with his being so relaxed and speaking freely for 35 minutes. When the conversation ended, I felt that what he had told me couldn't wait for publication until Thursday, when my column would run in its usual position. So I spent Easter Sunday writing the column, then called DN editor Zack Stalberg at home and told him what I had. Zack connected me with Michael Days, the newly appointed managing editor, who ran my story the following morning with front-page promotion. It was then picked up by the New York Post and Investor's Business Daily, which gave my reportage on Secretary Lehman and profiling new legs.

I was invited to appear on CNBC's Kudlow and Cramer, and immediately after I shared my observations with Jim Cramer, the Department of Transportation (DOT) issued a statement, saying that what I'd reported was incorrect. Bizarrely, when I asked the DOT for a copy of the statement, they refused. That only made me want to dig deeper to learn about profiling in a pre- and post-9/11 world. What I found appalled me.

In the immediate aftermath of 9/11, the DOT fined four U.S. commercial carriers millions of dollars for alleged discrimination as they sought to prevent a repeat of the terrorism. Stunningly, those punished included United and American Airlines, which had lost two airplanes apiece and a combined total of more than 30 of their own personnel on 9/11. (Continental and Delta were the other two airlines fined.) The DOT, under Norman Mineta, initiated discrimination complaints against United and American that were settled for $1.5 million apiece. I read the litigation files and would later testify before a Senate subcommittee about what I had learned.

As I have previously summarized, the fact patterns were similar: Picture a pilot in the cockpit ready to pull back from the gate. He's got a schedule to keep. And he has a statutory obligation to see to it that anyone who is perceived to be "inimical to public safety" is removed from the aircraft. Then comes the knock on the cockpit door and the pilot is told, either by someone from the flight crew or by someone in law enforcement, that the person in seat 3C is of Middle Eastern descent, that he has been acting suspiciously, and that his name (or one very similar to it) is on a federal watch list. "What should we do, Captain?" And to the extent that the pilot agrees to have the passenger questioned while he goes ahead and departs, our government perceived his actions to be discriminatory and initiated legal proceedings against his airline. Had the DOT not challenged me for repeating Lehman's assertions in print and in my interview with Jim Cramer, I probably would never have written Flying Blind.

HOW TO GET QUASIMODO A DATE

Philadelphia Daily News, Thursday, April 22, 2004

LEGALIZE IT.

That's my reaction to the publication of the photos of 16 "johns" recently arrested for prostitution in Philadelphia.

What an outrage. Just who decided that the press should be judge, jury, and executioner? These men should be facing the wrath of wives and girl-friends, not the Fourth Estate.

Don't get me wrong. It's terrible that people wake up to the sight of used condoms on their stoops. The oldest profession has no business in residential communities. But the fact that this seediness is all around is just another justification for making it legit, which would let us control the location, the participants, and the revenue.

No politician is willing to say this. (Good thing columnists don't have to stand for election.) Instead, they'll talk about the need to protect neighborhoods by going even further to embarrass the johns, perhaps by putting their faces on cable TV.

Ridiculous, I say.

The mug shots published in the *Daily News* revealed a random sampling of American men: white, black, Hispanic, and Asian, of all ages. (My first thought: Poll them and find out who's really winning the presidential race!)

Of course, it's the school principal among them who is drawing most of the attention. No wonder the police department was reluctant to give up the information. You have to worry that one of these guys will kill himself as a result of this latter-day version of the stocks on the town green. That's happened elsewhere.

And what happens if one of the guys whose picture was published is exonerated? As Ronald Reagan's secretary of labor once asked: Where will they go to get their reputation back?

And the attention on the principal is misplaced. I'm more interested in the guy who turned out to have a rap sheet that includes a rape conviction. He did three to seven for it.

Having him pay for sex sounds to me like a good thing. What might he do if he had no place to go and get it? (Spare me the letters saying that rape is a crime of violence, not sex. As far as I'm concerned, when the rapist pays for sex, he's at least not abusing someone else.)

Want to get sex out of neighborhoods? Then legalize it.

Give those who want to do it a place to go far from our homes. Surely a country that says a woman can determine the fate of her fetus can let her decide to accept cash instead of a few drinks for sex. This way, we not only determine where it happens, but we regulate those involved.

Take a look at the adult-film industry in Los Angeles right now.

The business has gone dark because two stars were determined to have AIDS. This is a billion-dollar industry closing up shop on its own initiative. In L.A., the thousand or so porn stars are all tested monthly, and show the results before they can work. Is the system perfect? No. But it is a helluva lot better than the open season on many urban streets right now.

One of the porn stars returned from shooting a movie in Brazil on March 17. Unfortunately, Brazil doesn't exercise L.A.'s oversight of the industry. The day this guy returned, he tested negative. Falsely, it turns out, because of his recent infection.

So he went to work. When tested again on April 12, he was diagnosed. It's an ugly situation. Now 65 people are scared to death that they, too, are infected. But it could have been worse. At least the circle is defined and the initial case was caught within one month.

Imagine if that happened with the hookers on the streets of Philadelphia whose clients were outed last week. How long would it have taken for a diagnosis? How in the world could potential victims be identified?

And there's one more reason for legalization. Call it the Quasimodo conundrum.

Simply stated, some guys are never going to find companionship. I say guys because women never have this problem.

That's just the way we're wired. Aren't the Quasimodos entitled to a little happiness? Particularly in a world where sexual stimulation is all around us?

It's all about sex. And if that's tolerated, so too must a means of dealing with the effects.

AFTERWORD

Yes, legalizing prostitution is still my view, and I've repeated it in other columns. Beyond the Quasimodo factor, I'd add the following virtues to legalization: increased odds of sex workers' reporting crimes against them, a decrease in the spread of sexually transmitted diseases, and a decline in the number of sex workers—all of which came to pass after New Zealand decriminalized prostitution in 2003 (as detailed by a government-commissioned study of the impact). And it's not just the Quasimodos and sex workers I'm looking out for; I'm protecting politicians too! When in the spring of 2013, former New York governor Eliot Spitzer, the victim of his own prostitution scandal, sought to resurrect his career by running for New York City comptroller, I defended his right to run and said it could well pose the final referendum on sex scandals if he won, even though he didn't necessarily agree with me. (Maybe he was right; he lost.)

Guest-hosting one night for Chris Matthews on Hardball, I asked Spitzer whether we'd become too intrusive, and he said:

> Look, I'm not sure I'm the right person to ask, because I have a perspective that is so tailored to what I have been through. And I might separate those questions. Have we become too intrusive? Have we lost all sense of privacy? Yes. I think that's a larger issue that we as a society need to confront. . . . I think maybe there's an important conversation there. Is it the end of the sex scandal? No. Am I in any way condoning what I did? Absolutely not.

I'd argue that we lose potentially good public servants when we evaluate their work capabilities through the prism of their private lives. That's not a defense of Spitzer's patronizing hookers but rather an opinion that his inability to honor his marital vows is not necessarily a reflection of his ability to comport himself as a city comptroller. Which is why I told Spitzer that while his wife should have thrown his clothes into Central Park, I didn't think his stint as Client No. 9 was a job impediment. The following day, again anchoring Hardball, I delivered a commentary and said this:

> I would argue that it's time to bring the world's oldest profession above-board in communities willing to allow it, clean up the trade, and clamp down on the exploitation. Let government share in the revenue, but otherwise stay out of the private affairs of consenting adults. Beyond the role of the taxman, prostitution doesn't warrant the involvement of federal authorities.

That commentary earned me a negative headline at the right-wing website News Busters: "Smerconish Fawns over Spitzer." No, I was just defending the idea that his sex life was his wife's business, not ours.

A BRUSH WITH GREATNESS, THANKS TO A LITTLE TRUANCY AND SOME CONNECTIONS

Philadelphia Daily News, Monday, June 7, 2004

I ONCE SKIPPED SCHOOL just to meet Ronald Reagan. No regrets.

It was the spring of 1980. I was a senior at Central Bucks West and about to vote for the first time. Despite my age, the presidential race had captivated me, largely because of my fondness for a guy running for the office who was 50 years older than I was.

A week or so ahead of the election, a friend named Charlie Gerow, then a regional campaign coordinator for Ronald Reagan, called to say that Reagan would tour the Italian Market in South Philadelphia the next day. He told me that if I was standing inside Esposito's Meat Market at exactly 2:50 P.M., I'd probably get to shake his hand. I decided to try. I recruited a buddy from my neighborhood, Mike Stachel Jr., and together we rode the train into the old Reading Terminal shed. Then we hoofed it down to 9th Street.

The scene was bedlam. The go-go '80s were just beginning, but this was old-school politics. Buttons. Bands. Banners. And open access to a man who might be the next leader of the Free World.

From a distance, we watched Ronald Reagan get out of a town car in front of Giordano's, at 9th and Washington. It was hard to see, much less get close to, the man who people still addressed as "Governor." So we walked a block or so north and headed into Esposito's. There was no one around.

"Are you sure he's coming in here?" my friend asked. I had my doubts. Things were too quiet. Then I spied a large catering plate with a huge length of sausage spelling out "Reagan." It was a good sign. I figured we must be in the right place.

Sure enough, minutes later, in walked Ronald Reagan and what we then thought was an army of Secret Service, although when viewed through 2004 glasses, it was really just a few guys. That was it. Ronald Reagan. Some security. The meat cutters from Esposito's. And the two punks from Bucks County who should have been in class.

I had a pocket Instamatic in my hood. They were all the rage at the time. I asked Ronald Reagan for his permission before we used it.

In person, Reagan was a big, broad-shouldered fellow with inviting eyes. And he was a gentleman. "Hold on fellows, I need to blow my nose," I remember him saying. We did. Then we snapped away as he smiled and gave the feeling that he had all the time in the world for two young men barely of age

Left to right: **Elia Esposito, Senator Richard Schweiker, Louis Esposito Sr. (background, with glasses), unidentified man (background), Ronald Reagan, Helen Sposaro, and Jules Esposito.** Photo courtesy of Louis Esposito.

to vote. The guys from Esposito's presented the sausage, while we were flies on the wall.

I'd never heard the word "gravitas" back then, but I knew that Ronald Reagan had something special. Something tough to put into words that I immediately felt from being in his presence for a few moments in a meat store in the heart of the Italian Market.

Call it Ronald Reagan's gift. It was a feeling that he exuded. "Grandfatherly" might sum it up. To be close to him was to trust him, and to feel that he had your back. He emitted strength. And an air of sincerity, a rarity among all people, but particularly in our public servants. Even bad news would be welcome if it were to come from his lips. And while he'd made his name on celluloid, and carried with him a certain formality, he nevertheless had a rugged sense of American independence and grit. He was a man's man.

We were like giddy schoolkids when we got back on the train. Hell, we were schoolkids! But a few days after the trip to the Italian Market, I was crushed. I hadn't wanted to carry the flash attachment on the train and, as a result, the photographs were of a terrible quality. I didn't know it then, but I would soon get another chance.

Late that summer, Charlie Gerow called again. Ronald Reagan, now the Republican Party candidate for president, was coming back to Philadelphia; this time, for a fund-raiser at the Bellevue with Arlen Specter, the GOP nominee for the U.S. Senate. The date was August 18, 1980—the price was $500 per person! Gerow told me that, if I played my cards right, I might be able to crash. There were no guarantees. I put on my only sport coat and headed back into the city. With a purloined nametag, I quickly gained admission. (Ah, the good old, pre-9/11 days!) This time I had not only my pocket Instamatic, but also my flash. I handed the camera to a stranger when Reagan worked the rope line and the mystery man snapped just one shot. That's all it took. I look at it often. It's me with a fat, '70s-era tie and a full head of hair, standing with the Gipper. I treasure it to this day.

While I would be in his presence on several occasions, none would equal the initial feeling I had inside Esposito's.

Those struggling to understand the enormity of the loss his death represents surely won't include people who got a chance to meet him.

AFTERWORD

When Charlie Gerow turned 60, Lou Esposito surprised him with the photograph of the unique sausage gift for the future president. Fortunately, he made me a duplicate! It's just the way I remembered all these years.

Meeting Ronald Reagan in the Bellevue Stratford, August 18, 1980.

JIM BEASLEY,
THE PEOPLE'S LAWYER

Philadelphia Daily News, Thursday, September 23, 2004

A LEGAL GIANT will be laid to rest today. But we'd be doing Jim Beasley a disservice if we were to recall him as a great "Philadelphia lawyer," a moniker that may still carry a connotation of skill and competence but also conjures up privilege, white shoes, and Ivy League degrees.

Jim Beasley was none of that. He spent most of his 78 years slaying dragons. He was a trial lawyer, and damn proud of it, even when it became a term of derision.

For 50 years, he reigned as the preeminent litigator in all of Pennsylvania. The range of his clients and breadth of his cases was unparalleled. Google "Jim Beasley," and you'll read about his beating the *Philadelphia Inquirer* twice on behalf of Dick Sprague. Or his representation of the family of Holly Maddux against the man who murdered her, Ira Einhorn. He made headlines when he obtained a judgment against Iraq for 9/11 victims. Many thought of suing, but it was Jim Beasley who figured out how to serve the members of the Taliban with legal papers.

But there also were the everyday unpublished stories of thousands of clients who were united only in their status as the underdog: Injured workers. Victims of medical neglect. Consumers injured by unsafe products. Beasley gave a voice to ordinary people who otherwise would never have had the ability to take on large insurance companies and Fortune 500 corporations.

Size mattered to Beasley: The smaller the aggrieved party, the more apt he was to become their champion. And his outrage was palpable. In this day of blow-dried pettifoggers, the jury felt—and shared—his sense of outrage.

Lawyers desperate to learn the secret of Beasley's success would travel great distances to watch him try a case or host a seminar. "You have to believe in your case," he'd say, "because a jury can tell when you don't."

But the skills that he used so effectively in court didn't come from a textbook. His roots were the key to his success. His humble upbringing and thorough preparation gave him a unique ability to speak simply and convincingly.

Jim Beasley was once a kid born on the wrong side of the tracks in the midst of the Depression. He grew up poor in West Philadelphia, the son of a factory worker. He spent his summers working his grandparents' Mississippi farm. At 17, he dropped out of high school to join the Navy. After his discharge in 1945, he worked briefly as a cop, and then returned to Philadelphia.

He drove a truck, a cab, and a Greyhound bus, and quickly realized that he had to go back to school. So he enrolled in a VA program and put himself through Temple law school (which now bears his name) by working at night. Then came the stuff of legal legend.

Like when he represented the teenage victim of an airline crash and walked into court holding a phone. During his closing speech, Beasley brought out the phone and invited the jurors to imagine themselves in the boy's home so they could "overhear" the call in which his parents learned of their son's death.

With the power of his spoken words, he crafted an image of cinematic size that was as poignant as it was vivid. Then, with a blend of common sense and a not-insignificant bit of flair, he told the jury that they would control the message in a call yet to be made—in which the airline lawyer would report the jury's verdict to the plane's manufacturer. It would be up to the jurors, he said, to decide what would be reported in that call.

I sat at his elbow and watched him treat all clients, from the mayor of Rome to a welfare mom from North Philly, with the same dignity and respect. Beasley didn't care about skin color. He wasn't interested in your politics. Your station in life was irrelevant. His only interest was the plight of his clients. And for them he was a gunslinger.

These days, it's enough to sneer contemptuously at "those trial lawyers," as if the title itself connotes dishonesty or opportunism. No need to qualify the title with an adjective ("dishonest")—it's bad enough to just call someone a "trial lawyer." No doubt some will see the career of Jim Beasley as one spent in an attack on American commerce.

But that would be a mistake. We can thank Jim Beasley for the fact that our cars are as safe today as they have ever been, newspapers think twice before publishing something that destroys a reputation, hospitals have implemented protocols that save people from getting the wrong medicine, and factories use machines that are less likely to injure working people.

People who think we would be better off without trial lawyers have simply been fortunate to never need one.

And somewhere, somebody should now be chiseling: "Here lies James E. Beasley, Trial Lawyer."

AFTERWORD

Pennsylvania lawyers have a continuing legal education (CLE) requirement that commands us to spend 12 hours every year listening to lectures about ethics and the conduct of the legal practice. Ever since Jim's passing, I'd had an idea to present a CLE program focused on him. In March 2015, working to-

gether, David Arena and Lisa Muench at the Pennsylvania Bar Institute and I staged a three-hour seminar entitled "Lessons Learned from the Legendary James Beasley, Sr." I moderated the discussion in front of a roomful of lawyers in Philadelphia that was simulcast to attorneys all over Pennsylvania. The participants included the Honorable Sandra Mazer Moss from the Philadelphia Court of Common Pleas, in front of whom Jim had often appeared; James E. Beasley Jr., who now runs the Beasley firm; Shanin Specter and Tom Kline, both of whom were mentored by Jim before creating one of the most successful trial practices in the nation; and Peter Hoffman, a defense attorney against whom Jim had tried many cases. The legendary Richard Sprague, Jim's close friend and former legal client, sat in the audience.

As is the custom for such programs, the speakers prepared written materials for the attendees. My contribution was a lengthy memo that I nevertheless described as a thoroughly INcomplete list of things I'd learned in my 10-year association with Jim. Most were tips for lawyers, such as the Beasley style of writing a letter ("You know that I know that you know . . ."), the way Jim liked to interview prospective clients, how he'd get them to summarize their claims in writing, his aggressive style of taking pretrial discovery, how he'd interview prospective jurors during voir dire, his special skill of persuasion, and his work ethic.

But under the heading of "Friendship," I also offered this:

> Outside the court room, Jim could be prickly. He maintained a very small social circle, but for those allowed to enter he was a good friend and better dinner companion. He enjoyed a glass of wine. Loved to tell stories. Relished a dinner debate. When our wives joined us, he would view my spouse's presence as an opportunity to sound her out on potential cases. Christmas seemed to matter to him—he never missed that gift exchange. I recall when my kids were young, we surprised him at his remote Villanova home on Halloween, and sans candy, he responded by going into his pocket for a $20 bill. He also acknowledged the birth of each of our children with a note. And I will always remember him making an unsolicited call to the delivery room at Lankenau Hospital during the birth of our first son—making it clear to the nursing station that "Jim Beasley was calling to make sure everything is all right."

I was touched, but also maybe a little concerned the OB would drop my son upon hearing who had inquired!

DREAMING OF A
WHITE (HOUSE) CHRISTMAS

Philadelphia Daily News, Thursday, December 23, 2004

ALLOW ME TO TELL YOU about a memorable night at the White House last week.

One which included my telling the president that he'd been mentioned in a letter sent to Santa by one of my kids. The occasion was a White House Christmas party attended by my wife and me. What a thrill.

We have four children—three boys aged 4, 6, and 8 and a teenage daughter (who's 16 going on 30). Our 8-year-old son met the president at a campaign rally in Yardley just days before the recent election. I emceed the event, and when it was over, Senator Rick Santorum introduced me to the president. My son was at my side. I had my digital camera, and so when the president greeted my namesake, I took a photo of them, albeit not at the best angle. Chalk that up to suddenly unsteady hands.

No wonder my son voted for W in his school's mock election. And he hasn't stopped talking about his chance encounter. Even when writing to Santa, he told Old Saint Nick that he "means as much to me as the President of the United States."

I thought the president would get a kick out of the note to Santa. My chance came soon after my wife and I entered the East Wing and joined the receiving line at the Christmas party.

After a "Welcome to the White House" greeting from a uniformed staffer, we'd walked past a photo display of the Reagans at Christmas, beyond the first of many beautifully decorated Christmas trees, and through a room with first lady portraits.

Standing in the receiving line, I had my son's letter to Santa in my pocket, along with the photograph I'd taken of him with the president. Now my dilemma.

The event was structured with military precision: We would be formally announced as we greeted the president. We'd shake hands and pose for a picture. In other words, keep moving.

"Michael and Lavinia Smerconish," someone called out.

There we stood shaking hands while a photographer clicked.

"Our son wrote to Santa Claus to say he respects him as much as he respects you," I said.

He asked me my son's age. I took it as an opening.

"You met him during the campaign," I said, and pulled out the letter and picture to show him.

My eyes were fixed on the president, who seemed touched to hear the report. My wife told me later that I gave the Secret Service a stir when I reached for the letter to Santa.

The president asked if he could sign the picture to my son. I told him it wasn't necessary. He ignored me, asked his name, and penned a greeting.

We were then free to explore 1600 Pennsylvania Avenue. The entire first floor was open without restriction. Gone were the stanchions that limit the public tour. We were able to navigate the rooms, sit in the furniture, and get a close look at the breathtaking art collection. The trees were all white, and lit with candlelight bulbs. (The president has yet to join my colored-light brigade.)

This was clearly a red-state party. Most people posing for their own photos wanted them taken under the Ronald Reagan portrait, or near the crèche in the East Room. (There was no waiting line at Hillary's portrait.)

The menu was a mixture of some politically correct low-carb stuff: western-style wraps, some tame sushi, and a dish or two of pasta. Red and white wine flowed, nothing French. The egg nog tasted good—and spiked.

Karl Rove was circulating. But the cloak-room staff provided more interesting conversation. When retrieving my wife's coat, I said I felt sorry for the president having to pose for pictures all night.

One fellow told me that the Reagans had the party down to a science. "When they wanted you to leave, the band would strike up 'Hit the Road Jack' and people did."

AFTERWORD

My wife and I did a few of the White House Christmas parties with the Bushes and were together for one with the Obamas their first year in the White House. Then she said she'd had enough: "Take the kids." So I did. In subsequent years, I took each of our four children, and then my mother, and finally, my brother. The only close family member I did not get to take was my dad; we had planned to go in the final year of the Obama administration, but he was unable to travel and so neither of us attended. Good thing I was able share the experience with so many, because I am not anticipating any similar invitations from President Trump!

COS CASE: IT'S KOBE ALL OVER AGAIN

Philadelphia Daily News, Thursday, February 17, 2005

TOLD YOU SO.

With Kobe, I mean. From the start of that case, I said it didn't pass the smell test.

All I needed to hear was that the alleged victim showed up for a rape test the next day with semen that didn't belong to Kobe on her shorts. Huh?

And now I'm ready to say the same thing about "the Cos." This one doesn't wash, either. It defies logic that a woman wakes up feeling that she's been drugged and violated, but doesn't call the police. And then, one year later (according to her father), only after receiving training on the ethical boundaries of massage therapy, she realized that she should call the police? That, plus the fact that the Philadelphia police sexual assault report says, "According to the Canadian [police] interview, her recollection is poor," tells me any criminal case is a loser.

I know, this makes me an insensitive male. But there will be other insensitive males on the jury, and they'll never buy it.

And on the gender bias that seems to dictate perception of these cases: I'm tired of the argument that those of us who are circumspect about an alleged sexual-assault claim do a disservice to future victims. I say it's actually the initiators of weak claims who do future claimants a disservice.

Remember: If claimants in sexual-assault cases never lied, we'd never see acquittals! But we do.

Bottom line: This is a criminal case that won't be filed. And if it's filed, it'll never succeed. On the civil side of things, maybe she files, and he pays her to go away.

Bruce Castor, the Montgomery County DA, is perfect for the Cosby case. He's tough. And a straight arrow. He won't be intimidated by the possibility of a celebrity defendant, nor will he cower in the face of those who want the man charged. If you need a reference on his work, just seek out Craig Rabinowitz, Caleb Farley, or Guy Sileo.

But Castor is now the subject of criticism for comments he made about the case, some of them on my radio show. I've heard his words twisted by people who claim that Castor tipped his hand. I checked the tape. He did nothing of the kind. Here is what he did say:

You will find no place that I said the case is weak or anything of that nature. What I said was that, under Pennsylvania law, delay in reporting inures to the benefit of the defendant unless there is some good reason why the victim waits to come forward.

There is a presumption in the law that a "prompt complaint" goes to the credibility of the person complaining. The reverse is also true. Juries tend to believe that a delay in reporting means that the victim did not think that what happened was so bad, and that some intervening event made her decide she wanted to go ahead and complain. Where you see juries sympathetic to delay is the type of case where you have a child complaining.

Was he tipping his hand? Was he insensitive to the alleged victim? Hardly. He was simply explaining the legal realities of the review he is duty-bound to apply.

Consider this. After a Pennsylvania jury in a case of alleged sexual assault hears all the evidence, here is one of the instructions read to them by the judge:

> The evidence of delay in making a complaint does not necessarily make her testimony unreliable, but may remove from it the assurance of reliability accompanying the prompt complaint or outcry which the victim of a crime such as this would ordinarily be expected to make. Therefore, the delay in making a complaint should be considered in evaluating her testimony and in deciding whether the act occurred with or without her consent.

That's what Castor was talking about. He was explaining that this is something he must consider when deciding whether to charge Cosby in a case that would appear to be a he said/she said.

But some people wear blinders on this topic. They think that if the conduct involves sex, the credibility of an alleged victim should be off limits. Which is ridiculous if all you have to go on is her word.

This same logic applies to the latest voice in the case, the lawyer from California who now claims that 30 years ago, the Cos assaulted her, too.

Where has she been? In part, defending herself against disciplinary charges in front of the California bar. Are we supposed to ignore those revelations when all we have to go on is her word? I think not.

Here is one final way of looking at it. Bill Cosby is presumed to be innocent. This is a case where she claims he did something, and he claims he didn't.

One of them is lying. If he is presumed to be innocent, it means she is presumed to be lying, until shown otherwise. She has to move the needle. And based solely on that which has been printed about the case to date, I doubt she can do it.

AFTERWORD

Yikes. In my defense, I wrote this column long before 50 or so women came forward and told similar stories about Cosby. Nevertheless, I did later write about the way Cosby was treated by the judicial system, specifically how, despite a confidentiality agreement in a long-settled civil suit, a federal judge allowed the release of portions of his sworn deposition testimony, truly "the" decision that opened the floodgates for those many accusers to come forward. I still think that decision was wrong. As I wrote for the Sunday Inquirer *in July 2015:*

> *That Bill Cosby will be forever known as a serial abuser of women wasn't determined by the findings of a jury. It didn't come down to evidence such as forensics, DNA, or even a blue dress. Instead his fate was sealed in the court of public opinion by an adjudication of his hypocrisy. Beyond the legalese, that was the true predicate on which Judge Eduardo C. Robreno based his decision to unseal documents related to a civil suit filed against Cosby 10 years ago.*

> *I was referring to the fact that in his ruling to release portions of Cosby's testimony from the civil case, the judge reasoned that Cosby had "thrust himself into the vortex of these public issues" and had therefore "voluntarily narrowed the zone of privacy that he is entitled to claim." One of the ways Cosby had done so, according to the judge's footnotes, was by giving a speech about personal responsibility in the black community on the 50th anniversary of* Brown v. Board of Education. *In other words, had Cosby stayed out of the public policy arena, the deposition excerpts might have remained sealed. But because he was a public moralizer, he opened the door to be refuted by discovery motions and their supporting documents from 10 years earlier. I didn't buy the logic then and I still don't.*

My willingness to offer that nuanced legal defense of Cosby in his prosecution surely played a role in what happened just before the start of his criminal trial. In May 2017, my iPhone rang on a Friday afternoon while I was preparing for the following day's CNN program. On the line were Andrew Wyatt, a public relations professional, and his client—Bill Cosby. They wanted to offer me audio for use on my radio program that consisted of two short statements of support from Cosby's daughters, Erinn and Ensa, and a lengthy interview that Erinn recorded with her father. Would I like to play some of the sound on my radio show? they asked. "Maybe" was my reply. I wasn't about to commit to just playing sound that I hadn't heard and suspected was biased in support of Cosby. But what did interest me, I said, was to interview Bill Cosby himself. To my surprise, Wyatt and Cosby told me that was possible. The following Monday, at noon, I taped a 30-minute interview with Cosby that aired the following day (May 16) uncut and uninterrupted by commercials on my SiriusXM radio show. I prepared for the interview as I would a deposition, and with the knowledge that merely speaking with him would earn me scorn. (It did.) My intention was to be fair but direct, courteous but not a lackey. And mostly, to let him speak.

The biggest revelation was Cosby's telling me he had no intention of taking the stand in his own defense. ("No, I do not.") While I'd seen plenty of news footage showing Cosby slowly entering the courthouse to face charges for aggravated indecent assault, the man I spoke with, possessing an unmistakable hearty laugh, was not mentally infirm. He told me that he regarded himself as "unsighted," but his 79-year-old mind was sharp. And though his answers were often meandering, he nevertheless made his points. He dismissed my question about whether he was seeking to influence jurors ("You can't aim at jurors") but kept his eye on his goal ("Well, things were rescinded, and I'd like to get those things back"). He was partially accepting of his daughter Ensa's opinion that there is racism at play ("Could be, could be. I can't say anything, but there are certain things that I look at and I apply to the situation. There are so many tentacles, so many different—'nefarious' is a great word—and I just truly believe that some of it may very well be that") and said he'd been subjected to media bias ("I also feel that there are many filmed things and writing as well that people can take what you say and insert it and it will mean something altogether different"). He presented himself as a victim of a gang-up by accusers ("I think that the numbers came because the numbers prior to the numbers didn't work") not only intent on denying him the reputation he has earned but also willing to punish those still willing to pay to watch him perform ("But I will ask this question, If no matter what happens, if a man is then free to go where he wants to go, free within the law to do what he wants to do, and he offers himself in concert for people to buy tickets, why would people threaten the hall, threaten the people who booked the show, when in fact the people who are coming are those who are buying tickets?").

The conversation got huge play. Patrick Reilly, the head of corporate communications for SiriusXM, distributed an internal e-mail calling the pickup of the interview "massive." I'll say. He reported that in the ensuing 48 hours, the audience for the national television segments discussing the interview totaled nearly 20 million viewers; in addition, the interview played on local news outlets in more than a hundred cities across the country. There were many headlines generated by the interview. As I explained in a subsequent Sunday Inquirer *column:*

> *Many outlets, like the* Inquirer *and* Washington Post, *highlighted that Cosby revealed he would not testify on his own behalf. Several, including the* Huffington Post, *noted that he regarded the volume of accusers as "piling on." Others, like* People *magazine, reported that he said he "never" lost the support of his wife. All of that is true. But to me, who conducted the interview, they miss the bigger takeaway from the discussion. Considered in total, the half-hour conversation was a roadmap of Cosby's defense.*

At the end of the interview, Cosby said, "I just hope I'm not in trouble now, man," which became a headline in the New York Post. *I thought his concern was justified given that he'd invoked race and revealed his trial posture. I'm not sure he helped me personally when within hours of the airing of the interview he tweeted me thanks for "integrity, ethics and clarity," but it was clear that he believed he'd made his points. One month later, a mistrial was declared when the Cosby jury could not agree on the verdict in his case.*

AIR-TRAVEL SCREENING STUPIDITY—TIMES 4

Philadelphia Daily News, Thursday, March 10, 2005

'M PREPARED TO CROWN A WINNER. Of what, you ask? My competition for best horror story involving airport security screening since 9/11.

In the six months since I published *Flying Blind: How Political Correctness Continues to Compromise Airline Safety Post 9/11*, I've been overwhelmed with anecdotes from all over about the ridiculous nature of passenger screening.

I've heard it all. Military folks returning from the front lines (in uniform and with papers) who take a commercial flight only to get searched after being selected for random screening. Or people with pacemakers and documents that say metal detectors might cause a heart hiccup who are nevertheless "wanded" and asked what they're hiding in their chest!

I've heard from eyewitnesses to the full-scale screening of government leaders like Senator Joseph Lieberman and former secretary of defense William Cohen. There's been the full complement of seniors with walkers and young kids on whom we've wasted precious resources.

But none compares to the experience of the Yocum family, from Boothwyn, on October 28, 2002, at the Phoenix airport. Frank and Claire Yocum's visit to Arizona was due to her quadruple pregnancy. The plan was to deliver at Good Samaritan Hospital in Phoenix because that's home to Dr. John P. Elliot, nationally recognized for his delivery of quadruplets.

Claire's delivery was nine weeks premature. The babies then needed two months in the ICU. Their immune systems were compromised, and they had to be kept germ free. A cold could have killed them. The Yocums were eager to return to Pennsylvania. Their doctors were nervous about the travel. Airplanes, with their recycled air, are not the most sanitary of environments.

After consulting the physicians and American West Airlines, they decided to make the

Photo courtesy of Frank and Claire Yocum.

trip on a late-night flight when there would be few other passengers. American West was so sympathetic, it offered to fly the entire family free. So sensitive was the situation that the Yocums had to take CPR training before the hospital would permit the travel.

Frank Yocum, a cop's son, was meticulous about planning for the journey. The morning of the flight, he actually made a test run so he knew exactly where to go, minimizing the babies' contact with other people.

On the day of the flight, the nurses and doctors prepared the Yocums for their seven-hour trip. They organized bottles, medicines, and other necessities. (Extremely important because the babies were all on different formulas.)

Each of the babies was on a heart monitor, and the darkness of the night flight was expected to make the necessary maneuvering quite a challenge. The trip from the hospital to the airport was smooth until it came to airport screening.

By now, I'm sure you've guessed that the newborn Yocum quads were selected for additional screening! Nineteen Arab look-alikes wreaked havoc on the United States on 9/11, and four newborns from Philadelphia are the ones getting the hairy eyeball.

The babies, wrapped tight in blankets with a net covering their safety seats, were removed from their medical equipment and searched. All of their bags, prepared and organized by the nurses, had to be removed. Worst of all, the screeners woke the sleeping babies. Frank and Claire never again got a handle on the situation and the flight home was chaos. Everything was thrown back into bags to sort out later, which never happened.

Unlike the screeners, the other passengers had common sense. They voluntarily moved to the front of the plane and gave the Yocums about 20 rows to themselves. Says Frank, "I can only imagine what it was like for the other passengers with four crying babies, and heart monitors going off on a five-hour flight."

A member of Congress recently told me the TSA has backed off the random screening of children. But when I tried to confirm this with the TSA, they reported no change in policy.

TSA says the policy of selecting passengers for secondary screening by the individual air carriers occurs in one of two ways: random selection by the carrier, or selection based on a screening profile that looks for "trends in travel." Children under 12 who are selected randomly MAY be "de-selected" at the carrier's discretion and a parent need not be screened in place of the child.

The stupidity continues.

AFTERWORD

I'm happy to report that the Yocum quadruplets—and their parents—are doing well. During the 2016–2017 school year, the now-14-year-old Claire, Frank, Jake, and Judy were all honor students in the eighth grade at Garnet Valley Middle School. Their father, Frank, confirmed that all four kids are "very healthy," which seems like a miracle given their susceptible immune systems as babies. Frank went on to tell me more about each kid, including:

> *Claire plays field hockey and lacrosse for the school team [but] Judy runs track and cross country. The girls wanted to do separate sports but are inseparable otherwise. Jake is six [feet] tall and is crazy about politics and is Hillary Clinton's biggest supporter. Frank plays baseball and basketball for the school team and loves sports.*

Meanwhile, Claire, the children's mother, went back to work as a gifted teacher in the Chichester School District less than two years after the children were born. Understandably, Frank is concerned about paying for college.

Jake, Judy, Frank, and Claire in 2016.
Photo courtesy of Frank and Claire Yocum.

POSTCARD FROM GLADWYNE

Philadelphia Daily News, Thursday, July 21, 2005

YOU THINK YOU HAVE ISSUES in the city? Be glad you're not out here on the Main Line this summer. It's a jungle.

In case you haven't heard, Bill and Laura just got news that their lease isn't being renewed, which means they're getting the boot by the end of summer from the shack that Laura runs with Doris, unless things change, and that's unlikely because Connie owns the place, and he's committed to Maurice so that Maurice can expand his salon into what's now the kitchen, which has everybody angry. In fact, there's a website up called savethelunch.com, where you can find talk of boycotting OMG, and—as if that isn't enough—when a local reporter went to Connie for comment about throwing out Bill and Laura, he says Connie mumbled something about "home invasion" and brandished a pistol.

It's enough to make you want to move back to the city.

Bill and Laura Faust own Gladwyne Village Lunch. They have terrific, inexpensive food, basic stuff hard to find out here, where even short-order cooks think of themselves as artistes. Eggs with pork roll. BLTs. Cheesesteaks.

Even SOS in the colder months. Laura won't make it in the summer, although I've never dared ask why. I never got around to asking her anything until the controversy began. That was the beauty of the place. You could go in, eat, and be left alone if you chose.

But now everyone who stops by is conversing. Mostly about Maurice next door. And Connie down the block.

Maurice is Maurice Tannenbaum, the hairstylist to the rich and famous in these parts. He once shaved my head. I'd had a few drinks at the Guard House and finally decided to do it. Maurice obliged. It cost me a C-note. I always say that if Bill Clinton stopped traffic for a haircut out here, no doubt it would be Maurice with the shears in his hands. His salon is called OMG, as in "Oh, My God." (I couldn't make this stuff up.)

Needless to say, Maurice is a character. He drives a yellow Hummer sixtenths of a mile to work from the home he shares with his significant other, John, according to his website.

He says that when he arrived in Gladwyne, Bill Faust was rude to him. In the same post (which began, "Don't hate me because I am beautiful"), he also said that the gardening rigs and delivery trucks cause the traffic jams on the block, not his clients with their BMWs and Porsches. Which gets to the heart of the controversy.

Maurice's clients do drive fancy cars. And while I suspect that most of Maurice's customers eat at Village, I doubt many Village customers reciprocate. Some of the Village customers drive fancy cars, too, but many also command those gardening rigs.

All are equal at Gladwyne Village Lunch. Smack dab in the middle of one of the 50 richest ZIP codes in America are six highly coveted bar stools open to anyone. On them, you can find the fannies of cops, accountants, lawyers, doctors, mechanics, grocers, landscapers, retirees, and school kids. Joe is the guy who checks my oil at Gladwyne Texaco. But he is a salt shaker away at breakfast. Think Famous Deli without the politicians.

Memories get made here. Parents with their kids. Kids who return with their kids. Bill and Laura have run it for about a decade of its 60 years. The building was the first post office for Gladwyne's predecessor, Merion Square, back in the Civil War era.

Which is why it will be a crime if it closes. I've asked Maurice to reconsider. No way. He intends to open OMGorgeous, a tiny day spa, just what the area doesn't need.

Maurice also told me that Connie Barker, who owns the shack and the block on which it stands, would just find somebody else.

When Richard Ilgenfritz of the *Main Line Times* went to Barker to find out if this was true, he said Barker pulled out a pistol, although he made it clear that Barker didn't point it at him.

I believe Ilgenfritz. He's an ex-Marine and has seen guns before. Barker is another local character. Which is all the more reason that the place should stay open. We characters need a clubhouse.

Six stools. I'm picturing Maurice. Another for his partner, John. Laura and Bill. One for Connie. And one for yours truly. Maybe I'm dreaming.

AFTERWORD

Gladwyne Village Lunch ended up moving less than half a block up to 951 Youngsford Road into what had previously been the Merion Square Coiffure. About a month after this column ran, I took a copy I'd had framed and presented it to Laura as a bit of a housewarming gift, thinking that she would hang it in the new location. When she didn't do so after a few weeks, I asked why. She said she was so angry about what had happened to the old spot that she refused to post a visual reminder in the new luncheonette. Bill and Laura decided to retire in 2011 and move to Florida after 18 years of owning and operating Gladwyne Village Lunch. They sold the restaurant to one of their patrons, the Gladwyne resident Sam Stanford, who renamed the spot the Gladwyne Lunch Box. Sam subsequently sold it to Theo Gerike, who remains the owner, and I'm still a customer. I recommend the tuna "scoop" salad for lunch.

GOOD WITH A PEN,
AS WELL AS A FOOTBALL

Philadelphia Daily News, Thursday, August 11, 2005

IT WAS 30 YEARS AGO, but I remember it like it was yesterday.

I rode my yellow, banana-seat bicycle, the one with the monkey handle-bars, the three blocks from my house to the Artic Market, in Doylestown. It was a Saturday, and an important day in the neighborhood. A new Philadelphia Eagles wide receiver was coming to town, and those of us who imitated our favorite Eagles when we played Nerf football on Mercer Avenue were excited to meet him.

I remember our awe when he walked in the same door we'd usually enter with our folks and shopping carts. He was a giant. There was 6 feet, 8 inches of him. But he wasn't intimidating, not even to young kids half his size. He had a disarming smile, and a gentle nature. He was gracious. And he was accommodating. He seemed to understand and appreciate that it was a very big deal for my friends and me to have the chance to shake his hand and ask him to sign his picture.

His name was Harold Carmichael.

There were a handful of us neighborhood kids who showed up that day to get his autograph and be present for a grand-prize drawing. As luck would have it, No. 17 pulled my name out of a hat, and I won a pair of tickets to an Eagles preseason game at Veterans Stadium. I remember being thrilled and a little embarrassed, but very anxious to share the news with my parents. When I didn't have a dime to call home from the pay phone outside, the big guy himself reached into his pocket and gave me one.

I guess that's why I never stopped cheering for Harold Carmichael. On and off the field, he was what little kids thought pro football players were made of.

I was thinking about my encounter with Harold Carmichael this past Monday, when reading about the kids with their fathers who showed up last Sunday at Lehigh expecting that Terrell Owens would sign autographs as per the Eagles player-signing schedule. To me, it's inexcusable that T.O. stood them up.

Off the field, T.O. is no Harold Carmichael.

Up until this point I haven't had a rooting interest for, or against, T.O. in his attempt to breach his contract with the Birds. He says he's worth more than the negotiated amount he is to receive in an agreement which still has wet ink. I keep wondering if that means he's willing to refund the Eagles if he underperforms? We all know the answer to that one.

HAROLD CARMICHAEL   PHILADELPHIA EAGLES

But now I feel different. T.O. crosses the line when he disrespects fathers and sons—kids like I was three decades ago at the Artic Market—who make the drive to the Lehigh Valley with an expectation of getting his autograph at a designated place and an appointed time. Frankly, he's not worthy of their admiration. Instead, he's everything bad that sports have become. He's a big, spoiled, petulant pain in the ass. And I can't understand why everyone is this town is so afraid to say so.

Yes, he can catch. So could Harold.

And Harold could sign autographs, too.

AFTERWORD

This reflection on the positive value of celebrity reminds me of another column I wrote, in 2003, for the Daily News. *I recounted a night spent in Camden, New Jersey, in the company of two disparately famous characters: Pete Rose and Ted Nugent. I had been invited to Campbell's Field, the beautiful home of the Riversharks, to introduce Pete Rose to thousands of fans there to watch his No. 14 being retired in a minor league ballpark. The greatest baseball player of our time didn't know my role as we mingled at a pregame event. And what a sight he was. His close-cropped Moe haircut was an unnatural shade of orange. He wore a pair of sweats that would make a South Philly gangster proud. Gold chain with alligator clips suspending a pair of eyeglasses. You get the picture. My buddy Paul Lauricella had a great line: "Pete Rose now looks like what you'd get if James Caan and Pete Rose had a baby. What would ever lead you to conclude he had a gambling problem?"*

Unfortunately, Pete was really an ass. He refused to sign anything other than the paid-for pictures he was peddling, including the baseball I'd carried to the game: a onetime foul ball I'd snagged one-handed (while balancing a beer in the other) in that same stadium. He changed his tune only when we met again under the concourse and he saw me with a microphone in my hand and realized my role just before we walked onto the field.

A few minutes later, and a couple blocks away, I stood backstage with Motor City Madman Ted Nugent. Quite a contrast. Hair down to his butt, guitar in his hand, guns on his mind. Nugent was thrilled to put his pen to my copy of Kill It and Grill It, *which you could call his recipe for life. I wrote in the column that Nugent was "much more the embodiment of the American Dream than Rose."*

> *The rocker owes his place to hard work, and he didn't screw up along the way. Rose's legacy may have been born in America's pastime, but he no longer conjures up visions of hot dogs and apple pie. Nugent, on the other hand, has distinguished himself by being an unabashed flag-waver who is stone-cold sober in an industry of antagonists and miscreants.*

Years later I become disgusted with Nugent's vitriol ("subhuman mongrel") directed at President Barack Obama, but that night in Camden, he was the better man.

SMALL GESTURE FOR
A REAL AMERICAN HERO

Philadelphia Daily News, Thursday, September 15, 2005

JOSE MELENDEZ-PEREZ, one of the great unsung heroes of 9/11, felt a roomful of Brotherly Love last week. Arguably, it's Melendez we can thank for the fact that Flight 93 never completed its mission of striking a symbol of democracy in Washington and instead crashed into a field in western Pennsylvania.

Melendez was feted at a luncheon in his honor sponsored by my radio station, the Big Talker 1210, at the Union League.

A confab of conservative Republicans? Not exactly.

Particularly when Representative Bob Brady, head of the city Democrats, stood up to present Melendez with a flag he flew in his honor over the Capitol and thank Melendez for saving his life.

Still, no amount of recognition could ever fully thank Melendez for what he did while performing his job back on August 4, 2001.

It was Melendez, an immigration inspector, who stopped Mohamed al Kahtani when he tried to enter the United States at Orlando International Airport. Kahtani was a Saudi national who was directed to Melendez because he had incorrectly filled out a customs declaration. Kahtani claimed not to speak English. Melendez put Kahtani into his computer, and it came up negative. His documents seemed genuine. A check of his possessions was unremarkable.

But Melendez still didn't let him pass. Why? "My job requires me to know the difference between legitimate travelers to the U.S. and those who are not," he told the 9/11 Commission. "This included potential terrorists."

Keep in mind—this is a month before 9/11.

Through my INS training and military experience, my first impression of the subject was that he was a young male, well groomed, with short hair, trimmed mustache, black long-sleeve shirt, black trousers, black shoes. He was about 5 foot 6 and in impeccable shape, with large shoulders and thin waist.

He had a military appearance. Upon establishing eye contact, he exhibited body language and facial gestures that appeared arrogant. In fact, when I first called his name in the secondary room and matched him with papers, he had a deep staring look.

With Governor/Secretary Tom Ridge and Jose Melendez-Perez at the Flight 93 Memorial on the 8th anniversary of 9/11 in 2009.

As Melendez would later tell the commission, "He just gave me the creeps." And the would-be terrorist, who claimed not to speak English, suddenly was able to say, when Melendez rejected him, "I'll be back." The next time we encountered Kahtani, he was fighting in Afghanistan. He's now at Guantanamo.

Here's the kicker: What we now know is that at the moment that Mohamed al Kahtani was being given his walking papers by Melendez at the Orlando Airport, there to pick up the new arrival was 9/11 ringleader Mohamed Atta. That was one of the more interesting details to emerge from the work of the 9/11 Commission, and why Democratic 9/11 commissioner Richard Ben-Veniste told Melendez that his conduct may have spared the Capitol or White House an attack. Ben-Veniste reasoned that, with the added muscle of Kahtani on Flight 93, the terrorists could have fended off the passenger revolt and continued to Washington.

No wonder Bob Brady wanted to thank Melendez, and that City Councilman Frank Rizzo was present to extend recognition from the city, and that state representative Denny O'Brien did likewise for the Commonwealth.

Alice Hoglan, mother of Flight 93's Mark Bingham, sent a greeting from California. Debra Burlingame, sister of Chic Burlingame, pilot of American Flight 77, which crashed into the Pentagon, and Ellen Saracini, wife of Victor

Saracini, captain of United Flight 175, which hit the South Tower, both came to extend their gratitude.

From the moment that Lauren Hart sang the national anthem, it was one of those events that no written description will ever be able to fully describe.

And when it was finally time for Melendez to address the crowd, he choked back tears and told the crowd, "I wish my father were here to see this."

Jim Murray, the former Eagles GM and founder of the Ronald McDonald House, then stood to offer a benediction. Murray paused, and said, "Jose, your father was watching today."

There were no dry eyes.

AFTERWORD

Jose retired in October 2013 after 40 years of service to his country. He spent his last 15 months on the job teaching a basic course for new Customs and Border Patrol officers at the Federal Law Enforcement Training Center in Glynco, Georgia. He has since shared with me that he greatly enjoyed aiding in the development of new officers, but I still wonder whether the skills he possessed aren't innate (as opposed to something one can be taught). My hunch is that Jose was born with a gift for reading people, an "instinct," which is the word I used when I wrote a book about him in 2009. (We donated all proceeds from the book, Instinct, to the Flight 93 National Memorial in Shanksville, Pennsylvania.) Jose also said that though he was reluctant to hang up his uniform, his retirement life is great. Having successfully fought cancer, he now spends his time on home projects, some travel, and visits with family and friends. He has two sons and two daughters—one son has retired as a lieutenant colonel in the U.S. Army and the other is a police officer in Puerto Rico. Every time there is a terror incident anywhere in the world, his mind drifts back to the day, one month in advance of 9/11, on which he altered the course of history.

DUKE CASE:
REVENGE OF THE NERDS

Philadelphia Daily News, Thursday, April 13, 2006

WHEN I WAS A COLLEGE FRESHMAN a quarter-century ago, rape charges were brought against virtually every guy who lived in the fraternity housing the football team.

The story was huge news. I watched as about two dozen guys had their lives turned upside down by one woman who claimed they had all raped her.

They were all exonerated a few years later, but by then it had faded to a B-section story—no Page 1 for that. I see the same thing happening at Duke. The press coverage is totally one-sided against the lacrosse players and in support of the "victim." You have to search for anything resembling investigative journalism concerning the accuser.

For example, this tidbit was aired Friday on WRAL-TV in Raleigh, North Carolina, but given scant attention elsewhere:

> New information about the victim has been divulged. . . . According to a 2002 police report, the woman, currently a 27-year-old student at North Carolina Central University, gave a taxi driver a lap dance at a Durham strip club. Subsequently, according to the report, she stole the man's car and led deputies on a high-speed chase that ended in Wake County.
>
> Apparently, the deputy thought the chase was over when the woman turned down a dead-end road near Brier Creek, but instead she tried to run over him, according to the police report.
>
> Additional information notes that her blood-alcohol level registered at more than twice the legal limit.

In spite of that incident, her lawyer at the time, Woody Vann, asserted that the incident should not cause people to question her character. He said she is "a decent and credible human being."

Just imagine if it came to light that one of the lacrosse players had received a lap dance and stolen a taxi and tried to run over a cop. Page 1 again, all the way from Durham to Philadelphia.

The DNA results? Negative. No match between DNA taken from the 46 white athletes and the samples taken from the exotic dancer's body or belongings.

And photos from the party have come to light. In one, the "victim" is smiling at the camera, in another she's lying down on the back porch of the house.

Most controversial, the time-stamped photos indicate the woman was bruised on her legs and face and had cuts on her legs, knees, and feet when she came to the party, before the rape allegedly occurred.

It was in July 2003 that Kobe Bryant was accused of rape after having what he considered a consensual encounter with an employee at a Colorado hotel. Bryant was crucified in the media, while the "victim" went unnamed and unsupported by evidence. DNA in this case showed that she had a sexual encounter with someone else shortly after she was with Bryant.

A judge finally dismissed the case a year later, but Bryant paid heavily with loss of reputation and lucrative endorsements.

We've just seen a similar case more recently right here—that of Gary Neal and Michael Cleaves.

In June 2004, these basketball players from La Salle were charged with having sexually assaulted/raped a woman, 19, over a bathroom sink while she was heavily intoxicated and throwing up.

The "victim" had left a party and met players attending summer classes on campus, who invited her back to their house. The unnamed woman admitted to downing eight shots of high-proof booze in an hour. She started to feel sick, and went to the bathroom. Her blood alcohol content was a whopping .23.

The woman admitted never saying no or offering real resistance. As the case raged on, prosecutors contended that she was too drunk to consent to sex. Defenders claimed that the sex was consensual and the woman created the allegation out of embarrassment.

In November, a jury acquitted both men of all charges.

These cases share the characteristics of race, gender, and, perhaps most important, social standing.

The question: What drives this hostility toward athletes? Why a rush to judgment every time a ballplayer is accused of sexual indiscretions?

I say it's the revenge of the nerds. Most journalists would never be chosen for a pickup game of hoops, let alone a varsity sport. So they take perverse pleasure in bringing down the BMOC, however undeserved.

What went on in the Kobe case and at La Salle and now at Duke? The unathletic are getting their chance to vent at those who are. And they crucify these young men with gleeful speed.

While the "victims" are allowed to remain anonymous and aren't prosecuted for their tales, the athletes they accuse don't get the same treatment. These young men are the real victims, no quotation marks needed.

AFTERWORD

I was skeptical about the Duke lacrosse case from day one and said so on radio and in print. The investigation began a day after the alleged incident, on March 14, 2006, but the story broke wide open on March 29. That morning, the New York Times *put the burgeoning scandal on its front page, and I read the story aloud on my radio program, voicing my reservations about the quickly spreading narrative of a gang rape by boorish athletes. In the article, Durham County district attorney Michael B. Nifong criticized team members for their lack of cooperation: "The thing that most of us found so abhorrent, and the reason I decided to take it over myself, was the combination gang-like rape activity accompanied by the racial slurs and general racial hostility." How could he be so sure? I wondered. I would later have similar doubts about the alleged gang rape of a woman in a University of Virginia fraternity that proved to be a hoax.*

Part of my skepticism stemmed from my distinct recollection of a separate incident that I note at the beginning of this column. In the spring of 1981, I was a second-semester freshman at Lehigh University. That April, 14 men, including 13 Lehigh University students, were charged with the rape of a 19-year-old woman from a neighboring college (Muhlenberg). They were members of a fraternity, Delta Tau Delta, a football house, which was immediately suspended for four years, during which it was converted into co-ed student housing. One of the guys, a 20-year-old, was from my hometown, and his name, like all the others, was sprayed across the local newspapers. Ultimately, they were all exonerated for rape. Nine were cleared before trial and one was admitted to an accelerated rehabilitation program for the charge of open lewdness. Four went to trial and were acquitted. But the damage was already done to their reputations. And even though the case occurred in a pre–social media world, I still had no trouble recently accessing the old newspaper accounts via Google. Don't get me wrong. Guys can be pigs, and sexual assault is a real problem on U.S. campuses. Those who take liberties need to be severely punished. But equally inviolable must be the rule of law, which affords the accused the presumption of innocence.

Because of his handling of the Duke lacrosse case, Nifong was ultimately disbarred. And the accuser, Crystal Mangum, while never facing legal repercussions for her false allegations in the Duke case, was arrested for attempted murder of her live-in partner in 2010 (she was later convicted of lesser crimes) and in 2013 was convicted of second-degree murder in connection with the 2011 stabbing death of her boyfriend, for which she is serving a 14- to 18-year prison sentence.

SETTING THE RECORD STRAIGHT

Philadelphia Daily News, Thursday, May 18, 2006

MAY 14, 2006

Dear Wilson:

Congratulations on receiving your First Holy Communion today. It brought a tear to my eye to stand with you as you accepted the sacrament, and it was obvious to your mother and me that you have taken your religious education very seriously.

I saved a copy of the church bulletin distributed at Mass today as a keepsake, and I'm writing this letter in the hope that you'll keep it attached to the bulletin as an explanation. You see, my name appears in an insert to the bulletin distributed throughout the archdiocese on the day you received communion, and not in a favorable light.

The situation caught me by surprise. It was unsettling to sit in a pew as we prepared for your special moment only to look at the flier and see my name under the banner of a group called Pro Life Union Inc. They mentioned my name in a story about a recent symposium at Penn.

At the invitation of bio-ethicist Arthur Caplan, I participated and posed questions to experts on the subject of death and dying. But the assertion that I was at Penn to "celebrate" the death of a woman named Terri Schiavo was untrue. I found that characterization offensive. While I refused to let it mar your day, it warrants an explanation.

Terri Schiavo was a woman who collapsed without warning in 1990, at 26. She never recovered. Her husband, Michael, discovered her at their home in the early morning after hearing a thud. She was later diagnosed to be in a persistent vegetative state. Two years after the event, Michael successfully asserted a malpractice action against Terri's doctors for failing to diagnose an underlying eating and nutritional disorder that led to her cardiac arrest and caused irreversible brain damage.

While the jury made financial awards in a number of areas (medical expenses, lost earnings, loss of consortium), they awarded nothing for Terri's pain and suffering. In other words, after hearing the evidence just two years after the tragedy, the jury concluded that Terri was then feeling no pain and not suffering.

Soon afterward, there came an ugly battle between Michael and Terri's parents, the Schindlers. The judge in this dispute concluded that it was about money from the malpractice action. But it soon morphed into a battle over Terri's end-of-life wishes, since she could no longer speak for herself. On this issue, there was a factual dispute between Michael and the Schindlers.

A court listened to evidence for five days and determined that Terri's wish was to disconnect her feeding tube. The appeals process upheld that view.

Things got ugly. Many outsiders tried to affect the outcome. One of those was the pro-life community, which embraced Terri's parents and voiced opposition to taking away her feeding tube.

I supported the right of the individual to have her wishes fulfilled. I regarded Terri's case as one involving the right of a person to die on her own terms. I believed that the affected person could make the decision free of any outside involvement, including the government's.

I never looked at Terri's case in the conventional pro-life vs. pro-choice terms. But as the dispute continued, I began to wonder whether the pro-life agenda was to support "life" even in a situation where someone in a permanent vegetative condition would want otherwise.

Terri Schiavo left this earth in 2005. An autopsy showed that she was in a permanent vegetative state, that she had been for many years, and that the cause of her death was brain damage due to anoxic brain injury. An inquiry by a Florida state's attorney found an absence of any evidence that her initial collapse was caused by criminal actions.

I wish my name had not appeared in the church bulletin on the day of your first communion.

I love our church and the fulfillment it has provided each member of our family. But I am your father first, and I am not about to let this moment pass without providing you with a frame of reference for how your dad views the controversy, even though I recognize it will be inappropriate for you to read this for a number of years.

Let no one tell you that your father celebrated any death. Your old man is supportive of self-determination. In the case of Terri Schiavo, I kept saying, "There but for the grace of God go I."

If that outcome should come my way, I certainly don't want some individual or group, pro-life or pro-choice, imposing their view of end-of-life issues on me, or anyone else.

The fact that one such group would proclaim, in a church bulletin on the day of your First Holy Communion, that I celebrated death by my support of Terri Schiavo's right to determine her own fate tells me all I need to know about this group's lack of respect for individual rights.

They wanted to call this shot for Terri. Well, please don't ever let them decide for me.

Love,
Dad

AFTERWORD

There is one aspect of the Terri Schiavo case about which all should agree— everyone needs to specify his or her own end-of-life wishes. I'll support anyone's individual desire, and I will oppose those interlopers who seek to overturn an- other's desire. After Schiavo passed away on March 31, 2005, in lieu of a typical column, on April 7, 2005, I published a pro-forma, Pennsylvania standard living will that I'd filled out for myself. I encouraged readers to copy the format I had published or send me a self-addressed, stamped envelope in which I'd return a standard version for their usage. After 15 years and more than 1,000 columns, that remains one of my most popular. Months later people were still asking me for a sample living will. I'd like to think I spared someone the family squabble that was the hallmark of the Schiavo case.

A DOG NAMED WINSTON

Philadelphia Daily News, Thursday, July 6, 2006

IN THE LATE 1980S, I had a humiliating experience.

I was trying to make my way as a real-estate developer when the market collapsed. I was overextended with several Center City properties. I was on the brink of filing for bankruptcy.

My only hope was to arrange a deal with my bank, First Executive, then headed by an amiable Israeli named Zvi Muscal. In advance of our sit-down, he'd asked for an itemization of my monthly living expenses.

In my moment of truth, there sat Zvi, with furrowed brow and oversized glasses at the end of his nose, bearing down on my list. His finger had been running over the page when it stopped on one item. What was it? I wondered. My cable bill? Amex? PECO? The Union League fees?

"Eh, Micccchael," he asked in his heavy accent. "What is dis dog-walking expense of $15 per day?"

Of all the money flowing out of my pocket, my banker thought that paying a woman to come to my apartment and walk my young cocker spaniel, Winston, was my most extravagant expense.

Little did he know that I'd have sooner gotten rid of the TV set, cut off the power, or quit the Union League than deprive my little guy of a leg stretch while I was at work. Zvi and I still joke about my refusal to budge on that expense.

I'm thinking a lot about that, and other memories of Winston, because I had to bury him this weekend. He died suddenly on Sunday morning after living a very full 16 years. His life was amazing, considering all that he went through, not that it makes it any easier for me to grieve.

My wife told me I've given myself an impossible task if my goal is to try to express to you the meaning of his life and our time together. She's right. Too many others have done too good of a job explaining that bond between people and their pets, not the least of whom is John Grogan in *Marley and Me.*

Still, if my alternative subjects today are flag-burning, an Iraq exit strategy, Santorum vs. Casey, or next year's mayoral race, I'd rather tell you about Winston. He's way more interesting.

Getting Winston was the suggestion of a long-ago girlfriend. I'd never had a dog and was leery of the responsibility. In fact, I decided to bring him home only when the breeder told me he was born on Christmas. But that's not the real divine intervention.

This is: Soon after, the girlfriend was gone and my wife entered the picture. She too had a cocker, named Rudy. We quickly established that Rudy and Winston were brothers, having been bought from the same breeder at the same time. But Winston's Christmas birth was thrown into doubt when my wife told me the breeder, thinking she was Jewish, told her that Rudy was born in the middle of Hanukkah!

Winston was to become a walking advertisement for managed care. For a while, he was a regular at the Penn vet school ER, making me wish I hadn't scoffed at a brochure offering health insurance for pets during his first visit. During his life he'd require eye surgery, a urethrotomy, and a hip realignment by the nation's foremost dog orthopedist after he was hit by a truck. He also needed emotional therapy for separation anxiety, not that I think even Blue Cross has a plan that would have covered that.

There was also the afternoon he cornered a baby bunny in our backyard. He had it in his jowls and must have panicked when I shouted, because down the hatch went the bunny. This too necessitated a trip to Penn, where on X-ray, the bones of Brer Rabbit were discernible.

And those were the real problems, not the false alarms. Like the night he woke me from a dead sleep with what I thought were convulsions. Imagine my embarrassment over at Penn when they told me he had a severe case of the hiccups.

My love for him was such that I went to great lengths to try to breed him. That too was an eye-opener. First, my wife and I took him to a dog show at Ludwig's Corner, naïvely thinking we'd match our prized possession with someone else's.

But the dog Nazis at the show demeaned the length of his ears, the shape of his nose, and the size of his belly. So we implemented Plan B: a personal ad titled "Sleepless in Philadelphia" giving an honest approximation of his physical attributes. That too was a loser. No replies.

Finally, we found an evangelical Christian from Lancaster who said she'd let Winston have a go with her Tootsie, as long as WE paid $1,200. Praying that Zvi the banker wouldn't find out, we made the deal. Then fate dealt Winston a most unkind blow.

Two weeks before his date with Tootsie, we were down the shore and noticed he wasn't peeing. A quick trip to the vet revealed he had a kidney stone in his bladder, or as our then 6-year-old daughter put it, "Winnie has a rhinestone in his platter."

I'm left with lots of other memories, too, most still too raw to revisit. They're no substitute for not having him at my feet when the time comes to plan my next day's radio show or write my weekly column, but my life was greatly enhanced every day of those 16 years that Winston was at my side.

AFTERWORD

I never had a dog growing up. My father was supportive, but my mother held a veto that she exercised throughout my childhood, although she too came to love Winston. He was, as I describe, my first dog, but certainly not our family's last. In fact, there was a time when under our roof, we had four kids and four dogs, or as I liked to say, 10 beating hearts in one home. Checkers was our white lab and she lived a full life to age 14½. Mr. Lucy is our miniature dachshund, who is at my feet as I type this note. Floyd, a companion dachshund for Mr. Lucy, met an untimely demise because of my lack of awareness when driving my pickup truck out of our driveway one weekend. The thought of that day still pains me. Over the years, many have asked how Mr. Lucy got his name and I want to share that story here.

Mr. Lucy was a birthday gift from me to my wife in honor of her 42nd birthday. Her birthday is in December, and this one came just months after the tragic passing of one of our close friends, the Honorable Jay C. Waldman, a federal judge based in Philadelphia. So now you are wondering, "Why would you name a dog 'Mr. Lucy' for a man whose name was not Mr. Lucy?" Fair question. First let me tell you a little about Jay.

I met Jay C. Waldman when I was a summer legal clerk at the law firm of Dilworth, Paxson, Kalish, and Kauffman, after my first year at Penn Law. I was the lowest man on the firm's totem pole and spent most of my time performing rudimentary legal research. Jay C. Waldman, in contrast, was at the top of the firm's food chain, having just joined the firm—as a partner—after leaving his post as counsel to Pennsylvania governor Dick Thornburgh. I think it says a great deal about Jay that he was open to a friendship with a person who was then so far from being his professional equal. Politics was the initial basis of our relationship. We both craved political action. His experience was at a much higher level than mine. Over the years, we became very close.

Jay died on May 30, 2003, after a valiant battle with cancer. His passing left many of us, including my wife, Lavinia, and me, devastated. At the time of his death, he and his wife, Roberta, were two of our closest friends. We ate together every week for the last 15 years of Jay's life and vacationed together as well. In fact, Jay married us in 1994. We'd invited all our friends to a party we billed as an engagement affair, but at 10 P.M., Lavinia went into a changing room and put on a gown, and when she came out, we shocked the crowd by having Jay, in his role as a federal judge, preside over the surprise ceremony.

He was a brilliant man. Jay, we liked to say, was able "to see around corners." That's why his political and personal counsel was always in demand. He was not only Dick Thornburgh's right hand, including during the Three Mile Island scare, but also Rudy Giuliani's long-standing confidant. The two had known each other since their days as young prosecutors in the Justice Department, and I think we can credit Jay for Rudy's run for mayor as a Republican. I don't rely on Jay in saying this; I rely on Rudy's recollection as presented in his book, Leadership *(2002).*

At the time of his death, Jay was a U.S. district court judge (appointed by Ronald Reagan) who had been appointed to the Third Circuit Court of Appeals by President George W. Bush but not yet confirmed by the U.S. Senate. In an odd but appropriate twist of fate, in 2004 President George W. Bush nominated Paul S. Diamond to the federal bench, effectively enabling Paul to fill Jay's position. Paul Diamond was also a former Dilworth partner and one of Jay's close friends. Paul used to be a frequent guest of my radio program on legal matters, whom I invited because of his acerbic wit, but he decided to stop doing the show when he realized he might one day require Senate confirmation and that what plays in the morning drive might not play in the hallowed halls of the Senate. Too bad for me. He was a great radio guest, and I would always introduce him as "my smartest friend."

Jay C. Waldman's send-off was quite an event. I had the privilege of serving as the master of ceremonies. Those who eulogized Jay included Governor Dick Thornburgh, Mayor Rudy Giuliani, and Senator Arlen Specter. Another speaker had been a friend of Jay's since childhood, a lawyer named Daniel Shapira. Believe it or not, this is where Mr. Lucy comes in. Danny Shapira is a gifted orator. He stood in front of a packed funeral home auditorium and told poignant and humorous stories about life with Jay. One of the best concerned a childhood poker game involving a young Danny, a young Jay, and an old-timer in their neighborhood named, you guessed it, Mr. Lucy. I couldn't do the full story justice here and I don't know that it's all that appropriate for me to do so, either. Suffice it to say that Mr. Lucy might not have been the most honorable poker player. What I do know is that Jay was the sort of fellow who liked to live life below the radar. For that reason, we didn't want to give our new beloved pet his moniker, but we did want to pay him tribute with our new family member. So, to honor Jay in a style with which we thought he would approve, we called our new friend Mr. Lucy and think fondly of Jay when we are in his company, every day.

As Paul Harvey would say, now you know the rest of the story.

ROGER WATERS:
THE PINKO IN FLOYD

Philadelphia Daily News, Thursday, September 21, 2006

FOR THE SECOND TIME IN MY LIFE, I'm writing a column about Pink Floyd. Specifically, about the man I've always considered to be the brains of the band: Roger Waters. The first time I wrote about him was 26 years ago when I was a high school senior at Central Bucks West in Doylestown and editor of the school paper, the *Chatterbux*.

Back then, I was one of the lucky few to see Pink Floyd perform *The Wall*, live at the Nassau County Coliseum on Long Island, New York. My review earned me an invitation to the principal's office. I was encouraged to write a retraction on the grounds that I'd promoted a band whose lyrics the principal associated with drug use.

It was a moment straight out of "Another Brick in the Wall, Part 2." "We don't need no education" indeed. I told the principal to pound sand. Maybe even called it a matter of "free speech."

For three decades, the Floyd has never left my playlist.

In fact, I have done what I call "the cycle" for every Floyd and Roger Waters recording, meaning I bought it in all forms in which it was released: album, 8-track, cassette, and CD. I once made a London taxi driver take me to the Battersea Power Station just so I could photograph the image that appears on the cover of my favorite album, *Animals*. No one was more pleased when the band reunited to headline at Live 8. And in the never-ending debate among Floyd fans on David Gilmore vs. Rogers Waters, I've always sided with Waters.

My affinity for Waters has always been in spite of his politics. Chalk that up to spending too much time studying song lyrics back in the day when they printed such things. I thought rock stars had all the answers.

Fast-forward 25 years.

Last Wednesday, I sat in the front row for a Roger Waters performance at Madison Square Garden. (The same show came to the Tweeter Center in Camden Saturday night.) The crowd was diverse, but mostly like me: white middle-aged guys with receding hair and expanding waists.

It should have been a night to have a few beers and enjoy the soundtrack of my life. Instead, I sat there in my expensive seat and heckled the guy whose music I know by heart.

Waters's politics are no longer just liberal; they're over the top.

I was expecting the line about "incurable tyrants and kings" when he sang "Fletcher Memorial Home," and I knew there'd be references to Margaret Thatcher and Ronald Reagan.

What I wasn't prepared for was a photo montage featuring Osama, Saddam, and George W. Bush. Especially not two days removed from the anniversary of September 11 in the city where the most death and destruction occurred.

I'm sick and tired of entertainment types arguing a moral equivalency between our president and the Butcher of Baghdad and the architect of 9/11.

It's not that I object to the criticism of the president or his policy. But Waters and others lose all credibility when they treat Bush and bin Laden the same way. And that was before Waters announced he was beginning the "controversial" part of the show.

I held my breath as he introduced "Leaving Beirut" with a long-winded story about his teens. Then came:

Are these the people we should bomb
Are we so sure they mean us harm
Is this our pleasure, punishment or crime
Is this a mountain that we really want to climb
The road is hard, hard and long
Put down that two by four
This man would never turn you from his door
Oh, George! Oh, George!
That Texas education must have f—— you up when you were very
    small.

This is Waters's ridiculous ode to some guy who gave him a lift and a meal when he was hitching in Beirut at 17. According to the logic of his lyrics, because he received this courtesy, we're supposed to overlook the murder of innocents at the hands of radical Islam, including the close to 3,000 who died almost five years to the day, and just blocks from where I was hearing him sing.

I couldn't take it anymore. "Go visit Ground Zero!" I shouted from the front row. He heard me, and proceeded to avoid our corner of the stage except to oblige a hottie who wanted to take his picture with her cell phone.

Then the pig came out.

I refer to a giant inflatable pig, a hallmark of many Floyd shows, and the symbol of my aforementioned favorite album. Only this time, the pig was a billboard for Waters's twisted priorities. "Habeas Corpus Matters," it said,

A certain bald fan watching from the front row as Roger Waters performs *Dark Side of the Moon* **live at Madison Square Garden, on September 13, 2006.** Photo by Paul Lauricella.

among other things. How appalling. I wondered how many in the New York audience had lost relatives or friends in the 9/11 attack and now were witness to his call for more rights for the murderers?

"Go visit Ground Zero," I yelled again.

Roger Waters still has free-speech rights. Bald, bespectacled, and willing to shell out for a front-row seat, so do I.

AFTERWORD

Time for another mea culpa. Roger Waters toured North America in 2017, during which time I had the opportunity to spend a few hours in his company and came away with a more nuanced understanding of his thinking than I'd gleaned from the front row. Of course, he would say that only means I hadn't been paying close attention all those years I'd been listening to him and reading his liner notes.

Before hitting the road, Waters was interviewed by Jon Pareles for a New York Times "TimesTalk" in Midtown Manhattan. Waters was on the verge of releasing a new album—Is This the Life We Really Want?—and embarking on the tour he dubbed "Us + Them." He showed footage of a recent perfor-

mance in Mexico City with virulently anti-Trump images and made clear that both the album and the tour would have significant political overtones:

> Unfortunately, we're all forced to think about current events because we feel the impact of current events. We could go on about your nincompoop president all night. It might be somewhat redundant; he's doing a good job on his own without any of us interfering in his condemnation of himself.

As I listened, I wondered whether Waters worried about his ability to sell seats in red states, and when it came time for audience questions, I stood up and raised the issue. He responded: "You know, just because it's a red state, and it's apparently very conservative, Kansas City, doesn't mean that there isn't a viable resistance to this administration in that city."

He also noted that he'd be playing "a bunch" of Pink Floyd songs for which there was great audience attachment, including the song from the legendary Dark Side of the Moon album for which the tour had been named.

> "Us and Them" from Dark Side of the Moon, you know, "with, without, and who'll deny that's what the fighting's all about." You can't get any more contemporary than that. . . . We better start working together cohesively or we're all fucked.

I wrote a Sunday Inquirer column predicting that the tour would be the most politically charged of the summer season. By then I had re-evaluated my treatment of Waters eleven years earlier:

> Five years post 9/11, I wasn't bothered by the idea of presumed terrorists sitting in Guantanamo Bay without having been charged with a crime. . . . At the end of the Obama administration, 41 men were still held at Gitmo out of the 779 people imprisoned there since 2001. Of the 41, 31 were being held without charges. That's not right. We're better than the status quo.

I ended the column saying: "Sometimes listening to great music means listening to someone whose message makes you uncomfortable."

The column made clear that while I still had political disagreements with Waters, that which separated us had narrowed. And I wasn't finished exploring the outlook of a singer-songwriter whose solo projects and work as the chief lyricist for Pink Floyd I'd been listening to since my teens. I soon made contact *with Fran DeFeo, Waters's longtime publicist, and asked to interview Waters for CNN while he was on tour. She was very accommodating and invited me to do so in Miami, where Waters was performing on July 13 at the American Airlines arena. The plan was for me to interview him at his hotel the night before the show, and then to have a CNN crew shoot some B-roll of me watching Waters do a sound check the night of the show, preferably as he rehearsed with local school kids who would participate in a dance routine during "Another Brick in the Wall, Part 2."*

The afternoon of the interview, we met by happenstance in an otherwise deserted gym at the Mandarin Oriental, where we both were staying. I'd never have known the fit and trim Waters was 73 to see him working out with a trainer and his body man. A few hours later, he sat for my 30-minute interview in a hotel room CNN had cleared out for the occasion. I asked whether he was concerned about alienating longtime fans with his virulent anti-Trump message.

"It would be a lot easier to be on tour if I weren't doing any of this, if I didn't have opinions," he said.

When I asked him what he might say to someone looking for escapism rather than politics at a rock concert, he was quick with the reply: "Go see Katy Perry."

I was pleased with the interview and only sorry that because of time constraints, we could not play it all. With commercial breaks, it would have filled the entire hour (which would have suited me just fine, but not CNN). I enjoyed being in his company and even when we disagreed on subjects like the "war on terror" (I'm using scare quotes because when I said that phrase, he bristled), I still found him to be civil, bright, passionate, and engaging. I left thinking I could have spoken to him for hours more about politics. Unbeknownst to me, I'd soon get that chance. Twice.

The next day, the afternoon of the Miami show, DeFeo told me that the Miami Beach Parks Department had just canceled the participation of its Teen Club in Waters's show that night. The adults had decided to deny the kids the opportunity to perform a dance routine they'd been rehearsing because the adults had determined that Waters was anti-Semitic, a charge that has long dogged the rock star. The story of the cancellation was quickly gaining steam in the blogosphere. So as I sat watching Waters perform his sound check from the fifth row of an otherwise empty basketball arena that seats 21,000, I suggested to DeFeo and Kate Watkins, who works with Waters's manager, that they allow me to record a brief response to the cancellation on my iPhone that I would post on my Facebook page. After they consulted with Waters, he agreed. By now, the doors to the arena were opening, the show was 90 minutes from starting, and my eldest son had joined me at the venue. The two of us were ushered backstage so that I could ask Waters about the abrupt cancellation of the kids. Sean Evans, Waters's videographer and the director of the extraordinary 2014 documentary movie The Wall, *recorded our conversation. Waters seemed to relish the controversy and was very eager to set the record straight. "Peeved" is probably the word that best describes his mood. He said that in every city, he goes out of his way to recruit kids from disadvantaged backgrounds to perform with him and that this was first time there'd been a cancellation.*

> At 3 this afternoon, one of the local newspapers posted a story saying that these children had backed out of doing the show with me because I'm an anti-Semite and the show is all about hatred blahblahblah, which was a lie. These kids didn't back out of anything; it was the mayor who called the organization partly funded by the city and said, "Your kids cannot perform in the show."

I asked Waters to respond to those who were already complaining to me that I should not be affording him a platform on CNN.

"I'm not an anti-Semite, obviously," he said. "To call me anti-Semite is malicious propaganda."

The interview went viral. Within days it racked up nearly half a million views. And the show went on. Somehow, by the time he hit the stage a little more than an hour later, Waters had recruited another dozen kids, who did a fine job performing "Another Brick, Part 2". The show was amazing. People might disagree about the very few numbers that got very political, but no one could dispute the sound and production values.

Afterward, I joined the band for what they called the "Golden Trough" celebration back at the hotel. I was seated at a dinner table next to Waters, and we had a very spirited conversation about U.S. politics and international affairs. The following day I flew home to Philadelphia, and that Saturday, my interview aired. I didn't hear from Waters or anyone on his team immediately after and thought he must not have liked his treatment. But the following month, DeFeo contacted me when Waters came to Philadelphia for three shows at the Wachovia Center. I had already planned to take my youngest son to the first show. He was 17, a Waters/Floyd fan, and this would be his first concert. He loved it. The next day, Mark Fenwick, Waters's manager, called and said Waters had asked to see me after the second night's performance. I didn't go to that show, but I met him afterward in the bar of Lacroix at the Rittenhouse Hotel, which had been closed to all but a handful of the band and support staff. Waters walked in and motioned me to join him at a table for two. This was not a working meeting—the CNN interview was long over and had already aired. Over my beer and his wine we had an animated discussion touching on music and politics, with me wanting to talk mostly about the former and him mostly about the latter. By now I was much more familiar with the new album than I'd been when I first saw him in Miami. I told him that "Wait for Her" was my favorite song on the new recording. We ended up closing the place. I left only when the bartender flicked the lights. Three hours later I got up to deliver my daily radio program and did so without so much as mentioning what I'd done the night before.

THE GARDEN
OF ETERNAL VIGILANCE

Philadelphia Daily News, Thursday, October 5, 2006

I'S AMAZING WHAT NEIGHBORS can do when united in purpose. On Saturday, in Lower Makefield Township, Bucks County, several thousand gathered in what used to be a nondescript field to rechristen the Garden of Reflection, a tribute to 9/11 victims. Fellow citizens spent five years planning and fund-raising to bring to life what is now a showpiece for the nation.

Bucks was the hardest hit of Pennsylvania's counties on September 11, and Lower Makefield bore a particular brunt because it's a commutable distance to New York City. Seventeen Bucks Countians died that day, a statistic that enabled state representative David Steil to get the commonwealth to designate the garden as the official Pennsylvania memorial.

From the outset, the garden was a collaborative effort of neighbors united by tragedy whose mission seemed guided by divine purpose. How else to explain that on a cold day in January 2002, family survivors Grace Godshalk, Fiona Havlish, Ellen Saracini, and Tara Bane went looking for a site and found a lonely American flag wedged in some bushes on Woodside Road. They knew at once they'd found the spot. Two years later, Lower Makefield named the proposed site Memorial Park.

When it came time to review potential designs, they flowed in from all over, but it was a local woman, Yardley's Liuba P. Lashchyk, who conceptualized the final plan. The level of her deliberation is readily apparent.

Visitors to the garden are first confronted with a several-ton piece of twisted steel from the wreckage of the Twin Towers. This remnant of Ground Zero intentionally faces the direction of New York City.

Symbolism is everywhere. Seventeen maple trees on an outer berm acknowledge the Bucks County residents lost in the attack, and 42 lights along the spiral labyrinth walk remember each of the Pennsylvania children who lost a parent that day.

The names of all 2,973 victims are etched in a glass semicircle leading up to the inner sanctum.

At the heart of the garden is a reflecting pool where two recessed squares represent the footprint of the Twin Towers and serve as the basis for dual ascending fountains that rise as a metaphor for the soaring spirit of the victims.

I'm not a message kinda guy, but even I get the garden. It's a special place, worth the drive from anywhere in the region.

The dedication befitted the creation. Local firefighters and American flags lined the approach. Valerie Mihalek, a local woman, coordinated the event with military precision. Literally. How else to explain the C-17 that dropped out of the sky and tipped its wing, flown by yet another local, U.S. Air Force major Samuel Irvin III of Wrightstown.

The ceremony was appropriately devoid of politics. Representative Mike Fitzpatrick, in a tough re-election battle, was the emcee. His role was deserved, given his procurement of $750,000 to build the garden. But he just did his job and was never formally introduced. It was that kind of low-key day.

The speakers were emotional. They included Tara Bane (who lost her 33-year-old husband), Grace Maureen Godshalk (who lost her 35-year-old son), and Ellen Saracini (whose husband, Victor, was the captain of United Flight 175). The Commencement Brass played "Holy, Holy, Holy," and the Pennsbury High choir sang "You'll Never Walk Alone."

We all had goose bumps.

Go see the garden. It's just five minutes from the New Hope–Yardley exit of I-95. When you get there, you will see that the site is ringed with athletic fields where children will play for future generations, which reminds me of the most significant aspect of what these neighbors created.

We've all heard it said that, with regard to the events preceding that fateful day, the most important failure was one of imagination.

Well, sitting at the dedication on Saturday, it occurred to me that for more than 99 percent of the country, September 11 was a day never experienced directly. To be sure, we were all witness in a way and everyone now has images and ideas based on the film footage, but only a few experienced directly the ramifications of what occurred.

The garden not only honors the dead, but offers their sacrifice as a way of protecting against any failure of imagination in the future. It's a living reminder of what occurred so that never again will there be a similar lapse of attention.

Long after we're all gone, the Garden of Reflection will form images and ideas in the minds of those who follow us of a horrific event that will not have been seen or experienced directly by anyone then living. So let's hope that, in that way, it will safeguard future generations against a repeat failure of the imagination.

AFTERWORD

All the proceeds from my first book, Flying Blind: How Political Correctness Continues to Compromise Airline Safety Post 9/11 (2004), *went to the Garden of Reflection, where I remain an active supporter and benefactor. It's just two turns off of I-95. Make the trip if you've never been. And read more about the Garden here: www.9-11memorialgarden.org.*

MANHUNT FOR OSAMA
DROPPING ON U.S. AGENDA?

Philadelphia Daily News, Thursday, October 26, 2006

HAVE THE BRAKES been put on the hunt for Osama bin Laden? Just back from the CENTCOM region, that is my hunch.

The effort to find bin Laden was one of the many questions I had about the war on terror as I joined a Pentagon-sponsored military immersion program called the Joint Civilian Orientation Conference.

This was to be a unique opportunity for 45 civilians to learn about CENTCOM, a geographical territory encompassing the most dangerous spots in the world, and I was looking forward to being a mental sponge on a subject that has preoccupied me since 9/11.

I have done thousands of hours of talk radio and written numerous columns and two books about the war on terror, but never before had I seen it being waged.

The weeklong activities did not disappoint. The daily agenda was packed and the presenters were stellar. We heard from the defense secretary, the vice chairman of the Joint Chiefs of Staff, the vice admiral of CENTCOM, and other high-ranking war commanders.

Our days began at 5 or 6 A.M. and didn't end until 10 or 11 P.M. We traveled 15,000 miles and spent time in four nations. We ate meals with soldiers, fired the best of the Army weaponry in the desert, toured classified Air Force surveillance aircraft, and were educated about the latest in efforts to counteract the dreaded IEDs (improvised explosive devices).

I came home with the utmost of respect for men and women throughout the ranks of all five branches of the service who are committed to eradicating the forces of radical Islam.

There was only one area of disappointment. I refer to the hunt for bin Laden and his deputy, Ayman al-Zawahiri.

I began to think of it as the Lord Voldemort of the trip—which Harry Potter fans will recognize as the individual whose name shall not be uttered. The search for bin Laden and al-Zawahiri was not part of the agenda, and when I did ask questions looking for a status report, there was no information forthcoming except a generic assertion that, indeed, the hunt continues.

For example, when we were briefed at Andrews Air Force Base by Vice Admiral Nichols—the No. 2 to Army general John Abizaid—I asked him whether the hunt for bin Laden was, at this stage, completely dependent upon

Pakistani president Pervez Musharraf. He told me we respect national sovereignty and described the search as "difficult and nuanced."

I took that as a confirmation of my concern about outsourcing.

When, in Bahrain, I put the same question to Marine brigadier general Anthony Jackson, he told me that the search was the equivalent of finding one man in the Rockies, an analogy that I heard repeatedly from men I met overseas. He also said that "no one is giving up" and that my question was better put to the guys in special ops.

So when we got to the special ops headquarters, in Qatar, I raised the matter yet again, this time with Colonel Patrick Pihana, the chief of staff to the Combined Forces Special Operations Component Command. He offered nothing substantive on the issue. There were other places we visited that I am not at liberty to discuss where one would expect it to be a focal point, but it wasn't in our briefings.

I want to be clear here: Nowhere did anyone ever tell me the search for bin Laden is over. But I am worried that the days of aggressively hunting him have ended. I say that based on the lack of response to my repeated questions in the context of other sensitive briefings, the fact that the CIA reportedly closed its bin Laden desk, called the Alec Station, and the agreement reached between Musharraf and tribal leaders in the northwestern part of his nation wherein he has agreed to give them continued free rein.

I might be wrong. The prospect certainly exists that the hunt continues and yours truly, a blowhard from Philadelphia, was deemed unworthy of any information. That would be fine with me—I am not one who believes Americans have a right to know secrets—but I would have hoped that along the way, someone would have said so. In light of a great deal of sensitive information that was shared with my group, and the total absence of anything about bin Laden, I don't think this is the case.

I may be right. To be sure, if we catch a break I am certain we will grab him and kill him, but maybe our Special Forces have repositioned their precious resources. And why might this be the case? Well, for starters, because our limited manpower is desperately needed in Iraq. Perhaps they're hiding in Pakistan and we are respecting their borders, even with the knowledge that Musharraf is limited in what he can or will do to find him.

Why would we respect Pakistani borders to the exclusion of finding and killing the most wanted man in the world? Because as weak as Musharraf might be in assisting us in finding bin Laden and al-Zawahiri, he is probably the best we can hope for in Pakistani leadership. Forcing his hand might lead to his undermining, and end up with a friend to radical Islam running the country.

There is another consideration. More than one individual with whom I spoke—and no one that I have named here—raised with me the question of what would happen to public support for the war against radical Islam if we were to find and kill bin Laden and al-Zawahiri. Would the American people then expect the military to pack up and go home? they wanted to know from me, who spends 17.5 hours a week answering phone calls from the public.

Again, I need to be blunt. No one ever told me that we are not hunting bin Laden because killing him would cause Americans to want to close up shop in Iraq and Afghanistan.

But this possible ramification is absolutely on the minds of our warriors as support for the war in Iraq dissipates.

I pray my gut is wrong. I hope that somewhere in Pakistan there are some bad-assed special ops guys wearing veils and burkas moving through villages, cutting deals, using sophisticated spy gear, and doing whatever is necessary to bring the bastards' lives to the most heinous of endings. Bin Laden and al-Zawahiri are mass murderers responsible for 6,000 deaths—3,000 on 9/11, and another 3,000 from events tied to that. The search must never end.

AFTERWORD

It would be six more years until Osama bin Laden would be killed, on Monday, May 2, 2011. Like many Americans, I remember exactly where I was when I heard the news. That night I was at a Neil Young concert at the legendary Tower Theater with my buddy "Liberal" Paul Lauricella. As we drove home, Twitter began exploding with tidbits about something big that had happened. We went back to my house at midnight and watched as President Barack Obama announced the news to the nation:

Good evening. Tonight, I can report to the American people and to the world that the United States has conducted an operation that killed Osama bin Laden, the leader of al Qaeda, and a terrorist who's responsible for the murder of thousands of innocent men, women, and children.

I remember going on radio the following day and saying I wish that I knew who killed him so I could buy him a beer, prompting several callers to say we would never know the names of the heroes. A few years later, I was able to interview two members of Seal Team Six who played critical roles in the mission: Matt Bissonnette (aka "Mark Owen") and Robert O'Neill (the guy who actually killed bin Laden). Both were memorable. I still hope to buy each that beer.

SHOULD FREE SPEECH ALLOW
HOLOCAUST DENIAL?

Philadelphia Daily News, Thursday, January 11, 2007

"IF WE REALLY WANT to know the truth about history, we need to allow freedom of speech."

So I was told by David Duke in an interview three weeks ago via a scratchy connection from Tehran. He was in Iran to participate in Mahmoud Ahmadinejad's Holocaust conference.

I've followed Duke's career and find his repeated condemnation of Israel and its supporters to be abhorrent. And I knew that accepting an invitation to interview the former Klan Imperial Wizard would cause a stir. But I was willing to speak to him because I was on the verge of visiting the most deadly of all Nazi extermination camps, and I wanted to hear what a self-described revisionist had to say.

The fringe represented by Duke argues that laws in Europe prohibiting Holocaust denial inhibit an analysis that could otherwise reveal the Holocaust to be a historical exaggeration that exists to justify the legitimacy of Israel. No Holocaust, or exaggerated description? Then there's no justification for the creation of the state of Israel in the minds of these few.

Now that I'm back from my visit to Auschwitz, I find that I agree with Duke that Europeans should be free to debate the Holocaust, but not for reasons he would agree with. Having seen the ghastly evidence, I believe it's far easier to defeat the deniers with fact and logic rather than risk fostering the skepticism that comes from making those views illegal. It is through the clash of truth and falsity that the truths of the Holocaust are most readily seen.

My trip had been planned for nearly a year. I'm one of a half-dozen Philadelphia friends, three Jewish, who regularly travel after New Year's to historic sites.

We began in Berlin at the Wannsee villa where, on January 20, 1942, 15 officials of the Third Reich plotted the "final solution." In their meeting room, we read the protocol written by Adolf Eichmann that set forth the plan to murder European Jews.

Then we visited Track 17 in the fashionable Grunewald section of Berlin, at the former station that was the point of departure for Jews from the area being sent to the camps. Listed next to the tracks are the dates, number of passengers, and destination of the railcars.

Next stop: the other end of those tracks, in Poland.

On a raw, dark, rain-swept day, we spent four hours walking the grounds of Auschwitz I and Auschwitz II-Birkenau.

We saw it all. At Auschwitz I, we walked through the infamous gate ("Work Brings Freedom"). We toured the surviving crematorium. We saw the ghastly displays of human hair, personal effects, suitcases, even shoe polish, all confiscated from the prisoners who'd packed in haste under the ruse of "resettlement." Also there: empty canisters that held pellets of Zyklon B, the agent used to exterminate human life in the crematoriums.

At Auschwitz II-Birkenau, we stood on the platform where Jews were divided between those who were to be immediately gassed and those who would live for, at least, a while. We also surveyed the ruins of crematorium II, the most prolific of the death machines, largely destroyed by the Nazis in an effort to hide their crimes against humanity.

The critical question: If the evidence of the Holocaust was right before my eyes, should all argument to the contrary be outlawed? Close to 20 nations say yes, and ban Holocaust denial. Austria only recently released the historian David Irving, imprisoned for this very crime. Our guide was one of many who believe those laws justified. She thinks they're a safeguard for properly educating future generations about what occurred.

I agree, we must ensure the understanding of future generations. But I don't see these laws as a way to do it. Banning Holocaust debate would be like America disallowing argument on the wacky 9/11 Internet conspiracy theories.

There are many credible-looking websites that have become clearinghouses for rumor and innuendo about the attack on the Pentagon. A missile, some argue, not an airplane. (What then happened to American Airlines Flight 77 and its passengers?)

The most effective way of dealing with such propaganda is to discredit it point by point, not to make it unlawful, which runs the risk of fueling skepticism. *Popular Mechanics* did so exquisitely in magazine and then book form.

It should be the same with Holocaust revisionists. The way to combat their mindset is with total openness and a climate of candor about all aspects of World War II. That includes providing full access, even to those locations that run the risk of cultivating morbid curiosity.

In Berlin, we stayed in the Hotel Adlon at the foot of the Brandenburg Gate. The concierge provided me with a walking-tour map of the neighborhood. Included were both the Reichstag, home of the German parliament, and the Memorial to the Murdered Jews of Europe. Missing, however, was any reference to what's beneath a nondescript parking lot just 100 yards behind the hotel: Hitler's bunker.

Not until the World Cup came to Germany last year was there any sign to note the significance of the spot where Hitler killed himself as Russian troops stormed the Reichstag. That too is the wrong response to a hideous chapter of German history. Not only should the location of the bunker be noted, it should be unearthed and opened to the public.

Those were my views upon arriving back home. But my reflection wasn't over.

I then had the chance to question one of the world's foremost historians, Sir Martin Gilbert, official biographer of Winston Churchill and author of *Auschwitz and the Allies* and *The Holocaust: A History of the Jews of Europe during the Second World War*. I asked him if he thinks Holocaust denial should be against the law.

"This is a very difficult question," he said. He attended almost every day of the trial that convicted David Irving.

> And I heard from the mouth of the Holocaust denier the most terrifying racism and anti-Semitism. I thought to myself, if this person is allowed to spread his word to ignorant audiences or audiences who want to be prejudiced, that's a bad thing.
>
> So when the Austrian government imprisoned him for his denial, I thought, "Well, he knew the law, he broke the law, and the Austrians have a right to feel that this is something inflammatory and wrong."
>
> I think every country has the right to its own laws. . . . As you say, free speech is tremendously important in our society, and debate and argument, and I'm all for that. I'm all for every Holocaust denier being able to speak in a forum where there's someone who is going to challenge him or her. At the same time, countries like Poland know that Holocaust denial, anti-Semitism, racism take on a life of their own.

I told Gilbert that I believe we give credibility to the minute number of deniers by not allowing that kind of dialogue. I worry that there will be a level of skepticism in future generations who'll ask why we're able to debate anything but that.

"I think the key word is 'dialogue,'" Gilbert said.

> I'm totally in favor of every Holocaust denier being able to speak, provided he or she allows there to be a dialogue. I'm willing to travel the

world or get up at the crack of dawn in order to be present at such a debate. And many other historians, Jews and non-Jews, will do the same. So that's fine.

And the other thing I feel . . . is that Holocaust denial is really quite a minor thing. I mean it has its fling on the Internet; it has its few adherents who travel everywhere, as they did to Ahmadinejad's anti-Holocaust conference—they made a pathetic showing actually there.

I think that what is important is the amount of material about the Holocaust, much of that you'd have seen in the Auschwitz bookshop, published by Auschwitz itself: records, diaries, the enormous number of superb memoirs. . . . These things are available, they're taught in school. American schools have a very good record mandating Holocaust teaching.

I told Gilbert about my Berlin experience and suggested that the Fuehrerbunker be opened to the public. He agreed.

When I traveled around Europe with my students about 10 years ago, and I wrote a book about that called *Holocaust Journey*, . . . I was myself astonished, and I mentioned in the book, that there wasn't a plaque there. I'm glad to hear there is, albeit only a small one. . . .

There should be complete transparency and the bunker should be open for the world to see. . . .

So let the bunker be open, let it become a place of pilgrimage, if you like, and a place of learning, as so many Holocaust sites are today.

Finally, I shared all this with a close friend who lost family in the Holocaust. We discussed whether free speech should exist on the issue of Holocaust denial.

He was unsure. But he acknowledged that laws banning Holocaust denial are probably an insufficient blanket to put out that fire.

AFTERWORD

Early in 2015, controversy arose over whether the third-ranking Republican, House majority whip Steve Scalise (R., La.), had once attended a 2002 convention for a white supremacist group—EURO (European-American Unity and Rights Organization)—that had been founded by David Duke. (It is Scalise who was later shot at a June 14, 2017, congressional baseball practice.) For a program on January 2, 2015, Duke was invited to be a guest of mine on CNN. My producer told me that Duke would do the show but wanted to be wined and dined, which is how I ended up eating lunch at the bar of the Landmarc Restaurant in the Time Warner Center with the former Imperial Wizard. What I remember is that he was no different in private than he was in public. Everything he said at lunch came wrapped in his worldview. It was impossible to engage him in a conversation with no political overtones. I didn't know it until compiling this book, but he recounted the meal on his blog:

> I actually liked the host personally; found him intelligent and iconoclastic and immediately understood the depth of his innate rejection for political correctness. I am anxious to read his book on PC. He was kind enough to invite me to a long two-hour lunch after the show. He truly wanted to understand why and what I believe. He asked me so many questions, I could barely chew the food. If he had a seven-hour dinner with Fidel Castro, I guess he saw no harm in spending two hours with me.

In the CNN interview, Duke said he didn't recall whether Scalise attended the meeting in question ("Frankly I'm not sure; I was in Russia at the time doing research for my dissertation and have since gotten a Ph.D."). And we had a spirited exchange on camera after I tried to get him to acknowledge the occurrence of the Holocaust. ("I believe in the 'quote' Holocaust," he finally said, his words diminished by his adding the air quotes.)

After the program, my weekly postshow drill was then to get on the subway beneath the Time Warner Center and ride to Penn Station, where I'd catch an Amtrak train back to Philly. On this particular day, I rode the subway solo, got to Penn Station, ate a slice of pizza at a favorite spot downstairs (Rosa's), and then found a seat on my train to Philly. No sooner had I settled in than I saw David Duke walking down the aisle of my train, whereupon he spied me and jumped into the seat as though we were long lost friends. He was as talkative as ever on the train ride, and I was desperately trying to turn the subject away from politics for fear that his comments would be overheard. It's one thing to have a provocative conversation with him in a CNN studio where that's expected but quite another on a train surrounded by other passengers. I remember I asked him what other interests he had and whether he liked music. He told me he liked classical music and rattled off a list of German and Austrian composers he thought I should follow. Again I tried to divert the conversation from his worldview and asked whether he liked classic rock. I volunteered the name of a *few classic rock bands on my playlist, and with his southern roots in mind, I said I was a fan of Lynyrd Skynyrd. Another wrong turn. Duke told me a story about having once received a flattering letter from its leader, which I took to mean Ronnie Van Zant, who died in the famous plane crash on October 20, 1977. I have no idea whether his claim is true. Only when the doors opened in Philadelphia was I a free bird.*

2007–2011

GUILTY AS CHARGED:
I DON'T SUPPORT IMUS'S FIRING

Philadelphia Inquirer, Sunday, April 15, 2007

L ET'S GET THE ESSENTIALS out of the way.

Don Imus said something indefensible. He needed to be punished. The public flogging he has suffered, plus the two-week suspension his bosses initially announced, should have been sufficient. I do not believe that MSNBC (where I often appear) or CBS Radio (my employer) should have fired him. And I cannot fathom how Al Sharpton and Jesse Jackson became the arbiters of appropriateness, given Tawana Brawley and "Hymietown," respectively.

Only Imus knows for sure what was on his self-admittedly drug-damaged mind when he said those things. His apology sounded sincere. I myself do not believe he said something racist per se. It was a reach for a cheap laugh, not something said to be injurious to the Rutgers women.

Ah, but the floodgates are now open. The cyber-lynching by faceless, nameless bloggers of talk-show hosts like me has begun.

Individuals who hide behind the anonymity afforded by the Internet are seeking to squelch the First Amendment right of people whose identities are readily known and who, unlike their cowardly critics, put their names and credibility on the line each and every day on matters of public concern. Left unconfronted, it is a dangerous practice in the making.

The very day Imus was fired at CBS, I was alerted to a posting on Media Matters for America, a sophisticated website instrumental in stoking the flames for Imus's departure. The posting, titled "It's not just Imus," identified me as one of seven talk-show hosts in America who bear observation:

> As Media Matters for America has extensively documented, bigotry and hate speech targeting, among other characteristics, race, gender, sexual orientation, religion, and ethnicity continue to permeate the airwaves through personalities such as Glenn Beck, Neal Boortz, Rush Limbaugh, Bill O'Reilly, Michael Savage, Michael Smercon-ish, and John Gibson.

I have done talk radio for about 15 years, have written two books, authored hundreds of columns, and have appeared on every major television program in which politics gets discussed, from *The Colbert Report* to *Hard-*

ball with Chris Matthews. This week alone I was responsible for 17.5 hours of content on my own radio show, wrote two newspaper columns, guest-hosted Bill O'Reilly's radio show nationwide, and found time to make television appearances on the *Today* show, the *Glenn Beck Program*, and *Scarborough Country.*

Needless to say, I was anxious to see which of my words, among the millions I have offered over all these years, have been documented by these blogger-watchdogs as "bigotry" and "hate." What exactly puts me in a category with the likes of Michael Savage?

Well, let's evaluate the quality of the evidence. For me, they identified three examples:

EXHIBIT A. "Substituting for host Bill O'Reilly on the April 4, 2006, broadcast of Westwood One's *The Radio Factor,* nationally syndicated radio host Michael Smerconish repeatedly discussed 'the sissification of America,' claiming that political correctness has made the United States 'a nation of sissies.' Smerconish also claimed, several times, that this 'sissification' and 'limp-wristedness' is 'compromising our ability to win the war on terror.'"

Guilty as charged. America is getting muzzled. Those among us who assert their own brand of political correctness while sacrificing the rugged individualism that has been the hallmark of our nation are seeking to mute the words and actions of others, make them conform to a standard of correctness that is not just silly but also toxic. In the past, this sanitization of that which we say and do would have been debate-worthy, but in truth, only a minor irritant to our quality of life. But I believe that in the post-9/11 world, these trends represent a cancer that has metastasized into the war on terror, where it threatens our very survival. We debate the comfort level at Gitmo while Nick Berg gets decapitated. We've become sissies in that regard.

EXHIBIT B. "On the Nov. 23, 2005, broadcast of *The Radio Factor,* while guest-hosting, Smerconish took issue with a decision by the New Jersey Sports and Exposition Authority to provide a designated prayer area at Giants Stadium. The decision was in response to a Sept. 19 incident involving the FBI's detention and questioning of five Muslim men who were observed praying near the stadium's main air duct during a New York Giants football game. Smerconish stated: 'I just think that's [the men's public praying] wrong. I just think they're playing a game of, you know, mind blank with the audience. And that they should know better four years removed from Sept. 11.'"

Guilty. When five Muslim men in attendance at the Meadowlands in September 2005 for a Giants-Saints game that was also a Hurricane Katrina fund-raiser, with George H. W. Bush in attendance, saw fit to pray in an area near food preparation and air-duct work, I think it was a case of mind blank. That's a form of terrorism in itself.

EXHIBIT C. "On the Nov. 23, 2005, edition of *The Radio Factor,* Smerconish interviewed Soo Kim Abboud, author of *Top of the Class: How Asian Parents Raise High Achievers—and How You Can Too.* . . . Smerconish asserted that 'if everyone follows Dr. Abboud's prescription . . . you're going to have women who will leave the home and now get a great-paying job, because you will have gotten them well-educated.' He continued, 'But then they're not going to be around to instill these lessons in their kids. In other words, it occurs to me that perhaps you've provided a prescription to bring this great success to an end.'"

My favorite—and truly an assertion that shows how asinine this situation has quickly become. Guilty!

Two Philadelphia-area Asian sisters wrote a great book explaining the success of their upbringing. The bottom line was their parents' hands-on approach. I not only hosted them on the air but also honored them at a book club meeting with several hundred attendees. It occurred to me that if their advice were followed, it would create more "high achievers" with better educational opportunities and job offers, which would, ironically, take them out of the home where they could instill those same values to their own children. But now, that insight is sexist.

How long before they start burning my tapes?

AFTERWORD

Here's a head-scratcher. Immediately after I wrote this column critical of Don Imus but arguing that he should not have been fired, MSNBC invited me to sit in his chair and anchor his old program. How could they not have known I'd taken this position? Or did they not care? Or did they figure it out after inviting me? I still don't know. I ended up spending a week guest-hosting the old Imus show. As I wrote in my book Morning Drive: *"Instead of getting up at 3:15 A.M. to do morning drive in Philly, I got up at 2 A.M. to do morning drive in Philly, simulcast to everyone else from the MSNBC studio in Secaucus, New Jersey." The week went well, but MSNBC gave Imus's spot to Joe Scarborough (for whom I had often guest-hosted at 10 P.M.). He was my last guest while I was temporarily in that slot. My producer, TC, helped engineer quite a national television debut of my radio show. My other guests that week included Rudy Giuliani, Camille Paglia, Richard Clarke, Pat Buchanan, John McCain, D. L. Hughley, Larry Kane, and Jon Anderson from YES. Anderson closed the Mon-*

day show by singing "Roundabout," after which it was announced on set that Steve Capus, the president of NBC News, was on the telephone. I momentarily thought he was calling to congratulate me on a high-quality program. Actually he was calling for Jon because he too is an uber YES fan.

For my Sunday Inquirer *column that immediately followed my week filling Imus's old spot, I published a diary of what my crazy week had entailed. The column ends: "Camera lights go dark and mic cut. Five days over, no glitches, no gaffes. Time to slide off the national stage and head back to the place where I've been content for all my 45 years."*

Not long thereafter, I began guest-hosting Hardball *for Chris Matthews on MSNBC, a role I then consistently played for five years. Finally, in 2014, CNN gave me my own television program.*

THE WAR COMES HOME

Philadelphia Daily News, Thursday, May 10, 2007

THINGS LIKE THIS don't happen here. That's what I was thinking while standing at a parking lot at State and Hamilton in Doylestown last week.

It's a location I know well. I used to walk through this spot most mornings on the way to high school at C.B. West, when the school was known for being a football powerhouse. Across the street is my mother's real-estate office. Catty-corner is La Maison cheese shop, where I often stop for a bite. Down the block is Kenny's News Agency, where we used to line up for Spectrum concert tickets. Still visible in the distance is where Bert's Bicycle Shop once sold my parents my banana-seat bike. Two blocks away is the County Theater. I remember the night in the 1970s when Kevin Benstead "streaked" after the *Bad News Bears* let out. Main Street merchants. High-school hijinks. That's the normal stuff of Doylestown. Not what I witnessed on Friday night.

Ladder 79 of the Doylestown fire company raised an American flag above a crowd of a few hundred. And as the clock (a gift from the Rotary Club marking Doylestown's founding in 1838) was about to strike 8, someone called for a moment of silence.

In front of the crowd was a fit, immaculately groomed man wearing a blue Oxford shirt. He was on the verge of tears. His wife, in black, was already over that line. Equally distraught were their daughter and son-in-law. No one could blame them, or understand their loss.

They were Colonel Thomas Manion, Janet Manion, Ryan Borek, and David Borek—the family of Travis Manion.

The night was to be First Friday in Doylestown, a monthly ritual for dining out and shopping. But the evening had been recast as a vigil for Marine first lieutenant Travis Manion, who died in Iraq on April 29.

But by the time it began, its purpose had changed yet again. Now it wasn't to honor just Manion but also another man from town as well, Army first lieutenant Colby Umbrell, who died May 3. Neither fit the ID of who's fighting in Iraq.

They were 26, scholars, athletes, warriors, patriots, and from Doylestown. Young men who could've done anything with their lives. Now there were two condolence books to sign, and, silently, the crowd did so. As we waited, a young woman named Christy Jefferson sang "Amazing Grace."

Major Adam Kubicki is the commanding officer of Military Transition Team 20. He was Travis Manion's commanding officer and was at his side when he died. He wrote a letter to the family, which they shared with me.

Major Kubicki wrote:

Know that Travis meant a great deal to all of us in his unit. He was an incredible officer, a true warrior, and an example and inspiration to us all. He was also an honorable man, willing to pursue the right path no matter the difficulty. His enthusiasm and abilities were apparent to everyone, including the Iraqis with whom we live and serve.

Meanwhile, an Associated Press story ran in this newspaper on May 1 under the headline "April's Toll: 104 Troops."

It's the sort of story I would have read in passing. I doubt I would've paused when I got to the paragraph that said, "A Marine died in combat Sunday in Anbar province, a Sunni insurgent stronghold west of the capital, the military said."

But the Marine who died in Anbar was Travis Manion. And when another story is written giving the final count for May, there will be one more Doylestonian in those ranks, Lieutenant Umbrell.

It's difficult to localize a war fought around the globe when daily stories describe a death toll pushed upward by often-faceless, nameless soldiers killed in combat.

But things have changed. Never again will I read a headline on war dead and see only words. The war has now come home.

AFTERWORD

Five years later, tragedy revisited the Manions when Travis's mother, Janet, passed away from lung cancer, but by then, she'd ensured the legacy of her son by establishing the Travis Manion Foundation (TMF), which continues to thrive. As described on the foundation's website, travismanion.org, "Travis' legacy lives on in the words he spoke before leaving for his final deployment, 'If Not Me, Then Who . . . [?]' Guided by this mantra, veterans continue their service, develop strong relationships with their communities, and thrive in their post-military lives. As a result, communities prosper and the character of our nation's heroes live[s] on in the next generation."

In 2014, Travis's father, Tom, teamed up with the journalist Tom Sileo to write the book Brothers Forever, *which tells the story of Travis and his Naval Academy roommate and best friend, Lieutenant Brendan Looney, who died in a helicopter crash in Afghanistan. Together, theirs is a sad and amazing story, and one that I have also written about. The two men are buried beside each other at Arlington National Cemetery. Brendan Looney's widow, Amy, opened what was then the second of TMF's four offices in San Diego shortly after his death in 2010. And on Memorial Day in 2011, President Barack Obama visited the graves of Lieutenants Manion and Looney and told their story during his address at the Arlington National Cemetery:*

> *The friendship between 1st Lieutenant Travis Manion and Lieutenant Brendan Looney reflects the meaning of Memorial Day. Brotherhood. Sacrifice. Love of country. And it is my fervent prayer that we may honor the memory of the fallen by living out those ideals every day of our lives, in the military and beyond.*

UNEXPECTED MEMORIAL DAY LESSON
FROM DECORATED MARINE

Philadelphia Inquirer, Sunday, May 27, 2007

THOUGHT I HAD a great idea for a Memorial Day Weekend column. I believe that the men currently fighting in Iraq are an unheralded bunch no less deserving of our thanks and praise than those of the so-called greatest generation who fought World War II.

My plan was to contact some of the highest profiles of that generation and see whether they agreed. I had in mind men like Bob Dole, who, as a member of the Army's 10th Mountain Division, tried to rescue one of his platoon's radio men while fighting in the hills of Italy and almost paid with his life; or "Wild Bill" Guarnere of Easy Company, a D-Day hero immortalized by the historian Stephen Ambrose in his book *Band of Brothers*.

I hoped they'd share a few stories, praise fellow soldiers, and offer a word of remembrance.

That was the plan. Except I never got past the first interview.

I started and ended with Jack Lucas. Lucas became known to me when I visited the USS *Iwo Jima* last October while she sailed in the Persian Gulf. I was a military tourist, and on landing aboard ship by helicopter, I found myself on what's called the Jack Lucas Airfield. Naturally I inquired: Who is/was Jack Lucas? Well, shame on me for not knowing his story.

Jack Lucas remains the youngest recipient of the Medal of Honor since the Civil War. Today he is 79. But he was recognized for his conduct at age 17. Lucas finagled his way into the Marines when he was just 14 by forging his mother's signature on the consent papers. Six days after his 17th birthday, he threw himself on top of two grenades to save three fellow Marines. He was one of 22 Marines to receive the Medal of Honor for service at Iwo Jima.

"I was fortunate that one was a dud. The other tore me up pretty bad but I survived it, and so did the three men who were with me, and they enjoyed a full life," he told me this past week. When the war ended, and his body had healed, Lucas kept a promise made to his mother upon enlistment: He returned to high school (ninth grade), now sporting a Medal of Honor and driving an Oldsmobile convertible!

All of which is column-worthy in itself. But things got even more interesting when I said to him: "You know, Mr. Lucas, we think of you as a member of the greatest generation, and as I become more familiar with the gentlemen who have given their lives in the war in Iraq, I believe that they, too, are a great generation."

As expected, Jack Lucas agreed with me. But then he offered a 10-minute discourse on Iraq, which was not what I expected from this larger-than-life Marine.

He began by reminding me that, in the Second World War, 400,000 young men lost their lives and an additional 900,000 were wounded. He thought that was a horrible price to pay, but necessary because we'd been attacked. Vietnam and Korea, by contrast, were wars that were "really not necessary" but were "brought upon us by politicians who thought we needed to go to war. We were not attacked."

> Each life given for America is most valuable, and most precious, and I do not want to put that down. But for comparison, consider the viciousness of World War II: We lost 5,320 men in the first two days of combat at Iwo Jima. And in just 36 days, 6,820 men killed at Iwo Jima and 19,000 wounded. Just 36 days.
>
> In Iraq, we are going on five years, and lost 3,300 men and 25,000 wounded. So you see the difference in the violence of the war.

On Iraq, Jack Lucas was just getting started.

He recognized that Saddam Hussein was a dictator, albeit not one who attacked us, and who possessed no weapons of mass destruction.

> We have gone in and caused our young men to lose their lives.
>
> Our men are very precious, and we don't need to be losing lives for something we should not be in, in the first place: Iraq.

Lucas bristled at the notion that Iran may be a future point of conflict and argued that if we'd kept Saddam Hussein in power, he'd be dealing with Iran, and we wouldn't have to.

He told me about a trip he'd taken to Bethesda Naval Hospital, where he saw young men with no arms and legs: "It makes me sick." He deemed it "heartbreaking" and "unnecessary."

"We should have gone into Afghanistan with sufficient troops, and got bin Laden, and wiped out al-Qaeda, and crushed the Taliban," he said, before finally pausing to catch his breath. When he did so, I remembered the initial purpose of my call.

"Mr. Lucas," I said. "Do you agree that the service of these men is no less noble than your own?"

"You got that exactly right," he said with authority.

And I do not want to equate it otherwise. Everyone who serves this great nation, in peacetime as well as wartime, are our most noble young people, and we do cherish them, and want to look out for our young men.

And when we want to get them out of harm's way, people want to call us "liberal" or "pantywaist," and I ain't never been no pantywaist, but I want my boys out of Iraq.

Lucas's message for Memorial Day?

Just remember all of the young people who lost their lives in this great country, everybody, and bow your heads, and think about them, and inscribe their names on your hearts.

All the while Lucas spoke, I was thinking of a friend who told me that wars are fought by people who are infinitely wiser and braver than the people who start them.

AFTERWORD

Jack Lucas died of leukemia in 2008 at age 80. His obituary in the New York Times *says:*

> *Big for his age and eager to serve, he forged his mother's signature on an enlistment waiver that would have allowed him to join the Marines at 17 rather than the usual 18. But in fact he was by then only 14, though the military did not learn of that until censors discovered it through a letter he had written to his 15-year-old girlfriend.*

I didn't know that part about the girlfriend or I surely would have written it in my column. But I'm glad I did describe the image of Lucas returning to the ninth grade wearing a Medal of Honor and driving an Oldsmobile convertible. The obituary also pointed out that in the 1960s, Lucas rejoined the military and became an Army paratrooper to conquer his fear of heights. Apparently, on a training jump, both of Lucas's parachutes failed but he survived, thanks to his stocky build and a last-second roll as he hit the ground.

My friend Mark O'Connor, the proprietor of the Irish Pub in Philadelphia, raises money for a group called Marine Corps Law Enforcement Foundation.

Every year he hosts Medal of Honor recipients for a raucous and worthy fund-raiser. I've met and interviewed several of them at these events, including Barney Barnum, Tom Norris, John Cavaiani, Sal Giunta, Brian Thacker, and Mike Thornton. In my interviews, I of course referenced their heroism and intrepidity and often read from their official award citations. To a man, they never want to discuss their own accomplishment but always stand ready to describe another, more "worthy" recipient.

THE WORLD
ACCORDING TO BRUNO

Philadelphia Daily News, Thursday, July 5, 2007

HE REMAINS the Living Legend.

The distinctive voice of Bruno Sammartino, a native of Abruzzo, Italy, sounded just fine when I caught up with him this week at his home outside Pittsburgh, recovering from back surgery.

"I had two [operations] before this one, and I came back strong. I will be back in training within a matter of a few weeks, and I'll be good as new, I hope," he said. He sounded like he has plenty of fight left in him, particularly when the subject is the current state of his old profession.

> I finally got disgusted and walked away because it seems like nobody cares. People keep dying, keep dying, keep dying. But nobody cares.

Like many across the country, and in this area in particular, I grew up watching the man tangling on Saturday mornings with the baddest the World Wide Wrestling Federation had to offer. He had no equal.

Sammartino's career spanned four decades. He was the longest-reigning champion in WWWF history. He headlined at Madison Square Garden on 211 cards, and 187 were sellouts!

I wondered what Sammartino was thinking as he watched the Chris Benoit tragedy play out. Investigators in Atlanta believe Benoit strangled his wife, Nancy, and their 7-year-old son, Daniel (who suffered from fragile X syndrome, an inherited mental disability).

Their bodies were discovered with Bibles beside them, which authorities believe Benoit put there before hanging himself with a weight-machine pulley. The Canadian Crippler was just 40.

Sammartino told me that steroids have ravaged the sport he loves. Citing data from Irvin Muchnick's book *Wrestling Babylon: Piledriving Tales of Drugs, Sex, Death, and Scandal*, Sammartino said there have been about 90 premature deaths in professional wrestling over the last generation. He added:

> And it blows my mind that there are all these investigations in baseball, football, and what have you where there have been no reported

deaths, and yet when it comes to wrestling, it just goes on like it doesn't matter, it's not important, it doesn't exist.

I asked the man I still admire about the steroid culture in his era. He said that he first heard of steroids while training at a gym in the early- to mid-1960s when he was impressed by a bodybuilder. When he asked about the guy's regimen, Bruno was told he was using steroids. Sammartino had no idea what that meant.

"I was 275 pounds at the time, and I got there by training my guts out," Bruno said. By the 1980s, things had changed. Sammartino said the mindset of today's wrestlers has been tragically refocused: "The mentality of any wrestler today is that to make it, you have to be juiced up. Now, who's discouraging of that?"

He was quick to point at the ringleader overseeing wrestling's devolution. He says Vince McMahon deserves "great blame" for failing to discourage the steroid culture rampant in his business.

Sammartino believes McMahon doesn't explicitly encourage steroid use but protects its destructive culture by keeping the sport's drug testing in-house. And he remembers when McMahon admitted to using steroids himself during a 1994 trial:

> If the head of the organization is known to be a steroid user like that, can anyone believe the inside drug testing that the organization does? I find it extremely difficult for anybody to take that seriously.

There used to be more to pro wrestling than the size of the competitors. It was all about Chief Jay Strongbow's determination, Victor Rivera's athleticism, and George "the Animal" Steele's . . . animalism. I loved it, but when the latest incarnation comes on the TV and I'm with my sons (who are at the age when I first got hooked), I change the channel.

Sammartino understands it. "I'm glad to hear that," he said. "Because today there's so much vulgarity, profanity, nudity. That puzzles me more than anything else." He also worries about kids emulating the steroid use they see rewarded.

> Today, young kids are very knowledgeable, and they hear about so-and-so and how strong they got and how they can improve by using these chemicals. And they're not thinking of the serious dangers that go along with that.

Anybody who knew Bruno Sammartino, they would know better than to ever suggest that I should ever take anything, or anything like that.

A living legend, indeed. Pro wrestling has long been a ghost of its former self. I hope the sport will soon take the ultimate good guy's concerns to heart.

AFTERWORD

Not long after I wrote this column, a sponsor of my radio program—a cigar store in Philadelphia—invited Sammartino to come to town for an appearance. I was thrilled to be his escort for the day at a time when I was still practicing law with the legendary James E. Beasley. The firm is located in the ornate and aptly named Beasley Building at 12th and Walnut Streets in Philadelphia. The building was constructed in 1894 by the Episcopal Diocese of Pennsylvania and served as its headquarters for many years. The headquarters fell on hard times before Beasley bought the building in 1986 and painstakingly restored it. The building was—and remains—a showpiece. The afternoon of Bruno's appearance, I took him to my normally staid law office, thinking it would be the ideal spot for him to spend some down time before the event. But from the moment he entered, he was immediately recognized by lawyers and support staff, all of whom were eager to share stories of his influence on their upbringing. Word spread through the five floors that there was a celebrity in the building, but not everyone understood who it was. Finally, on a microphone normally reserved for fire drills, our receptionist announced that "the living legend Bruno Sammartino" was in the house. A line quickly formed outside my office for photos and autographs. In 10 years of practicing law at a firm that saw many noteworthy clients come through its doors, I don't recall any other moment that so energized the office.

AN IMMIGRANT'S DREAM
STILL MEANS SOMETHING

Philadelphia Inquirer, Sunday, July 15, 2007

THE DAUGHTER of the shoemaker to King Nicholas Petrovich of Montenegro is on her deathbed. She is 101 years old. She is my grandmother.

Word of Victoria Grovich's (nee Ivanisevich) imminent passing came to me last week on the same day I reviewed the latest Pew Global Attitudes Project Survey. The study noted the continued decline of the United States' image throughout the world. The same day, the president's approval rating in one poll plummeted to 29 percent, while Congress's rating is lower still.

Maybe the silver lining to the passing of the shoemaker's daughter is the antidote her story offers to increasingly negative perceptions of the United States. Let me explain.

Nikola Grujicich was my maternal grandfather. He left the Balkans in 1906, at age 14, for America. He was accompanying his father to seek jobs in the coal mines of West Virginia. Grujicich quickly became Grovich. After World War I, Nikola returned to the Balkans and, not long thereafter, wed my grandmother in an arranged marriage. Her father, Milo Ivanisevich, was the town cobbler in Cetinje, Montenegro. He made boots for the king, a fact proudly trumpeted in the window of his shop on a dirt road.

After the marriage, Nikola returned to work in America, leaving behind my grandmother and their newborn until he could afford to send for them. That happened in 1927.

My grandmother made the 12-day journey with their firstborn and arrived at Ellis Island. She left behind her roots and parents she would never see again. Awaiting her was a limited network of fellow Slavs. She did not speak English. She once told me that while sailing for America, she was homesick and frightened and wished the ship would turn back. Lucky for me, it didn't.

My grandparents briefly operated a boarding home for miners in West Virginia and then relocated to Hazleton, in Pennsylvania's coal region. There, they raised 11 children (eight girls, three boys) before my grandfather succumbed to black lung.

Those 11 children are still alive, which is itself an extraordinary testament to American health care. The 11 have led comfortable lives. Each has been formally educated and consistently employed. Each owns a home and a car. They have traveled extensively. Their children have had it even better. My cousins'

Portrait of King Nicholas Petrovich, the last king of Montenegro, in the national Museum of Montenegro, in Cetinje, wearing boots presumably made by my great-grandfather.

educations extend well beyond those of their parents. Their homes today are larger than the ones in which they were raised. None wants for any basic necessity.

They are leading typical American lives. This is not only a story about my grandmother, but also about many of our forefathers.

What a land of opportunity! This takes me back to the way we are regarded.

In the last Pew Global Attitudes Project survey, the United States' favorable ratings declined in 26 of 33 countries. Anti-Americanism is extensive and has been for the last five years. There are a few surprises as to where we are well-received—more favorably in some of the Third World than with former World War II allies, for example. Another tidbit: Americans are more popular than America. (See the report at http://pewglobal.org/reports.)

No one should be shocked to learn of rising hostility toward the United States, given the situation in Iraq. Nor the corresponding decline in the president's popularity.

I'm concerned about the way we are perceived around the globe. And I am worried about the way we regard our own nation. My hunch is that the negativity from abroad and the vitriol directed toward our president here at home are causing an American loss of self-respect. I sense a collective tail being placed between our legs in response to a constant barrage of all that is wrong with America. I may be mistaken.

My evidence about how we view our own country is visceral and anecdotal, not quantitative. (I did, however, see a recent CBS survey that found that 72 percent of Americans believe that if the Founding Fathers came back, they would be "disappointed" rather than "pleased.")

Don't get me wrong: We've certainly got our share of problems, Iraq chief among them. Fixing them and our standing in the world should be a never-ending goal.

But it's healthy to take stock of all that we are afforded in this country—namely, an environment in which we can still live free and pursue dreams. Frankly, that is why we have an illegal immigration problem.

Despite what *Paris Match* and the *Manchester Guardian* say about us, millions are still breaking barriers to go where the streets are figuratively paved with gold.

They want what the shoemaker's daughter experienced.

AFTERWORD

On Mother's Day in 2015, I wrote a Sunday Inquirer *column under the headline: "Thanks to Mom for Opportunity." It was about the importance of the decision both my parents made when they were young to move to Bucks County, Pennsylvania. I continued the family story begun here by noting that my mother, the onetime Miss West Hazleton High School, married my father when both were living in that Luzerne County coal community. Soon they moved to Lykens, in Dauphin County, where my father was hired to teach school. My brother was born shortly thereafter. By the time I arrived four years later, my family had moved to Doylestown, which is where my brother and I grew up. In that Mother's Day column, I told a couple of stories about Mom:*

> *Like the time when Mom drove my brother and me to Little League baseball and decided to step into the batter's box, only to hit one over the left-field fence. Or how, at our urging, the night before a rock festival was staged in our small town, she drove us slowly in our '66 Chevy so we could spy the "hippies" sleeping out in tents. We might laugh about the night she dragged my brother out of a dance after seeing some "hoodlums" smoking outside. While my brother and I most feared my father as a disciplinarian, it was usually Mom who meted out justice, with a yardstick she acquired from Cross Keys Hardware.*

And I wrote about her incredible business success:

> *When I was in the eighth grade, the state of Pennsylvania raised the credits required to sit for the real estate exam. That change spurred my mother, a high school graduate, to take weekend classes and take the*

test. My job was to follow her around our house, posing questions from a manual supplied by the Schlicher-Kratz Institute. The day of the test she was so nervous she didn't want to get out of bed. But she did and she passed. It was the start of a spectacular career that continues today.

My mother has twice built thriving residential real estate business-es. Her hard work and success as a Realtor afforded our family a life-style (and me an education) we would otherwise not have enjoyed. Today I'll thank her for that, and for guidance, and for unconditional love. But now I'm adding something new to the list. I want to thank her for not only how she raised me, but also where. I always suspected I had an advantage growing up in Doylestown—now there is data to prove it.

Then I drew on recently released research from the Harvard economists Raj Chetty and Nathaniel Hendren on the relationship between where children grow up and their future well-being. Their findings support those of previous studies revealing that growing up in good neighborhoods produces better long-term outcomes for children. According to the data, Bucks County ranks among the most advantageous in the nation for upward mobility, while the county where my folks were raised, Luzerne, is at the other end of the spectrum. My brother and I didn't grow up poor. When Dad was a guidance counselor and Mom was a secretary (before selling real estate), we were decidedly middle class. My family's experience only reinforces my belief that the combination of good schools with better test scores, intact families, and civic engagement provides a big boost for those who want to climb the economic ladder.

Or as my mom, the Realtor, would say: "Location, location, location!"

PROOF A SON'S HEAD IS FAR
FROM DISMAL ADULT EVENTS

Philadelphia Inquirer, Sunday, August 5, 2007

JUST PICKED UP my 11-year-old namesake from sleepaway summer camp in New Hampshire.

He'd been away for five weeks, and writing letters is not his forte, so I wasn't sure what to expect when his grandfather and I picked him up.

The second I saw his Mohawk haircut, I knew all was well.

Notwithstanding his mother's shock and horror, I'm elated. And not just due to follicle envy.

My son's restyling told me his head had been in the right place while playing sports and living in the woods. Better there than where we adults have been, swamped in some dismal headlines this summer of 2007.

He's been swimming, boating, playing tennis, making friends, and eating Fluffernutter sandwiches, far removed from significant events during what are normally quiet months. So when he asked me what was "new" on the way home, I had to weigh which of the following was worthy of the attention of a preteen:

the uncovering of another U.K.-based terror plot earlier this summer;
the record pace of homicides in Philadelphia;
professional wrestling's latest plot twist, the murder-suicide of Chris
      Benoit;
the Delaware County native who works as an NBA ref and is now
      the focus of a law-enforcement inquiry;
or that Michael Vick is being charged with being involved in dog-
      fighting?

I decided instead to lead with the news that the Phillies are hanging tough despite continued pitching woes, and the Eagles are back at Lehigh with Donovan McNabb looking strong. I figure my son will have plenty of time later in life for the heavy lifting.

This is not to say that his recent exploits have been totally free of stressors.

He's had no Internet, played no video games, and watched no TV for weeks.

And the 13-year-old barber who created his Mohawk gave him a bit of a scratch on the back of his neck. (Chalk that up to salon immaturity.)

Son no. 1 sporting a Mohawk at Camp Tecumseh, Moultonborough, New Hampshire, summer 2007.

It could have been worse. After all, there's that poor camper who lost in a game of Truth or Dare and had to read the daily mail list in front of other campers on a day he'd had to put Icy Hot on his private parts. ("That was rough," my son tells me, "because it was a day when there were lots of packages, Dad.")

What exactly do you do with 20 or so bunkmates who may need to get up in the middle of the night? Well, a couple of guys had to run morning sprints because they did not walk the full 20 paces mandated by the unwritten camp rule spelling out the distance one must travel if getting up in the dark and needing some relief.

Speaking of sleeping, every night when his head hit the pillow, in a bunk in a cabin just off a glimmering lake, he had to contend with the knowledge that the crimes of the infamous Mary B had never been solved. The counselors not only revealed the camp's origins as what they called a "funny farm" (PC they are not) but also felt it appropriate to share the legend of Mary B with the younger campers. She was an escapee who returned years ago to wreak havoc on the more recent generations of campers. ("It was a huge story a while back," said my son, with more than a hint of surprise that his columnist/talk-show host/news pundit/father had missed this whopper.)

And it had to be true, because one of her victims was the brother's sister's cousin's niece ("or something") of one of the current counselors.

So it all checks out.

By now, of course, it did sound familiar. Only my recollection was that Mary B had an accomplice who had a hook for an arm and ended up terrorizing local couples on Lovers' Lane.

Perhaps you're wondering if my son was staying at Camp Granada. No, it was Camp Tecumseh, but Allan Sherman sure would have been proud to hear his tales.

Not even a seven-hour delay at the airport when it came time to fly home could have spoiled my pride.

Maybe that's because there have been many recent days I've wished I had a Mohawk, and not just because I'm bald.

AFTERWORD

I recently asked my son whether Tecumseh has changed. He sadly reported hearing that "the Widow" had undergone modification. That's the nickname for the lavatory that had six commodes facing one another, sans doors. He said it made for interesting conversations but suggested I confirm with one of his classmates, Jack Keffer, a Tecumseh lifer. Jack is a camper-turned-counselor. His dad, grandad, and great-grandad attended the same camp. Jack reported that indeed a giant wall was installed in the Widow to separate the previously open stalls, adding that the move was "a big hit to the integrity of the place." He added:

> *It also pains me to tell you that there is no more Fluffernutter offered in the dining room. It's even more painful to tell you that no one reads the packages list at lunch anymore because of the havoc and rowdiness it would cause. Basically, the mail boy would get up in front of the dining hall, say, "Packages," and the entire camp would scream "PACKAGES" in the most outrageous ways possible for roughly two minutes, making it virtually impossible for the mail boy to read out the names of anyone who had received a package that day.*
>
> *But other than these minor changes, Tecumseh lives on! There are still no cell phones, TVs, or video games, despite pressure from parents for camp to publicize daily activities on social media, so the Tecumseh Instagram page has been a big emphasis and photos are sent to parents weekly. Through all this, they still do a great job of making good boys better.*

A NAVY SEAL'S GUT-WRENCHING
TALE OF SURVIVAL

Philadelphia Inquirer, Sunday, August 26, 2007

WHEN FOUR U.S. NAVY SEALS surreptitiously tracking a high-level Taliban official in Afghanistan encountered three wandering goatherds, they faced a dilemma with perilous consequences: Were the herders harmless civilians or Taliban scouts? What should be done?

One hour after deciding to let the three go, the SEAL team was surrounded by 80 to 100 Taliban fighters, and in an ensuing gun battle, three of the four SEALs were killed.

The lone survivor was Lead Petty Officer Marcus Luttrell, hence the title of his best-selling book. President Bush awarded him the Navy Cross for combat heroism, and Luttrell's account of what happened in the Hindu Kush in June 2005 is now the buzz of book clubs across the country. It asks us: When war obscures your vision, what do you do? And as Luttrell offers his explanation, his story shows how the fog of war can spread beyond the battlefield.

Luttrell recounts that the SEALs voted on whether to let the goatherds live or to kill them. According to Luttrell, the tally was 2–1, with one abstention, in favor of letting them go. Petty Officer Second Class Matthew G. Axelson was in favor of killing the herders, Luttrell writes, while Petty Officer Second Class Danny P. Dietz was noncommittal. Lieutenant Michael Murphy wanted to release them, and Luttrell agreed with his superior officer, breaking the deadlock. About that decision, he writes:

> It was the stupidest, most southern-fried, lamebrained decision I ever made in my life. I must have been out of my mind. I had actually cast a vote which I knew could sign our death warrant. I'd turned into a f——ing liberal, a half-assed, no-logic nitwit, all heart, no brain, and the judgment of a jackrabbit.

After Luttrell repeated those sentiments recently on the *Today* show, a *Newsday* article said that Daniel Murphy, Lieutenant Michael Murphy's father, believed Luttrell's published account differed from what Luttrell told the Murphy family during a condolence call. Michael Murphy was gunned down by the Taliban in the midst of the firefight after voluntarily entering an unprotected area to call for reinforcements. For that bravery, he is reportedly under consideration for the Medal of Honor.

Lone Survivor is a searing narrative, one that elicits an emotional commitment to the SEALs, and any reader will be pained to think that friction might now exist between Luttrell and the family of a man with whom he served. This reader decided to call Mr. Murphy to find out more.

Daniel Murphy began by telling me:

> There's a controversy that is not really a controversy. When Marcus came to our house, he . . . told us Michael was adamant that the civilians would be released, and they were released. . . . Michael's decision . . . is what carried the day.

I asked him if Luttrell mentioned there having been a vote. Daniel Murphy said no. He also told me he thinks it's a "disservice" to Axelson for Luttrell to suggest that he wanted to kill the goatherds, or that Dietz was "ambivalent" about the choice.

Still, Daniel Murphy assured me that he bears no hostility toward Luttrell; to the contrary, he "loves" him. As for why there is a discrepancy between the book's account and what Luttrell told him previously, Lieutenant Murphy's father said he believes he knows the answer: Luttrell, he thinks, is burdened by the guilt of surviving.

> [Marcus is] acting like his friends would be alive if it wasn't for him and his actions. And that's not what happened. And Michael would not want Marcus to believe that, and we don't want Marcus to believe that. We love Marcus. I just think he's taking too much guilt for what happened by saying, "You know, if we had killed these civilians, my friends would be alive."
>
> And I've tried to tell him that's not what we believe, and that's not what happened.

The father's appraisal of his son's character makes sense and rightfully honors the heroic men we lost as well as the patriot with his guilty burden. In addition to Murphy, Axelson, and Dietz, eight other SEALs and eight Army specialists died that day when an MH-47 Chinook helicopter sent to help was shot down. That day brought the largest loss of life to Naval Special Warfare forces since D-Day. Murphy said:

> I don't think Michael could have lived with himself. To kill innocent people, . . . it is such the antithesis of the character of my son Michael, who I've known for 29 years. It would not have even occurred to him.

I hung up, admiring the father, just as I admire his son and those he served with in the SEALs. And I kept thinking about that decision made two years ago on a mountaintop 8,000 miles from home. So last week, I asked Marcus Luttrell to revisit that fateful decision concerning the goatherds.

Luttrell, too, admired the son. He said:

> I mean, obviously, Mikey was in charge. He had the final word no matter what, but he was a great officer, and he used every man and all the talents they had and he did it well. That was our decision, and we all got together and that's what we came up with.
>
> That takes nothing away from Mikey. He could have run that whole thing by himself, but like I said, he was a great officer and he used all the information he had.

Finally, I believe, my confusion has cleared: America lost 19 heroes that day in Afghanistan, and Marcus Luttrell had the good fortune to survive. But good fortune can exact a price—even though he knows he did not make the fateful decision alone, he cannot escape his sense of responsibility to the ones who died. The fog of war can obscure the truth even when the combatants come back home.

AFTERWORD

The Lone Survivor *story has long captivated me, and I have made it the subject of numerous columns and radio and television commentaries. I'll also never forget hosting Marcus Luttrell for one of my book club events, on May 21, 2008, at the Scottish Rite Auditorium in Collingswood, New Jersey. When tickets for the event went on sale, the 1,050-seat venue was sold out within 48 hours. You could have heard a pin drop for the entire 90 minutes Luttrell spent recounting to the audience and me what had happened in the Hindu Kush. Over the years I have hosted many live events with authors in front of large audiences under the guise of my "book club" but none with the emotional punch of that night.*

I was pleased when President George W. Bush posthumously awarded Lieutenant Michael Murphy the Medal of Honor and presented the medal to his parents, Daniel and Maureen Murphy, on October 22, 2007. Daniel is himself a wounded veteran, of the Vietnam War. In May 2010 my friend Mark O'Connor and I hosted Daniel and Maureen at the Irish Pub in Philadelphia, where we met to celebrate Gary Williams's tribute to Lieutenant Murphy, a book called Seal of Honor.

"ANTI-SEMITIC" LABEL
CURBS TALK ABOUT ISRAEL

Philadelphia Inquirer, Sunday, September 9, 2007

ONE YEAR AFTER 9/11, I visited Israel as a guest of the *Jerusalem Post.* In the midst of the intifadah, the hard-line newspaper arranged for me to broadcast my daily radio show from Jerusalem. At the time, I was also filing one-minute commentaries for KYW-AM (1060). One of them caused some consternation at home. Here is what I said:

> Yesterday, an Israeli guide was anxious to show me the community called Gilo.
>
> "Look," he said, "at the sandbags that these people have to place in their windows to shield them from sniper fire from a neighboring village called Beit Jala."
>
> Sure enough, there were sandbags in windows and bullet holes in walls. Thinking of my kids, I said, "That's no place to raise a family."
>
> Today, I had a different guide with a different perspective. He wanted me to tour an Arab neighborhood in the West Bank.
>
> "Look at where Israeli tank fire has destroyed these homes," he said to me. I looked. The devastation was terrible. "This is no place to live," I said to myself.
>
> "Where are we?" I asked.
>
> "This is the village called Beit Jala," he told me, "and the tank fired from over there, in Gilo"—where I had been the day before.

I ended the commentary by saying: "And so it goes."

My intention was only to present a form of geopolitical glass half empty/half full, not to assert any moral equivalency. But that didn't spare me an onslaught of e-mail from Jewish listeners disappointed in what I had said, or what they thought I was implying. Some told me my "comparison" was anti-Semitic, which stunned me, given that my entire trip had a palpable, pro-Israeli tone.

I was reminded of that experience this week while considering the backlash against the release of *The Israel Lobby and U.S. Foreign Policy,* by John J. Mearsheimer and Stephen M. Walt. Mearsheimer is a political scientist at the University of Chicago. Walt is a professor at Harvard University's John F. Kennedy School of Government.

Their book is an outgrowth of their lengthy online article on the same subject, and of a 40-page essay published last spring in the *London Review of Books*. Their premise is that the United States has set aside its own security to advance the interests of Israel, owing to the existence of a "lobby," which they define as a loose coalition of individuals and organizations who actively work to steer U.S. foreign policy in a pro-Israel direction.

Among their observations is that anyone who criticizes Israel's actions or argues that pro-Israel groups have a significant influence over U.S. policy stands a good chance of being labeled anti-Semitic.

Labeling has become all too common in today's political debate, overlooking that few of us can neatly be compartmentalized under words such as liberal or conservative. Speak against same-sex marriage? You must be a "homophobe." Oppose affirmative action? That sounds "racist."

Similarly, to question U.S. support for Israel runs the risk of being branded "anti-Semitic." Perhaps it's only a small minority who assign the labels. Still, each debasing generalization stifles conversation about issues of the day. The shame is that some people, who already have a seat at the table, resort to such language as a way to prevent those of different views from even getting to the table at all.

Here's hoping that, six years removed from 9/11, Mearsheimer and Walt can initiate a reasonable conversation about Israel. No subject with implications for U.S. security should be off-limits. Among their words worthy of debate are these:

> Saying that Israel and the United States are united by a shared terrorist threat has the causal relationship backwards: the United States has a terrorism problem in good part because it is so closely allied with Israel, not the other way around.

Of course, others conclude that the origins of America's terror problem are much wider in scope than Israel alone; they argue that disdain for America's relationship with Israel long preceded the modern terrorist threat. I say let's air it out.

Mearsheimer and Walt's arguments sound similar to words spoken to me by Michael Scheuer, author of the book *Imperial Hubris* and a man who spent 22 years with the CIA. From 1996 to 1999, he ran "Alec Station," the Osama bin Laden tracking unit at the CIA's Counterterrorist Center. He told me he agreed with Mearsheimer and Walt that the Israeli lobby had "distorted and burdened" U.S. foreign policy and added:

The most dangerous aspect of the Israel lobby is that it threatens free speech in America. Very few Americans will exercise their right to free speech if criticizing Israel earns them identification as an anti-Semite.

Which reminds me that after I recently interviewed Scheuer, a blog posting said:

> He won't out-and-out claim he hates Jews, but everything he criticizes centers around Israel and the "dual loyalty" of neo-cons. You would be smart to avoid using this man as a reference. Soon he will reveal himself to be the true anti-Semite he is.

Scheuer argues that he was hired by the CIA not to be guardian of the world but to be a guardian of the American people and that our foreign policy should be designed to protect Americans first. This is exactly what Mearsheimer and Walt say we have abdicated.

Hardly an anti-Semitic view, and these well-credentialed academics have gone to great lengths to defuse any accusations of personal animus toward Israel. As they write in the *London Review of Books:*

> In its basic operations, the Israel Lobby is no different from the farm lobby, steel or textile workers' unions, or other ethnic lobbies. There is nothing improper about American Jews and their Christian allies attempting to sway US policy; the Lobby's activities are not a conspiracy of the sort depicted in tracts like the *Protocols of the Elders of Zion.*

Their words are falling on deaf ears in certain quarters. A number of potential forums for discussion with the authors have turned down or canceled events. According to the *New York Times,* these include the Center for the Humanities at the Graduate Center at the City University of New York, the Chicago Council on Global Affairs, a Jewish cultural center in Washington, and three organizations in Chicago.

This would seem only to strengthen their argument.

AFTERWORD

I have a vague recollection of my editor telling me I had "guts" to write this column at the time I filed it. That caused me to reread it before publication, but because I saw no problem in describing the book and the issues it raised, I made no changes. Well, he was prescient about the reaction. The blowback I received only underscored the observation that many have made that there is more robust debate about Israel within Israel than is tolerated in the United States. For some, support for Israel 99 percent of the time isn't enough. Two particular reactions among many stand out in my mind. The first was an angry phone call I received from a close family member who is Jewish; he really let me have it. Someone in his Florida synagogue had shown my column to him, and while he could point to nothing specific that I had said, he was nevertheless insulted that I'd even written about the book. The second was even more upsetting. I was livid when I learned that coverage of the release of the book in the Jewish Exponent, a Philadelphia-area newspaper, targeted me because I wrote this column. The article was complete with my photograph and a defamatory headline. The fact that I was so inconsequential to the story that my name didn't appear until the 11th paragraph didn't stop them from running my name in the headline next to the word "Lies," along with accusations of anti-Semitism within the story. I wrote to the executive editor who authored the story to express my dissatisfaction, and he replied by doubling down on his baseless accusations. I ended my participation in the e-mail exchange by writing, "You, sir, are an ass . . . and I intend to continue to support Israel despite you."

THE FACE OF SEPTEMBER 11, 2001

Philadelphia Daily News, Tuesday, September 11, 2007

THERE ARE EVENTS in our lives that will forever be entwined with the person who broke the news.

I doubt you can recall the passing of a loved one without remembering who first told you. Any mention of JFK's assassination reminds me of an emotional Walter Cronkite informing the nation of the passing of our 35th president. And few Philadelphians can think of the Broad Street Bullies without hearing Gene Hart repeating, "The Flyers win the Stanley Cup!"

Today, as I have for each of the last five anniversaries, I carry a mental image of Aaron Brown on 9/11. I see him standing on a New York rooftop in brilliant sunshine against a smoldering backdrop while providing an extemporaneous human dimension to the death and destruction whose extent was then unknown.

I just rewatched much of his work at YouTube. I wish all Americans would do likewise. It's the perfect, unifying antidote to the partisan division that fighting the "war on terror" has become.

Sobering. That's how I regard his reports. Brown was always an intelligent journalist. But that day he spoke with an added somber clarity. Typical was this observation after the collapse of the World Trade Center's South Tower:

> There has just been a huge explosion. . . . [W]e can see a billowing smoke rising. . . . I'll tell you that I can't see that second tower . . . but there was a cascade of sparks and fire and now it looks almost like a mushroom cloud . . . about as frightening a scene as you will ever see.

I've often wondered how Brown himself regards his work that day, and what thoughts he might have now that he is unbridled by the limitations of being a reporter. So I called him to ask.

He'd just started at CNN at the time of the attack, having been hired to create and manage a national newscast and breaking news. Brown was driving to work when he heard radio reports of an airplane hitting the North Tower. He said he assumed it was an accident, but knew he'd be reporting what happened, regardless of the cause.

I dropped the car [off] . . . and was racing . . . to where the CNN building was and just thought, "Calm down. Whatever is about to unfold here, you need to be calm."

When I said I thought his work that day stood apart from that of his "competitors," he was quick to point out that on 9/11 no one was motivated by any thought of competing. On another day, sure, but on 9/11, Brown said, there was an unprecedented level of cooperation among those all trying to do the same thing.

But he recognized that his broadcast had the advantage of being live from a rooftop in sight of Ground Zero, instead of inside an antiseptic studio.

When I asked what he remembered about that perch, he repeated what he'd once said to Peter Jennings:

The thing that stays with me . . . is how I could smell it. . . . We were outside and could rarely see the monitor because of the sunlight. We could smell the tragedy. I can still smell it in many ways.

I suspect Brown will never fully shake 9/11. When I replayed audio of his words that day and asked for a comment, his voice quaked as he told me that it was only the second time he'd re-listened to his reporting. The first came in a class at Arizona State University, where his students in a TV course asked to analyze his work. Brown spent three classes reviewing an hour of his 9/11 coverage.

And I thought I was over the emotional power of it, but I'm clearly not. I suspect that 20 years from now, if God is kind enough to keep me alive that long, I will hear that tape and still have trouble putting together a complete sentence.

Brown recalls the events of 9/11 in three parts: the morning "all-hell-breaking-loose" phase, the middle when "all of us, reporters and citizens," tried to figure out exactly what had transpired that morning, and the end of the day, when the president finally addressed the nation.

That night, Brown stayed in a hotel. The following morning, he recalls the deathly silence that consumed New York City, "as if saying something would have been disrespectful to the 2,500 people or so who died."

Today, just like the rest of us, Aaron Brown tries to make sense of what he reported, and we watched unfold. He thinks we continue to lack a "civil national conversation" about how to deal with this tragedy. He says:

We have been angry, and we should have been, and there were things that needed to be done. But we can't kill all of these people; we can't even come close. And so we need other strategies, smarter strategies, more thoughtful strategies, or my kid is going to have this conversation with your kid.

Which makes sense to me. And if we don't follow that script, then no doubt a future Aaron Brown will be standing on another rooftop offering somber descriptions of another smoldering building.

AFTERWORD

On the 15th anniversary of 9/11 in 2016, Brown, then living in New Mexico, was interviewed by my CNN colleague Brian Stelter and said he still hears from viewers who thank him for his coverage that day. I'm not surprised. Aaron Brown's work was stellar on 9/11, but even more so considering that it was his first day on the job at CNN. It was also the first day on the job for Ben Sliney as Federal Aviation Administration national operations manager. It was Sliney who made the decision to ground all planes in United States airspace that day.

Like Brown, Sliney is a very impressive guy. I met him when we were both participants in a 9/11 remembrance at the Garden of Reflection on September 11, 2013. And I interviewed him close to that anniversary on my SiriusXM POTUS program. "Looking at weather on TV that morning," he told me, "there were no issues from Maine to Florida. . . . I thought, 'This is going to be a very easy day for me.'" Soon, he would be ordering a complete "ground stop" of all airplanes in the nation, so that none could take off. As he contemplated the chaos that might ensue if he forced those in the air to land, the situation worsened and he ordered that all airplanes in the United States be grounded, and that the borders be closed. The process took about two hours to land all 5,300 airplanes then in U.S. airspace, and all the while, Sliney and his team in Herndon, Virginia, watched a large screen showing the plane movements with a counter ticking down the number still airborne. Sliney was asked by the director and producers of the movie United 93 *to help ensure the accuracy of that depiction and ended up playing himself in the movie. He was as steady and competent in the film as he was on 9/11.*

HOW RUSH BECAME
THE KING OF TALK

Philadelphia Daily News, Thursday, October 18, 2007

THE MAESTRO ONSTAGE at the Academy of Music one week ago wielded a microphone instead of a baton. And while the Philadelphia Orchestra was nowhere in sight, you could say the evening's selection was a version of "Fanfare for the Common Man."

The conductor? Rush Limbaugh. He was in town at the behest of the station that airs his program locally (and mine), the Big Talker 1210/AM. This was Rush unplugged, working without commercials, and letting it rip for 90 minutes in front of a sold-out crowd of "dittoheads."

The packed house was a fraction of the millions he reaches every week via 600-plus stations as America's most-listened-to radio personality.

Of course, Rush brought with him a lesson plan from the Limbaugh Institute for Advanced Conservative Studies, but after watching his tutorial on Broad Street, it became apparent the strength of his appeal lies in more than his message.

Rush Limbaugh is radio's Riccardo Muti. He is an entertainer par excellence, and it is his gift of communication that sets him apart. The message, his politics, is his encore.

To be sure, Limbaugh is an unapologetic conservative. He has single-handedly made that ideology fashionable in a medium where it previously had no home. His worst critic would have to concede that his legacy is one of having reshaped the media landscape, starting with talk radio.

I recognize that by now Limbaugh antagonists either have relegated this *Daily News* to the birdcage or are thinking of it.

I get it. You like him or you don't in the same way you condone or condemn the senior U.S. senator from New York. But give the big man his just due.

Two decades ago, "the media" consisted of the big three networks and CNN, conventional radio, and traditional print. There was no Fox News, and Al Gore had yet to invent the Internet. Conservative media voices were the odd few. And there certainly was no dominant voice on the right. Rush Limbaugh filled that void when he was syndicated in 1988.

He'd been honing his craft since 1967, when he began as a high school student with the moniker of Rusty Sharpe on KGMO in his hometown of

Cape Girardeau, Missouri. After college, he worked his first radio gig in McKeesport, Pennsylvania, as a Top 40 DJ at WIXZ. By 1972 (as Jeff Christie), he was on Pittsburgh's KQV. After a stint with the Kansas City Royals, he returned to radio at KFBK in Sacramento—and changed the broadcast business.

Philadelphia was the last major market to welcome Limbaugh. He came aboard WWDB-FM on September 21, 1992. Eight years later, he moved to WPHT.

The *Inquirer*'s Joe Logan wrote:

> Finally, finally Philadelphians are about to hear the radio talk show that the rest of America has been talking about for several years. For the uninitiated, Limbaugh is 320 pounds of conservative bombast. He attacks liberals, feminists, environmentalists, animal-rights types, just about anybody who doesn't worship Ronald Reagan.

Those words are typical of how Limbaugh has been typecast and misunderstood by those who don't get (or are frustrated by) his appeal. Detractors assume he draws strength from positions that divide, when in fact the Rush Limbaugh onstage at the Academy of Music accentuates all that unites Americans. Last week he said:

> Look at the greatness. Look at the inventions. Look at what happened to the world in the 20th century, because most of it happened in this country. A level of achievement—human achievement—that advanced lifestyles, extended life spans . . . unknown in the hundreds of years prior.

With decidedly pro-American pitches like what he offered in Philadelphia—with some fun at Hillary's expense sprinkled in for good measure—Rush showed how he created a clubhouse for a significant segment of society that believed their views were unwanted and unrepresented in the media. That demand didn't start with Rush, but no one before him was able to meet it.

Before Limbaugh, no one was able to harness the widespread discontent with the mainstream media. He did it by having a message. But, equally important, Rush became a phenomenon based on the strength of his personality, and a jovial one at that. He's a man who likes to laugh and who knows how to deliver a punchline. He's also a master of self-deprecation. (And a ladies' man. Limbaugh didn't leave the Academy stage without completing a "ring check" of a shapely blonde who'd been particularly appreciative of his speech from her perch in the front row.)

Rush onstage is more ringleader than Republican, more entertainer than conservative. Unassailable is his status as a headliner. You don't attract 15 million-plus listeners a week—or 2,000 for a night on Broad Street—by being anything less.

AFTERWORD

What I remember most about this night (just a little more than a year before the 2008 election) is that I was feeling increasingly uneasy about my long-standing support for the Republican Party and was on the verge of leaving the reservation. As I detailed in many columns and radio commentaries, I was by now convinced that the George W. Bush administration had lost interest in killing those responsible for the events of 9/11. Rather than focusing on the perpetrators hiding in Afghanistan and Pakistan, we'd taken a draining and disastrous left turn into Iraq.

One year earlier, I'd participated in the Pentagon-sponsored Joint Civilian Orientation Conference, a military immersion program that began in 1947 with the goal of building citizen awareness of military functions. I was part of a hand-selected group of about two dozen Americans who, in the span of one week, traveled 15,000 miles and visited four Middle Eastern countries. Our itinerary included a briefing by Defense Secretary Donald Rumsfeld at the Pentagon, boarding the USS Iwo Jima by helicopter in the Persian Gulf, firing the best of the Army's weaponry in the Kuwait desert (just 10 miles from Iraq), driving an 11-kilometer Humvee obstacle course designed to protect against IEDs, boarding the Air Force's most sophisticated surveillance aircraft in Qatar, and touring a military humanitarian outpost in the Horn of Africa. I returned home from the immersion impressed with the men and women who wear the uniform of our country but convinced that we were no longer making the hunt for Osama bin Laden a priority. More than anything else, this realization led to my support of Barack Obama for president, especially after I spoke several times with Senator Obama and received his assurance that he'd take the hunt for bin Laden into Pakistan if necessary—which he did.

So when my friend Mike Baldini, the radio station's general manager, asked me to introduce Limbaugh at the Academy of Music, I passed. I was off the GOP talking points, didn't want to be in that position, and thought many of the hardcore Limbaugh supporters in the audience would not want me emcee-ing the event anyway. It just didn't feel right. But I wanted to help, so I wrote a speech for Baldini to recite and he nailed the delivery. I took my father to the event as my guest. We ate steaks at the Palm before the show, then met Rush backstage, where we exchanged brief pleasantries and took a photo before taking our seats in the audience.

One more thing: Limbaugh really liked this column. He thought it captured him. I know because he referenced it on more than one occasion on his program and spoke of our backstage greetings.

WHY RUDY WASN'T IN IOWA
ON TUESDAY

Philadelphia Daily News, Thursday, November 29, 2007

IOWA CAUCUS–GOERS will cast their first ballots in the 2008 presidential race in just five weeks, and Rudy Giuliani, trailing rival Mitt Romney in the Hawkeye State, needs to spend every available moment campaigning there.

Yet on Tuesday, Rudy could instead be found in a state whose April primary has for years meant little to the presidential nominating process. He was drawn to Pittsburgh by matters of friendship, loyalty, and respect—concepts seldom broached with focus groups and direct messaging.

"I needed to come here today," he said to me.

Rudy came to the Iron City to honor a friend we had in common, the Honorable Jay C. Waldman, who left this earth at age 58 in 2003 after a battle with lung cancer. Judge Waldman sat on the federal bench in Philadelphia for almost 15 years. He was formerly general counsel to Governor Dick Thornburgh.

Governor Thornburgh has since donated his papers to the University of Pittsburgh, where the Dick Thornburgh Forum in Law and Public Policy has been established. Within that facility, Thornburgh honored Judge Waldman with the naming of the Judge Jay C. Waldman Seminar Room, which was dedicated in a private ceremony on Tuesday.

I think the fact that Rudy Giuliani would interrupt his presidential campaign at a time when he is in a dogfight with Romney to pay homage to an old friend who has been gone for more than four years speaks well of Rudy's character. And it offers more insight into him than any combination of 30-second ads or debate appearances ever will.

Seeing him in this context was a reminder that I had seen the way he supported his friend in the direst of circumstances a few years ago. When our good friend Jay was terribly and fatally ill for several weeks in the winter and spring of 2003, Rudy was there, too.

Even then, he was enmeshed in a schedule that could only be described as world-class, yet he came to Thomas Jefferson University Hospital—far from the cameras, pollsters, and advance men—to participate in a process for which there is no playbook. Without fanfare, he constantly made himself available and provided comfort, caring, and compassion.

I know. I watched. And was touched.

Rudy and Jay met in 1975 when both were young prosecutors in Gerald Ford's Justice Department. They were drawn to one another by their love of law, their intellect, and ethics (and probably a little cigar smoke).

Jay was a Pittsburgh native who earned an undergraduate degree from the University of Wisconsin and his law degree in 1969 at Penn.

He clerked for a state court judge in Pittsburgh before briefly entering private practice. He joined the federal prosecutor's office in Pittsburgh in 1971.

Thornburgh was then the U.S. attorney, and it was in this era that Jay met Rudy.

In 1988, Jay was nominated to the federal bench by a man both he and Rudy admired: Ronald Reagan. And one month before Jay passed, President George W. Bush nominated him to serve on the U.S. Court of Appeals for the Third Circuit.

When Jay died, Rudy told the *Inquirer* that he so valued Jay's political advice that he consulted him before deciding to run for mayor of New York. "I think he had the brightest political mind in the country," Rudy said of our mutual friend.

I remember that one of Jay's dying wishes was to dance at Rudy's wedding. He never got that chance. Only Rudy was more brokenhearted than Jay.

I wish the people of Iowa knew where Rudy was on Tuesday.

AFTERWORD

I wrote this column about Rudy at a time when I held him in the highest regard. As an American, I was proud of his leadership in New York City on 9/11 and thereafter, and we were both grieving the loss of our close mutual friend Jay C. Waldman. Rudy was compassionate and very loyal to Jay until the tragic end. Back in 2008, I thought Rudy was presidential timber. But today those sentiments are gone. Several statements and incidents associated with him in the past few years have disappointed me, but the tipping point came on February 18, 2015. That night, Rudy stopped by a presidential campaign event for Wisconsin governor Scott Walker at Manhattan's 21 Club that was attended by 60 conservative Republicans and members of the media. From published accounts of the event, it's not clear to me that he was a scheduled speaker or that his remarks were planned. Nevertheless, Politico *reported the following:*

> "*I do not believe, and I know this is a horrible thing to say, but I do not believe that the president loves America,*" *Giuliani said during the dinner at the 21 Club, a former Prohibition-era speakeasy in midtown Man-*

hattan. "He doesn't love you. And he doesn't love me. He wasn't brought up the way you were brought up and I was brought up through love of this country."

I found what Rudy said appalling, the epitome of the never-ending vicious campaign against President Barack Obama intended to cast him as an "other"— not one of us, but a representative of some sinister force brought here like a Manchurian Candidate. In a word, I thought it was the statement of someone who was unhinged. Remarks like those have made me realize how much Rudy misses not only Jay's friendship but also his guidance. I don't think Jay, as much as he loved Rudy, would have had much tolerance for the way he questioned the patriotism of an American president.

SPECTER PRACTICES—
AND ENDORSES—CIVILITY

Philadelphia Inquirer, Sunday, December 16, 2007

I HAVE WATCHED ARLEN SPECTER, now Pennsylvania's longest-serving U.S. senator, deliver countless speeches. But never had I seen him talk quite as he did when he addressed 1,000 people December 8.

The setting was the Grand Ballroom of New York's Waldorf-Astoria Hotel, site of the Pennsylvania Society's 109th annual dinner. That is the centerpiece of a weekend during which the Keystone State's political movers and shakers gather in pomp and collegiality.

That night, Specter was the 99th recipient of the Society's Gold Medal for Distinguished Achievement, awarded every year since 1908 to a figure of unfailing leadership and wide-ranging contributions. Former awardees include Presidents Dwight Eisenhower and George H. W. Bush, sports figures Arnold Palmer and Joe Paterno, and media figures Bill Cosby and Chris Matthews.

He began his remarks as he so often does—by taking off his wristwatch, placing it on the lectern, and telling the crowd he wished to "give you a false sense of security that I am paying attention to the time."

He continued by showing some of the humor that recently earned him second place in an annual Washington celebrity comedy contest, complete with references to Bob Dole and Viagra. Having watched his performance on YouTube, I was disappointed he didn't reprise one particular one-liner on Dan Quayle. ("He thought 'harass' was two words.")

But then he reached inside his tuxedo pocket and withdrew a few index cards. I knew immediately he had something important to say—and that he wanted to get it just right—because Specter rarely, if ever, speaks from notes. Despite dining with my friend Jack Daniels, I'm glad I had the presence of mind to jot down a few of my own.

This was Specter as Pennsylvania elder statesman, anxious to deliver a message about the need for

A little blurry, yes, but nonetheless a shot of me with Senator Arlen Specter at the Waldorf Astoria the night he delivered the speech that is the subject of this column.

civility and compromise, not shrillness and contempt. He spoke like an ideological moderate fed up with the left-right extremism too often seen on the
split screens of America today. And he thought the future should have more
of the camaraderie so evident in New York City that night.

> The importance of courtesy and civility is critical at all levels—interna-
> tional negotiations, national, state and local government. This week-
> end is exactly the kind of time when we should all reflect on how much
> we have in common and how much harder we should try to get along.

And then came this key line:

> If you can lift a glass together with your colleague from across the aisle
> on a Saturday night here in New York, you can lift your pen with that
> same colleague across the hall on Monday morning in Philadelphia,
> Pittsburgh, Harrisburg, or any place in our state.

His introduction had been accompanied by a video presentation that rolled
through the stages of his career—from hard-charging district attorney to Warren Commission staffer to unsuccessful gubernatorial candidate. Included in
the high-tech scrapbook were images of Specter on the world stage—with Fidel
Castro and Yasir Arafat—which prompted a round of guffaws from the audience.

It occurred to me that his office had no doubt supplied those images to
underscore his point that we live in times requiring more, not less, dialogue.

That became evident when he praised President Bush for writing a letter
to Kim Jong Il that began, "Dear Mr. Chairman," calling that greeting of
respect a good move as we strive for better relations with North Korea. He
cited President Ronald Reagan's successful arms-reduction treaties with the
U.S.S.R. even after Reagan had tagged that country the Evil Empire. And he
credited diplomacy for the deflation of Libyan leader Moammar Gadhafi's
terrorist tendencies.

Sitting on the dais through all of this was Governor Rendell, himself an
actor in Specter's sketch of cooperation. Specter shared a story from his final
days as district attorney in Philadelphia. Riding in an elevator in City Hall, a
young Ed Rendell told his boss he planned to make a career in public service.
Specter offered to introduce the young prosecutor to city Republican leader
Billy Meehan, at which point Rendell informed Specter that he was a Democrat. Before that, Specter said, "I did not know—or, for that matter, care—
about his political registration."

He also shared a story in which Chief Justice Earl Warren shook the hand of Jack Ruby, already convicted for the murder of Lee Harvey Oswald. Later, in connection with the work of the Warren Commission, Warren lent Ruby his eyeglasses.

The goal in all these anecdotes, he told me a few days after his speech, was to inspire those in attendance to transport the nonpartisanship evident in the bar rooms of New York to the courtrooms, war rooms, and chambers of Pennsylvania.

Tweaking a Barry Goldwater line, Specter told the crowd:

> Moderation in the pursuit of virtue is no vice and is the approach which must be extended to our county courthouses, to Harrisburg, to Washington and beyond to international conferences. This is the approach that will ensure that, when you future gold medalists stand in my place on a future second Saturday in December, you can declare, as do I, that we still live in the greatest country in the history of the world.

AFTERWORD

I miss Senator Specter, who passed in the fall of 2012, immensely. He was an intellectual giant with ethics beyond reproach and a work ethic second to none. He earned a better exit from electoral politics than he was afforded. In 2010, having changed parties, he lost a Senate primary to Admiral Joe Sestak, who in turn lost in the general election to the current senator Pat Toomey. Specter's change in party was precipitated by his 2009 vote for the stimulus package, which he regarded as the most consequential vote he ever cast. In his book, Life among the Cannibals, *he says, "As proof mounts that the stimulus saved the country from a depression, that vote, which cost me so dearly, should count as the most important of my ten thousand Senate votes—hard to compare with trebling NIH funding, but in the same league."*

Our final meeting was over martinis and dinner at a Stephen Starr restaurant in Philadelphia called Barclay Prime. That conversation stands out because I was encouraging him to take his vast knowledge of the Kennedy assassination on the road the following year, marking the 50th anniversary of that event, and he gave me the unsolicited advice of running for his seat in the 2016 election. Neither of those things came to pass. Within months he was gone. I was honored to be one of his pallbearers.

MR. CHROME DOME
GETS FUZZY

Philadelphia Daily News, **Thursday, January 10, 2008**

IT SPROUTED ON CHRISTMAS DAY, though not because I had planned it that way, or intended it at all.

That's just the way it began.

Christmas is obviously an atypical day. My wife and I sleep only until the first of the kids awakens, and from the moment one of them comes into our bedroom, nothing that follows mirrors the usual daily routine, or even that of a weekend.

Instead of heading for the shower, we all go downstairs for coffee and gift-opening.

That process is a lot like Thanksgiving. It takes my wife four hours to cook a meal we eat in about four minutes, including the moment it takes to say grace. The time it takes to open packages? Feels like the same four minutes.

When the gift-giving had ended this year, I decided to stay in a sweat-shirt—and unshaven.

The day after Christmas, I got into the shower but didn't draw the razor. Not for any particular reason, and again, without a plan. I just didn't feel the need.

By Day Three, I needed to leave the house, and at that point my joyride became a plotted course: I'd decided to grow a beard. At least until I had to return to work.

Well, it's been two weeks. I'm back at work, and the beard is staying. At least until my wife acknowledges I have one. So far, she has said nothing.

I've been bald since college, so hair decisions have been few. Five years ago, I shaved my head, and it was one of the better things I've ever done. I only wish I'd done it sooner.

That decision was also born of unusual circumstances. I had taken my wife to the Old Guard House Inn in Gladwyne for dinner in honor of her birthday.

Albert Breuers, the chef/owner, gave me some homemade schnapps as an after-dinner drink. When we left his place, my wife—who was also the desig-nated driver—noticed that her then hairdresser, Maurice, was still open for business across the street.

She said she needed to make an appointment.

So we walked in together, and Maurice took a look at me and suggested I come for an appointment, too. Which is when the schnapps kicked in. I said OK.

The following Saturday, I got my hair "done." In a salon full of Main Line women, I sat while Maurice gave me a military-style buzz cut. Then the women voted, unanimously, that he keep going.

When it was over, my head was totally shaved, and I became the only man to ever pay $125 for the honor. (My wife explained that Maurice had a reputation that commanded such prices.)

I wasn't sure how I felt about the new me when I left. Two weeks later, I found myself in Cuba, having dinner with Senator Arlen Specter and Fidel Castro.

I think my new look was why Fidel took me for a military/CIA/Bay of Pigs organizer. Nonetheless, all I needed was a little sun on my noggin. Once I had that, there was no looking back.

Since then, guys contemplating the full monty of haircuts often seek my advice, which is fourfold: (1) Buy an anti-steam mirror. (2) Use the mirror to shave in the shower. (3) Use a multiblade handheld razor. (4) Find the right lather. (I recommend Helan Natural's Vetiver and Rum Sapone da Barba.) I get it online from an old-school apothecary in Chicago.

So as 2008 begins, I'm now sporting a Seamus McCaffery up top and a Jerry Garcia down below. Actually, it has yet to grow to that level, and I have no idea if it will. So far, it's salt and pepper in color, so I guess that's politically correct.

I still have some decisions to make, such as length.

I intend to trim it somewhere between a Pat Croce goatee and ZZ Top/ Rip Van Winkle look, and I'm unsure of how high it should grow up toward my ear.

I've yet to decide if it will still be around when the Phils hit Clearwater. That will probably be determined by if and when my wife acknowledges it.

You'll know it's staying when you see my column photo change. Happy New Year.

AFTERWORD

As you might know from seeing me on television, I still sport a beard and shaved head, and still get asked by listeners and viewers for my advice on grooming both. Have a good mirror and shave in the shower is my usual advice. For me, one of the great guy treats in life is to get a head shave and beard trim from a professional, and the best I've found are at Geo. F. Trumper, gentleman's barbers and perfumers in London, which opened in 1875. I don't visit England without making a stop. Go to the original shop located on Curzon Street in Mayfair. As described on its website (www.trumpers.com): "Trumper's original Curzon Street shop remains the same with its beautiful mahogany paneled private cubicles and stunning displays of grooming requisites." Famous clientele, past and present, include many British royals (Trumper's has received five Royal Warrants over the years), Winston Churchill, and JFK.

OBAMA SEES ROUTE
TO RIGHTEOUSNESS

Philadelphia Inquirer, **March 23, 2008**

ON TUESDAY, this son of Eastern European stock drove into Center City to bear witness to a speech about race delivered by a candidate who described himself in his remarks as "the son of a black man from Kenya and a white woman from Kansas."

Representative Patrick Murphy (D., Pa.), the product of Irish and Italian ancestry, had invited me as his guest to hear Senator Barack Obama. He also offered the possibility for me to conduct an interview with Obama for use on radio. That chance prompted my producer, a Mayflower-bred, Harvard-educated, Main Line mom, to offer to carry the sound equipment and drive us to the event in—what else?—her Volvo.

Immediately after the speech, lunchtime added to the bustle of the block at Eighth and Race, where I stood with my bald white head and my Black-Berry. Meanwhile, my lily-white colleague sought to retrieve her Cross Country wagon. Unfortunately, in her haste to exit the parking lot, she scraped an immaculate SUV in the adjacent space. (Her defense: She herself was on the phone, responding to a request from Fox News for me to react to the speech.) When I went to inspect the damage on the other vehicle, I took note of the Puerto Rican flag hanging from the rearview mirror.

A parking attendant responded to the fender bender. He was a black man wearing a bow tie and speaking with an African accent. I heard him tell my WASP-y producer she couldn't leave the lot until his manager arrived. While she was handling this development, I saw a Latino man with close-cropped hair and low-hanging jeans cross the lot, and upon seeing the damage to his 2007 Suzuki, he was instantly anguished. "Manny" (as we later learned he was named) was understandably upset to learn what had happened in his absence.

An hour earlier, I'd been watching Barack Obama. Now, I was caught up in an episode of *Curb Your Enthusiasm* with more metaphors than I could keep track of.

I'd walked into the National Constitution Center thinking like Howard Baker: What did Barack Obama hear from Rev. Jeremiah A. Wright Jr. and when did he hear it? I wanted to know what kept him coming back to the pew after two decades of toxic diatribes, and I wondered whether he was really taken aback at seeing the now-notorious YouTube clip of Wright, whether he'd been present for that sermon or not. After all, he had disinvited Wright from delivering the invocation at his campaign announcement for some reason.

I exited the speech thinking that if I ultimately do not vote for Obama, it will be for reasons other than his minister.

What I found most refreshing about the speech was Obama's willingness to give it at all—a totally unmuzzled talk about race. He spoke with customary elegance, in stark contrast to the angry rants of his pastor. How ironic that this powerful orator has been undermined not by his own words but by those of his pastor, and some of his critics. He has managed to distance himself from the angry extremists to his left and right, using something more than just grandiose language: substance. The transcript is definitely recommended reading.

His speech noted the reality of America's history of racial inequality, but also the legitimacy of some concerns of the white middle class. And he made admissions. ("Did I know him to be an occasionally fierce critic of American domestic and foreign policy? Of course. Did I ever hear him make remarks that could be considered controversial while I sat in church? Yes. Did I strongly disagree with many of his political views? Absolutely.")

Perhaps most important, Obama made clear where he believed Wright had been wrong:

> The profound mistake of Reverend Wright's sermons is not that he spoke about racism in our society. It's that he spoke as if our society was static; as if no progress has been made; as if this country—a country that has made it possible for one of his own members to run for the highest office in the land and build a coalition of white and black, Latino and Asian, rich and poor, young and old—is still irrevocably bound to a tragic past. But what we know—what we have seen—is that America can change. That is the true genius of this nation. What we have already achieved gives us hope—the audacity to hope—for what we can and must achieve tomorrow.

A point well taken. How can America be so fundamentally unfair and racist if one of Wright's very congregants is now positioned to capture the Democratic nomination for president? As Obama said, "I will never forget that in no other country on Earth is my story even possible."

Two blocks away after the speech, the lot attendant with the African accent returned to tell the WASP woman and the Puerto Rican man not to worry because his manager was en route. Sure enough, within a few minutes, a natty BMW pulled up and out popped "Mr. Tran," the Asian supervisor who had come to sort out the unfolding drama. All parties spoke civilly, co-operated, and parted company with handshakes all around. Which reminded me of something else I'd heard that day:

> We may not look the same and we may not have come from the same place, but we all want to move in the same direction—towards a better future for our children and our grandchildren.

AFTERWORD

After this ran in the Sunday Inquirer, *I posted it at HuffingtonPost.com, where, unlike with my newspaper columns, I get to write the headline. I used "Curb Your Enthusiasm Meets Barack Obama," which I like more than "Obama Sees Route to Righteousness." I just think it better captures the scene I experienced. I could see Larry David and Jeff Garlin caught up in a moment like my producer TC's fender bender with half the U.N. involved. The speech was one of the pivotal moments of Senator Obama's primary campaign against Senator Hillary Clinton. Had it been poorly delivered or received, I think it would have been a negative turning point of the campaign. Instead, the content and delivery kept him forward moving. I wrote in the column that Representative Murphy invited me because he was trying to facilitate an interview for me with the senator. It did not come to pass that day, but it did soon thereafter, when we had a memorable Good Friday conversation that I wrote about in* Morning Drive. *I have since returned to the relatively small auditorium at the National Constitution Center where this speech was delivered, including to host Libertarian governors Gary Johnson and Bill Weld there in 2016. And whenever I am in the room, I find myself looking around remembering the Obama speech on race and thinking this is where I witnessed history being made.*

HOW I GOT THE BIRD

Philadelphia Daily News, Thursday, April 3, 2008

A NOTHER SOUTH PHILLY GUY is in the news for getting jammed up. And while everybody else is wondering what one Dougherty's guilty plea means to another Dougherty, I'm thinking about the eagle on my desk.

Until the end of last week, I hadn't kept close track of the criminal case against Donald "Gus" Dougherty. Like everyone else, I've now read that he's pleading guilty to 98 of 100 counts of theft and tax offenses—just not the two that allege illegal payments to John J. Dougherty.

I know both Doughertys, although one far better than the other. I've known Johnny Doc for years. I think I met Gus Dougherty only once, but it's a day I won't soon forget. That's when he gave me the eagle.

Mike Baldini introduced us. Baldini is another Philly guy (Father Judge, La Salle University), but not one in any trouble with the feds. He's a Runyon-esque fellow in his early 40s who used to run sales for my radio station, and now does the same at KYW.

He was born in South Philly, grew up in the Great Northeast, and is raising his family in a Montgomery County town with "ville" at the end of it. I have a hard time picturing him in the burbs.

Baldini is fun to watch: fast-talking, mind always racing, constantly sizing up people he meets with an innate sense of street smarts. He's perfectly suited for his sales-manager job.

He's a people person. In a previous life, I could see him working as a maître d' at one of the big casino showrooms, making sure that Sinatra had enough Jack in his dressing room while simultaneously deciding who sits where out front.

One day a few years ago, Baldini said he needed me for a sales call in South Philly with an electrical contractor named Dougherty. I told him I already knew Johnny Doc. Baldini said this was another South Philly guy named Dougherty who also knew a thing or two about fuses.

I said I'd go if he took me to lunch at Shanks. He agreed.

Gus Dougherty's office was special. It was one of those environments where the women were especially pleasant, called you "hun" and wanted to know if they could "get you a cup."

Upstairs, Gus had a plush suite with sports memorabilia, a big fish tank, and a comfortable leather sofa, which is where he held court—and where I first spied the eagle.

It's a gold likeness about a foot high with its wings fully extended, sitting on a plain wooden base. It's not real gold and isn't a trophy awarded for a particular event or exploit, but to see it is to know it has history. I told Gus I thought it was beautiful. He immediately told me he wanted me to have it. I told him I couldn't.

Then he said, "It used to belong to Leonard Tose," referring to the former owner of a team full of Eagles. I've had a soft spot for Tose since I was a kid and spotted him riding his bike and wearing a green velour tracksuit on the Atlantic City boardwalk.

We chatted that morning and he was awfully nice to me, a young boy. His aide de camp, Jimmy Murray, has since told me endless stories of Tose's kindness and charity. I'll bet Tose would have liked Gus, but I don't think they ever met.

I asked Gus how he got Tose's eagle. He said that Tose lived his final days at the Warwick Hotel on 17th Street, and that Tose had given it to the hotel doorman as a sign of appreciation. The doorman gave it to Gus for reasons that were unclear—or I have since forgotten.

Now Gus wanted to give it to me.

I hemmed and hawed, then finally accepted. I rationalized my acceptance by thinking that Tose would like knowing that the newest keeper of the eagle appreciated his contribution to the city, and was once thrilled to meet him down the Shore.

It was a gracious gift from a guy who's now jammed up. Gus could do time, which is sad.

"The bird"—formerly owned by Philadelphia Eagles owner Leonard Tose—which Gus Dougherty gifted to me.

And me? I'm recording the provenance of the eagle while sitting on my desk and wondering who'll get it when I'm gone. I hope it's someone who appreciates what a small town this is.

And maybe it will end up on Senator Dougherty's desk in Harrisburg.

AFTERWORD

In August 2010, a Philadelphia developer named Steve Solms died and I wrote about him for the Sunday Inquirer. *Solms was the driving force behind Historic Landmarks for Living, a real estate service that changed the complexion of the city for the better by converting countless factories and industrial spaces into luxury apartments. As I noted at the time, "I knew him only peripherally, but always got a kick out of his joie de vivre." He was for me the epitome of a Philly guy: a character. Steve was feast or famine—or both. I remembered seeing him in the midst of a real estate crash looking no worse for wear sitting poolside at Caesar's Palace in Las Vegas with a wad of cash buying a drink. I then reflected on the number of "characters" I've been privileged to know, having spent my entire life in Philadelphia. And believe me, I use the term "character" as a compliment. I named only a few that I'd crossed paths with or had come to know: Charlie Bowser, Hardy Williams, Jim Beasley, Jay Waldman, Thacher Longstreth, Russell Byers, Ed Rendell, Pat Croce, and Zack Stalberg. I concluded with this: "I don't know what it's like to live in Phoenix or Dallas, Indianapolis or St. Paul. But I have a hard time believing they can match us man for man. Hopefully it stays that way."*

Well, Leonard Tose, the generous and dapper NFL owner and four-time husband who consistently violated the cardinal rule of the casinos ("Bet with your head, not over it") should have made that column too. Like those I reference there—Messrs. John Dougherty, Gus Dougherty, and Mike Baldini—Tose was pure Philly. So too was his alter ego, Jimmy Murray, who was the Eagles' general manager under Tose during my childhood. One of the highlights of my youth was rooting for Tose's Eagles despite many losing seasons in the 1970s, especially when Roman Gabriel was briefly their quarterback. The team fortunes, and that of the city, changed when Tose hired head coach Dick Vermeil, who took us to the 1980 Super Bowl. Sadly, Tose never got to raise the Lombardi Trophy.

Tose's life deserves the full movie treatment. For now, we have to settle for a short but fabulous ESPN 30 for 30 documentary directed by another Philly guy, Mike Tollin, called Tose: The Movie.

The bird on my mantle is a tribute to Leonard Tose and all Philly characters.

RUSSERT-BRAND DISCOURSE VS.
CABLE CARNIVAL SHOUTFEST

Philadelphia Inquirer, Wednesday, June 18, 2008

A FEW WEEKS BEFORE the Pennsylvania primary, I received an e-mail from an associate producer for a national cable-television program, who wanted me to appear on a show about Barack Obama. Her e-mail said: "We're looking for someone who will say, 'Yes, he's cocky and his cockiness will hurt him, if not in the primary, definitely in the general election against McCain.'" I passed.

She responded by asking if I would instead say Hillary Clinton was untrustworthy. I said no.

A few days later came another invite: "We wanted a person to go after Hillary and how often she lies, how it's easy for her, etc." Although I again said no thanks, I am sure in each instance someone filled the prescribed role.

I was thinking about those exchanges while watching the many tributes to Tim Russert, whose memorial service was scheduled for today. How ironic that the same journalism community that feted Tim Russert after his death Friday has so many members who don't follow his lead.

Russert never practiced the brand of journalism upon which many radio and television careers today are predicated. It seems almost hypocritical that he should be extolled by those who don't emulate his example.

Tim Russert didn't become the preeminent political journalist in the nation by browbeating, condescension, or debate-stifling. He was a facilitator of intelligent, political conversation, not an enabler of the stark left-right, black-white, Democrat-Republican, liberal-conservative cable world in which we now live.

That doesn't mean Russert asked guests to check their partisanship at the door, or that he was devoid of strong views. To the contrary, his was a forum where clear difference would emerge, but minus the edge that has otherwise become commonplace. Through direct discourse, not shouting and cross-talk, he guaranteed that all sides would be represented—and not in a carnival atmosphere. Russert was forceful, yet deferential. He'd ask the tough questions, and then afford an opportunity for a response.

Perhaps reflective of his law-school training, you could always count on him to bring up the prior inconsistencies of a guest's various statements. But unlike so many of his would-be successors, he'd always follow up with a willingness to listen to an explanation or reflection.

Russert combined an intellectual understanding of the intricacies of government and policy with street smarts about the electoral process, honed no doubt from his days of service to both New York governor Mario Cuomo and Empire State senator Daniel Patrick Moynihan.

That combination of comportment, political acumen, and wit made Russert a unique bridge—someone to be relied upon for guidance about matters of great importance, and yet, you wished you could seek that wisdom over a beer or two.

I interviewed Russert twice, after each of his books, *Big Russ and Me* and *Wisdom of Our Fathers*, was published. He was as impressive on the receiving end of questions as when he was the questioner.

Perhaps his greatest gift was his humble, down-to-earth nature, which he likely gleaned from his father. When we last spoke—almost a year ago—Russert told me he admired "the quiet eloquence" of his father's hard work. Well, like father like son.

Not long after I interviewed Russert about *Big Russ and Me*, I selected it to be read by a small, informal book club to which I belong—eight guys who get together every few months. We read, yes. But, more important, we drink, eat, and enjoy one another's company.

I had asked Russert if he would mind telephoning our gathering and chatting with the group for a few minutes. The host of the most-esteemed talk show in America obliged.

That night, in a small private dining room at a Georges Perrier restaurant on the Main Line, his call arrived. He was on a cellphone in his car, and we lost the connection soon after it began. But the guys were thrilled, and Russert seemed to get a kick out of their interest in his book.

Months later, I met him at an NBC party in the Rainbow Room high atop Rockefeller Center, where we spoke for a few minutes. I was eager to talk politics; he wanted to know more about my book club.

I painted the picture of our end of the call, especially the camaraderie he'd inspired. Tim Russert seemed to genuinely enjoy the fact that for one night, he'd been a catalyst of such friendship.

AFTERWORD

Eight years after his passing, Russert's words still mattered. In a sophisticated conference room high atop the Time Warner Center in Midtown Manhattan, CNN worldwide president Jeff Zucker shared with network talent, including me, the network statistics for 2016, which was CNN's most-watched year ever among total viewers (CNN ranked no. 1 in ALL of TV—cable and broadcast—

on election night in prime time, among both total viewers and the coveted de-mographic of adults aged 25–54). But when, after celebrating the past, it was time to look forward and talk about CNN's relationship with the incoming Trump administration, Zucker put on the video monitor the words of his former NBC colleague Tim Russert:

> *The primary responsibility of the media is accountability of govern-ment, whether it's about lying under oath, which upset Democrats, or the mismanagement of responding to a hurricane, which happens to upset Republicans.*

REQUIEM FOR AN ERA

Philadelphia Daily News, **Thursday, August 21, 2008**

I**T'S MONDAY NIGHT,** and I've just joined the end of a long line waiting to enter a viewing in South Philadelphia. The obituary in the *Daily News* said it began at 6. When I arrived at 7, the line was already wrapped two full blocks down Reed Street. I've been up since 3 A.M., and hosted two radio shows, but I don't regret the wait.

It's not often that you see an outpouring like this. Especially when half the town is down the Shore. It's a good thing for the several hundred of us snaking down the South Philly sidewalks that this August night isn't a particularly humid one.

But it is a uniquely Philly scene. There's an old-time feel (the BlackBerry I'm tapping as I record these thoughts doesn't quite fit in) even though the crowd is fairly young.

Every age group is represented, but most look to be in their 40s and 50s. Lots of closely cropped hair. Guys in suits, sport coats, or open dress shirts. Women wearing what women wear when guys dress like that. Several hold mass cards. There are plenty of appointed and elected officials. Many more are on public payrolls.

I stand for a while in front of a row house with a Flyers banner hanging in the window alongside a sign saying: "Parking for Italians only, all others will be towed."

Next door, an older woman in shorts, white sneakers, and white socks sits on an immaculate stoop. There's a pot filled with colorful artificial flowers and an American flag. I'm thinking she cast a couple of votes for Frank Rizzo.

Cars are doubled-parked everywhere, but something tells me that'd be the case even without the funeral.

I'm sure it's somber inside the Rogers Funeral Home, but out here people are friendly and chatty. They know each other or know somebody who knows somebody. Lots of "How ya doin'?" and "Whaddya been up to?"

It's a glimpse of the way the city used to look 30 years ago. Very white and ethnic. And, in fact, I'm thinking that many of these people won't have far to travel to get back home, even if their kids are headed back to Cherry Hill or Broomall after the viewing ends.

A scene like this reminds me how much the city has changed. The parents of those around me used to control City Hall, but those days are over.

They don't have the votes anymore and haven't since the late 1970s. But they're together tonight to mourn the passing of the mother of two public figures. It's a matter of respect. The sort of thing we could use more of these days.

I wasn't sure whether I'd come. The kids are going back to school soon, and it would've been a nice night to grill. I didn't know the decedent. But I'm glad I'm here. I'm always glad when I get there. I've never regretted paying respects, but I've often been sorry when I didn't.

It's dark outside an hour and 20 minutes later, but I've rounded the corner at South 3rd Street. Near Garrett, a big-screen TV flickers through a picture window that sports a star for somebody serving overseas. People are still arriving. The line is even longer than when I first joined it, but it's time to turn off the BlackBerry and go inside.

A well-respected woman has passed. And so has an era.

AFTERWORD

I referenced this column when signing off from the Daily News *in 2011. I wrote:*

> *Of all that I've written in nearly a decade at the* Daily News, *I'm most proud of . . . "Requiem for an Era."*
>
> *In it, I tried to capture how the city had changed in the last few decades based on observations I jotted down while standing in a viewing line as it snaked along a South Philly street.*
>
> *I wrote the entire column on my BlackBerry, using my thumbs. I never said whose funeral it was because I thought it would distract from my observations, but I was paying my respects to [the union leader] John Dougherty after the passing of his mother, Mary Theresa, so I'm closing that loop now.*

McCAIN FAILS
THE BIG FIVE TESTS

Philadelphia Inquirer, Sunday, October 19, 2008

I'VE DECIDED.

My conclusion comes after reading the candidates' memoirs and campaign platforms, attending both party conventions, interviewing both men multiple times, and watching all primary and general-election debates.

John McCain is an honorable man who has served his country well. But he will not get my vote. For the first time since registering as a Republican 28 years ago, I'm voting for a Democrat for president. I may have been an appointee in the George H. W. Bush administration, and master of ceremonies for George W. Bush in 2004, but last Saturday I stood amid the crowd at an Obama event in North Philadelphia.

Five considerations have moved me:

TERRORISM. The candidates disagree as to where to prosecute the war against Islamic fundamentalists. Barack Obama is correct in saying the front line in that battle is not Iraq; it's the Afghan-Pakistan border. Osama bin Laden crossed that border from Tora Bora in December 2001, and we stopped pursuit. The Bush administration outsourced the hunt for bin Laden and instead invaded Iraq.

No one in Iraq caused the death of 3,000 Americans on 9/11. Our invasion was based on a false predicate, so we have no business being there, regardless of whether the surge is working. Our focus must be the tribal-ruled FATA region in Pakistan. Only recently has our military engaged al-Qaeda there in operations that mirror those Obama was ridiculed for recommending in August 2007.

Last spring, Obama told me: "It's not that I was opposed to war [in Iraq]. It's that I felt we had a war that we had not finished." Even Senator Joe Lieberman conceded to me last Friday that "the headquarters of our opposition, our enem[y] today" is the FATA.

ECONOMY. We face economic problems that are incomprehensible to most Americans; certainly they are to me. This is a time to covet intellect, and that begins at the top. Jack Bogle, the legendary founder of the Vanguard Group, told me recently that McCain's assertion that the fundamentals of the economy were "strong" was the "stupidest statement of 2008." In the light of the unprecedented volatility in the market, who can dispute Bogle's characterization and the lack of understanding that McCain's assessment portends?

VP. I opined here that Sarah Palin demonstrated the capacity to be president in her speech to the Republican convention. Sadly, there has been no further exhibition of her abilities, and she remains an unknown quantity. We are left questioning the judgment of a candidate who bypassed his reported preferred choices, Lieberman and former governor Tom Ridge, and instead yielded to the whims of the periphery of his party. With two wars and a crumbling economy, Palin is too big of a risk to be a heartbeat away from a presidency held by a 72-year-old man who has battled melanoma. Advantage Joe Biden.

OPPORTUNITY. In a speech delivered on Father's Day, Obama lamented that too many fathers are missing from the lives of too many children and mothers. Look no further than Philadelphia for proof that the nation has a fatherhood problem at the root of its firearms crisis. And no demographic is affected by this confluence of factors like the black community. Among the many elements needed to address this crisis are role models, individuals whom urban youth can aspire to emulate. Little more than a year ago, Charles Barkley told me: "I want young black kids to see Barack on television every day. . . . We need to see more blacks who are intelligent, articulate, and who carry themselves with great dignity." Obama can be that man.

HOPE. Wednesday morning will come and an Obama presidency holds the greatest chance for unifying us here at home and restoring our prestige around the globe. The campaigns have foretold the kind of presidency we can expect from each candidate. Last Friday in Lakeville, Minnesota, McCain himself had to explain to a supporter who was "scared" of an Obama presidency that those fears were unfounded. Another told McCain that Obama was untrustworthy because he is an "Arab." Those exchanges were a predictable byproduct of ads against Obama featuring tag lines such as "Too Risky for America" and "Dangerous," and a failure to rein in individuals at McCain events who highlighted Obama's middle name, all against a background of Internet lore.

Last Saturday at Progress Plaza, I heard Obama say: "The American people aren't looking for somebody to divide this country; the American people are looking for someone to lead this country."

AFTERWORD

This was one of the more consequential columns I have written. I deliberated about whether to be public about my election choice, knowing I had the option of remaining mum. But I'd grown increasingly uncomfortable with the direction of the Republican Party, and I felt I owed it to my audience to explain what

I was doing and why. Perhaps what is most significant is that I didn't feel I could fully explain myself in 850 words, the length my Inquirer *columns were then running. So I wrote a 5,625-word essay for Salon.com that ran on September 11, 2008, under the headline "Why This Lifelong Republican May Vote for Obama." I focused solely on the issue of hunting down bin Laden and which presidential candidate was willing to do what it took to capture him. You can check it out here: http://www.salon.com/2008/09/11/hunting_binladen/.*

THEIR STANLEY CUP
RUNNETH OVER

Philadelphia Daily News, Thursday, November 20, 2008

STREET HOCKEY was once the stick ball of suburbia. In the Philly suburbs in the early 1970s, it was an after-school sport that lots of kids played.

The Flyers were the rage, and we each had orange-and-black jerseys emblazoned with our favorite players' names and numbers.

We'd imitate Bernie Parent and Bobby Clarke. And every class bully became the team's Dave Schultz. A guy in my neighborhood took metal from a swing set and made two goals, using sewn-together burlap bags for netting. Goalies had foam-rubber pads. It was teenage bliss.

Long before organized soccer, kids would face off in parking lots, on tennis courts, and anywhere there was a lip around a flat surface to stop an errant Mylec ball. Each neighborhood and subdivision had its own loosely affiliated team, and pick-up games were easily hatched without any formal league and were free of adult oversight.

I once played at the Burpee Playground, named for the local family of vegetable-seed fame. It had a fenced-in basketball court, making it the ideal rink. The team from the Burpee neighborhood had a guy named Joel Gingras. He was a "ringer" who played ice hockey at the Face-Off Circle in Warminster, and in college for St. Bonaventure.

Unfortunately, Joel died in 1988 of a brain tumor at 27. The next year, family and friends established the Joel Anthony Gingras Jr. Memorial Fund to increase awareness of brain-tumor research and raise money to help combat this deadly affliction. In 20 years, the JAG Fund has given more than $806,000 to the American Brain Tumor Association. It's a silver lining to a sad story. And it's just gotten better.

Enter Bill Clement.

Clement is, of course, the former Philadelphia Flyer and now a Versus and NBC broadcaster. It's his voice you hear on EA Sports NHL '09.

Clement lives in Bucks County, not too far from where Joel Gingras grew up. He's one of the guys whose jerseys we wore playing street hockey when he was a member of both Flyers' Stanley Cup teams in 1973–1974 and '74–'75.

Today, the NHL has a grand tradition of entrusting the Stanley Cup to each member of the championship team for 24 hours, but that tradition

Celebrating with Lord Stanley and my boys at the home of Bill Clement on November 15, 2008.

didn't start until after the Flyers won their back-to-back championships. A couple of years ago, Clement started thinking about trying to bring the Stanley Cup to Bucks County. When the NHL and Hockey Hall of Fame graciously agreed, he began organizing a charity fund-raiser.

Four years ago, Clement heard of the JAG Fund from a co-worker at ESPN named Jay Altmeyer, a college classmate of Joel Gingras's. Clement decided that the visit by the cup would benefit the JAG Fund and NOVA, which aids crime victims in Bucks County.

"When I knew I was getting the cup for a day, the first person I called was Johnathan Gingras," one of Joel's brothers, Clement told me. "I am also close to NOVA, and the two charities seemed like naturals. I wanted to keep the money local because of my affinity for Bucks County, where I have lived for 20 years."

The visit was scheduled for last Saturday.

On Friday, when flights from Toronto to Philadelphia were canceled due to weather, the event was in jeopardy. Within a half-hour of learning of the transportation dilemma, Altmeyer called a buddy in Canada named Joe Duplantis, who works as a PGA caddy, and in no time, he and a friend were in a car, with the cup and its minder (Mike Bolt), headed for Bucks County. They arrived at Clement's house at 4:15 A.M. Game on!

Later that day, at the Middle Bucks Institute of Technology, a few thousand dads and sons were happy to pay a buck or two to see the cup. By mid-afternoon, police were directing traffic away from the school. The crowd of several thousand was already so large that they couldn't fit any more people in.

Clement said it was one of the best days of his life, and that the event raised more than $55,000.

"Some people might not believe this, but Saturday for me was better than winning the cup," he said. Johnathan Gingras's take? "I truly believe that Joel had something to do with this weekend's success."

AFTERWORD

What I didn't report in the column is that Bill Clement's display of the Stanley Cup for charity was so successful that, on the day of the event, I drove with my three sons but couldn't get near the school where it was held. There were too many people. Bill had no way of knowing that and, before the event, had mentioned to me that he'd be hosting friends at his home that night for a private viewing of the cup. It was an awfully nice invitation, but I had no intention of taking him up on it because I suspected it was for his closer friends and wanted to respect his private time with the cup for the short time it would be in his possession. But after dinner that night, with the boys' afternoon disappointment lingering in my mind, I felt differently and decided to accept the invitation after all. With my wife and three sons in our car, I found what I thought was the Clement residence outside of New Hope, Bucks County, and drove down the driveway. There were a few cars outside, but not so many that we knew definitively that there was a party going on inside. It was a chilly night, and I remember leaving the car running with my wife and sons in it while I scouted the situation. I walked up onto a porch and peered inside the house. Lo and behold, I was looking into Bill Clement's kitchen, and sitting on the counter was the Stanley Cup! I ran back to the car and excitedly told my gang. The boys scrambled out of the car. My wife thought we were interlopers and the whole thing a bit ridiculous, so she didn't join us. We went inside and, within minutes, Bill had us drinking champagne from the Stanley Cup!

MY DINNER WITH PERVEZ

Philadelphia Daily News, Tuesday, January 27, 2009

ON SUNDAY, I had dinner with ex–Pakistani president Pervez Musharraf, in town for a talk at the World Affairs Council, courtesy of Raza and Sabina Bokhari. Raza is a past president of the Pakistani American Public Affairs Committee.

I've written many times on my frustration with U.S. policy on Pakistan. We've outsourced the hunt for Osama to Pakistan, which lacks the will and motivation to get the job done. I voted for Barack Obama in part because on this issue he promised change.

I was seated at Musharraf's right and across from Senator Arlen Specter, who explained to Musharraf my media role, including my radio show. Musharraf told me he wasn't doing interviews. He'd had a contentious interview with CNN's Wolf Blitzer, but had no intention of doing any more. So I didn't use my recorder, or take notes, but Musharraf gave me permission to ask whatever I wanted.

I said that many of us wanted to know how the Pakistani government could reach an accord with the leaders of the tribal region in fall 2006, about the time it was revealed that the United States was sending $80 million a month to Pakistan to fight al Qaeda.

Musharraf spoke decent English in a low but audible voice. He didn't look at me, but interrupted his meal and stared straight ahead while speaking. It was a conversation only between the two of us.

Defiant is probably the best description of his tone. He said many Americans were naïve. People don't understand Pakistan, he said. There are Pakistani troops in those tribal areas (overlooking my point that they weren't doing anything) and 1,500 Pakistani soldiers had died in the war on terror. There are important matters of strategy, he said, and, "Don't tell us what to do in our country."

I wanted to know what we had to show for the $11 billion the United States had paid the Pakistani government for its counterterror efforts. He said that this was very "frustrating," that there had been many successes by the Pakistanis in the war against terror and that many leaders of al Qaeda had been killed.

He lamented that in his own country he is perceived as a U.S. "lackey," and in the United States, he is seen as "double-dealing."

Incidentally, the buzz in the room is that he's not well-off. More than one individual surmised over cocktails that for all the money that was paid to Pakistan, you'd think Musharraf wouldn't need to do the U.S. lecture circuit, which is the reason for this visit.

I told him of my trip to Qatar, and how I had visited CENTCOM headquarters and seen the maps depicting military activity in real time, including how all U.S. troop activity stopped at Pakistan. I told him that soldiers told me of frustration at not being able to pursue al Qaeda when it retreats into Pakistan.

He said that wasn't true. Soldiers had crossed the border, but it's foolish for them to do so. Because of the terrain and the nature of life in the tribal areas, they could get sucked in and killed in great numbers. According to Musharraf, crossing from the Afghanistan border was not an option for American troops. He also said that terrorism was created in Afghanistan and imported to Pakistan, not vice versa.

With some reluctance because I was sure he'd heard it thousands of times, I asked where bin Laden was. In the Swat valley? He laughed and said no. In Waziristan? More grimly, he said, "I don't know."

I asked what he thought when Barack Obama said in August 2007 that if Musharraf didn't act on intelligence regarding high-level al Qaeda targets, the United States would. Musharraf said they are doing that. He said we mix up strategy and tactics. Tactics, he said, are how to deal with al Qaeda. There is disagreement there, he said, but overall, strategically, we agree.

I expected him to say that Obama was wrong to make that assertion. He did not, but did offer that personality changes don't change policy, only changes in policy do. He said that the aims he had pursued with President Bush were the best policy. He also said that through last March, things in his country were "pretty good," which I found to be odd. (He left office in August.)

I asked if Pakistani condemnation of U.S. Predator strikes are simply to save face. Musharraf took this as an opportunity to tell me how angry Pakistani people are with the Americans. He said the man on the street doesn't like the United States, but the United States needs Pakistan and vice versa.

When I asked what we Americans don't understand about the situation in Pakistan, he said that the Mumbai coverage had been all about the Pakistani role, with very little said of the Indian role.

He said that Americans didn't appreciate the danger posed by India, which had sided with the Soviets during the cold war, and that for more than 40 years, we'd been allies of the Pakistanis, and people were too quick to question Pakistan's loyalty to the United States. He repeatedly made a case for continued U.S. economic aid to Pakistan.

Taking former Pakistani president Pervez Musharraf along as I voted in Montgomery County, Pennsylvania, on November 2, 2010. Photo by Raza Bokhari.

By then, others had taken their places at the table. I felt I was monopolizing the conversation. Switching to a lighter topic, I asked him how he relaxed. He mentioned reading and tennis, describing himself as a good defensive player. He also sang the praises of bridge.

So what were my other impressions?

He was most anxious to defend his policies. From my first words, he was very forceful. Measured, never ungentlemanly, but very determined.

And, in the bigger picture, as our limited foreign-policy attention focuses on Gaza, Iraq, and Afghanistan, real American security is being determined in Pakistan, where the same forces who killed 3,000 seven years ago continue to have free rein.

AFTERWORD

This column was one of nearly a dozen that I wrote expressing disenchantment with the way the Bush administration was pursuing Osama bin Laden by placing too much responsibility on President Musharraf. I said the same thing on radio and television. It still stuns me to think about my friend Raza calling and saying, "Why not come to dinner with him?"

Two days later, after I gave a recap on radio that Raza heard, he called me and said the president had enjoyed our dialogue and had consented to a formal interview with me. One day later, I returned to Raza's house, where, in his wine cellar, I recorded a lengthy discussion with Musharraf. On the record, I did my best to summarize how I saw the situation and expressed my concern that we'd taken our eye off the ball with respect to bin Laden.

His immediate response was "None of what you are saying is true."

We then had a 40-minute, wide-ranging conversation that left me second-guessing some of my long-standing criticism. He seemed earnest. And honest. I left wondering whether perhaps he was the best dance partner we could find in that part of the world. For the next few years, Musharraf went into a self-imposed exile in Dubai and London, but he continued to return to the Phila-delphia Main Line to stay with Raza and Sabina, who took to referring to their back patio as the "Musharraf deck."

When a Musharraf visit in 2010 (during which he was in exile) coincided with our U.S. midterm elections, my wife suggested I take him with me when I voted. (He's the second most important person to ride in my car; one morning I drove Phillies skipper Charlie Manuel down the Schuylkill to Citizen's Bank Park.) At my quaint polling place in Lower Merion Township, we walked past yard signs for Pat Toomey, Joe Sestak, Tom Corbett, and Dan Onorato while I told him about American voter apathy and bragged that I had never missed an election. I will not forget his reply: "You said you've always voted. Let me shock you by saying that I have never voted—except in the last eight years [while president]."

The people manning my polling place could not have been more gracious. They allowed me to enter my polling booth accompanied by President Mu-sharraf and I took delight in showing him our means of casting a ballot. When we exited, Musharraf told me that because of the number of illiterate Paki-stanis, they record ballots for symbols, not parties or individuals. He also said that he would compete in Pakistan's 2013 election. He'd already settled on his party's symbol: a shaheen falcon. "It flies higher than all other birds," he told me. "It doesn't fly in a flock. It is independent. It flies alone. It doesn't come back to a nest, . . . so I think it's a symbol which shows independence, which shows courage, which shows confidence." Musharraf did return to Pakistan in 2013 after four years in exile but was disqualified from taking part in the election.

JACK KEMP'S
WINNING GAME PLAN

Philadelphia Daily News, Thursday, May 7, 2009

I HAD MY LAST CONVERSATION with Jack Kemp in October.
No surprise, our focus was to be on tax policy. But the part of our dialogue that will always stay with me had to do with football and his family.
I asked him if he could still throw a spiral at 73. "I can throw a spiral," he assured me.

> I can't throw it very far anymore. I used to be able to throw it—believe it or not—about 90 yards. But, you know, I've aged a little bit. I was in Vail, Colorado, last summer with my grandsons, and they put the ball on the ground, ran out for a pass, and said, "Grandpa, Grandpa, throw me a pass!" By the time I picked up the ball, they were 50 yards down the field, and I said, "Hey, come back to around 15!"

Kemp was the Republican quarterback who tried to rewrite the party's playbook. Others will remember Kemp as a professional football player, nine-term congressman, secretary of Housing and Urban Development for Bush 41, and VP candidate for Bob Dole.

I'll remember him as a onetime boss.

In 1991, HUD was divided into 10 regions, and I was a federal housing commissioner responsible for the one that included Pennsylvania, Delaware, Maryland, Virginia, West Virginia, and Washington.

This was at a time when HUD, under Kemp's leadership, was trying to transfer ownership of public housing to the tenants. One of the first was to be Tyler House, a Washington development.

That's where I met Elaine Johns. Ms. Johns, then approaching 70, was a tenant leader who had invited Kemp for a tour of Tyler House in June 1989.

Kemp was so disgusted by the conditions ("The rats are so bad here you find them in the hall; you get up in the morning, and you find them dead in your apartment," Johns said at the time) that he described them as "scandalous." He vowed to make it a poster child for his homeownership initiative.

Before my meeting with Ms. Johns roughly two years later, I remember being told by a colleague that I needed to be particularly attentive to her. When I asked why, I was told that whenever Ms. Johns called Kemp, he took the call.

That was classic Kemp. He wasn't politicking for the sake of appearing populist. He was accessible because people like Elaine Johns were at the heart of the two most important causes in his political career—incentive-oriented economics and equality-oriented politics.

Kemp was a believer in giving people—especially minorities—a bigger stake in their own future. That's why he pushed his initiative to sell public-housing tenants their apartments "with the fervor of a Southern Baptist preacher," as a *New York Times* reporter wrote in 1996.

It's also why he became a lone GOP voice urging the party to apply the principles of fiscal conservatism to address urban problems and reach out to minority constituents. Kemp, a self-described "bleeding-heart conservative" working in an administration perceived as inattentive to urban issues, received three standing ovations during a speech at the NAACP's annual convention in 1989.

"You see, real leadership is not just seeing the realities of what we are temporarily faced with, but seeing the possibilities and potential that can be realized by lifting up people's vision of what they can be," he wrote in a letter to his 17 grandchildren published a few weeks after our October conversation.

Unfortunately, too many of those now playing the games that Kemp did—athletics and politics—are in it for the stats or the sound bite.

They'd be better off running the routes recommended by Kemp, the GOP quarterback so invested in his playbook that a consultant once told him: "If I could remove two-thirds of your knowledge and three-fourths of your vocabulary, I could make you into a decent candidate."

AFTERWORD

I first met Representative Jack Kemp when I was an undergraduate at Lehigh University and dropped into his Capitol Hill office with a paperback copy of his book An American Renaissance: A Strategy for the 1980s *tucked under my arm. His gatekeeper and longtime office manager, Sharon Zelaska, let me in to see him. I was excited to meet him and eager for him to sign the book, so much so that I became flustered when he asked me where I was studying. I said "Lehigh," and when he asked me to spell it, I got tongue-tied and said, "L-e-i . . . sorry, L-e-h-i-g-h" but it was too late. The resulting inscription reads: "Best wishes to you and Leihigh YRs—from a 'fellow soldier' and friend, Jack Kemp." A decade later, he called to invite me to serve as one of his 10 regional administrators in the Department of Housing and Urban Development, clearly having forgotten that not so long before, I had trouble spelling the name of my own school.*

CHECKING IN WITH SMOKIN' JOE
TO THANK HIM FOR HIS DIGNITY

Philadelphia Inquirer, Sunday, May 17, 2009

HARD TO BELIEVE. It's already been a month since the great Harry Kalas passed away.

The Phillies—from the memorial cigarette to the black H.K. uniform patches to that famous home-run call now playing after each hometown dinger—offered him an honorable tribute. So too did the fans, thousands of whom visited Citizens Bank Park to pay their respects. Only Jack Buck and Babe Ruth got similar send-offs. Harry the K got his just due in death.

But as usual, it came a little late. Too often the accolades flow when the recipient is no longer around to hear them. We've all lost people close to us and regretted never having told them what they meant to us in life. It's true for both noncelebrities and celebrities.

Take Joe Frazier. HBO's *Thrilla in Manila* depicts the bitter feud behind the three epic fights between Frazier and Muhammad Ali. That era and those bouts have been well documented, but *Thrilla* is different. It shows us what the battle looked like from Smokin' Joe's corner.

Like the fact that the two rivals had once been friends. Or that Frazier gave Ali money when the latter's boxing license was revoked in the late 1960s, and that Smokin' Joe lobbied President Richard Nixon in support of Ali's reinstatement.

Ali's return to the ring, however, brought a change of attitude. He mocked Frazier in public. He called him stupid and ugly. He race-baited for the cameras, calling Frazier an Uncle Tom and a tool of his white backers. "He's the other type of Negro," Ali asserted. He riffed about Frazier as a gorilla and sparred with a man in a gorilla suit—all as the cameras rolled.

In other words, he took the prefight schtick way too far. And while Ali would later apologize to Frazier's son Marvis, he's never offered a personal apology to Frazier himself.

Too bad it's taken more than 30 years to get a glimpse of that era through Frazier's battered eyes. Ali has long been feted as one of the greatest sportsmen who ever lived. Smokin' Joe, meanwhile, lives in a room above his gym in a North Philadelphia neighborhood labeled the Badlands. As Ali biographer Thomas Hauser notes in the film: "It's an interesting look at how America treats its sporting icons. Some are accorded special status, and others are largely forgotten."

I hope Joe Frazier, now 65, doesn't feel forgotten. Where possible, the icons among us should be told today just how we feel about them. It shouldn't take Tim Russert's passing to spark a conversation about civility in today's media world. Or Jack Kemp's death to inspire the GOP to make an honest effort in his name at reaching out to minorities and urban communities.

And it's not limited to the rich and famous. Each of us has family and friends to whom we owe gratitude—or perhaps people with whom we need to reconcile. It shouldn't take a memorial service or a funeral for us to think about doing so.

A few weeks ago, I called Smokin' Joe Frazier to tell him what he meant to my youth and how he'd helped cultivate my appreciation of the sweet science. I thought he should understand that there are millions of people who acknowledge his commitment to the sport and the dignity with which he's always carried himself. Unfortunately, what *Thrilla* made clear is the reality that Frazier's sense of dignity and sportsmanship has gone unheralded since he left the ring.

He told me he's concerned with influencing "the young one who's growing up to be a young man or young woman as time goes by." He added, "We're

Two guys who dig hats: with Smokin' Joe Frazier in my radio studio, May 2009.
Photo by TC Scornavacchi.

going to have to represent them right so that they can carry on the right way. If we're not right, how are we going to make our kids right?"

I then asked the former Olympic and heavyweight champ if he's happy, and the response was vintage Joe Frazier. "The Lord's been good to me," he said, before telling a story about a car accident that caused him significant pain and resulted in multiple surgeries on his neck.

"From that day on, I've been walking with a little hippy-hop, but I get around the best I can, so it's no problem," he said.

I was glad I made the call.

AFTERWORD

Joe Frazier passed on November 7, 2011, after a battle with liver cancer. He was just 67 years old. While saddened over his death, I was pleased that I had picked up the telephone two years earlier to tell him what he meant to me. For two days—a Friday and Saturday—Frazier lay in state at the Wells Fargo Center, home of the Philadelphia Flyers and 76ers. Like thousands of others, I drove to the South Philadelphia sports palace to pay my respects. Smokin' Joe was laid out at what would be center ice, in a closed white casket. A black cowboy hat, which he fancied wearing later in life, was sitting on top of the casket and nearby was one of the fight posters from his legendary March 8, 1971, fight against Muhammad Ali at Madison Square Garden (often referred to as "The Fight of the Century"). Ali was among the 4,000 mourners on the following Monday who attended Frazier's funeral service at the Enon Tabernacle Baptist Church in Philadelphia. If you have not yet seen it, I highly recommend an HBO Sports documentary about that initial Frazier v. Ali fight called Ali-Frazier I: One Nation . . . Divisible. It tells the story of the remarkable fight between two undefeated heavyweights in largely political terms that helped me appreciate why, when I was just nine years old, our white suburban Philadelphia family was in Frazier's corner, not Ali's.

1-800-POLITICAL-VENOM

Philadelphia Daily News, Thursday, September 3, 2009

'M ON VACATION this week. It couldn't have come soon enough. This is the first time-off I've had in eight months, and 2009 has been an incredibly exhausting and newsy year.

I was looking forward to some neglected leisure activities and projects around the house. I promised our sons that we'd go kayaking on the Delaware, and told my wife that I'd finally clean up a makeshift pet memorial in the backyard.

The to-do list also included trying to get new home-phone service straightened out with Verizon. On Tuesday, I called Verizon and was connected to "Annie" (not her real name).

She asked what number I was calling about, and I offered one of several that might get her to my account. She told me that line had been disconnected (even though I'd just used it)—and that it had last been called by "Obama for America," cavalierly sharing her access to far too much information.

Too bad she didn't let it go at that. "He's not for America," she volunteered. "Excuse me?" I said. She repeated herself, then casually told me the president "is a communist," a "Marxist-Leninist."

Of course, I'm no stranger to discussing politics by phone. I make a living fielding calls and debating the issues with my listeners. But I didn't field this call; I made it. And having initiated it, I couldn't exercise the radio host's prerogative and hang up on myself.

Even worse, I didn't make the call to talk politics. I just wanted to get my phone fixed. I'd done nothing to invite Annie's diatribe, yet she was insistent that I listen to her robotic regurgitation of the talking points she'd likely absorbed hours earlier.

I told her I found her comments inappropriate (if not outright offensive). But she didn't let up. She proceeded to tell me that the president's parents and individuals in his administration were also communists.

So convinced of the righteousness of her beliefs, Annie was ready to espouse them to anybody who called. It was as if she fancied herself a talk-show host ready to do battle with her callers—even though her audience was simply those people whose phone lines needed Verizon's attention.

This is the sorry state of political discourse in America today. Annie was so certain of the opinions that someone else had told her that she was ready to regurgitate them to any hapless caller, the brazen audacity that transformed so many town-hall meetings into shouting matches.

I told Annie she should save her views for after hours and concentrate on my phone. When she persisted, I told her I wanted her last name, and the names of her supervisors. She initially demurred on supplying her own name, but readily offered two names—one male, one female.

When I asked to be connected to the woman, she said she was off. When I requested the man, our connection ended.

By then, the kids were dressed for the kayaks, and the last thing I wanted to do was get into a squabble about politics while on vacation, much less wait on hold to recount what had just happened.

But there was no way I was letting this pass. So I called the same 800 number, and tracked down her male supervisor. He heard me out but seemed more intent on telling me to calm down than getting my name or phone number. I demanded he take both. He promised to look into the situation.

That day on the Delaware, I told my sons what had happened. I explained that I complained to Verizon just as I would have if an operator had volunteered that George W. Bush lied about Iraq or offered some equally reprehensible view from another political extreme.

And I explained that I viewed this as more than just an aberrant woman in a company call center.

As we paddled, and I recalled our conversation, what stood out was not only the outlandish charges against the president, but the ease with which she recited them. To a stranger. And while on someone else's dime.

It was as if the mention of the president's name—which she herself brought up after accessing my billing records—had pushed a button that caused her to spin out of control.

And the manner in which she stated her views told me she was someone who viewed her own disparagement of our nation's leader as some kind of a badge of patriotism.

Well, Annie, you're no Tom Paine. Nor is there a war being fought for independence.

And if the venom being spewed against the president isn't reined in soon, I fear your mind-set will give aid and encouragement to some sicko who thinks it's his place to protect the republic through the barrel of a gun.

Just before the business day ended, my cell phone rang. It was some big mahoff in Verizon's Pittsburgh call center. He wanted to apologize on behalf of the company.

I told him I appreciated the call, that I had no ill will toward Verizon, and that I hoped the call had been recorded "for training purposes" and would indeed be used for that.

I suspect that when Annie is confronted with my complaint, she won't hedge but will readily admit her behavior because she believes she is fighting for some principle higher than her job.

I conveyed my suspicions to the mahoff.

His chuckle told me I was correct.

We are truly in a sorry state. Can you hear me now, Annie?

AFTERWORD

On a subsequent occasion not long after my phone call with Annie, I had a problem with my telephone service. When I called and wasn't getting satisfactory service, the Verizon representative at the other end of the line said, "What are you going to do? Get me fired, too?" Apparently word had spread within Verizon that I'd written this column. So I'm sure they heard me.

SORRY, BUT FOR ME,
THE PARTY IS OVER

Philadelphia Inquirer, Sunday, February 21, 2010

IT TOOK ONLY THE SINGLE TAP of a computer key, and just like that I'd exited the Republican Party after 30 years of active membership. The context might sound impulsive, but I'd been thinking of becoming an independent for a long time. I just hadn't expected that a trip to renew my driver's license would mark the end.

Just before my photo was snapped, I was asked if I wanted to register to vote. For me, the question was borderline offensive. I first registered after turning 18 in the spring of 1980 and haven't missed an election since. And I'm not just talking presidential races. I mean all elections. Congress, town council, school board, whatever.

"I'm already registered," I offered. Next came the unexpected question of whether I wished to change my political affiliation. I'm not sure why that is asked of someone renewing a driver's license, and I question whether it is even appropriate for most. But in my case, it was the only impetus I needed.

Years ago, I grew tired of having my television or radio introduction accompanied by a label, with some implied expectation that what would then come from my mouth were the party talking points. That was me 26 years ago, when I was the youngest elected member of the state delegation to the Republican National Convention, but not today. I'm not sure if I left the Republican Party or the party left me. All I know is that I no longer feel comfortable.

The national GOP is a party of exclusion and litmus tests, dominated on social issues by the religious right, with zero discernible outreach by the national party to anyone who doesn't fit neatly within its parameters. Instead, the GOP has extended itself to its fringe while throwing under the bus long-standing members like New York assemblywoman Dede Scozzafava, a Mc-Cain-Palin supporter in 2008 who told me she voted with her Republican leadership 90 percent of the time before running for Congress last fall.

Which is not to say I feel comfortable in the Democratic Party, either. Weeks before Indiana Democratic senator Evan Bayh's announcement that he will not seek reelection, I noted the centrist former governor's words to the *Wall Street Journal*'s Gerald Seib. Too many Democrats, Bayh said in that interview, are "tone-deaf" to Americans' belief that the party has "overreached rather than looking for consensus with moderates and independents."

Where political parties once existed to create coalitions and win elections, now they seek to advance strict ideological agendas. In today's terms, it's hard to imagine the GOP tent once housing such disparate figures as conservative Barry Goldwater and liberal New Yorker Jacob Javits, while John Stennis of Mississippi and Ted Kennedy of Massachusetts coexisted as Democratic contemporaries.

Collegiality is nonexistent today, and any outreach across an aisle is castigated as weakness by the talking heads who constantly stir a pot of discontent. So vicious is the political climate that within two years, Senator John McCain has gone from GOP standard-bearer to its endangered-species list. All of which leaves homeless those of us with views that don't stack up neatly in any ideological box the way we're told they should.

Consider that I've long insisted on the need to profile in the war against terrorists. I believe that if someone like Khalid Sheikh Mohammed has actionable intelligence on future terrorism, you try the least coercive methods to extract it but ultimately stop at damn near nothing to get what you need to save American lives. I want the U.S. military out of Iraq, but into Pakistan. I'm for capital punishment. I think our porous borders need to be secured before we determine how to deal with the millions of illegal immigrants already within them. Sounds pretty conservative. But wait.

I think that in 2008, the GOP was wrong to adopt a party platform that maintained a strict opposition to abortion without at least carving out exceptions in the case of rape, incest, or danger to the mother's life. I was appalled that legislators tried to decide Terri Schiavo's end-of-life plan. I don't care if two guys hook up any more than they should care about my heterosexual lifestyle. And I still don't know what to think about climate change.

I think President Obama is earnest, smart, and much more centrist than his Tea Party caricature suggests. He has never been given a fair chance to succeed by those who openly crow about their desire to see him fail (while somehow congratulating one another on their relative patriotism). I know he was born in America, isn't a socialist, and doesn't worship in a mosque. I get that he inherited a minefield. Still, the level of federal spending concerns me. And he never closed the deal with me that health insurance is a right, not a privilege. But I'm not folding the tent on him. Not now. Not with the nation fighting two wars while its economy still teeters on the brink of collapse.

All of which leaves me in a partisan no-man's-land, albeit surrounded by many others, especially my neighbors. By quitting the GOP, I have actually joined the largest group of American voters. According to the latest *Washington Post*–ABC News poll, 39 percent of Americans identify themselves as independents—compared with 32 percent who say they are Democrats and 26 percent who are self-described members of the GOP. Nowhere is this more pronounced than locally, where a shift away from the Republican Party has taken place in the four bellwether counties surrounding Philadelphia.

I will miss casting a ballot in the spring, as current state election law prohibits unaffiliated voters from voting in GOP or Democratic primary elections. Instead, I'll join the others who bide their time until fall, when we can temper the extremes of both parties.

"My decision should not be interpreted for more than it is: a very difficult, deeply personal one. . . . I value my independence. I am not motivated by strident partisanship or ideology."

Those are Bayh's words, not mine. But he was speaking for both of us.

AFTERWORD

As I wrote in the column, my exit from the GOP was a long time coming and I'm now much more comfortable being registered in Pennsylvania as "non-affiliated," the Commonwealth lingo for Independent. I did rejoin the GOP briefly in 2016 because I couldn't stand the thought of sitting out the presidential primary. I cast a ballot for John Kasich and then promptly left the party again. Of course, my transition begs the question: Did I leave the GOP or did the GOP leave me? Well, probably a little of each.

There's no doubt that as I have gotten older, my views have moderated on several important issues, including abortion, climate change, same-sex marriage, and gun control. But both parties have become increasingly inhospitable to ideological nonpurists, which is an enormous change since I came of age politically. Don't take my word for it. Consider that for nearly three decades, the Na-tional Journal took the ideological pulse of the Congress, and in 2014–2015, for the fourth straight year, the Journal found that every Republican in the Senate was more conservative than every Democrat and every Democrat was more lib-eral than every Republican. The House was similarly divided. But that isn't the way it's always been. As recently as the 1980s, on Ronald Reagan's watch, 60 percent of the Senate was made up of moderates. There were so many moderates on the Republican side of the aisle that they had their own weekly gathering, called the "Wednesday Lunch Club." Members included Bob Dole, Alan Simp-son, Bob Packwood, Ted Stevens, Nancy Kassebaum, John Heinz, and my friend Arlen Specter. Today, there are no moderates left in the Senate. For this, I pri-marily blame the polarization of the media. There is no coincidence in the fact that since the early 1990s the media have become more polarized, and so has Washington, and it is clearly a matter of causation. Too many elected officials take their cues from men and women with microphones who wield outsized influence in the primary process.

There are other drivers of the polarized divide—money, social media, geography/gerrymandering, and self-sorting, each of which has contributed to the skewing of our debate. But more than any other cause, I fault the desire of those who stir the pot for ratings and mouse clicks without regard for governance, which requires cooperation and compromise.

And here's confirmation of what I see: the National Journal, *which used to publish that annual assessment of Congress, stopped publishing its weekly magazine in 2015 after 46 years in print, which the editor Ronald Brownstein, under the headline "Facts, RIP," attributed partly to the partisan climate.*

"But mostly," Brownstein writes:

> *I think the magazine's position deteriorated because the market for its core product eroded as our political system has grown more rigidly partisan. Fewer elected officials now follow the sequence of gathering objective information and then reaching a decision; usually they follow ideological or partisan signals to reach decisions and then seek talking points to support them. With that change, Washington reporting has evolved further toward sports reporting that partisans consult mainly to see whether their side is "winning" each day's competition. The* National Journal *could never entirely compete in that world.*

YARD SALE 101

Philadelphia Daily News, Thursday, May 13, 2010

WHILE FEDERAL REGULATORS spent last weekend unsuccessfully hunting for the cause of last Thursday's momentary financial meltdown, I was monitoring a classic American enterprise.

It featured a partnership agreement, product development, and market research, not to mention an advertising plan, pricing strategy, concessions, negotiations, and money handling.

Unlike the current financial markets and their fluctuations, this one didn't require a Ph.D. in economics to follow. It was a yard sale run largely by our three sons, ages 9, 12, and 14.

Weeks ago, I'd proposed that they manage the sale with a twofold purpose: first, to relieve our garage and attic of all the stuff we'd accumulated but didn't need or want. And, second, to use it as a device to teach them some of the rudiments of economics.

Now that it's over, I think Wall Street can learn more from the boys than they can learn from Wall Street. The lesson would be about returning to basics.

First, the boys had to work out their partnership. Would they split the profits equally? Or was the eldest entitled to a larger share of the take? Would Dad get reimbursed for using his truck to haul the goods?

Second, they needed product. Good thing their "Uncle Pat," better known as "Cap'n Pat," was willing to rid his own garage of some items, including a vintage Coca-Cola sign. They had flowerpots, books, CDs, toys, a go-kart, two bikes, and an old-fashioned radio.

Their market research consisted of visiting a few sales on the weekends before their own. At one, the homemade brownies seemed to do a brisk business. Suddenly, food became a consideration.

Marketing consisted of two newspaper ads and some road signage for the morning of the event.

As for the negotiating strategy, I recommended they cut whatever deals were necessary in order to spare us a trip to Goodwill. My wife and I promised to stay off the floor as best we could, leaving the boys to run their own show. That meant they'd handle all the money.

Immediately, the ethics of business confronted them.

While they were setting up the night before, a man arrived, newspaper ad in hand, saying his son was graduating from high school the next day. He was hoping to get a look at the Coca-Cola sign.

Was it proper to sell before the sale started?

The boys didn't hesitate. The sign went for full price. The buyer offered a $5 tip for allowing him to make the purchase, which only reinforced the boys' belief they'd sold it too cheap. "I wonder if he uses the line about the son's graduation the night before all sales," our eldest said.

The boys' grandmother had been generous in emptying her own cupboard. A blender I recognized from my childhood had an asking price of $5. I heard a man offer $2. One son countered at $3, but another shouted out $2.50, exposing frailties within the partnership.

The asking price on the go-kart was $50. There was an offer of $40 and a counter of $45, which closed the deal.

Dollar books were popular. So were CDs, flowerpots, and framed wall hangings.

But not the lamps or the jackets. Ditto for the old radio. Electronics—the phone, TV, and printer—were slow movers as well.

Interestingly, everyone asked for jewelry. The boys had none in stock.

And while the brownie idea had given way to hot coffee and cold water, neither moved on such a mild day.

The gross was $713 (split three equal ways). But they seemed to learn several business lessons aside from calculating their take.

How every Smerconish yard sale ends.

Besides the product procurement, marketing, and pricing, they also learned about shifts. One brother could take a break only if the two others were on the job.

They also paid attention to their client base. I let political correctness be damned as they observed that the nerdy Asian guy bought the video games, the gay guys acquired the empty Tiffany boxes, and the Hispanic family purchased some used clothes.

What's clear to me now is that garage sales are a slice of entrepreneurial Americana unspoiled by the masters of the universe on Wall Street.

In fact, here's hoping those operating in the world's financial capital take a lesson from the kids. Namely, that they made money selling tangible items—bikes, flowerpots, lacrosse sticks, and wrapping paper. Their products could be understood and purchasers knew exactly what they were getting— whether it was a used copy of Walter Isaacson's *American Sketches* or a slightly scratched Andreas Vollenweider CD.

For one morning at least, they were engaged in real work, facilitating a real exchange of goods.

I'm reminded of the words of Jack Bogle, founder of the Vanguard Group, the largest mutual-fund manager in the world. In his book *Enough*, which is about to be re-released because of its timeless message, he laments that this country produces fewer tangible products and depends more on pushing paper than ever.

> Over the past two centuries, our nation has moved from being an agricultural economy, to a manufacturing economy, to a service economy, and now to a predominantly financial economy. But our financial economy, by definition, deducts from the value created by our productive businesses.

Bogle, a true captain of industry who seeks real measures of value and simplicity in financial markets and in life, probably loves a good yard sale.

AFTERWORD

The boys' yard sales were a summer ritual for a few years running. And while the annual event has ended, my sons still swap stories about lessons learned and some of the personalities who were repeat customers. Their goal was to make money; my wife and I were simply eager to have them get rid of stuff we'd accumulated that no longer had value to us. This cycle led to a new family vernacular—"yard sale material"—appropriately used when one member of my family sees another making an imprudent, impulsive purchase. I'd like to think the regular use of that admonition has curbed our profligacy. That, and the fact that each sale was inevitably followed by the embarrassing placement on our curb of whatever didn't sell, alongside a spray-painted sign on plywood that simply said: "Free." We'd debate how many days had to tick off the clock before the unsold item disappeared and wonder about those who had attended the sale and were disturbed by the gratuitous offering.

THE POWER OF PIN MONEY

Philadelphia Daily News, Thursday, September 9, 2010

HOW COULD ANYBODY hate Steven Singer, given the generosity he's exhibited toward the construction of the Flight 93 National Memorial in Shanksville, Pennsylvania?

Over the past year, the man whose unique marketing campaign is ubiquitous on Philadelphia radio and billboards has become a fund-raising superstar for this worthy national project.

His role began last September, when I published *Instinct: The Man Who Stopped the 20th Hijacker.* The book tells the story of Jose Melendez-Perez, the immigration inspector who on August 4, 2001, refused to allow Mohamed al Kahtani—the intended fifth hijacker on Flight 93—into the United States. (Neither Melendez-Perez nor I earned a penny from the sale of the book. All author proceeds were donated to the Flight 93 National Memorial.)

Singer, the prominent jeweler here in Philly and a sponsor of my radio program, told me he was inspired to do something.

"Since September 11, 2001, I, like most Americans, felt helpless and very much wanted to help make a difference in some small way," he said.

So he designed the 9/11 "Never Forget" lapel pin pictured herein, and began to sell them to my radio audience for $10. He donated every cent to the Flight 93 memorial, covering the production costs and the manpower needed to sell and distribute them—even the shipping fees.

Last year, our effort raised more than $30,000. Three weeks ago, he told me he had a goal for this year. I did, too.

Mine was $50,000.

Singer scoffed—and said his was $100,000.

Well, with two days to go before the ninth anniversary of 9/11, I'm thrilled to say that he was right, and I was wrong. We just surpassed $100,000, with orders shipping to all 50 states.

The response has been staggering. One individual wrote to Singer:

I love the pin. Being a firefighter who was on standby for the 9/11 tragedy, it holds a place in my heart that I will never forget that day and everything about it and am a full supporter of the Flight 93 Memorial.

Another wrote:

> As a survivor from the 105th floor of 2 WTC, I must tell you that your pins are an incredibly fitting tribute to those lost that day and an outstanding way to help us all "never forget." . . . I now have a small but significant tattoo on my right wrist, the hand I cross my heart with, that is a replica of the pin. It is my way of "marking" my experience and always remembering.

Alice Hoglan, the mother of the Flight 93 hero Mark Bingham, called the effort "thrilling" and "absolutely special." Which is the highest praise.

Hoglan is a woman of remarkable strength, and her son was a shining example of the rugged individualism that defined Flight 93 and its legacy. Bingham was a 6-foot-5 rugby player who was gay. He and his fellow passengers stopped Flight 93 just 20 minutes shy of a strike on Washington, D.C.

In the weeks and months after that day, a makeshift memorial overlooking the crash site was created as thousands of people streamed to Shanksville to pay their respects. They have never stopped.

According to Jeff Reinbold, the memorial project's site manager, almost 1.5 million people have visited the temporary memorial since 9/11.

And although construction of the permanent memorial is now under way (the first phase will be completed by next year's 10th anniversary), the fundraising efforts for a second phase are continuing, Reinbold told me.

Plans for that expansion include a visitor center and 40 groves of trees representing Flight 93's 40 heroes. Those purchasing Singer's pins will be directly contributing to the completion of this phase by the planners' goal of 2014.

That will mean a permanent record of the bravery displayed by people like Hilda Marcin, another passenger on Flight 93.

For more than a year, Marcin had been planning to move to California to

Steven Singer presenting a check for the Garden of Reflection to Ellen Saracini, widow of Victor Saracini (captain of United Flight 175), on the 15th anniversary of 9/11.

live with her daughter, Carole O'Hare, and Carole's husband, Tom. They were to begin that new chapter of their lives on September 11, 2001.

"These people were not soldiers, yet they fought a war—at 35,000 feet. That has to mean something," Carole told me when I asked what the national memorial will mean to her.

> I think history many years from now will treat it as a defining event in our nation's history.
>
> But for now, for the families, the purpose of the memorial is to remember, reflect, and honor people they loved in a very personal way, realizing it's much bigger than all of us.

To purchase your pin and make your $10 donation to the Flight 93 National Memorial, visit IHateStevenSinger.com, or call 1-800-350-1104.

You can also visit Steven Singer Jewelers at the (other) corner of 8th and Walnut in Center City and buy them in person.

AFTERWORD

Steven Singer is not only a longtime radio advertiser of mine but also a friend. Over the many years he has sponsored my program, I have come to admire his work ethic, mastery of advertising, and—as this column details—his generosity. I'll get back to that last attribute later. First, let me tell you that Steven started in the business at age 17 while still in high school, when his job was selling jewelry wholesale on Philadelphia's Jewelers' Row. Steven then completed courses at the Gemological Institute of America, making him an expert in the disciplines of diamond residency, color stones, gem identification, and cultured pearls. In 1980, he opened his first eponymous jewelry shop. By his early 20s, he had already distinguished himself in the nation's oldest and second-largest jewelry district—despite having the smallest store on the block. He outgrew that space and several that followed. And that was before he realized his brand's great potential through radio advertising.

As Steven explains in a profile in the Wall Street Journal *published in the late 1980s, he noticed the buzz that Howard Stern was getting on radio. According to the* Journal:

> *[Mr. Singer] mortgaged his house and opened more than 20 new credit-card accounts. The ads cost about $1,000 a minute, he says. Some weeks, he could afford only two or three spots. His wife—and his accountant—*

thought he "was nuts," Mr. Singer says, but both went along grudging-
ly. "I made it my business to get in good with that show," he says.

The rest is history.

I know firsthand his brilliance from my perspective as a broadcaster. So many times over the course of my radio career, I've been asked by advertisers, through radio salespeople, to make sure that, in the span of a fleeting 60 seconds, I say certain words and phrases before repeated reference to the telephone number and "the ask." If the spot ran 57 seconds, some advertisers would want a three-second credit. And if all the parameters in the written copy were not met, they would also complain, even when their ad had been given an effective read. Then there were those who would insist, "We really want your personality in this one," only to script so much of the 60 seconds that there was no place left for me to leave my imprint.

Enter Steven Singer. The guy who built a jewelry empire with the worse-than-self-deprecating line, "I hate Steven Singer." Steven was unlike any advertiser I'd ever met. "Just say my name," he told me early in our relationship. "Huh?" I replied.

"Do whatever you want to do for 60 seconds, just say my name." That was his only request.

As I said, a genius. By giving me the freedom and flexibility to say what I wanted to say, he was guaranteeing that his ads would be different, that I wouldn't sleep through a one-minute read, and that by giving me the flexibility to do less, he was actually ensuring he would get more. I'm not saying I've hit a home run with every one of his spots, but on the whole, I think I've given him more than his money's worth.

Most important, I know Steven to be a very generous guy, as illustrated in this column. As of this writing, Steven Singer has contributed $538,221.43 to 9/11 charities over the span of just seven years. For the first three years, his donations went to the Flight 93 National Memorial in Shanksville, and for the past four, to the Garden of Reflection in Bucks County. How could anyone hate a guy like that?

FAREWELL, MY *DN* FRIENDS

Philadelphia Daily News, Thursday, February 3, 2011

EDITOR'S NOTE: *Michael Smerconish made history here at 400 N. Broad when, six years after starting a column for the* Daily News, *he also began a weekly column in the* Inquirer. *To our knowledge, no one has ever contributed to both papers in quite the same way. In this and so many ways, Smerconish is one of a kind.*

But starting next week, having taken on more work for the Inquirer, *he'll be found exclusively in that paper. While this is his last column for the* Daily News, *we will always consider him a People Paper person.*

To see why, check out Philly.com/topsmerconish for a selection of our favorite Smerconish columns.

MORE THAN NINE YEARS AGO, at the invitation of then-editor Zack Stalberg, I penned my first column for the *Daily News*. And today is my last, since I'll be increasing my work at the *Inquirer*.

I was proud of my first column byline on November 13, 2001, when I made the case for Rudy Giuliani to run the Department of Homeland Security, and have remained pleased with my association here ever since.

I've written hundreds of columns since then. Many stand the test of time; others don't. I've taken positions on countless controversies. Most but not all of my views still hold.

For profiling. Against Mumia. For Katz. Against Street. For Ted Nugent. Against Pete Rose.

I recently perused those many columns. Some are forgettable. Others I wish I could dial back. I'm disappointed that I got carried away with a conspiracy theory linking the Oklahoma City bombing to Middle Eastern terrorists.

But I'm proud that on January 2, 2003, I wrote: "I am terribly disappointed in the Bush administration's public case for the war against Iraq."

I called the Duke lacrosse case from the start. ("It's the revenge of the nerds. Most journalists would never be chosen for a pickup game of hoops, let alone a varsity sport. So they take perverse pleasure in bringing down the BMOC, however undeserved.")

And every once in a while, I asked a provocative question. Like, if Alfred Kinsey was correct in saying that 10 percent of the population is gay, why did so few same-sex partners emerge seeking compensation from the September 11th Victim Compensation Fund?

For rebuilding the Twin Towers as they existed. Against the zoo balloon flying so close to the Schuylkill. For keeping the Barnes in Merion. Against the Cuba embargo.

I once wrote that they could fix the sagging ratings of the Miss America pageant if they'd "bring back the busty baton twirler."

That was probably my favorite line. Others have not been so pleased with my work.

When I was critical of John Street for not firing an aide who reportedly said, "All of these teams are Jews—Jew lawyers and Jew architects—and we need to do something about that," I found myself on the receiving end of a lawsuit by that speaker. (It was thrown out.)

Other attention was more favorable. Remember the kidnapping of Erica Pratt, the plucky little Philadelphia girl who eventually escaped? After I wrote that those close to her were as much to blame as those who kidnapped her, Bernard Goldberg called to say he was using the column in a book, which he did (*Arrogance*).

For colored Christmas lights. Against white ones. For legal prostitution. Against women with tattoos.

It's been interesting to reread my old columns. I was reminded that my disgust with the politicization in the country has been building for a while. After the presidential election in 2004 I wrote:

> In every green room in the country, there was a "liberal" and "conservative" at the ready, who, even if uncomfortable with those labels, were willing to be accepted as such for the sake of getting their mugs on camera.
>
> Televised politics now caters to the ideologues, the doctrinaire types. Lost in the screaming is any chance for a reasoned discussion. People at home take their marching orders from them, then parrot what they've heard. And so it goes.

For buying fireworks in Pennsylvania. Against banning beer at Wawa.

Probably the most popular column I ever wrote came during the Terri Schiavo controversy, when I used my column space to publish a sample living will. People still occasionally write and ask for a copy of it.

Certainly the most significant item I published was on April 12, 2004, when I examined a question former Navy secretary and 9/11 Commission member John Lehman had asked Condoleezza Rice at a 9/11 hearing:

Were you aware that it was the policy . . . to fine airlines if they have more than two young Arab males in secondary questioning, because that's discriminatory?

Little did I know that Lehman's single question would spur me to write my first book, *Flying Blind*.

For a Christmas Village at City Hall. Against a blank check for Pakistan.

Of all that I've written in nearly a decade at the *DN*, I'm most proud of something published on August 21, 2008, under the headline "Requiem for an Era."

In it, I tried to capture how the city had changed in the last few decades based on observations I jotted down while standing in a viewing line as it snaked along a South Philly street.

I wrote the entire column on my BlackBerry, using my thumbs. I never said whose funeral it was because I thought it would distract from my observations, but I was paying my respects to John Dougherty after the passing of his mother, Mary Theresa, so I'm closing that loop now.

Speaking of untimely death, I will never forget editor Michael Schefer for allowing me to use a column to eulogize the passing of my first dog, Winston, evidence of his being both a friend and a savvy editor.

And I'll always be a proud *Daily News* alum.

AFTERWORD

Something had to give. With four kids (and four dogs) at home, I was getting up at 3 a.m. to deliver a three-hour daily morning-drive radio program, appearing more and more often on cable television news, writing books, and cranking out two columns a week, one for the Daily News *and one for the Sunday* Inquirer. *Even with the able assistance of my colleague John McDonald, it was just too much and I knew I had to choose which newspaper association I'd continue. The wider circulation and prominence of the Sunday* Inquirer *was certainly a consideration in my choice, but so too was the fact that I was no longer living in Center City, Philadelphia, but had moved back to the suburbs. I thought I was better suited to writing about issues that appealed to my suburban neighbors; hence my decision to discontinue my columns for the* Daily News. *Still, I remain grateful to Zack Stalberg and the* Daily News *for giving me a platform at the People Paper. I like how this recap sign-off perfectly encapsulates my good times at the DN and have emulated the style since in several end-of-year columns.*

2011–2016

INVESTMENT GIANT ON LIVING WELL— AND MADOFF

Philadelphia Inquirer, Friday, March 4, 2011

THINGS HAVE A WAY of coming full circle for Jack Bogle, founder of the mutual-fund leader the Vanguard Group.

At the midpoint of his sophomore year at Princeton, he was struggling in economics with a D-plus average, which placed his scholarship in jeopardy.

The basis of his difficulty? The first edition of what would become the seminal college economics text written by Paul Samuelson.

Later, in search of a topic for his senior thesis, Bogle recalled, he read on "Page 116 of the December 1949 issue of *Fortune* magazine" a story about mutual funds titled "Big Money in Boston."

Inspired, Bogle proceeded to write about an industry that he said could be so much better. He argued that sales charges and expense ratios should be reduced and that funds should be run in the most honest, economical, and efficient way possible. Funds should be run for the benefit of shareholders and not managers, he wrote, and they should make no claim for superiority over market indexes.

Years later, that same *Fortune* would proclaim Bogle one of the four investment giants of the 20th century. And Samuelson, author of the legendary economics text, would write the foreword for Bogle's first book, *Bogle on Mutual Funds*.

Samuelson, the first American Nobel laureate in economics, was both a personal and professional proponent of Bogle. In 2005, Samuelson wrote Bogle a note: "Any small influence on you has been more than offset by what Vanguard has done for my six children and 15 grandchildren. May Darwin bless you!"

That same year, Samuelson delivered a speech that ranked Bogle's financial invention with the "wheel, wine and cheese, the alphabet, and Gutenberg printing: a mutual fund that never made Bogle rich but elevated the long-term returns of the mutual-fund owners. Something new under the sun."

On Monday, Bogle regaled a full house at the Bryn Mawr Film Institute with such anecdotes from his past while celebrating the release of his newest book, *Don't Count on It!*

At 81, Bogle was sharp as ever, displaying no evidence of having just been hospitalized for a touch of the flu. In fact, Bogle recently celebrated the 15th anniversary of his heart transplant, yet shows no signs of slowing down or curtailing the messages he has espoused for decades. Why should he? So much of what he has said for years has come true.

Bogle's sense of serendipity extends to things he has preached for decades: ethics and giving value to clients.

He is the antithesis of Michael Douglas's character Gordon Gekko, who famously said that "greed is good" in the movie *Wall Street*. To the contrary, while extolling the virtues of entrepreneurship, Bogle is quick to point out: "No, greed is not good. Ambition is good." Bogle laments that college finance courses and business schools often assert that the only incentives that move the world are financial.

> Isn't living a worthy life an incentive? Isn't being a good member of the community an incentive?
>
> I read a wonderful quote the other day. It said the great thing about money is that it will buy you all you want of anything in the world that is totally unimportant. It cannot buy you what is important.

The day of his Bryn Mawr presentation, *New York* magazine released a jailhouse interview with the disgraced financier Bernie Madoff. "Everyone was greedy. I just went along. It's not an excuse," Madoff told the writer Steve Fishman, adding that banks' and hedge funds' willingness to work with him—and collect their fees—despite obvious irregularities with his business had amounted to "complicity." Bogle agreed:

> Well, of course there was [complicity]. Why was there? I will give you one example. These fund managers who used Madoff did not do any due diligence at all, and they were paid over three to five years just for pointing their fingers to invest "over there" $600 million. So of course they ignored all the warning signs. . . . Some of these guys I hope will go to jail.

Sprinkled into Bogle's remarks were a number of thoughts from a business giant looking at a life well lived.

His mantra, "Press on, regardless," was adopted from the name of his uncle's boat. Bogle emphasized how important it is to follow that credo no matter how tough—or how easy—times may be.

And there was: "You deal with what is and not what might have been."

And: "Live life a little with blinders on. You have the task in front of you. Don't be disturbed by peripheral things around you. March to your own drummer, do your best, focus on the task at hand."

And perhaps the most Boglesque: "If you have a good impulse, do it."

AFTERWORD

On November 16, 2016, Jack Bogle, at age 87, was among the first recipients of the Philadelphia Inquirer's *inaugural Industry Icon Awards. I read with interest his acceptance remarks. As one who has read many of his dozen books, hosted him for radio interviews and live events, and had the privilege of visiting him in his Vanguard offices in Malvern, Pennsylvania, I was not surprised by anything he said. At the outset, the man who founded a company that had grown to nearly $4 trillion in assets felt compelled to defend the title of his remarks:*

> The idea of "Big Money"—the title of my remarks this evening—has never motivated me. My goal in this business was not to build a colossus. It was to give investors a fair shake.

After walking through a timeline of his life in business, he closed by saying this:

> The idea of fiduciary duty, honest disclosure, and candor, along with our simple mutual structure and our simple index strategy that followed—all of which, as it happens, are Quaker in spirit—have become "the way." We now effectively serve the needs of the 22 million human beings who have entrusted us with their investments, their hopes, and their confidence. We are proud of our heritage, and faithful service to investors has always been my primary goal. If "Big Money in Philadelphia" suggests that we have accomplished that goal, well, so be it! Thank you again, . . . Philadelphia Inquirer, for the honor that you bestow on me and Vanguard this evening.

That's pure Bogle. There's an underutilized, old-school word that sums him up: scruples. *To the extent we use the word today, it is most often as a pejorative, to describe what someone lacks, as in, a moral hesitation. He's the opposite. Every step he takes seems guided by his Quaker faith and sense of what is just. And that is the way he has run his phenomenal business.*

Jack Bogle has achieved tremendous deserved recognition during his life. In

2004, Time *magazine named him one of the world's 100 most powerful and influential people.* Fortune, *in 1999, called him one of the investment indus-try's four "Giants of the 20th Century."* And Institutional Investor *presented him with its Lifetime Achievement Award.*

In his book Enough: True Measures of Money, Business, and Life, *Bogle quotes Joseph Heller as telling Kurt Vonnegut at a billionaire's party, "I have something he [their host] will never have: Enough." I get the sense that even without the many accolades, Jack Bogle, the proud Princeton alumnus who built a business on an idea he voiced in his senior thesis, had already had enough.*

A LESSON IN GUMPTION,
AND ITS REWARDS

Philadelphia Inquirer, **Sunday, April 3, 2011**

FOR YEARS, my family has vacationed in the same Florida town. In fact, we just returned home after spending a week of spring break there with our three sons.

Many nights, we take the same scenic drive to dinner at a favorite restaurant. As we travel along Gulf Shore Boulevard, we admire a combination of small beach apartments, swanky high-rises, and spectacular homes.

A few years ago, we noticed that whenever we drive this particular route, there are always two men sitting in front of the same third-floor window of a low-rise apartment building that overlooks the road. All that is visible from the road are their two silhouettes. Even during off-peak months, they've always been there.

Over the years, we've had great fun speculating about who they are, whether they're having a drink, and if so, what they fancy, where they're from, and what they might be discussing. Our guesses have become a modern form of car bingo. Widowers? Retirees? Partners? We've run through the gamut of possibilities.

Eventually, I started beeping the horn as we passed. We'd wave. Our new friends would do likewise. There was something comforting in seeing them. In a world of constant change, it's been nice to look up and see that they are there, same as we remembered from our last visit.

And then last spring, we drove by and they were missing. The apartment was dark. No one was visible in the window. Funny thing, we grew worried about two people we'd never met. Where did they go? Was everything all right? A new round of the guessing game. Too bad, because we had started to joke about dropping in on them to fill in the missing pieces.

On our last trip at Christmastime, we were relieved to see them once again. We were driving past about 6 P.M., and there they were at cocktail hour. I told my wife that I suspected they were gin drinkers and said we should buy them a bottle. She said that if I bought it, she'd deliver it. I said, "Tomorrow."

So I bought a bottle of Bombay, and en route to dinner at dusk the next night, we speculated with our three boys as to their names and why they had disappeared during our last visit.

Approaching the usual stretch, we were pleased to see the light was on.

This time, there were three images in the window, not two. Our friends were entertaining. I pulled over.

My wife, accompanied by our 10-year-old, boldly got out, clutching the gin, and headed toward the stairs to their door. I remained behind with the other two boys, and parked across the street. Then she disappeared from our line of sight.

In a scene reminiscent of Hitchcock's *Rear Window*, we watched as one of the men rose to answer the door. Then he, too, was out of the camera frame. After a few minutes, he returned to show his two friends the bottle that had just been delivered. Soon, another of the men went toward the door, presumably to meet whoever had paid them a visit. Then we saw both men return and show the bottle to their guest.

A few moments later, my wife and son returned to the car.

She said Phil and Helmut (one of the boys had guessed "Phil" correctly) were appreciative of the gift (and I was correct about their fondness for gin!). They couldn't have been nicer and encouraged us to stop next time for a drink. Yes, they'd seen our car and had heard the greeting of the horn. And while they appreciated our concern over their absence in the spring, they had just been away on vacation.

As we started the car and continued along the beach to dinner, my wife and I were happy that a throwaway line about delivering a bottle of gin to our Florida friends had yielded a lesson to show a little gumption and take some initiative. After all, you never know when you could become a comforting constant for somebody else.

Last week in Florida the apartment was dark. But we're not worried. I beeped anyway.

AFTERWORD

I'm sad to report that Phil and Helmut are no longer where we saw them in Naples. We still vacation in the same place and take our normal route to dinner. But for several years, the drapes have been pulled in their apartment and there have been no signs of life, at least when we've been in town. We miss seeing them in the window, while imagining their conversations as we pass in the night. Instead, we now speculate on what became of them. Did their relationship end? God forbid, did one of them pass? Or maybe they just settled on another unit or in another town? Regrettably, I confess to not having learned the lesson of my own column: taking a risk with new relationships. I failed to ensure they read this story. We didn't return to Florida for several months after I wrote this column, and when we did go back, I forgot to pack it. Lacking an e-mail or street address for Phil and Helmut, I never made them aware of what I'd written.

CAN YOU IMAGINE
HOW CHRISTIE'S SON FEELS?

Philadelphia Inquirer, Sunday, June 5, 2011

T WAS NO SURPRISE TO ME that Chris Christie took heat for using a state helicopter to attend his son's baseball game, but I'm not thinking of the wrath of New Jersey taxpayers. If his house is anything like mine, he has bigger problems on the home front for the poor decision he made.

Last Tuesday, Christie flew from Trenton to Montvale to watch his son Andrew play baseball in a state playoff game. Upon arrival next to the field, Christie was shuttled about 100 yards in a dark town car with tinted windows to the stands. Then, after the fifth inning, play was halted so he could depart in order to travel to Drumthwacket, the governor's mansion, to dine with some Iowans who were courting him to run for president.

The state police superintendent said the pilots would have been training in the new $12.5 million craft without the governor, so there was no additional cost to the state police. In similar circumstances, the *Star-Ledger* reported, Governors Jim McGreevey and Christie Whitman repaid the state. After initially saying that he wouldn't do likewise, Christie and the state Republican Party announced Thursday that they, too, would pay their own way.

But I'm thinking that satisfied only one segment of his critics. Here's why.

I drive two vehicles: a 2004 F-150 that I own and a 2011 Jaguar XJL, which is provided to me by a sponsor of my radio program.

I was first offered the Jaguar when the model was released, and so I was among the first to drive one on the Philadelphia roadways. The car is spectacular—the finest I have ever driven. It's both ultra-luxurious and a smooth ride. So imagine my excitement to pick up our sons from school. Our boys are this week finishing the fourth, seventh, and ninth grades.

I arrived in this brand-spanking-new $80,000 car, only to have the first of them get into the passenger seat and slump down.

"Dad, I can't believe you picked us up in this!"

Only when we cleared the school grounds did he and his brothers sit up straight and appreciate the interior beauty of the car.

The following day, I thought it best to get them in the F-150. Another surprise.

"Dad, how many pickup trucks do you see other than ours?"

Answer: none.

The lesson here was that at this age, they wish to fly beneath the radar—pun intended—which is not so easy with a father prone to the limelight.

So I can only imagine what it was like for Andrew Christie.

It must be bad enough that the opposing pitcher knows he is the governor's son when he comes to the plate. You can imagine him deciding to put a little more heat on the ball. And now, to have added attention heaped on him thanks to a hovering helicopter, not to mention a town car apparently needed to shuttle dad 300 feet? How embarrassing.

I have to believe he was none too happy with dad's arrival ceremony for a high school baseball game. Good thing his team won.

This also reminds me of a story I often was told by a friend and neighbor from Doylestown, Jack Ernst, who passed away a few weeks ago. Jack was one of the funniest men I have ever known. It runs in his family.

Jack grew up in Lockport, Illinois, with two brothers, Jimmy and Joey. The Ernsts had little money. Consequently, the family car was a late 1940s Ford coupe with a banged-up fender and an "88" Jimmy had painted on its side to resemble a stock car. The family was perpetually getting ready to get rid of it.

One day as teens, Jack and Joey had a date at the movies with two local girls. As they approached the theater in the family jalopy, they asked their father to drop them off a block away so the girls would not see the car. Dad obliged.

But when the boys got to the front of the theater, their dad suddenly pulled up, rolled down the window, honked the horn, and said, "I'm Mr. Ernst and this is my car!"

One can only imagine the horror the boys felt. Like mine did when I pulled up in the XJL and then the F-150. Like Andrew Christie no doubt did when his dad flew to the ball field.

Next time Chris Christie should drive. I'll let him borrow the Jag.

AFTERWORD

My purpose in this column was to tell a funny story and show some empathy for Governor Christie as a fellow dad. Well, he missed the joke. Instead, I was dead to him for having written it, a fact that became clear when, in the spring of 2015, Tom McGrath, the editor of Philadelphia *magazine, asked me to write a July cover story on Christie and he refused to cooperate. It was bizarre. I had taken Christie's participation for granted because he was so famously media accessible, and up until then, I'd interviewed him a half-dozen times and had often spoken and written about him in a complimentary manner, especially* when he first ran against Jon Corzine. During that campaign I had called foul on Corzine's use of slow-motion footage in a negative ad depicting Christie ambling along, because I thought the tape was slowed to accentuate his weight. Plus, this Philly Mag cover story would reach South Jersey in the midst of his reelection campaign. It seemed like a no-brainer. Well, my radio producer, TC, then reconstructed a ticktock of all dealings she'd had with Christie's press office, how our cordial relationship and his frequent radio appearances had come to a grinding halt, immediately after this column ran. I published that recounting in a January 2015 column for the Sunday Inquirer, where I wrote:

> Pre-helicopter, the staff was quick to respond and always courteous ("We'd like to get the governor back on with Michael once we start doing radio"). Post-helicopter, only one of many invitations got a reply ("Will be in touch about the next time we can get some time for the governor").

Still, I wrote the cover story without Christie's cooperation and I think I treated him fairly. Nine months after its publication, at the first GOP presidential debate at Simi Valley, I was present for CNN when Christie did a sound check and we had an awkward encounter and handshake. What a shame. For having once suggested he'd embarrassed his son—as I had done to my own three—I'd been tossed under the bridge, so to speak.

"MORMON ISSUE"
STILL HANDICAPS ROMNEY

Philadelphia Inquirer, Sunday, June 12, 2011

MUCH HAS CHANGED since Mitt Romney last ran for president. The economy has gotten worse, the Phillies assembled the best starting rotation in baseball, and the United States killed Osama bin Laden.

Sadly, one thing that hasn't changed is the reluctance of a significant number of Americans to vote for him because of his Mormon faith. In a nationwide poll last month by the Pew Research Center for the People and the Press, 25 percent said they would be less likely to support a Mormon for president, compared with 30 percent in February 2007.

Who are they? It seems that reluctance to vote for a Mormon is about the only thing on which many evangelical Protestants and liberal Democrats agree. The former, of course, present a significant stumbling block for Romney and fellow Mormon Jon Huntsman, the former Utah governor and potential presidential candidate, given the number of evangelicals in early caucus and primary states such as Iowa and South Carolina.

Romney was optimistic earlier this year during an interview with CNN's Piers Morgan. He said:

> I can't judge the politics. I don't know the answer to that. My experience so far, in Massachusetts running as a Mormon guy in a state that's overwhelmingly of other faiths, is it didn't seem to get in my way there. But most people in the country recognize that, in fact, the nation itself was founded on the principle of religious tolerance and freedom.

My interaction with radio callers tells me he is overly optimistic. I've heard from many voters willing to state their hesitancy to vote for a Mormon, including "Sean," a self-described Catholic from Indianapolis.

"I'm in that group that won't vote for a Mormon," he told me. Why? "Because I think it implies poor judgment and critical-thinking skills."

Sean's critique didn't surprise Anthea Butler, a religion professor at the University of Pennsylvania. "Most Americans don't know the basic history and beliefs of their own faith, let alone any of the major religious traditions," Butler told me.

Sean, and those who make up the quarter of the country unwilling to elect a Mormon, believe the followers of Mormonism are insufficiently dubious about their own religion.

How else to explain Mormons' adherence to a faith founded by Joseph Smith, who told his followers that he had been visited at age 14 by God the Father and Jesus, who instructed him not to join an established church? A few years later, Smith would translate the Book of Mormon, based on inscriptions on gold plates buried in the ground, with a "seeing stone." Today, participants wear special undergarments to remind them of the tenets of their faith and to protect them. They also refrain from consuming coffee or tea, which the sect refers to as "hot drinks."

Sean's group knows better than to believe this, as well as whatever might underpin the faith of Jews, Muslims, Buddhists, and even Scientologists.

Take Scientology. This church is predicated upon events of 75 million years ago when an intergalactic warlord released millions of soul-like beings into Earth's atmosphere. Those beings, called thetans, harbor confusion and conflict, which they use to wreak havoc on the individuals they come to inhabit. In 1951, Scientology founder L. Ron Hubbard introduced the electropsychometer, or E-meter, to aid in detecting the unhealthy and potentially damaging subconscious memories these thetans carry with them.

No doubt Sean can just imagine what the Buddhists say about the Scientologists. These thetans were reincarnated from what, exactly? When did they go through their cycles of birth, life, and death? And how did they learn to release their attachment to desire and the self so they could attain Nirvana?

And no way Sean would be comfortable with all that Muslim stuff. Islam's holy text includes reference to Allah's creating man from a clot of blood, not to mention angels adorned with as many as four pairs of wings. Muslims believe it takes unwavering belief in God and a lifetime of good deeds to reach Paradise.

Perhaps Sean is more comfortable with Jewish beliefs. Jews readily understand that the Earth was created in six days (and that God rested on the seventh). And they appreciate Noah's survival of a great flood after building an ark big enough to hold two of each animal, the drowning of the oppressive Pharaoh's army after Moses parted the Red Sea, and the conquest of Canaan, complete with walls toppled by shouts and the sun standing still in the sky.

Still, they, too, can learn a few things from Christians.

Chalk it up to a sense of logic and common sense that comes from understanding a virgin birth, complete with a star over Bethlehem that served as a marker to three wise men, not to mention how decades later, this son of

God would walk on the water of the Sea of Galilee, convert water into wine, and rise from the dead after being crucified in front of scores of witnesses.

Critical thinking is, after all, in the eye of the beholder. Amen.

AFTERWORD

I thought the point of the column was pretty obvious; reread the last line if you have any doubts. Still, I should have known from experience that I would receive backlash from readers who either didn't get my point or hadn't read the column in its entirety. A few years earlier, on January 24, 2008, I published a Daily News *column in which I similarly attempted to employ satire to point out the hypocrisy of people of any religion judging Scientologists and Mormons, by restating some of the beliefs of my own religion, Catholicism. (Specifically, my brand of cafeteria Catholicism!) The backlash to that column was also swift, sure, and once again, oblivious to the point I was actually making.*

I wrote this column the year before Mitt Romney captured the Republican nomination and, in retrospect, I think his Mormon faith limited his potential only to the extent he allowed. I think he should have tried to use it more as a campaign asset. If viewers of the 2012 Republican National Convention in Tampa remember any of the speeches that week, chances are it's the Clint Eastwood improv with a chair at about 10 P.M. on the night Romney himself spoke. Eastwood's meandering moment made for a disjointed finale and overshadowed what happened earlier that night when fellow Mormons provided testimony about how Romney had impacted their lives with his caring and faith. They were remarkable. Their stories legitimate tearjerkers. Especially the story of an older couple from Massachusetts, the Oparowskis, who recounted how Romney, then the pastor at their church, had befriended their 14-year-old son for the seven months that he fought cancer before his death. At the boy's request, Romney sat beside his bed and wrote his will to ensure that his property went to friends of his choosing. When David Oparowski died of lymphoma, Mitt Romney delivered the eulogy at his funeral.

The only trouble for the Romney campaign was that they had buried the Mormon testimonials out of prime time, and after Eastwood spoke, he, and not Romney's faith, became the story of the night.

9/11 GENERATION IS HIGHLIGHT
OF SPEECHES

Philadelphia Inquirer, Friday, September 16, 2011

WAS INVITED to deliver several 9/11 10th-anniversary speeches in the last two weeks. I accepted them all. Two stand out.

One week ago today, I spoke to nearly 3,000 students in two local suburban high schools. In the morning, I spoke to the entire student body of Central Bucks East in Buckingham, and in the afternoon, it was the entire student body of Central Bucks West in Doylestown.

The speeches came just after I'd completed a full week of guest-hosting for Chris Matthews on MSNBC's *Hardball*, and yet I found it more intimidating to speak to local high schoolers than go live on a national cable channel. I graduated from C.B. West in 1980. The thought of returning to my alma mater, as well as visiting our crosstown rival, was thrilling and daunting.

How do you say something meaningful about a day teenagers have heard a great deal about but only vaguely remember themselves? After all, the only current high school students you'd expect to have a clear recollection of 9/11 are those who were then in Sandra Kay Daniel's second-grade class at the Emma E. Booker Elementary School in Sarasota, Florida, with President George W. Bush when he got the news.

The early-morning program at C.B. East was marked by approbation and patriotism. Principal Kevin Shillingford choreographed a moving 90-minute presentation that featured students and local dignitaries. Red, white, and blue—the school colors—were everywhere. Many students were wearing "We remember" T-shirts that they'd been selling in support of the Garden of Reflection, Pennsylvania's official 9/11 tribute in Lower Makefield. Representative Mike Fitzpatrick (R., Pa.) delivered a video presentation. Grace Godshalk, who lost her son William in the twin towers, thanked the students for their concern. A steel artifact from ground zero was presented by an honor guard.

At both schools, I tried to deliver a message focused on the role of individuals on a day remembered for its enormity. I also wanted to highlight the way in which judgments made in a matter of seconds had monumental consequences.

At C.B. West, my remarks came at the end of the day when Principal Kevin Munnelly introduced me in the school's auditorium, which was packed with the 1,400-member student body. Football players anticipating a game that night against William Tennent were wearing their legendary black-and-gold jerseys.

The vibe was less formal than at C.B. East but no less respectful. Feet tapped and bodies swayed as two guitarists and a drummer warmed up the crowd, then played a stirring rendition of the national anthem. I asked Munnelly about his current crop of students and listened as he made a bragging reference to the wholesomeness of Lake Wobegon.

What I learned was that West students had something in common with their rivals at East. Each student body seemed eager to listen and learn about a seminal day in American history. They were respectful, reverential, and intellectually curious. All of which made me think about the difficult climate for both students and teachers. Too often both are underappreciated, while the aberrant get all the attention.

I was happy that John Marmor, my junior high school football coach, introduced me at C.B. East. It gave me the opportunity to tell him privately that I think about him often and now value the lessons he instilled many years ago—even if I didn't appreciate them at the time.

Unfortunately, at C.B. West, I did not realize until I was finished that Regina Wild, now Mrs. Franchois, was in the audience. She was my high school speech teacher more years ago than either of us cares to count, and I have never forgotten her advice about giving an address: Tell them what you are going to say, say it, and then tell them what you just told them. I've been following her advice for years. I hope I did so in her presence.

Mostly I keep thinking about the students. Too often we're quick to judge future generations based on things such as their use of social media. But looking at their faces, it occurred to me that the only thing that has changed is the technology.

Vice President Joe Biden spoke at the Pentagon on Sunday and referenced "an entire new generation of patriots—the 9/11 Generation."

Many of them were just kids on that bright September morning. But like their grandparents on December 7, 1941, they courageously bore the burden that history had placed on their shoulders. And as they came of age, they showed up—they showed up to fight for their country, and they're still showing up. Two million, eight hundred thousand of that 9/11 Generation moved to join our military since the attacks on 9/11, to finish the war begun here that day.

He's correct.

The kids are all right.

AFTERWORD

I do a great deal of public speaking all across the country, primarily through my affiliation with the Washington Speaker's Bureau. These are paid gigs. I've had many productive encounters with large groups that have engaged me for my analysis: business leaders in Orange County, California; government relations executives in New York City; the bar association in Erie, Pennsylvania; health care executives in Kansas; trial lawyers gathered in Montreal; farmers in Illinois; reinsurers in New Jersey. You name the type of group and, chances are, I have spoken to them. I generally enjoy the experience, and I never mail it in. I take each event seriously and try to be timely with my stories and commentary. But of all my speaking engagements, this column concerns the two that most stand out. And while my only payment for those appearances was personal satisfaction, in that regard I was overcompensated.

To return to my high school alma mater and our crosstown rival on the 10th anniversary of 9/11 was deeply moving. At each, I told the story of Jose Melendez-Perez, the immigration inspector who denied the presumed 20th hijacker admittance to the United States a month before 9/11 and spared the Capitol a strike that fateful day. I noted that he'd had only seconds to make a gut decision about Mohamed al Kahtani when he first saw him at the Orlando International Airport on August 4, 2001. And I cited other instances where a difference of seconds determined life or death on 9/11, like the actions of the passengers on Flight 93. And then I said:

> *The question now is what you will choose to do with the seconds, the minutes, the hours, the days, and years of your lives, to best honor those we lost on 9/11.*
>
> *We hope you will never be called upon to make split-second decisions like Mr. Perez, or Mark Bingham and the other passengers confronted aboard Flight 93.*
>
> *But choices will confront you. As students, you may view the future in terms of years and decades. But ultimately, those years and decades are simply made up of seconds.*
>
> *When you think about 9/11, consider how every one of those seconds counted. Realize that an individual's actions—and inactions—can at a moment's notice have serious consequences for yourself and others.*
>
> *And always make it your goal to maximize those chances you do have left. In so doing you will honor those we lost on 9/11.*

IT'S TIME TO BREAK THE MOLD
ON TALK RADIO

Philadelphia Inquirer, Sunday, September 18, 2011

O N FRIDAY, I delivered the keynote address at a convention of the National Association of Broadcasters in Chicago, the people who own, run, and program the nation's talk-radio stations. And unlike the spontaneity required to work in the business daily, this invitation afforded me plenty of time to plan what I wanted to say.

I started by tracing my career path back to the old WWDB-FM (96.5), where the lineup of talkers then included Irv Homer, Frank Ford, Dominic Quinn, and Bernie Herman. Back then, it wasn't necessary to have ideology in common. What these headliners shared were engaging personalities. "Evil" Irv was an acerbic libertarian. Ford was an unabashed liberal. Quinn was erudite and had an unparalleled command of the English language. And Herman was billed as the "gentleman of broadcasting."

Sid Mark, the Philadelphia broadcasting institution who is about to celebrate 55 years on the air, recalls delivering his own talk program immediately after Ford. "I was worried that I would have to pick up on a new topic that was outside my realm, and he would say, 'Don't worry, I will leave you a full board of callers,'" Mark told me. "In other words, I could continue a conversation but not with the same perspective. There was collegiality."

Gentlemanly? Collegial? I can't imagine either being a winning brand in today's climate, which was the issue I addressed at the NAB.

Media polarization based on a faux ideological and partisan divide is having a horrific effect on Washington, where collegiality used to be commonplace but is now kryptonite. Before, politicians raised a glass with one another at the end of the day. Today, they raise their voices as if they're on a perpetual split screen.

And they get rewarded for it by each party's respective base—in the form of campaign contributions and increasingly important primary-election support. The more doctrinaire the view, the more likely it will be encouraged with campaign funds and interview requests.

That individualism is dead in D.C. is not subject to debate. The *National Journal* recently detailed how Congress is more divided today than at any point in the last 30 years. Gone are the days when Jesse Helms of North Carolina and New York's Jacob Javits were both Senate Republicans.

Today, every Senate Republican is more conservative than every Senate

Democrat, and every Senate Democrat is more liberal than every Senate Republican. The elected middle has vanished.

There are many reasons for this, including the diminished role of seniority, which allows telegenic ideologues to rise to positions of power.

Gerrymandering robs us of competitive races, while closed primaries cater to each party's base, further isolating moderate voters.

But the media are also big contributors insofar as they give voice to the extremes while ignoring the middle. That's because the loyalty derived from partisan listeners (as well as viewers or readers) is thought to outweigh the benefits of seeking to expand the listening tent.

It's time to change that business model, I argued to the NAB. A *Wall Street Journal*–NBC News survey conducted at the end of August found that 40 percent of Americans said their general approach to issues is "moderate." Indeed, the only people whose politics align perfectly with the right- and left-wing litmus tests are those discussing current events on radio and cable television. In my experience, most people are conservative on some points, liberal on others, and haven't reached an opinion on the rest.

But you'd never know they exist from listening and watching the media today, which extend themselves not to the middle but to the extremes.

Delivering the keynote address to the National Association of Broadcasters in Chicago on September 16, 2011. Photo courtesy of the National Association of Broadcasters.

It's a vicious cycle that robs us of substantive dialogue at a time when it is desperately needed, and political deal-making has been replaced with deadlock. There are even fights over which night the president will speak to Congress.

Substance need not equal boredom. I did not ask the NAB membership to sacrifice their business objective—namely, attracting listeners. Rather, I asked the broadcast executives to allow hosts to build an audience without being compelled to construct a political clubhouse in which every member must agree on every issue. Provide a platform to entertaining, compelling voices that might not fit the current mold.

For the sake of your stations, and the nation.

AFTERWORD

I recently reread my speech to the NAB and realized that it's even timelier now than when I delivered it. Here are the key thoughts I offered that still stand up:

> *I'm suggesting that now is the time for us to chart a new path. To embrace a new model that can benefit both our industry and the nation.*
> *. . .*
> *I'm not asking nor recommending you sacrifice your business priorities—namely, attracting listeners and viewers.*
> *But that you give consideration to entertaining voices that can expand the tent.*
> *Sure, we need our P1s—but are we excluding a potentially larger market share?*
> *In so doing, not only might you grow your market share, but you will also affect the tone in Washington and hence the future of the country.*
> *We can really do our kids a favor.*

My time spent in Chicago to deliver the NAB keynote address to a gathering of talk radio leaders is memorable for several reasons. First, my audience was warm but afterward did not heed my advice to break out of the polarized approach to talk radio for the sake of both the industry and the national discourse.

Second, while in the Windy City, I had a nasty encounter with the president of my then syndicator, who had grown increasingly uncomfortable with my unwillingness to deliver a doctrinaire, conservative, ideologically driven program. We reached a breaking point a year later when I was afforded a 30-minute, one-

on-one interview in the Oval Office with President Barack Obama in the final days of his campaign against Mitt Romney. Rather than promoting that conversation, my syndicator sought to hide it from the very stations that were carrying my program, which provided impetus for me to finally (voluntarily) move my program to SiriusXM.

Third, ironically, at the same confab where I was delivering the keynote speech, I was nominated for a Marconi Award, the radio equivalent of an Emmy or Academy Award. I was nominated in the Best Network/Syndicated Host category. The other nominees were Bob and Sheri, Clark Howard, Laura Ingraham, and Ryan Seacrest. Seacrest won. Smerconish out!

LESSONS FROM THE CHEAP SEATS

Philadelphia Inquirer, Friday, January 27, 2012

I HAVEN'T BEEN INTERESTED in the 76ers since the run at the Lakers in 2001. However, despite lacking a superstar, this year's young, passionate team is off to a tremendous start in an abbreviated season.

Two weeks ago tonight, I had dinner at a restaurant on 9th Street in South Philadelphia with one of our sons, who shares my interest. As we ate, he used his phone to keep tabs on the Sixers' score. They were host to the Washington Wizards and were up 54–40 when the game reached halftime, just as I paid our dinner bill.

"Let's go watch the second half," I said as we reached our car. He thought I meant on television. Instead, 10 minutes later, I wheeled into the lot at the Wells Fargo Center. Our late arrival was about to reap some reward.

"I just closed my register," said a woman at the parking entrance. "Just park anywhere."

I figured there'd be somebody outside with tickets at a deep discount, but there was no one around. So we headed into the ticket office where the seats, unlike the parking, remained at full price.

"Just get the $15 seats," said my son. I told him that I could spend more, and we could sit downstairs. He objected. I admired his frugality and did as I was told.

So we rode the escalator up, found our seats, and settled in for the third quarter. The Sixers have been on a tremendous roll lately and were having another good night. The attendance, however, had yet to catch up with their box score. As they continue to win, that will surely change. But from our perch high above, we could see plenty of seats on the lower level.

"Do you want to sit downstairs for the final quarter?" I asked.

"I'm fine," was the abrupt reply.

"But look at all the room. We can just slide down late in the game."

"No, Dad, these are our seats," came the reply. So we stayed put until the final buzzer.

The Sixers won the game, 120–89. In fact, because they also scored more than 100 points, we were entitled to a pair of Big Macs the next day just for showing our ticket stubs.

What a great night: The company of a son. Good food. Free parking. Cheap seats. Sixers basketball. And lunch the next day.

But since then, I've been debating what my son's contentedness with sitting upstairs says about him, and what my offer to "slide" downstairs says about my parenting.

Of course, I'm proud that he wanted to honor his real seat location, because I'd like to think the decision revealed his moral compass. When I told this story on my radio program, a woman quickly called and said, "Get him to run for office." Ethics, after all, will play a large role in his future path.

True, but he will also need to "ask for the order." That's my way of describing a willingness to take some risks, push the envelope, be a bit aggressive and adventurous, so long as it is not at someone else's expense. Some have told me I should be embarrassed for having suggested that we move to a better location—for the record, I am not. (Maybe it's because I remember being a small boy and having my father push my brother and me through the turnstiles at Franklin Field holding only two tickets.) Besides, I was not asking my son to join me in displacing someone from their location—but rather, to watch the final few minutes in a better and vacant seat.

He would have none of it.

On this night, at least, he was more his mother's son: cautious, lacking envy, and uncomfortable at the thought of occupying something that was not his. Those traits are going to serve him well. But hopefully he's got a little of dad's chutzpah, too. Because to fulfill his potential, I'm convinced he'll need both.

By the way, the Sixers are host to the Charlotte Bobcats tonight. We'll be there, sitting on the lower level, which tonight are our assigned seats.

AFTERWORD

Later that same basketball season, I met and befriended the Sixers' then-CEO Adam Aron, and his wife, Abbe. When I first met Adam at a Sixers game, I was again accompanied by my eldest son. Adam, having read this column, was quick to needle me while complimenting my son for his decision to stick with the cheap seats for which we'd paid. He then invited us into the owner's box. This time, my son didn't object.

The following season the Sixers hired Sam Hinkie as the team's general manager, and so began "The Process." Hinkie's already gone, but we're still optimistic that the groundwork he laid will soon pay off, and by most accounts, at least one legitimate NBA star has already come of it. Aron, meanwhile, is now the CEO of AMC Entertainment. He and Abbe remain my friends.

BURSTING A CLASS BUBBLE

Philadelphia Inquirer, Friday, February 10, 2012

CHARLES MURRAY thinks I live in a bubble, and it worries him. He believes that people like me are influential but detached, and that the level of isolation in which we live jeopardizes the well-being of society.

When he looks at me, here is what he sees: Main Line home, Ivy League law degree, kids in private schools, a Stairmaster in my office, and no domestic beer in my fridge.

I tried to convince him that he is mistaken, highlighting that I grew up in Doylestown in a three-bedroom, one-bath home (with only a tub, no shower) on a quarter-acre lot. I worked at McDonald's when I was 16 and attended the Central Bucks public schools.

So we put the issue of my detachment to a quiz contained in his new book: *Coming Apart: The State of White America, 1960–2010*. He told me the quiz was designed to show members of the new upper class how isolated they are. The questions, he said, could be answered by ordinary Americans in a heartbeat. Here are a few:

Have you ever walked on a factory floor?
Who is Jimmie Johnson?
Have you or your spouse ever bought a pickup truck?
Since leaving school, have you ever worn a uniform?
Have you ever watched an Oprah, Dr. Phil, or Judge Judy show all the
    way through?

(My total score was a 42; 77 is a typical score for a lifelong resident of a working-class neighborhood.)

Murray, a libertarian affiliated with the American Enterprise Institute, is best known as the coauthor of *The Bell Curve: Intelligence and Class Structure in American Life*. His new book is equally provocative. The focus is on class formation, which Murray writes is "a new form of segregation." Murray argues that America is coming apart at the seams, not from race but from class, which is why he focused on whites in his book, despite believing that the trends do cross racial boundaries.

When he looks at America, Murray sees a divide between locales such as Belmont, Massachusetts, and Fishtown, in the Lower Northeast of Philadelphia. While he fictionalizes both locales, the elements on which he draws are accurate—just exaggerated. The upper-middle-class residents of Belmont still embody the virtues of our Founders, while the white, working-class in Fishtown are sliding down the socioeconomic ladder. A large part of the problem is that the people in Belmont are no longer connected to the residents of Fishtown, denying the latter a needed form of social order.

Marriage, work, and community are important constituents of a satisfying life, says Murray, but those institutions are collapsing in Fishtown. This week he told me:

> We've always had classes in the United States. There have always been rich and poor folks who had somewhat different customs and mores. But there used to be a lot of interchange and it used to be that even the rich folks had grown up as either poor or middle class and knew what it was like personally. All of that is changing big time. It's going to get worse.

The danger seen by Murray is that power is concentrated in the hands of the new upper class, which lacks the requisite empathy to make decisions for the remainder of society. Given the impact the new upper class has on the economy and culture, it would be a "good idea," he told me, if its members could empathize with the rest of the country.

Murray views this as a continuation of themes he wrote about in *The Bell Curve* 17 years ago, a book that created a flash point because of its treatment of race and intelligence. He said:

> Brains are worth a lot more in the marketplace than they used to be. So when you get to these divisions of wealth, it's not that somebody is stealing money but that it is worth more to have a lot of ability in certain kinds of intellectual areas than it was 50, 60 years ago, and that's going to continue. And as that happens, you get development of what I call super zips—very affluent, extremely well-educated zip codes in which pretty much everybody is alike.

But his biggest concern is not my contemporaries. It's their children, who he believes are being raised completely detached from a society that they are being groomed to lead.

I asked him, sight unseen, to describe my bubble. He told me that the people who live around me don't watch TV like the rest of the country ("Some brag they don't even have a TV or use it only to watch videos or DVDs"), are more concerned about their weight, have different dietary and child-rearing practices, and bear very little relationship to mainstream Americans.

Sounds as if he just stepped off the R5.

AFTERWORD

Four years before the 2016 presidential race, this was my wake-up call. Too bad I missed it. I was dismissive of Donald Trump's campaign from start to finish. I never thought he'd run. After he announced, I thought he'd never file the requisite financial disclosures with the Federal Election Commission. I was certain his appalling comments about John McCain as a POW would sink him. I believed his proposed Mexican wall would crush him with Hispanics. I figured his "blood coming out of her wherever" comment about Megyn Kelly would ruin him with women. (And when it didn't, that the Access Hollywood Bush tape certainly would.) I believed that Hillary Clinton beat him in at least two of three debates. And despite his jumping all those hurdles, I still thought he'd tap out at about 240 electoral votes in a best-case scenario.

Had I thought more about Murray's book in a political context, I would have better anticipated the educational divide that defined the 2016 presidential election. Here's something to think about that tracks Murray's analysis, and I give credit to David Wasserman at the Cook Political Report *for the legwork. It's the Cracker Barrel versus Whole Foods way of viewing the 2016 race. And the statistics from this viewpoint are telling.*

The nation has roughly 3,100 counties. As of the 2016 election, there were 412 Whole Foods spread out in 184 counties, and 642 Cracker Barrels, located in 484 counties. They overlap in only about 90 counties, so they clearly build in different areas to reach different demographics. I'm convinced they take political data into account when they decide where to build. There is one of each in Plymouth Meeting, Pennsylvania, close to where I live, in Montgomery County. If you live in close proximity to both as I do, chances are you live in a swing area, like the Philly burbs.

Well, in the 2016 presidential race, Donald Trump won 76 percent of counties with a Cracker Barrel, and only 22 percent of counties with a Whole Foods—a 54 percent gap. In 1992, when Bill Clinton beat George H. W. Bush, the gap between the same counties was just 19 percent. It has grown steadily since the 1992 election, but the 2016 race represented the largest jump between two presidential races. Hillary Clinton surely paid a price for figuratively campaigning in Whole Foods Nation to the detriment of Cracker Barrel Country. And I'm sure Charles Murray would say that too many Americans who regularly patronize Whole Paycheck, er, I mean Whole Foods, need to spend more time eating at Cracker Barrel.

A SHATTERED SPIRIT

Philadelphia Inquirer, Sunday, June 3, 2012

I 'M ALBERT MILEY and I'm from Warminster, Pennsylvania I want you to contact my attorney Geofrey Fieger."

So read the note pinned on "Buddy" Miley by his younger brother Jimmy when Buddy was left in the care of a physician. But this was no hospital or medical office. It was Room 146 of the Quality Inn in Livonia, Michigan. And there was no insurance co-pay, just the payment of $46. And the physician was Jack Kevorkian.

Buddy Miley, 41, went to Michigan to die. By the time he got to Kevorkian, Miley had been suffering for 23½ years, significantly longer than the 17 he'd enjoyed while able to move his limbs.

On an overcast Saturday afternoon in September 1973, Miley, a standout quarterback for William Tennent High, was injured while running what had seemed like a routine option play. Tennent was playing a Suburban One League game at Plymouth-Whitemarsh. Miley, standing 6-foot-2 and weighing 170 pounds, gained a few yards before sustaining a blow that would leave him incapacitated. He suffered severe damage at C4/C5 of his vertebrae, or, in the vernacular of the time, he broke his neck.

Miley was initially the recipient of an overwhelming outpouring of sympathy. Eagles quarterback Roman Gabriel visited in the hospital. Eagles general manager Jimmy Murray arranged for a "hug on the telephone" from the quarterback Roger Staubach. Joe Namath, whom Miley idolized, sent signed memorabilia. Dallas coach Tom Landry visited the family home. Alan Ameche, a Heisman Trophy winner, sent Miley's parents on a Caribbean vacation.

But time moved slowly for Miley, who was in constant pain and required full care while living with his parents. His debilitating condition placed his large, tight-knit family under a tremendous burden, particularly his mother, Rosemarie. Nearly two decades after the accident, her frustration was evident in a letter she penned to *Sports Illustrated.* It began: "My son broke his neck 19 years ago playing high school football. Since then, our home has been hell on earth."

That's when Miley's plight became known to Mark Kram Jr., a reporter at the *Philadelphia Daily News,* who wrote a newspaper cover story titled "19 Years of Hell."

Kram now has meticulously charted the entire Miley tragedy in a new book called *Like Any Normal Day*. The result is a poignant account of family love and brotherly devotion. As Kram writes, the trip to Michigan was not the first taken together by Buddy and Jimmy. They'd previously flown to the shrine at Lourdes, France, in a "Hail Mary" bid for healing. The book also introduces us to Karen Kollmeyer, who would have had a first date with Buddy the night of the accident. While over the years their relationship ebbed and flowed, it was Karen whom Buddy talked to by phone while at the hotel awaiting Kevorkian.

Not long after that telephone farewell, there was a knock on the door, and in walked Dr. Death, wearing a black hat and dark glasses, and accompanied by two associates.

"So you're the celebrity?" Kevorkian said to Miley in recognition of Kram's *Daily News* cover story, which had been sent to him. And then, while his associates prepared Buddy to die, Kevorkian went into the hotel bathroom to prepare his lethal concoction. He emerged minutes later with a homemade device he called the Thanatron, which consisted of three glass bottles on a small frame, with a button that Buddy could use to hasten his own death while lying on the hotel bed.

It was now time for Jimmy to leave his older brother and fly home to Philadelphia.

Later than night, at the Miley family home on Acorn Drive in Warminster, Buddy's parents and siblings gathered to mourn while fearing the unknown. Would Jimmy get in trouble? Would the cops show up and lead him off in handcuffs? Thankfully, neither occurred.

As for Kevorkian, he died one year ago today after having been hospitalized for pneumonia and a kidney-related ailment. He was 83. Published accounts said that the music of Johann Sebastian Bach was played for him at the William Beaumont Hospital in Royal Oak, Michigan, so he could hear the music he loved as he was dying.

That sounds like health insurance. Hospital linens. Balloon deliveries. Balanced meals. The company of loved ones. Skilled practitioners. Familiar walls. Facing death with comfort.

Too bad our laws didn't, and still would not, permit Buddy Miley that level of dignity instead of a roadside hotel in the company of strangers. At least he had the best of brothers in Jimmy.

AFTERWORD

Mark Kram Jr. wrote an important book about dignity and death but also about brotherly love. The latter sounds like a cliché but that's really what he captured by recounting the story of Buddy and Jimmy. I was eager to encapsulate what he'd written for my column readers, but I don't recall why I didn't also offer my two degrees of separation to Buddy Miley. His injury occurred in 1973, when I was 11 and growing up a community away in Doylestown, Pennsylvania. In those days, the War Memorial Field stadium at my future high school, Central Bucks West, would be filled to a 10,000-person capacity every Thanksgiving Day, when "West" would play its crosstown rival, Central Bucks East. This really was our community at worship. The game was played in late morning to avoid interrupting family meals later in the day, and everyone in town turned out. Then, West was a powerhouse, and East, which opened in 1969, would wait until 1980—my senior year in high school—to win its first Thanksgiving classic.

Moments before one of those glorious, Rockwellian Thanksgiving days when I was a boy, I have clear recollection of Buddy Miley being wheeled onto the field to thunderous applause. He was from a neighboring town, but all the attendees, including the kids, knew his name and story. Many years passed before I'd hear his name again, in 1997, in stories about his death at the hands of Dr. Kevorkian. And so, when Kram wrote his book, I was naturally interested to learn the full history of the young man whom I, as a young boy, saw receiving that ovation. I played football (as did my brother) on the same field they wheeled Miley on that day in the early 1970s and today I can't help thinking, "There but for the grace of God go I." What a shame that later in life, when he'd had enough, there was nowhere for him to turn but to Dr. Kervorkian in a roadside Quality Inn.

WARREN'S SHAKY HISTORY

Philadelphia Inquirer, Sunday, June 10, 2012

ELIZABETH WARREN, the Democratic candidate for U.S. Senate in what is arguably the second-hottest race in the nation, Massachusetts's, was the recipient of a Lindback Award at the University of Pennsylvania in 1994. The awards, established in the name of the onetime president and principal owner of Abbotts Dairies, recognize distinguished teaching at Penn.

Warren's recognition was noted in a 2005 "Minority Equity Report." The document (still accessible online) was prepared by the Minority Equity Committee at Penn, which was established to "undertake a systematic review of the status of minority faculty at the university." Table 11 of the report lists the names of the 112 Lindback Award recipients from 1991 through 2004, eight of which appear in boldface italics.

Three of those professors are African American. Three are Asian. One is Puerto Rican. And then there is Elizabeth Warren, William A. Schnader Professor of Commercial Law.

That Warren's name appeared in bold and italics designated her as a minority, just like the African American, Asian, and Puerto Rican Lindback recipients.

Did Warren derive professional benefits from describing herself as a minority while she was at Penn and Harvard? That question continues to dog her candidacy. Her difficulty answering it has made it much more than the speed bump it might have been on a fast track to the seat once held by Edward M. Kennedy.

For nine years, while she was teaching at the University of Texas and Penn, Warren also listed herself as a minority in the Association of American Law Schools' directory. Who provides such information to the academic reference? The faculty members themselves.

Warren only stopped listing herself as such in 1995, just after she was hired by Harvard. But while she was at Harvard, the *Crimson* newspaper reported that the university's faculty included one Native American: Warren. And when she received tenure there, another *Crimson* story said she was the first woman with a minority background to receive tenure.

All of which would be well and good if Warren could substantiate her claim of Native American ancestry, which is a federal requirement when universities report diversity data. Thus far, she has not, and by her own admission, her connection to American Indians is remote.

Ever since this issue was raised by the *Boston Herald* in April, Warren has stumbled in her efforts to explain her claims of minority status. She initially sought to minimize the controversy by saying she had merely hoped "that I'd get invited to some lunch group or some—maybe some dinner conversation, and I might find some more people like me . . . people for whom Native American is part of their heritage and part of their hearts." That didn't silence the questions.

Finally, after five weeks of trying to dodge the matter, Warren sought to quell the controversy with an e-mail to supporters that read, in part:

> The people involved in recruiting and hiring me for my teaching jobs, including Charles Fried—solicitor-general under Ronald Reagan who has publicly said he voted for Scott Brown in 2010—have said unequivocally they were not aware of my heritage and that it played no role in my hiring. Documents that reporters have examined also show I did not benefit from my heritage when applying to college or law school. As I have confirmed before, I let people know about my Native American heritage in a national directory of law school personnel. At some point after I was hired by them, I also provided that information to the University of Pennsylvania and Harvard. My Native American heritage is part of who I am, I'm proud of it and I have been open about it.

In a subsequent conversation with the *Boston Globe*'s Brian McGrory, Warren insisted that the Harvard and Penn law schools hired her because of her scholarship and teaching abilities, not to increase the diversity of their faculties. She says she told the law schools she was Native American after she was hired. But she has not asked the schools to release hiring records that might substantiate her claim.

That her opponent, Republican senator Scott Brown, has kept up the pressure is no surprise.

"This goes right to the integrity and character of a person," Brown has said. "When you check that box, you're getting benefits [for] people who have historically been discriminated against."

He raises a legitimate point. The silence thus far from those minorities who are the intended beneficiaries of affirmative action is curious. If and when they demand to know whether Warren played the Native American card inappropriately, this issue could go from curiosity to deal-breaker.

AFTERWORD

I suspect I'm dead to Senator Warren for having written this column. Not long after CNN debuted my program on Saturday mornings, an acquaintance of my wife's reached out to me and (unsolicited) offered to put me together with Senator Warren. The intermediary was a woman with impressive credentials who had worked in a senior advisory capacity to Warren. "Are you interested in paying a call on her on Capitol Hill, and maybe doing an interview?" Of course. I remember that I tried to follow up, as did my producer, TC. But nothing ever came of the overture. I'm sure it was because someone on the senator's staff put both our names in a search engine and found this column.

I have great respect for Warren's intelligence and abilities as a retail politician, although I'm not convinced her progressivism can be sold nationally. Time will tell. Go on YouTube and watch her 2011 seemingly spontaneous "You didn't build it" speech at what looks like a coffee klatch in Andover, Massachusetts, and you can't help being impressed by her ability to communicate on her feet. In fact, when President Barack Obama tried to replicate that mantra during his 2012 campaign, he couldn't, not even working with a script. So she has some real, raw political talent, honed, I am sure, in Ivy League law school classrooms using the Socratic teaching method.

But this aspect of her resumé about which I wrote remains a blemish. She held herself out and was recognized as being a minority faculty member. Until and unless her employment files are released, I think it's fair to assume she made her "minority" status known to the schools at the time of her hire. Is this a deal breaker to her advancement? Only if minority groups to whom her identification could have been detrimental make it an issue—not just conservative outlets.

By the way, we tried to book Warren for my SiriusXM and CNN programs when she was in the midst of a publicity tour for her 2017 book, This Fight Is Our Fight. *No luck. As I said, dead.*

ZEPPELIN COMMUNICATION
BREAKDOWN

Philadelphia Inquirer, **Sunday, November 25, 2012**

DAVID PETRAEUS, Lance Armstrong, Led Zeppelin: All my heroes are falling.

The first two have gotten enough attention, so let me tell you a story about the third.

Led Zeppelin will be recognized with a lifetime achievement award from the Kennedy Center for the Performing Arts next weekend, which comes on the heels of the band's new concert movie, *Celebration Day.* The film was recorded in 2007, when the band reunited for its first headline show, a tribute to Atlantic Records founder Ahmet Ertegun. Eighteen thousand lucky fans saw the performance at London's O2 Arena; 20 million other requests for tickets were denied.

Zeppelin was one of those bands whose liner notes I studied in my suburban bedroom in the '70s. But I never got to see them perform before their career was cut short by the death of drummer John Bonham in 1980. That's why I was elated when they reunited five years ago, with Bonham's son Jason playing in his stead, amid talk that a tour would ensue. But the tour never happened.

So the closest I've ever gotten to the band was last month, when I attended the premiere of *Celebration Day* at the Museum of Modern Art in Manhattan. The screening was followed by a news conference with the band: Robert Plant, Jimmy Page, John Paul Jones, and Jason Bonham.

A journalist a few rows in front of me asked the band about rehearsing for six weeks to play just one concert. It struck me as a circuitous way of asking about the possible tour that was on everyone's mind, and there were a few murmurs in the audience suggesting that the reporter had identified the elephant in the room. But the band reacted as if he had told the emperor he had no clothes. The only answer came from lead singer Plant, who called the reporter a "schmuck." It didn't sound as if he was kidding.

A question or two later, I tried to introduce a little levity by saying I wanted to follow up on the question asked by the "schmuck." (No one laughed.) I then congratulated the band on the release of the movie, which I said was terrific. I was very reverent. "But," I said, I doubted it would "quench the thirst" of fans who want to see Led Zeppelin "in the flesh."

In response, one of my heroes started making a snoring noise. The rest sat in stony silence. Plant glared at me. Finally, after a few pregnant moments, John Paul Jones said softly, "Sorry." They hadn't refused to answer the question so much as they'd been completely dismissive of it.

I sat down a bit chagrined, though I was heartened when a reporter from CNN followed up on my question, as did the legendary classic rock DJ Carol Miller. (Neither got more of an answer.) And there was further proof that this was the most important question in the room, when both *Rolling Stone* and the *New York Times* focused on it in writing about the movie launch.

Leaving the news conference, I asked my field producer, Paul Lauricella, what had just happened. "Wow," he said. "Their contempt for that question was palpable. Shouldn't they be grateful we still care about them? Shouldn't they be dragging their 60-year-old butts on stage before Jason Bonham has grandchildren?"

Former Philadelphia DJ Denny Somach, the author of *Get the Led Out: How Led Zeppelin Became the Biggest Band in the World*, was also in the room. I later asked him whether he thought the band had played its last live show.

"I don't think they have," he said. "I think they are looking at what the Rolling Stones are doing—playing multiple dates in a few cities. I know for a fact that Jimmy [Page] is sitting at home playing his guitar and waiting for Robert to call."

If Somach is right, the band might indeed give the public what it wants. Just don't ask them about it unless you want to be treated like a schmuck.

Nobody withstands scrutiny anymore—generals, athletes, rock stars. Maybe they never could. Maybe it's time to stop scrutinizing them and just appreciate their talents.

AFTERWORD

In October 2014, "Liberal Paul" Lauricella and I returned to Manhattan for another Zeppelin-inspired event. It was Paul's birthday and I took him to a New York Times "TimesTalk" featuring Robert Plant. I'd been to a few TimesTalks, and they are a terrific opportunity to get up close to cultural icons in a beautiful setting inside the Times Building on 41st Street. (I once saw the entire cast of Breaking Bad *with another friend, Greg Stocker, one memorable night in this same setting.)*

Plant had recently released the album Lullaby and . . . The Ceaseless Roar *and was interviewed by the* Times's *chief pop music critic, John Pareles, in front of a live audience of about 300 people. Well, Pareles didn't have the temerity to ask Plant about a possible Led Zeppelin reunion even though it was on every-one's mind. And when the audience was invited to ask questions, it looked as though none of us was going to confront the elephant in the room, either. Having been famously smacked down by the entire band as noted in this column, I had no interest in moving from my seat. But then, the final questioner, a fan who looked about 13 years old, indelicately did what all the adults were afraid to do, asking Plant, "What is your relationship with Jimmy Page and will you ever perform with him?"*

Surprisingly, Plant didn't seem agitated by this young fan and gave a thoughtful answer, as well as a little advice and encouragement. He said things like "You haven't felt this yet, but you might like somebody today and it might be difficult later on down the line" and "Very good question—and you brought the house down. Well done. . . . Nobody we knew asked you to say that, did they?"

It was the lecture equivalent of Plant finishing the evening with "Stairway."

By the way, if you want to watch me ask the band about reuniting, as described in the original column, you can view it here: youtube.com/watch?v=fpa-Zbt7Nqw.

THE TEACHER WHO
OPENED A MIND

Philadelphia Inquirer, Sunday, June 9, 2013

IT'S THE TIME OF YEAR when our attention turns to graduates and their commencement speakers. But at a lunch with a friend last Friday, our conversation was about the often unacknowledged: the teachers for whom we're grateful.

I said that I'd been fortunate. My list is long, a product of a sound, K-12 education in the Central Bucks public schools, followed by four years at Lehigh University and three more at Penn Law. There are so many to whom I owe so much. But one in particular.

David Curtis Amidon Jr.

Truth be told, I was admitted to Lehigh as a legacy by virtue of my father and brother having received degrees before me. Before I arrived on campus, a fraternity brother (of my own brother) recommended that I use an elective to "take anything" taught by Professor Amidon. So sound was the advice that I ended up taking a course with him every single semester—eight different enrollments. I've never read so much nor thought so deeply.

Professor Amidon's reading list was enough to bankrupt you in the university bookstore. It was nothing for him to require the reading of a half-dozen books per semester. The payoff for me came in the form of an academic awakening. My subpar SATs were forgotten when, four years later, I graduated Phi Beta Kappa, largely due to his tutelage, and was accepted at an Ivy League law school.

What I didn't tell my friend at lunch is that a few years had passed since I'd spoken to my mentor. So I called him that very afternoon and learned from his wife, Ann, that she'd been meaning to reach out to me. Professor Amidon is recovering from a stroke and is also dealing with the debilitating effects of diabetes at a rehab facility in the Lehigh Valley.

Last Saturday I visited unannounced.

Amidon will soon be 78. Despite the physical setbacks, his mind remains razor-sharp. I turned down the Fox News in his room so that we could have a political conversation of our own, and took note of the loss of his trademark beard. He'd always looked like Marx while speaking like Lincoln.

The first sign that he hadn't missed a beat came when an orderly walked into the room to check on him. My professor introduced the man to me by name, adding that he hailed from Cameroon and was desirous of being a doctor. That's pure Amidon.

See, the first day of class was always a treat. He'd slide his finger down the roster and proceed to tell each student more about their ethnicity and hometown than any of us knew ourselves. This was pre-Google. He could do that just by studying a surname. Ethnicity and genealogy mattered to him, and his interest was infectious. He was such a revered figure at Lehigh that they created a special platform—the Department of Urban Studies—consisting of one faculty member, him. And when he retired in 2008, after more than 40 years of instruction, so too did the department.

I used to access his office after hours, in Room 358 of Chandler-Ullmann Hall (circa 1883), via a rickety wooden stair, to find him always ensconced amid his books, which were stuffed floor to ceiling, each acting as a sponge for the aroma of his cigars.

But class is where he shone. Actually, "professor" doesn't fully describe him. He was a "lecturer" in the finest sense of the word. And each hour-long assemblage was a command performance. Thirty years later I can still recall the registrar's numbered listing of his courses, such as "US 363," which was a class called "Philadelphia: Development of a Metropolis." This was no recap of our Founding Fathers. We read George Lippard's 1844 novel, *The Monks and Monk Hall* (582 pages!), and E. Digby Baltzell's *Philadelphia Gentlemen*, among others.

And a class trip via a van he drove one Saturday morning bypassed the Betsy Ross House and Liberty Bell in favor of a stop at Laurel Hill Cemetery to read tombstones of prominent Philadelphia families. Lunch was at the Famous 4th Street Delicatessen, where, in a second-floor room, proprietor David Auspitz was our guest lecturer about the city's modern political scene. (My later friendship with Auspitz is something else for which I thank Amidon.)

"I feel like a spectator now," Amidon said from his hospital bed last Saturday. "I can't stir things up the way I used to."

He'd done plenty of that. Amidon himself had a personal political transformation from a Frisbee-throwing '60s leftist to a 1980s conservative. I knew him only in the latter stage. In a freshman seminar ("Paleo and Neo Conservatives"), he had us reading William F. Buckley's *God and Man at Yale* and George Gilder's *Wealth and Poverty* while studying the Laffer curve. I know we haven't voted the same way in the last two presidential elections and told him I suspected that disappointed him. He would hear none of it.

"I'm disappointed that you would think I would be disappointed," he assured me.

We had a few laughs, shared our concerns about Syria, and found common ground in the foreign-policy edicts of Ron Paul. Both of us fear foreign entanglements and worry that our interventions make us less safe.

Amidon was secretary of the Lehigh faculty when I graduated in 1984, and in that role, he signed my diploma. How appropriate.

"This was a lift," he said when, after more than an hour, I stood to leave. He was speaking for both of us.

AFTERWORD

Sadly, Professor Amidon passed on September 23, 2016, at age 81. When Lehigh distributed word of Amidon's passing, an alumni publication noted that, in 1977, he'd been recognized with the university's Stabler Award for excellence in teaching and how his out-of-the-way office "overflowed with books and often with students who came to arrange files or to ask advice on school, career and life."

I enjoyed sharing memories of him with his wife, Ann, and his four children at a luncheon/reception held after his funeral service at the Hotel Bethlehem, not far from the Lehigh campus. Many in attendance told me they remembered the column and when an open mic was made available for mourners to share memories, I went first and was pleased to read it aloud. Several of the other speakers did a tremendous job eulogizing Professor Amidon with fond remembrances and humor. I particularly liked the story a Methodist minister named Barbara Lee shared. She'd enrolled in one of Amidon's freshman seminars not knowing of his conservative political bent. After two lectures, she felt compelled to seek him out to voice her displeasure. "By then he had offended all of my feminist sensibilities," she said. After patiently listening to her ideological complaints, Amidon responded simply, "You've been duped." A conversation ensued, and before she left his company, she'd been offered a job in his office—and she accepted. "I haven't changed my opinions, but I've had to think about things more deeply," she told the crowd, many of whom nodded in acknowledgment.

When I noted his passing via social media, I received many warm responses. One stands out: "@jenylnham We've lost an icon @LehighAlumni. In memoriam: David C. Amidon, Lehigh urban legend." He'd have liked that—the one-man Department of Urban Studies was indeed an urban legend.

UNPAID BUT RICHLY REWARDING

Philadelphia Inquirer, Sunday, June 23, 2013

WHEN A FEDERAL JUDGE sided recently with two unpaid interns who later sought compensation, he worsened an already bleak employment picture for young Americans.

U.S. district judge William H. Pauley III ruled in favor of two men who worked on the movie *Black Swan* and then sued Fox Searchlight Pictures for wages. He ruled that it wasn't enough that the two interns received some benefits, "such as resumé listings, job references, and an understanding of how a production office works," because "those benefits were incidental to working in the office like any other employee and were not the result of internships intentionally structured to benefit them."

His decision came just as the U.S. Bureau of Labor Statistics reported that teen unemployment was at 24.5 percent in May, more than triple the national jobless rate. Teens are competing with young adults in a search for full-time jobs, and if Pauley's decision eliminates unpaid internships, there will be fewer unpaid opportunities for those who can't find paid summer positions.

That would be a shame for the likes of Joshua Belfer, Benjamin Haney, Alexandra Smith, Anthony Mazzarelli, and other talented people who have interned for me over the years without pay.

Pauley might accuse me of violating child-labor laws given that Josh first worked for me when he was entering ninth grade at what is now Barrack Hebrew Academy, née Akiba. His father used to drop him off at my radio studio or sometimes wait in the car. I knew immediately that Josh was wise and mature beyond his years. In no time, I had him archiving old radio shows and fact checking newspaper columns.

We were together six years, giving me plenty of fodder to write my most sincere recommendation ever when he applied to Penn, from where he has since graduated and gone on to Robert Wood Johnson Medical School.

Now Josh worries that forcing companies to pay all their interns could rob others of opportunities like the one he had. He told me:

I highly doubt you would have brought me on as a high school freshman if you were forced to pay me. It would've made no sense. And thus I would have not received one of the best learning experiences of my life.

He's right: I could not have paid him—in which case we would both have missed out.

Ben Haney agrees. Ben came to me after graduating from St. Joe's Prep and stayed two summers while attending Notre Dame. He's smart, ethical, and earnest.

When Ronald Reagan lay in state at the Capitol, Ben jumped in his car and drove down I-95 to pay his respects, providing my radio audience and me with reports all along. Today he's a real estate developer and part owner of Mac's Tavern in Old City. In his spare time, he does advance work for GOP candidates. I'm hoping he'll run for office.

Like Josh, he finds the ruling ridiculous. He said:

> A lot of the relationships I've made in business and politics exist be-cause of connections I made during the internship. In nearly every situation I encounter, I draw on my experiences.

Alexandra Smith told me she has mixed feelings about the recent ruling. Just two weeks ago, I was thrilled to see her chatting with Bill O'Reilly on television as the chairwoman of the College Republican National Commit-tee. Years ago, she was invaluable to me when I was writing a book. She said to me:

> You allowed me to participate in meetings and tasks I'm not even sure I would entrust to someone my age today. You bet big on my compe-tence and abilities as a teenager, and it became my number-one prior-ity to try to exceed your expectations every time.

Alex knows a thing or two about internships: She worked in nine of them during four years at Catholic University. She said:

> In the course of eight semesters and three summers, I only took two internships that were unpaid, because I felt that their value far out-weighed whatever small compensation I could receive elsewhere. Still, both of these internships were tough decisions for me financially. I had to plan far in advance in terms of my own personal savings and con-tributions from family to make them happen.

Then there's "Mazz." Anthony Mazzarelli is the senior vice president of operations and deputy chief medical officer at Cooper University Health

Care. But back in 2000, he was a 25-year-old medical student at Robert Wood Johnson and a law student at Penn. He wanted to intern in my law practice. I wanted him involved in radio. Our compromise? Both. Like the others, he has many memories.

> I remember the first time you had me on the air. There was a press conference about a local fire department that was getting heat for having a woman pose on a fire truck. I went to the press conference with my school backpack but asked questions along with the press corps. You were very happy with me because my questions cornered the guy a bit, and I remember the pride you had in me for pulling it off. I was hooked at that point.

Josh, Ben, Alex, and Mazz all told me they were grateful, but I was quick to disabuse them of any notion that I'm responsible for their success. After all, they came to me unsolicited, as strangers. My role was simply to channel their ambition and compensate them with the currency of experience. That served us all well.

When I asked Mazz to remind me of the span of his internship, he quickly e-mailed:

> I started in the fall of 2000 or the spring of 2001. . . . As far as an end date, does it ever end? . . . None of your former interns will ever stop being your interns, nor will you stop mentoring them.

True—but now as friends and equals.

AFTERWORD

I've changed my mind. A year after publishing this column, I rethought the issue and decided to start paying my interns. No one is getting rich working for me (what I pay is more beer money than salary), but it no longer felt right to have students spend weeks or months working for experience alone. Maybe I was shamed into my about-face. One of our sons worked one summer in Hollywood for the legendary television producer Mike Robin on the set of Major Crimes, *and even though my son offered to work for free, the show paid him, providing him with a greater sense of self-worth. My radio studio is a skeletal operation consisting of just the producer, TC, and me, and while it costs the show a few bucks, I like the new order. I find that the interns now feel better about their contribution, and I like the added responsibility that's imposed by a paid arrangement. I no longer feel that I'm asking for a favor when I give an assignment; instead, I'm handing someone a task for which I have a certain (high) expectation. Don't misunderstand, I'm not advocating for any hard-and-fast rule when it comes to paying interns. I'm sure there are many situations where experience is the only form of payment available, but my small shop is not one of them.*

PENNSBURY GRAD
MAKES A SPLASH IN D.C.

Philadelphia Inquirer, Sunday, October 27, 2013

W HEN IN THE MIDST of the government shutdown President Barack Obama decided to summon leading conservative journalists to an off-the-record White House meeting, he gathered the usual suspects: Fox News contributor and syndicated columnist Charles Krauthammer, syndicated columnist Kathleen Parker, *Washington Examiner* columnist Byron York, and Paul Gigot, editorial page editor of the *Wall Street Journal*. And sitting directly to the president's right in the Roosevelt Room for the 90-minute exchange was a 27-year-old Bucks County native, Robert Costa.

Costa is Washington editor of the *National Review* and a contributor to CNBC. But just 10 years ago, he was a suburban public school class president and architect of one our area's most celebrated rites of passage: the Pennsbury prom. Recently he explained to me:

> So many proms today become these almost antiseptic affairs in a hotel ballroom and just kind of bland and boring and corporate, but Pennsbury has it in the gym, and this school has been around since the '60s. A lot of people joke it looks like a prison, but it's our prison, and in Levittown, Pennsylvania, the whole community comes together and puts up posters and puts up decorations and makes the whole school transform.

So rich is the tradition that *Sports Illustrated* senior writer Michael Bamberger used the event as the backdrop for his 2004 *American Graffiti*-esque work of nonfiction: *Wonderland: A Year in the Life of an American High School*. And Costa, who as junior class president was charged with coordinating the senior prom, was one of Bamberger's favorite subjects.

Wonderland is replete with Costa tales of ambition, ranging from his pursuit of John Mayer to perform at the prom to corralling a parking space at school despite his lack of both car and license. Ten years ago, Bamberger wrote of Costa that he was "well-connected and unusually sharp. . . . He always seemed a step ahead of everybody else." Today, they're saying the same thing on Capitol Hill. Last week Bamberger told me:

Bob was a force of nature then, and remains so. But you'd never know it, so unassuming is he. Bob is everything I think a reporter should be, most notably a good listener. I don't think of him as a "conservative journalist." I think of him as a good reporter. One who could wind up doing anything.

Costa, a music aficionado, began his journalism career writing reviews of local concerts for the *Bucks County Courier Times*. By day, he would read daily announcements over the PA system and appear on student-run television (PHS-TV). By night, he would attend shows in the Philadelphia area. When his attempts at landing Mayer for the 2003 prom didn't pan out, he "settled" for Mayer's then opening act, Maroon 5. The Los Angeles band was just on the cusp of national stardom.

Post-Pennsbury, Costa attended Notre Dame, where he ran the school TV station and wrote for the campus newspaper. He then landed a fellowship at the *Wall Street Journal* editorial page before leaving for Cambridge, where he obtained a master's degree studying Winston Churchill.

After Cambridge, it was the *National Review*, where he has worked for the past four years. In high school, he might have been voted least likely to end up working for a leading conservative outlet.

In *Wonderland*, Bamberger recounts how Costa traveled to Ed Rendell's inauguration in Harrisburg amid a busload of Revolutionary War reenactors, whereupon he buttonholed the new governor and offered his own blessing: "Make us proud, Ed." But his real hero, wrote Bamberger, was President Bill Clinton, whom Costa traveled to Trenton to meet the day after the prom, using his PHS-TV press credential for admittance.

"Mr. President, I'm Bob Costa from Pennsbury High," he said, adding, "I'm a young Democrat." To which the president replied, "That's what you should be."

Costa told me recently the prospect of his classmates going off to war in Iraq and Afghanistan affected his views.

"That experience unsettled me," he said, "and for a few years, my politics drifted to the left."

Costa credits Representative Mike Fitzpatrick (R., Pa.), for whom he interned when Fitzpatrick was a county commissioner, with his interest in conservatism and registration as a Republican. He said:

These days, I'm a reporter first and last, and keep my opinions to myself. I don't have an agenda. Temperamentally and personally, sure,

I'm conservative. But that's not what drives me. I love covering politics and talking politics, and I'm happy to leave the editorializing to the columnists and bloggers.

When Obama was sworn in for his second term in January, Costa was in the front row, sporting a *National Review* credential. Nearby? None other than John Mayer, on the arm of Katy Perry. Costa was quick to reintroduce himself to the music superstar as "Bob Costa, Pennsbury High."

See, though Costa's efforts to land Mayer at Pennsbury in his junior year hadn't panned out, he did persuade Mayer to play at his senior prom the following year.

Which explains Mayer's response at the inauguration: "I'm not surprised to see you here."

Neither, I'm sure, is anyone from Pennsbury High, Class of 2004.

AFTERWORD

I didn't put it in the initial column, but I get a real kick out of the fact that, according to Costa, his father used to drive him to school listening to me doing morning radio in Philadelphia, before syndication and SiriusXM. I'd like to think that some of his appetite for current-events discourse was shaped on those rides. Since I wrote this column, he has left the National Review *and joined the* Washington Post. *He also makes frequent television appearances through his affiliations with NBC and MSNBC and is a regular on* Meet the Press. *Today, Robert Costa is one of the most influential political journalists in America, as evidenced by the role he played in the 2016 presidential race.*

Costa's name was in the byline of any number of front-page stories for the Post *that evidenced his unparalleled access to the critical players. Two months out from Election Day, on September 15, he wrote a prominent story revealing that Donald Trump remained "unwilling to say that President Obama was born in the United States." This revelation came in an interview Costa conducted aboard Trump's private jet while it idled on a tarmac in Canton, Ohio. When, one month before Election Day, the now infamous Billy Bush/Access Hollywood ("grab them by the p——y") tape surfaced, whom did Trump talk to on October 8 to announce he was staying in the race? Costa, of course. "I'd never withdraw. I've never withdrawn in my life. . . . No, I'm not quitting this race," Trump told the Pennsbury grad.*

Just two days before Election Day, the Post *gave great prominence to a lengthy Costa piece detailing his 350-mile trek across his native Pennsylvania.*

And finally, on election night, via his Twitter feed (@Costareports) that then reached around 150,000, Costa gave unique insight into what was transpiring inside the Trump Tower:

> *On the phone w/ Giuliani. He just left Trump's apt. Said Trump is "watching everything even tho I'm telling him not to." Drinking Diet Coke.*

And:

> *Giuliani thought about bringing platters of Italian food but decided against it. "He always sticks with the hamburgers anyway."*

For anyone else, writing front-page stories for the Washington Post *about a presidential election or detailing the inner workings of a president-elect's suite would cap a long career. But for the barely 31-year-old Costa, it's still just the beginning.*

In 2017, Costa was named the new moderator of PBS's Washington Week, *succeeding Gwen Ifill, who had passed away the previous November.*

NIGHTMARE ON HEALTH SITE

Philadelphia Inquirer, Sunday, December 1, 2013

'M IN HEALTH CARE PURGATORY. Since sunrise on the day of the launch, October 1, I've attempted to shop for health insurance at health care.gov. Almost eight weeks later, I still haven't been successful in accessing quotes online for insurance.

My experience has been a Kafkaesque nightmare of Internet denial and telephone roadblocks. And this is not some journalistic folly. I'm in the market for health insurance and have been optimistic about my ability to get a competitive rate as a result of the Affordable Care Act. Here's the most frustrating part: Apparently, there is a competitive rate for my family and me, but I haven't been able to examine it.

For the first few weeks, I couldn't even gain access to the site. I would log on to the Web address with no result. The screen was all white space with no information. Then one day—Eureka!—I got to the home page and was greeted by the smiling face of the woman whose image has become synonymous with the site (and led to her allegedly being cyber-bullied). After inputting my home state of Pennsylvania, I was at least able to access an application. But when I was next asked for a username and password, the screen froze.

Trying again later, I could get to a page that asked me to provide the answers to three security questions—only my screen didn't show me the questions. I tried every conceivable way of getting beyond that step. It occurred to me that the answers were what was important, not the questions, so I tried providing consistent answers to questions I'd never seen. No dice.

A few days later—Voila!—the questions appeared. I was elated, but no closer to results. That's because my next roadblock came when it was time to finalize my application. Data that I repeatedly inputted would not save. I was back to square one.

Finally, I called the toll-free number and walked through my application with an operator who told me she was in Texas. It took about 45 minutes for me to cover the basics—all of my personal information, and that of my wife and three sons. (Our daughter will be 26 in the spring and no longer able to be carried on our plan.) This was a nonintrusive, cursory "Q&A" except for a question about tobacco usage that did not differentiate between cigars and cigarettes (a distinction that has been recognized by my insurers in the past).

After receiving my information, the operator told me that there were nine plans available for me. I was ecstatic and began to scribble notes. ("Independence Blue Cross/Keystone HMO plan for $1,926 per month?/6k out of pocket/$0 deductible/$15 per-visit co-pay/$5 prescription. Slightly more: Independence Blue Cross PPO plan. Can pay half that for far less protection.")

She assured me that all of the information I had provided would be merged with my online endeavors through my Social Security number just as soon as the bugs were out of the website. Then I would be able to go online and review all nine plans available to me. Great news.

Except that a few days later, when I could finally access the website, none of the data I had provided over the phone was on my application. I had to start over—again.

OK, I thought, with the website up and running, it will take me half the time to input the data on my computer than it took me to do so through the operator. (Spelling S-m-e-r-c-o-n-i-s-h was a fatiguing process for us both.) So, again, I inputted all the data for our family, at the end of which I was asked to electronically verify my signature. There was no instruction provided on how to do this. When I finally figured out that it meant simply typing in my name (too bad it didn't say so), my application was not accepted. Why not? Apparently because all of my attempts at accessing healthcare.gov left the computer model convinced I was a fraud. To which I say, if any crook invests this amount of time in impersonating me, he's entitled to my health insurance.

Now it was back to the toll-free number, whereupon an operator told me that I should send a copy of my passport or my driver's license so that my identity could be confirmed. Huh? I protested, noting that would mean a several day turnaround. The alternative, I was told, was uploading an image of either document to the website. I did, and was told they'd be in touch.

One day later, I logged onto my still "pending" application and was greeted with this message:

"You have a notice available about your identity verification."

This was yet another reminder of the poor design of the website. Were I dealing with Amazon or Orbitz, that "notice" would have been imbedded in the message itself. No such luck here. Instead, there was only an "x" off to the side, so I clicked it. Guess what? The message went away. And so did my ability to try to figure out what it was.

Now it was back to the toll-free number, where I was told to expect an e-mail explanation. None has arrived. Out of curiosity, I asked whether she had a record of my prior calls. She did—six. Wrong again. The number is double that.

Most frustrating is to think there are nine different plans for me to consider. If only I could see them. Especially because mental health is covered, and about now, I'm in need of some.

AFTERWORD

The week after writing this column, I published a follow-up in which I wrote:

> *This past week I broke the logjam. The key was using a new feature on the website that allowed me to remove my existing applications, then, using a new e-mail address, I started from scratch. . . . The process was not intrusive. I provided background information of the name, rank, and serial number variety. And after just 20 minutes, I was looking at 24 offerings from Independence Blue Cross and Aetna. Not bad, especially considering that Pennsylvania did not set up its own exchange. . . . The plans are grouped into four categories depending on the total cost of coverage they offer (Bronze, Silver, Gold, and Platinum). . . . I need coverage for a family of five. . . . My current plan, provided via my affiliation with the Kline & Specter law firm, is an IBX Personal Choice that costs $2,246.90 with zero deductible and no out-of-pocket maximum so long as we stay within the network. (That plan includes our daughter.)*

The plan my family settled on was pretty much the same as our old plan through the Kline and Specter law firm. While mindful of and concerned about the escalating costs of the plan since I bought it, I was nevertheless able to experience a Travelocity-like market for the purchase of private health insurance as President Barack Obama had promised.

SECRET FACET
OF WESTBORO CASE

Philadelphia Inquirer, Sunday, March 9, 2014

"**M**Y CASE made the national spotlight. There are almost a million articles on the Internet and I have done interviews across the world, but they won't tell you the real story. Up until this point, I have kept the truth to myself, my legal team, some family and close friends."

So reads a handwritten letter I received nearly a year ago from Al Snyder, a man I had come to know and admire for his courageous legal battle against the Westboro Baptist Church. Snyder sued Westboro after church representatives protested at his son's military funeral.

Marine lance corporal Matthew A. Snyder was just 20 years old when he died in a one-vehicle Humvee accident in Iraq on March 3, 2006, just five weeks after his deployment. A half-dozen Westboro members picketed Matthew Snyder's funeral at a Roman Catholic Church in Maryland one week later. That none of the protesters had any personal knowledge of Matthew or his family didn't stop them from parading signs saying, "America is Doomed," "Fag troops," "Priests Rape Boys," and "Semper Fi Fags."

For calling his son gay and disrupting the funeral, Al Snyder fought Westboro all the way to the Supreme Court without publicly revealing a secret—that he himself is gay.

Only now has Snyder decided to tell his story, an extended version of which I just authored for *Politico* magazine.

Initially keeping the matter a secret was a decision Al Snyder made with his partner of more than a decade, Walt Fisher. According to Al, it was actually Walt who never wanted to make the lawsuit about their sexuality. Al told me recently:

> When we first started talking about it, I couldn't see where it would hurt. I remember saying to Walt, "I don't think people are really going to care about that." And he said, "What it's going to do is make this a gay issue and it's not." He was right.

Snyder might never have sued Westboro had the church's bad behavior been limited to picketing the funeral. But not long after burying his son, Al discovered an online screed written by a Westboro member titled "The Burden of Matthew Snyder," containing vile assertions about the way he and his wife had raised their son:

> God blessed you, Mr. and Mrs. Snyder, with a resource and his name was Matthew. He was an arrow in your quiver! In thanks to God for the comfort the child could bring you, you had a DUTY to prepare that child to serve the LORD his GOD—PERIOD! You did JUST THE OPPOSITE—you raised him for the devil.

That's when Al contacted two lawyers in central Pennsylvania, Sean Summers and Craig Trebilcock, who agreed to file his case. Last year Al wrote me:

> You see this wasn't just a father fighting a gay hate group, this is about a gay father fighting for the dignity and respect of my son. A father who hid the fact that he was gay from the media and the public.

Summers and Trebilcock were successful in keeping Al's sexuality out of the case and benefited from rulings by district judge Richard Bennett, an

Al Snyder and Walt Fisher in April 2011, three weeks before Walt passed, in Harrisburg, Pennsylvania. Photo courtesy of Al Snyder.

appointee of President George W. Bush's, which precluded the questioning of Al about his lifestyle. While Al knows now that Westboro learned he was homosexual during the litigation, that information was never made known to the jury. It was not something he had kept from his only son.

Matthew had known of his father's sexuality since he was 14, when he'd asked Al about his relationship with the man he called "Mr. Walt." Al told his son the truth. While accepting his father's reality, Matthew quickly affirmed his own attraction to girls.

Al Snyder sued Westboro content in the knowledge that Matthew would have wanted him to do so. When able to write from his basic training at Parris Island, South Carolina, he'd be sure to extend greetings to Fisher: "I'm getting used to the yelling already. I'm looking forward to being a Marine. . . . I love you. Tell Mr. Walt I said hi."

Despite the intense interest of national media in a proceeding that revolved around homophobic slurs, the relationship between Al and Walt remained a secret from the media and public through the first trial and the subsequent appeals. Not even the justices of the Supreme Court could have known that, when the case was argued on October 6, 2010, seated in the chambers amid family members were partners Al and Walt. By then, Walt was walking with a cane, having been told he was suffering rheumatoid arthritis, for which he was receiving physical therapy. Soon he would be diagnosed instead with small-cell carcinoma.

Al Snyder lost his Supreme Court case on March 2, 2011, in an 8–1 decision, and lost Walt Fisher two months later.

Three years later, the vitriol directed at Al Snyder continues. Last December, Snyder discovered a hateful, online Westboro posting that made reference to Walt, the first public mention that Al has ever seen to the relationship. ("All this while he moved in with his 'house mate'—a simpering swishing queer-as-a-three dollar-bill open fag.")

Today, Al Snyder doesn't regard the entire experience so much as a coming out for him, but rather, a coming out for Westboro:

> I lost my battle in the U.S. Supreme Court but, in the end, won the war with the American people and the U.S. lawmakers. The lawsuit did what I hoped it would do. It brought this hate group out to the public.

AFTERWORD

Sometimes columns beget columns. This one is a great example. By the time I caught up with the attorney Craig Trebilcock to discuss Al Snyder's story, he was Judge Craig Trebilcock of the York County Pennsylvania Court of Common Pleas. He is also a U.S. Army Reserve colonel who had just served nearly a year in Afghanistan with the Judge Advocate General's Corps, where he was director of the rule of law for the commander of Afghanistan. After we'd finished talking about Al Snyder, he said, "When you're finished with this story, I have another for you, something that deserves attention." And he delivered.

Judge Trebilcock turned me onto Veterans Treatment Courts, which I wrote about in my column on April 27, 2014. The courts, which began operating in 2008, are the brainchild of Judge Robert T. Russell Jr., who sits on the City Court in Buffalo, New York. He saw and acted on the need after noticing an increase in the number of veterans appearing on his drug and mental-health dockets. His reasoning was that veterans entangled in the justice system should appear in front of judges with a unique understanding of their problems. Trebilcock himself presides at one of the Veterans Treatment Courts, and he shared with me the case of Justin Slesser, a success story.

When he lost his access to prescription pain meds, Slesser had turned to heroin and a life of crime. After being drummed out of the military, he built a rap sheet and lost his marriage. Luckily for him, help arrived in the form of Veterans Treatment Court. Slesser worked with an attorney and a veterans' outreach officer to get his legal troubles consolidated. He received substance-abuse counseling in West Virginia and then entered a program for post-traumatic stress disorder. He graduated from that veterans' treatment program and is now employed, and clean. "Without the Veterans Court, I'd probably be dead," Slesser told me.

And when I told Slesser's story on my radio program, I was overwhelmed with reaction from veterans eager to share their stories of injury, opioid dependence, and in some cases, heroin addiction. For those interested in learning more about this important subject, I recommend Justice for Vets, a nonprofit whose senior director is Melissa Fitzgerald, a Philly native who's doing good for veterans after a successful acting career that included playing "Carol" on The West Wing.

SATS DON'T ALWAYS MARK
A SUCCESSFUL PATH

Philadelphia Inquirer, Sunday, March 16, 2014

I JUST EXPERIENCED the thrill of being invited back to the campus of my alma mater to speak to undergraduate students. The invitation came a few months ago from Jack Lule, the chair of journalism and communication at Lehigh University, from which I graduated in 1984. That someone in Lule's position would think students could benefit from listening to me for an hour gave me a measure of achievement and acceptance.

And I get why I was invited: the combination of my professional activities since graduation, including writing for the *Inquirer*, hosting a daily radio program nationwide on SiriusXM, writing five books with a novel on the way, and now hosting a Saturday morning program on CNN.

There's just one problem: According to my SATs, I was never Lehigh material.

Here are the bare facts. At Holicong Junior High School, and thereafter at Central Bucks West High School, I was a "sometimes" honor roll student. My grades were mostly B's with an infrequent A and an occasional C, frankly, more of the latter than the former. In a scrapbook somewhere I've got a few clippings from the *Intelligencer* listing the most recent honor roll with my name mentioned.

My public school record included some other attributes—sports participation, a few class presidencies, a stint as newspaper editor—and some liabilities, such as when I was disciplined for selling fake IDs to classmates. What can I say? I was always entrepreneurial, the kid who sold you Christmas cards and came to shovel your drive. Sometimes that ambition got me in trouble. Such as when Coach Carey demanded I stop an NFL betting pool out of homeroom, or when I got thrown in a police van at the Spectrum for selling Genesis bumper stickers in my senior year. (They cost me a nickel to print, and I sold them for a buck.)

My SATs were never commensurate with my respectable school grades. And it was no one-off. I took the test several times and never batted above the Mendoza line.

Nine-ninety. I still hate seeing it numerically represented: 990. I never even broke 1,000.

Lucky for me that my father received his master's from Lehigh and my brother was president of his Lehigh class the year I was applying. Otherwise, I'm sure my SATs would have sunk my application.

Driving back to Bethlehem Tuesday, I felt like George Bailey on the bridge toward the end of *It's a Wonderful Life*, when an angel shows the Jimmy Stewart character an alternative path. Bailey's angel was named Clarence. Mine was Samuel Missimer, then Lehigh's dean of admissions, who admitted me despite my mediocre SATs. What if my college acceptance had been determined by that test?

A rejection would have meant I'd have never met a faculty mentor named Dave Amidon, who sparked in me an academic fire I never knew existed. Missing from the Lehigh campus in the fall of 1980, I would not have met "Ambassador" George H. W. Bush when he toured Bethlehem Steel, an event that led to my working for Vice President Bush and a string of extraordinary political experiences, which in turn caused media outlets to solicit my commentary. No Lehigh? No Amidon. No Amidon? No double major and no Phi Beta Kappa. No Phi Beta Kappa? No admission to Penn Law.

The intervening years haven't softened my antipathy toward the SAT, not even the recent experience of a son who aced it. I'm encouraged that the College Board is attempting to change the nature of the exam in a way that will recognize evidence-based thinking that students should be gleaning in high school. Perhaps if I'd had an exam like the board now contemplates, I'd have scored more respectably. But maybe not. Better for students, parents, and colleges to scrap it altogether.

Today, out of roughly 2,800 four-year U.S. colleges and universities, about 850 make SAT or ACT submissions optional. A recent study by two former colleagues at Bates College, William Hiss, the former dean of admissions, and Valerie Wilson Franks, the study's lead investigator, found that there is a negligible difference between the performance of students who submit test results and those who do not.

The study, published under the title "Defining Promise: Optional Standardized Testing Policies in American College and University Admissions," looked at 123,000 student and alumni records. It found only a 0.05 differential between the GPAs of those applicants who submitted a standardized test score and those who did not—and graduation rates for submitters were only 0.6 percent higher than those of non-submitters. In other words, trivial differences.

When I shared my personal experience with Hiss, he told me by e-mail that the disconnect between my SAT scores and later academic and career success is "strikingly common." He added:

In our one study, there were tens of thousands of students whom any statistician would call "false negatives." That is, these students' SAT scores suggest they could not do strong work in college, when in fact they can. Simply put, our country cannot afford to throw away up to 30 percent of its talent.

AFTERWORD

My wife and I have four children. Three have completed the SATs and the college application process, and each has done very well, so my disenchantment with this standardized test is not born of sour grapes, at least not on their behalf. In fact, one of our kids achieved a "superscored" perfect SAT: 2400 points. Clearly, his mother's child. But not even that accomplishment has changed my view about the limitations of the SATs in judging college aptitude and future success. One of ours still needs to navigate this world, and I really feel for him. If he were able to redirect the time he will now spend on test prep to learning a musical instrument, he'd be proficient by the time he will sit for that exam.

WORTHY SUBJECT OF PROTEST
MAY TARGET WORKERS

Philadelphia Inquirer, Sunday, May 18, 2014

TWO WEEKS AGO, I spent the weekend in Los Angeles. I was there to give a speech, attend a book signing, and deliver a radio show. The speech was at a Monday luncheon, and upon arrival back at my hotel I could see there was a commotion across the street, but I wasn't initially sure of the cause.

Inside my room, I had a surreal experience watching the local news—there was the exterior of the hotel, complete with a shot that depicted my open door leading to a small balcony. It was then that I learned that Jay Leno was among a few dozen protesters complaining about the hotel's ownership. The landmark where I was staying, best known for five-star service and an iconic roofline that adorned the album cover of the Eagles' *Hotel California*, was the Beverly Hills Hotel.

Leno and company were calling attention to the fact that far up the hotel ownership chain sits the sultan of Brunei, who is in the process of instituting sharia law in his tiny, oil-rich nation. I had no idea of the ownership connection prior to my stay. The hotel website and my electronic key touted the "Dorchester Collection" of hotels and referenced several other well-known properties. I departed the night of the protest to catch a scheduled red-eye to Philadelphia, so I never had to confront the issue of whether I'd continue to stay at the hotel given my newfound knowledge.

The night after my departure, the Beverly Hills City Council passed a resolution (5–0) that "urges the government of Brunei to divest itself of the Beverly Hills Hotel and any other properties it may own in Beverly Hills." The hotel pays $7 million in annual bed taxes and an additional $4 million in city taxes.

Soon thereafter, at a town hall meeting for employees, the hotel management announced that all jobs and wages of employees are secure despite the decline in business. I was happy to hear that. I have no sympathy for the sultan—the idea of sharia is abhorrent—but I do for those workers.

News accounts say that 600 people work at the hotel, and over the span of two nights, I had interactions with many of them. Like the guy who needed to take an iron to my suit because it looked like a truck ran over it when I unpacked. Or the valet who helped retrieve my rental car. The housekeeping supervisor who saw a half-dozen of my books in my room and felt obliged to put a bookmark in each. And the concierge who gave me driving directions. They aren't members of Hollywood's rich and famous. I doubt any of them live in Beverly Hills. They're American workers, hustling to earn a living, who are now probably a bit fearful about their jobs in a tough economy. Despite management's assurance, one has to wonder whether a protracted protest will ultimately jeopardize their livelihood. The only certainty seems that the protest will have no impact on the intended target.

No protest of the Beverly Hills Hotel can impact the sultan's wealth. His country is only the size of Delaware and yet it's the fifth richest in the world. So wealthy that all of its citizens receive free education and health care.

A friend had joined me at the hotel. Only now am I remembering that, after he booked his room online, he kept tabs on the rate being charged and alerted me to two reductions enabling both of us to negotiate a savings. Perhaps that was attributable to cancellations spurred by the high-profile protest movement. Ellen DeGeneres is on board and so, too, is Sir Richard Branson. Project Care, the Motion Picture and Television Fund, and the Beverly Hills Bar Association have all canceled events. Steven Young, who is on the board of the association's charitable arm, told me he was "shocked" to learn of the hotel's ownership. Where his group "stands for the highest principles of justice," he said,

> the violations of human rights through the implementation of harsh criminal laws, including the chopping off of limbs, the stoning of homosexuals and adulterers, and the unconscionable treatment of women, all of which are an anathema to our American values, made it morally untenable to continue to patronize the hotel.
>
> In making the decision not to further patronize the hotel, there was a full recognition that innocent management and staff members of the hotel may be adversely affected.

Perhaps a better way to protect those innocents would be a response from the White House. Last March, President Barack Obama met with the sultan in the Oval Office, where he opened a media availability by remarking:

> Well, it is a great pleasure to welcome my good friend, his majesty the sultan of Brunei. . . . He is a key leader in the Southeast Asia region, but also widely respected around the world.

I can find no statement of condemnation by the White House or State Department on the implementation of sharia law in Brunei. Perhaps the Hollywood elite would be better served enlisting the support of a president whose ear they certainly have rather than putting American workers in the crosshairs.

AFTERWORD

Not long after I wrote this column and repeated my sentiments in a commentary on CNN, I was invited to return to Los Angeles to appear on Real Time with Bill Maher. *For a show like Maher's, airfare and accommodations are usually comped. When I told the show's booker that I wanted to stay at the Beverly Hills Hotel, she replied, "Well, do you know there is a protest under way?" "Yes," I said, "that's why I want to stay there." To* Real Time's *credit, they satisfied my request.*

Upon arrival at the Beverly Hills Hotel, I was struck by how empty the place felt. While checking in, I was greeted at the front desk by the director of guest relations, Steven Boggs. He escorted me to my fabulous room and said that the general manager hoped I'd join him for coffee the following day in the Polo Lounge. After I agreed, Boggs confirmed the 11 A.M. appointment with a handwritten note (classic BHH!). So, the following morning, I sat with Edward Mady, the regional director of West Coast USA for the Dorchester Collection, in the outdoor patio section of the legendary Polo Lounge. He was the top management official for both the Beverly Hills Hotel and Hotel Bel-Air, and a terrific guy. To meet him is to immediately appreciate his orientation toward detail. Nothing escapes his attention. Mady said he was very grateful for my support and explained to me some of the backstory of the dispute—how at its core this was not a dispute about sharia law but about labor. Neither the BHH nor Bel-Air was a union hotel, and advocates for their unionization had seized the sharia issue to bring pressure to bear, a point lost on the Hollywood protestors. Anyway, after about a half hour of tea and pleasantries, Mady excused himself from the table. I didn't think much of his brief absence, and when he returned, he asked me to join him. So I stood and followed as he exited through a gate that I hadn't noticed.

Within seconds, in a small grassy area adjacent to the hotel's famed bungalows, I found myself surrounded by every employee of the BHH then on duty, and they were applauding me for my support. It was a totally unexpected and overwhelming experience. Then, Mady presented me with a framed photograph of the exterior of the pink hotel, with all the employees standing in front. On the matting they had all signed their names and many had added a personal message. "WE ARE the Beverly Hills Hotel! Thank you for telling our story!" one of them read. Mady kindly shipped the framed photograph to my home and enclosed a note saying, "You have 647 fans at this hotel and 351 at the Hotel Bel-Air." Five stars indeed.

I have since returned to the hotel on several occasions and can report that to my untrained eye, it appears that business has been completely restored.

MYSTERY TIP THAT
BROKE SANDUSKY CASE

Philadelphia Inquirer, Sunday, June 29, 2014

N EARLY TWO YEARS AFTER a 15-year-old boy first reported being abused by Jerry Sandusky, the attorney general's investigation was moribund. Very little progress had been made since the office took over the probe. The victim's mother was understandably frustrated, and the prosecutor assigned to the case considered it "stalled."

It could have easily ended there, and Sandusky might be a free man today—if not for a concerned citizen whose name does not appear on any of the 339 pages of independent investigator H. Geoffrey Moulton Jr.'s recently released report to the attorney general.

The report of Victim No. 1, a ninth grader known as "A.F.," was made by his mother to school administrators in November 2008. County officials eventually referred it to the Attorney General's Office in March 2009. At the time, the report notes, the office was "heavily invested in . . . Bonusgate," a political-corruption prosecution. Also that month, then–attorney general Tom Corbett announced that he was exploring a run for governor.

Given that prosecutors deemed the first victim credible, Sandusky could have been arrested immediately. Instead, they decided to use the secret grand jury process to search for more victims and bolster the case.

In June 2009, A.F. appeared before the grand jury and testified that he had engaged in oral sex with Sandusky. He returned to the grand jury in November 2009, a year after his initial report, because prosecutors wanted to gauge his ability to describe the crime on his own rather than in response to a prosecutor's leading questions. He was able to do so.

As 2009 ended, Senior Deputy Attorney General Jonelle Eshbach believed she had sufficient evidence to have Sandusky arrested, but her supervisors disagreed. At least one grand juror wanted to know when there would be progress, according to Moulton's report, asking Eshbach, "When do you see this moving forward?"

In March 2010—16 months after the first report of abuse—Eshbach delivered a draft presentment recommending charges against Sandusky to Glenn Parno, who had temporarily assumed the responsibilities of Chief Deputy Attorney General Frank Fina, who was involved in an extended trial.

Months passed without a reply or significant progress in the case. In May

2010, the report says, Eshbach wrote to an investigator: "Despite asking, begging, pleading, I have heard nothing."

Still more time elapsed. In July 2010, Eshbach wrote to several colleagues:

The grand jury asked me again, as they have for the last four months, why we don't have that particular presentment for them. They are very anxious to approve it. Likewise, I continue to get calls and mail from the victim's mother and therapist. Can someone please tell me what the holdup is?

It had been 20 months since the first report that a 15-year-old boy had been abused by Jerry Sandusky.

The following month, A.F.'s mother wrote in an e-mail to Eshbach:

It's been a long time on this case, and another school year is coming up. Why has this not been dealt with already? This is causing my family a lot of stress and anxiety. Please let me know what's going on.

Eshbach forwarded that e-mail to colleagues with another request:

Does anyone want to answer my questions about why we are stalled since winter?

Fina replied:

We are still working on the case, looking for better corroboration of our single victim. We need to do everything possible to find other victims.

And so, on the verge of the fall of 2010, which would mark two years since A.F.'s credible report of abuse, Sandusky was a free man, and the investigation was at a standstill.

Then came the lucky break that may have saved the case.

On November 3, 2010, the day after Corbett was elected governor, Centre County District Attorney Stacy Parks Miller received an e-mail. "Ms. Miller," it said:

I am contacting you regarding the Jerry Sandusky investigation. If you have not yet done so, you need to contact and interview Penn State football assistant coach Mike McQueary. He may have witnessed something involving Jerry Sandusky and a child that would be pertinent to the investigation.

It was signed only "A Concerned Citizen."

The only information about this citizen supplied in the report comes in a footnote on page 62:

> According to the author of the e-mail, he had recently heard rumors that Sandusky was being investigated for child abuse and assumed that any such investigation would involve the Centre County District Attorney's Office. In addition, he had recently heard from a member of Michael McQueary's family that McQueary had firsthand information about Sandusky that would be relevant to such an investigation.

The tip broke the case wide open. A week later, investigators knocked on McQueary's door, and he agreed to cooperate. New resources were committed to the case. Subpoenas were issued. Evidence was assembled. And Sandusky was finally charged on November 4, 2011—32 months after the investigation had been referred to the Attorney General's Office.

Who was the mystery man who seems to have rescued the prosecution? A March *ESPN* magazine story identified him as Christopher Houser. The magazine reported that during a chat on a Penn State football fan website, McQueary's older brother had told Houser that Sandusky, who had recently retired from his charity, would probably never coach again. And he revealed that his younger brother had caught Sandusky with a boy in a locker room shower.

Unlike so many who had reason to suspect Sandusky but didn't act, Houser did—and thereby resurrected the prosecution of a serial pedophile.

And that deserves more than an anonymous footnote.

AFTERWORD

Too many adults in leadership roles dropped the ball in the Sandusky case when they should have been working to protect the young victims. At the time this column ran, three top Penn State officials—President Graham Spanier, Vice President Gary Schultz, and Athletic Director Tim Curley—had already lost their jobs and had been charged with various counts related to their alleged failure to report to police incriminating evidence about Sandusky that would have ended Sandusky's crime spree much sooner. After five years of maintaining their innocence, Schultz and Curley pleaded guilty to misdemeanor child endangerment and agreed to cooperate in the case against Spanier. In 2017, Spanier was convicted by a jury of misdemeanor child endangerment.

Head football coach Joe Paterno had been fired shortly after the scandal went public in late 2011. He died in January 2012 before seeing his statue removed from Penn State's campus several months later and before seeing the NCAA vacate all of his program's wins from 1998 to 2011 (a decision that would be reversed in 2015 after Penn State successfully sued the NCAA for due process violations). His statue remains in storage.

Mike McQueary was fired from his coaching position in 2011, but in October 2016 he won a lawsuit against Penn State for wrongful termination and other charges, resulting in a total payout of over $7 million. (Penn State's appeal is still pending.)

And in August 2016, a Pennsylvania jury convicted Pennsylvania attorney general Kathleen Kane of nine criminal charges, including perjury, finding that she had leaked grand jury information as a means of political retribution against the Sandusky prosecutor Frank Fina, and then lied about it. She resigned. By then she'd already lost her law license and was subsequently sentenced to 10 to 23 months in prison.

I have no update to report on the private citizen and Penn State fan Christopher Houser, the unsung hero of the Sandusky prosecution. But for him, Jerry Sandusky could still be preying on kids.

RECALLING GARY HART,
DEBATING NEWS POLICY

Philadelphia Inquirer, Sunday, October 12, 2014

GARY HART'S DOWNFALL in the run-up to the 1988 presidential election marked an important milestone on a journalistic arc that began with Watergate. Where, previously, the media fast track was greased by befriending politicians, now it was enhanced by bringing them down. Ever since, nothing has been out of bounds for media outlets large and small. Consider Kansas.

Paul Davis, the Democratic gubernatorial candidate, has been locked in a tight race against Republican incumbent Sam Brownback. Three weeks ago, a twice-weekly local newspaper with no website called the *Coffeyville Journal* revealed that, in 1998, Davis, then 26 and unmarried, was in a strip club getting a lap dance when the place was raided as part of a drug sting. Davis wasn't charged with a crime, but that won't stop the story's circulation through Election Day.

Matt Bai's new book, *All the Truth Is Out: The Week Politics Went Tabloid*, asks whether the all-is-fair-game standard has been in the nation's best interest. The focus is the Hart saga, about which Bai corrects what he regards as numerous myths. Bai writes:

> Even when insiders and historians recall the Hart episode now they recall it the same way: Hart issued his infamous challenge to reporters, telling them to follow him around if they didn't believe him, and then the *[Miami] Herald* took him up on it. Inexplicably, people believe Hart set his own trap and then allowed himself to become ensnared in it.

Bai says that's not how it happened. The *Herald* was already staking out Hart by the time his so-called challenge was published by the journalist E. J. Dionne. And, Bai says, that's not just a timeline clarification. The idea that Hart set the episode in motion made it seem as if he, not the press, had changed the boundaries.

Plus, you remember the photograph of Donna Rice sitting on Hart's lap? Chances are you think the photo was the smoking gun that killed his political career. Actually, the picture didn't come to light until nearly three weeks after he suspended his candidacy.

Four years ago, I interviewed Hart about a book he was then releasing. I asked him where reporters and observers should draw the line today on covering politicians' personal lives. He said:

> The standard that got changed I think 20 or 25 years ago was that a public person's private life was of importance only if it affected their ability to do their job. I think that was a pretty good standard, and it permitted some people who are flawed human beings, as we all are, to continue to serve their country.

Maybe he's right. After all, as Hart noted, if today's standard had been applied in decades past, the country would have been denied the service of Franklin Roosevelt, Dwight Eisenhower, and John Kennedy, among others. (Bill Clinton was missing from his list, but deserves mention, too.) Some might argue that by Hart's own standard, he was rendered unqualified to serve, that a president carrying on an extramarital affair could be compromised by enemies foreign and domestic. But that's only because we ostracize behavior, which is, arguably, none of our business.

Tom Fiedler disagrees. Today, he is the dean of the College of Communication at Boston University. But 30 years ago, he was a political reporter for the *Miami Herald* whose phone rang with the tip that would eventually sink Hart. Recently on CNN, he told me that Hart's challenge had been issued before Dionne wrote about it and that "Senator Hart himself raised that issue as really a measure of who he was, of his own authenticity."

I asked Fiedler about the propriety of three *Herald* reporters and a photographer literally cornering Hart in an alley adjacent to his home. He said they were there to confirm a tip that Hart was spending the weekend with Rice, adding, "You somehow make it sound like what we were doing was somehow out of the bounds of journalism. It was very much in bounds of what journalists do."

When I noted that the tip was about infidelity, he disagreed:

> The tip was about lying. He had lied to everyone, the public included, that he claimed he was not engaged in this kind of behavior. That was the tip—that he was, indeed, engaged in this behavior, and we checked out the tip. We felt that it's important that voters be able to consider— when they're looking at a person's fitness for office—they should be

able to take into account what his character included. And it included lying about, as it happened, infidelity.

When I shared that recollection with Bai, he was quick to respond:

When they were in that alley, on May 2, 1987, and four reporters and a photographer had the presumed Democratic nominee, the guy who was beating George H. W. Bush in the polls by double digits, and they have him backed up against a brick wall in a white hoodie, and they are peppering him with questions about the woman who they saw entering and leaving the home. The question was not, "You said you were not cheating on your wife, so how do you explain the lie?" What Tom Fiedler said to him is, "You held yourself out when you announced . . . as a politician who would hold himself to a high moral standard. Who is that woman in your house?"

Bai sees significance in the fact that Hart's announcement comments about the need for morality were in the context of addressing official misbehavior—Iran contra and a series of Reagan administration scandals. "He was not talking about his marital vows," Bai told me, noting that the *Herald* reporters made no such distinction.

Perhaps it was never for us to condemn Hart. That was a job for Lee, his wife. And how ironic that, after more than 50 years, they're still together.

AFTERWORD

In December 2016, I was offered an interview with Donna Rice (Donna Rice Hughes since her marriage to Jack Hughes in 1994) for my SiriusXM POTUS program. She's become a leading Internet safety proponent and is the president and CEO of Enough Is Enough, a nonprofit that lobbies for that cause. I was willing to afford her the opportunity to make her points about her cause but was eager to ask whether, these many years later, she thought Gary Hart had been treated unfairly by the outing of their relationship. She said:

Here's the thing. . . . [T]here had been an understanding, if you will, between people in politics, primarily men, and the media. And that changed in 1987. I think to some degree there was a perfect storm that was set up here. I don't know if the media was necessarily out to get him, but there had been hints that people were trying to get to who *he was because he was a bit aloof, from what I understand, with the media.*

I explained to her that what especially concerns me is that people avoid running for office because they know it will mean airing all their dirty laundry. And when I asked how small of a pool that really leaves, she replied, "We're all human and we can understand that people are not perfect and they're going to have things in their life that they're not proud of."

I also asked whether she had ever spoken with Hart again. She said:

He called me many years later during one of President Clinton's many scandals. And he called and asked for my forgiveness. And I really appreciated that and told him that a long time ago I had forgiven him and anyone else that was involved with that.

OVERREACTION IN C.B. WEST
HAZING CASE

Philadelphia Inquirer, Sunday, November 2, 2014

HAD YOU GOOGLED Central Bucks West before the October 23 suspension of its football season, I suspect you'd have found links to such noted alumni as NFL referee Scott Green, who officiated three Super Bowls; Kevin Ward, who played for the San Diego Padres; and maybe the recording artist known as Pink, who attended but did not graduate.

From its inception in 1952 until the construction of crosstown rival C.B. East in 1969, the school on West Court Street in Doylestown was known as Central Bucks High School. Graduates from that era include race-car driver Al Holbert, an inductee of International Motorsports Hall of Fame, and Fred Fielding, White House counsel to Presidents Ronald Reagan and George W. Bush.

Ask the locals about C.B. West's origins and they'll likely direct you to the placard and stone facade that stand in honor of the old Doylestown High School, counting among its progeny author James Michener and anthropologist Margaret Mead.

Of course, scholarship matters, but what has garnered the most attention for the school in the modern era is its extraordinary football program under the direction of coach Mike Pettine Sr., who amassed a record of 326–42–4 and four state titles while at the Bucks' helm. Today, his son and namesake, a graduate of C.B. West and the University of Virginia, is head coach of the Cleveland Browns.

It is sad that the school's reputation, earned over generations, is now in jeopardy—both from the bad behavior of student athletes and the overzealous reaction of adults.

In times like these, many of us have a tendency to reflect on the indiscretions of our own youth. But they can be compared only in context. The foolish things I did in my three years at C.B. West are evidenced only by the strength of memory. In the digital age, nothing is ever erased. Now, regardless of the outcome, the actions of the school board in an Internet age will always follow C.B. West.

In his written notification to the community, Central Bucks School District Superintendent David P. Weitzel said:

> Our inquiry determined that students new to the team were expected to participate in several initiations that were both humiliating and

inappropriate. The most personally invasive activity required a rookie to grab another player's private parts while fully clothed. These initiations took place in front of most team members.

The lack of specificity in the statement furthered the harm done to perpetrators and victims because it allowed minds to wander and rumors to spawn. Suddenly, C.B. West has been mentioned in the same breath as Sayreville High School in New Jersey, where sexual-assault charges have been filed against seven members of the football team. At C.B. West, no student has served a detention, much less been suspended, for the behavior alleged. A better course would have been a more complete disclosure of what was known—and if administrators believed there was not enough known to fully advise the community, then by definition no punishment was ripe to be administered.

People close to the events have told me that on August 16, at the end of a week of two-a-day practices, the players had a scrimmage at home against Abington. The scrimmage ended about 11:15 A.M. and was followed by a football parents' club picnic at noon. Last year, the picnic was held away from school, but this year, to save money, it was held on a playground adjacent to the campus. Most of the coaches—including head coach Brian Hensel—were not in attendance.

During the picnic, the players left the adults and walked a short distance to the team locker room. There, the hijinks commenced. Veterans gave haircuts to rookies. Some initiates were "sugar cookied," doused with talcum powder after walking through the shower. Worse, some mimicked the game "slap lick fondle" from the Comedy Central series *Tosh.0*. (Three individuals face one person, who has to choose one of those three options.) When the players returned to the picnic, there was no sign of distress. Many who'd had their hair cut took "selfies" with family and fellow players.

Exactly two months later, an investigation commenced into allegations that a player was punched for refusing to have his hair cut, an allegation determined to be unfounded. Thus began an investigation that uncovered the other conduct described. Then, with two games to go in the season, and on the eve of the homecoming game against C.B. East, the district superintendent announced the suspension of the season.

Justice Potter Stewart may also have been defining "hazing" when he said of pornography, "I know it when I see it." For me, forced haircuts and "sugar cookies" don't cross that line. But "slap lick fondle" clearly does. The perpetrators of that behavior should have been singled out and punished, and if their number was such that C.B. West could not field a team, then forfeiture was appropriate. Instead, the bad behavior in August has now been compounded by a school board, which, in its haste, issued what amounted to a capital sentence in an Internet world.

AFTERWORD

Brian Hensel was fired as head coach about two weeks after this column was published, but he still teaches science at C.B. West. The superintendent cited "lack of coach supervision" when terminating Hensel, who is now an assistant football coach at Hatboro-Horsham High School. C.B. West athletic director Sean Kelly ended up resigning in June 2015.

CAT STEVENS'S POLITICS

Philadelphia Inquirer, Sunday, December 14, 2014

WHEN I BUMPED INTO DJ Pierre Robert at the Tower Theater, he had more on his mind than music. It's something of a running joke—when I see him, he seeks to engage me in political discussion, while I try to steer conversation toward classic rock. On the night that Yusuf Islam, the artist formerly known as Cat Stevens, kicked off his first American tour in 38 years, those worlds collided. There were many of us at the show who were excited to hear the music, but wondering aloud about the performer's politics.

I've often said that if I screened my entertainment choices according to political bent, I'd be erasing my iTunes account and surrendering my cable subscriptions. (These days I'd have to add professional athletes.) So there I was, with my wife, circumnavigating the long lines outside in Upper Darby and working my way through metal detectors—something I'd never seen in three decades of attending Tower shows. (A Live Nation executive told me their presence was the mutual desire of both promoter and performer.) My trial-lawyer buddy, Paul Lauricella, offered the politically incorrect quip that it was the first time he experienced TSA-like screening to protect a Muslim from Americans.

When I said hello to state senator Daylin Leach (D., Montgomery) just before the lights dimmed, he reminded me that Yusuf had played at Steven Colbert and Jon Stewart's "Rally to Restore Sanity," for which Stewart had been called out by Bill O'Reilly. Media and issues advocate Larry Ceisler, who was seated a row behind us with his wife, quickly weighed in, telling me that as a strong supporter of Israel, he was willing to overlook (for a night) any indiscretions toward the Jewish state in the name of music.

Clearly, there were many of us thinking about more than just the set list. "The Wind." "Where Do the Children Play?" "Oh Very Young." "Moonshadow." "Wild World." "Another Saturday Night." "Morning Has Broken." "Peace Train." "Father and Son." "Sad Lisa." "Miles from Nowhere." The repertoire was rich, and the recent Rock and Roll Hall of Fame inductee exhibited a rare voice.

But the next day, not only were the songs ringing in my ears, but so, too, the questions raised by friends about Yusuf's worldview. My cursory Internet search revealed that before Philadelphia, Yusuf played in Toronto, an event he marked with a contribution to the *Toronto Star* where he says:

> At one time I wrote, "I'm being followed by a moonshadow—moonshadow—moonshadow." Today I would amend that to, "I'm being followed by a trail of misconceptions—misconceptions—misconceptions."

He referenced "dragon-sized myths," and directed fans to the lyrics of new songs, including "Editing Floor Blues":

> *One day the papers rang us up,*
> *T'check if I said this?*
> *I said, "Oh boy!*
> *I'd never say that!"*
> *Then we got down to the truth of it*
> *But they never printed that!*

On his website, yusufislam.com, he has a section titled "Chinese Whiskers," "dedicated to dispelling myths and rumors created around my bruising skirmishes with the media." Perusing the site, it became obvious that these days, Yusuf is catching it from all sides. One of the frequently asked questions is why he has stopped wearing Muslim robes.

In further addressing his faith, Yusuf comments that he feels "very fortunate that I got to know Islam before it became a major headline." And he offers an opinion as to why he was stopped from entry to the United States post 9/11:

> No reason was ever given, but being asked to repeat the spelling of my name again and again, made me think it was a fairly simple mistake of identity. Rumors which circulated after made me imagine otherwise. I'm now free to travel to the U.S., so whatever it was has been resolved.

But it was whether he'd once supported a fatwa against author Salman Rushdie that I'd heard most raised the night before, and I was pleased to see Yusuf offer context.

> Because of imaginary scenarios set by courthouse TV interviewers, in 1989 I was drawn into making stupid and offensive jokes about Rushdie on a program called *Hypotheticals*; however, they were meant to

lighten the moment and raise a smile—as good ol' British sense of humor occasionally is known to do—unfortunately for me . . . it didn't.

In 1989, during the heat and height of the *Satanic Verses* controversy, I was silly enough to accept appearing on . . . *Hypotheticals*, which posed imaginary scenarios by a well-versed (what if . . . ?) barrister, Geoffrey Robertson. . . . I foolishly made light of certain provocative questions. When asked what I'd do if Salman Rushdie entered a restaurant in which I was eating, I said, "I would probably call up Ayatollah Khomeini"; and, rather than go to a demonstration to burn an effigy of the author, I jokingly said I would have preferred that it'd be the "real thing."

Criticize me for my bad taste, in hindsight, I agree. But these comments were part of a well-known British national trait; a touch of dry humor on my part.

Yusuf claims to never have "knowingly" supported Hamas, and most important to me, he denounced terrorism.

(Like all right-minded people, I absolutely condemn all acts of terrorism, including the attacks of 9/11 and 7/7 [the July 7, 2005, bombings in London that killed nearly 60 people]. The actions of the terrorists were completely un-Islamic and against the teachings and example of the Prophet. It's everybody's responsibility to make this world a safer, more peaceful place.)

It was all the information I wish I'd have known the night before so that I would have celebrated the man as much as the music.

AFTERWORD

Another mea culpa coming.

First, something not in the column: For this concert, I paid more money for a pair of Cat Stevens/Yusuf Islam tickets than for any other concert I've attended in my four decades of seeing shows. Even more than I spent for the front row of Roger Waters at Madison Square Garden. And more than I paid to see the Grateful Dead's second-to-last show, billed Fare Thee Well, *at Soldier Field. That will also be sad news for the artist who went to great lengths to try to mitigate ticket scalping of his shows. In fact, this show that I saw at the Tower Theater was supposed to occur at New York City's Beacon Theatre, but Yusuf relocated it out of concern over inflated prices due to scalping in Manhattan. For me, this was bucket-list stuff. Forever, I'd hoped he would reemerge after 40 years of not touring, and there was no way I intended to miss it. My wife was with me, and we were in about the fifth row, dead center. Perfect. Coincidentally, our friends Larry and Lina were in the row behind us, two seats over. (Knowing Larry, he got the seats free. No way he paid what I paid.) Directly behind us sat a young couple, the female half of which did not stop screaming and singing loudly for the entire first half of the show. Not intermittently—constantly. I did my best to stay under control but I was doing a slow burn, and by the intermission, I was ready to blow. "I paid to hear him sing, not you," I finally said. Lina interceded and used her psychological training to befriend and ultimately quiet the woman and the second half of the show proceeded. Larry later told me they were a Hollywood couple that had flown in just to see the show. I truly do get flying across country to see Cat Stevens. But I don't get making the trip so you can shout over him and ruin the experience for everybody else.*

The column makes reference to Cat/Yusuf's having been stopped while seeking entry to the United States after 9/11. Left unsaid is that I defended that decision at the time. When I wrote this column, I didn't recall having written about Cat Stevens a decade earlier, in a September 2004 column with the headline "The Cat May Be outta the Bag," or I would have said so. That column is about the diversion of a flight carrying Cat Stevens/Yusuf Islam, and in it I say:

> *Islam's flight was diverted when it was determined that he was on a "no-fly" list, presumably due to his alleged financial connection to Hamas and support of Omar Abdel-Rahman, convicted in the first World Trade Center bombing. (The ex-conductor of the "Peace Train" also supported the death fatwah on Salman Rushdie.)*

I added that I hoped the handling of this flight represented a change in airline-safety protocol under transportation secretary Norman Mineta, which at the time included levying fines against airlines that engaged in actions similar to those taken toward Yusuf Islam. I was referring to specific instances in which American, United, Continental, and Delta Airlines were forced to pay millions of dollars for using their lawful discretion to boot passengers who the pilot believed were "inimical to safety." That was a subject I dealt with extensively in my book Flying Blind.

While I could not have known in 2004 that the Department of Homeland

Security was operating on bad information about Stevens/Islam, I nevertheless regret my role in the repeating of incorrect data. I have a vague recollection of making similar comments on radio at the time but no tapes I can listen to for recollecting. A series of successful Google searches, however, reminded me of what I said on television. On September 22, 2004, I appeared on CNN's Anderson Cooper 360. After the lead-in music—Cat Stevens, of course—faded out, Cooper tossed to a Justice Department correspondent, Kelli Arena, who provided background and then said:

> *His supporters say he's known for advocating peace. But U.S. officials say recent information suggests Yusuf Islam has knowingly financed terrorists through Muslim charities and has knowingly associated with potential terrorists. But officials would provide no specifics.*

And then, after I was introduced by Cooper, I said:

> *I think it was the right call. I mean, imagine if you were on that plane, and all of a sudden they have knowledge of the fact that somebody who is Muslim and on a terrorism watch list is on board as well. Do you want that plane to enter the airspace over New York City and Washington, D.C., where it was headed? The answer to that is no.*

Cooper then described my book as "pretty controversial" and said that what I was calling "terrorist profiling" would sound to some like "racial profiling." Here, from the transcript, is my final word:

> *SMERCONISH: Anderson, you know, "profiling" is not a dirty word to me. The bottom line is that on September 11, 19 individuals who had a lot of common denominators, race, religion, gender, ethnicity, and, yes, appearance, they are the ones who perpetrated that attack. And my view is that we ought to be taking those characteristics into account. I mean, look at the mug shots.*

I don't regret my 2004 words to Anderson Cooper, especially when viewed in the context of their being said three years after 9/11. Still, I am sorry that Cat/Yusuf was the subject of government misinformation that I played a role in spreading. I'm convinced he's a man of peace and that I jumped the gun in 2004 in defending the decision to deny him entry to the United States. While I regret the opinion I expressed years ago, I am pleased I was able to correct the record by writing this column. I still love his music, and when Yusuf returned to the States in 2016 with his Cat's Attic tour, his second date (of just 12) was in Philadelphia, and I was again there when the legendary songwriter, now 68 years old, walked on stage solo at the Kimmel Center and opened with "Where Do the Children Play?" I took my friend Mike Baldini as my date. Thankfully we were not seated near anyone who wanted to compete with the headliner.

GO OLD SCHOOL ON DRINKING?

Philadelphia Inquirer, Sunday, February 15, 2015

▌ **PULLED FROM A SCRAPBOOK** a Weekender column I wrote for the
Lehigh University *Brown and White* in 1982:

> Friday Happy Hours are at Lambda Chi Alpha, Pi Lambda Phi, and
> Zeta Psi. Later, there's Delta Chi, FIJI, and Alo-TLC, all at 10. Satur-
> day offers Alpha Sig, and Psi U at 9:30, Lambda Chi Valentine Grain
> Dance at 9:59, Delta Phi, Crow at 10, ATO at 11.

Pressure from the feds that made 21 the drinking age nationwide and liability concerns have limited that kind of lineup, and schools are still struggling to
strike a proper balance. Dartmouth College just announced a prohibition of
hard alcohol on campus, following the lead of Stanford, Colgate, and Swarth-
more. But maybe the solution lies in the past.

Like Dartmouth, Lehigh has a rich Greek tradition. When I attended in
the early '80s, Lehigh had as many fraternities (36) for an undergraduate
population of 4,000 as Penn State had for a community of 20,000. For Lehigh
freshman men, the question used to be which house you'd be pledging, not
whether. There were fraternities to suit every interest and personality: a football house (Delta Upsilon), a basketball house (Theta Delt), a Lax house
(Theta Xi), a WASP house (Kappa Sigma), a Jewish house (Sigma Alpha
Mu), a white-privilege house (Chi Psi), and even a nerd house (Psi Upsilon),
although it did own its own fire truck. My fraternity, Zeta Psi, was more of a
blend.

We were on tap 24/7. Thursday was pub night. On Fridays, the Interfra-
ternity Council would sponsor cocktails for students and faculty at one or
more houses. About once a month, we'd have a Saturday party, often themed.
Except for the rare event that featured grain alcohol, I remember very little
hard liquor. And given the constancy of the social life, there was no such
thing as pregaming. Guys didn't drink in their rooms; we drank among one
another, in our own bar while playing beer pong, or in the lounge watching
TV. Nobody drove. Everything was contained on campus.

Students with whom I have spoken tell me that the social life is still strong
at Lehigh, but no longer revolves around on-campus fraternities, the number
of which has decreased by one-third since I was there. One freshman told me

that social life is now "90 percent off campus." And when the fraternities do have parties, they need to be registered with the university so that wristbands can be distributed to the attendees who are 21 to ensure that only they drink the beer. A recent graduate, John Archibald, questioned the efficacy of the registration system, and confirmed the migration off campus:

> With the registered fraternity parties, kids start to consume more al-
> cohol quicker, trying to get drunk before the party starts at 10:30, so
> they consume a lot in shorter time, and it's more dangerous than it
> needs to be.

Archibald graduated in '13 and then received a master's degree in '14. (His father was a fraternity brother of mine.) He told me that in his senior year, 25 of the 27 members of his fraternity pledge class lived in five different off-campus houses within a block of one another. He said the social restrictions drove them off campus, denying the young men the camaraderie that used to come from living in a fraternity in senior year. Such is the demand for off-campus housing that Archibald and his roommates placed a security deposit for their senior year at the end of the first semester in their sophomore year. He told me:

> It would be safer if they allowed more drinking on campus because
> it's going to happen anyway, and now they go to off-campus houses,
> in an area for which students constantly get e-mails from campus
> police raising security concerns.

I don't envy Sharon Basso's job. As Lehigh's dean of students, it falls to her to fashion an environment that is both socially fulfilling and safe. Where only 20 percent of the undergraduates are 21, she said, the resulting gap sets up a cat-and-mouse game on campuses for which no one has yet found a highly effective solution.

> We take a harm-reduction approach that focuses on teaching stu-
> dents about healthy norms, dialogue about responsible consumption
> of alcohol and teach bystander intervention skills to step in and inter-
> vene when they see peers consuming alcohol dangerously, as opposed
> to a "crackdown, zero-tolerance approach."

By e-mail, I could not persuade her with my Old School solution. "I think the issue is much more complicated than this," she wrote, citing research

Delta Upsilon (DU) Beach Party, Lehigh University, spring 1986. The DU brother on fire is George Keefe ('86). Keith Curtis ('88) is on the left looking up. Lou Sofianakos ('87) is behind Keefe, and Dan Ezring ('88) is on the right, with a towel over his head. According to DU brother Brad McGowan (and Greek lore), then–Lehigh president Peter Likins had objected to the presence of the above-ground pool behind DU house and was reportedly en route to check that it had been removed, which prompted the brothers to plan this special welcome. Photo courtesy of Brad McGowan ('87).

concluding that more than half of students who experience hazing are forced to participate in drinking games; almost half of students had a high-risk drinking event in the last two weeks; and 43 percent of the sexual-victimization incidents involved alcohol consumption by victims and 69 percent involved alcohol consumption by the perpetrator. She also said the way in which students were partying had changed.

> On many campuses in 2015, students describe their parties as gatherings that last only two hours, and the entire focus is on getting intoxicated as efficiently as possible. That is why hard alcohol comes into the picture.

At Dartmouth, Nick Desatnick has concerns about whether the crackdown on hard liquor is the solution. Desatnick is a senior majoring in history and Asian studies. I caught up with him recently just after he finished his midterm in The Making of the Modern World Economy. He's also a member of Sigma Alpha Epsilon and the editor of the *Dartmouth Review*, the conservative newspaper on campus. He said:

> I know from experience that Dartmouth in the last two years has tried out a prohibition on Greek life for all freshman students during their first six weeks on campus, and what we've seen during the period is a great deal in the way of furtive drinking behavior with hard alcohol in dorms, which is in my opinion far more dangerous than anything you would see in a Greek basement. . . . [There] you at least have some control over liability as a brother who's looking after the well-being of guests, to avoid issues with the administration. But, also, just having a bunch of inexperienced drinkers around a bottle of vodka in a dorm room strikes me as a terrible idea.

On that, at least, we all agree.

AFTERWORD

My brother graduated from Lehigh four years before I did. He was president of the Class of 1980, and he, too, wrote the Weekender column for the Brown and White but did a much better job. For him, it was like covering a beat. We were both brothers at Zeta Psi—I was the house academic chairman; he was the house social chairman. My job was to file all the tests and quizzes in the house library for future reference by the brothers; his was to plan parties and come up with themes, like the one where the guys all wore X-ray-vision goggles. Anyway, he doesn't think my Sunday Inquirer column's opening paragraph listing a weekend's worth of Lehigh parties in the early '80s does justice to the social scene that he remembers from the late '70s. Some of what he recalls is mind-boggling when viewed through the lens of 2017.

For example, today, Greek Week means volleyball and dodgeball competition or a lip-sync dance contest or both, but in my brother's era, it meant the "Campus Crawl," an incredible test of endurance where contestants would walk up and down Lehigh's steep hillside and stop at each of 24 fraternities to chug a beer. Recalls my brother: "The perennial winner was a wrestler who could run and puke in stride. It was a thing of beauty!"

There was also "Nude Hoops" at the Beta house; an annual chugging contest; a beach party at Delta Upsilon facilitated by three or four dump trucks of sand around an above-ground pool into which a volunteer would dive after being doused with lighter fuel and ignited; a wet-T-shirt contest at Delta Tau Delta; and "Fiji Island," where the brothers would flood their basement and toss in goldfish for effect.

I recently read an archived 1985 story in the Allentown Morning Call about changes in the Lehigh social scene in which Lehigh's then dean of students, William Quay, is quoted. Quay suggests that the permissive era at Lehigh in the 1970s was a reaction to students' getting interested in the Vietnam War and other world affairs and successfully arguing to the faculty that they were mature and could take responsibility for their own actions. As Quay explains it, the administration bought that line of reasoning.

"It is like a seesaw," Quay says, noting that an incident will occur that causes the administration to become more restrictive, and then, four years later, a new generation of students will ask why they should be punished for something they did not do, and the restrictions will be lifted.

If he was right, maybe the pendulum will again swing. I'm not holding my breath.

MY DINNER WITH ROGER STONE

Philadelphia Inquirer, Sunday, August 23, 2015

"**O**H, I WENT to an orgy there once."

That was Roger Stone's response after I answered his question on my New York City hotel of choice. He's standing shirtless and wearing khakis inside his pied-à-terre on the Upper East Side, where we meet before going for a drink and dinner. The two-bedroom with hardwood floors is decorated with vintage martini shakers and political memorabilia, including a poster of Richard Nixon sporting an Afro.

Stone had just awoken from a well-earned nap. He's had a busy week. After three decades of advising Donald Trump, the two have just parted company and Stone has been busy fielding media inquiries. Whether he quit or was fired depends on which of the two men you ask.

Stone pulls a polo shirt (skull and crossbones, no alligator or man on a horse for him) over his bare back, which famously sports a tattoo of Nixon. But before we leave, he asks if I want to see the closet. Mine's an easy call given his appreciation for sartorial splendor.

After the death of Mr. Blackwell in 2008, Stone began publishing his own best-and-worst dressed list on an annual basis at his website Stonezone.com (full disclosure, I made the former in 2014).

A full wall of his bedroom is filled with neckties and his closet is packed with seersucker and bespoke suits, although he professes to not having purchased one in years. He tells me the *New York Times* has a profile of his fashion sensibilities scheduled for its men's style section in September.

"My tailor was a Chinese guy on 44th Street named Chen who was trained on Savile Row," he says. "He was skilled and knew to leave enough fabric in the seams for weight fluctuations."

Spending time with this practitioner of political dark arts is a steady diet of stories featuring household names. We begin with a drink at a neighborhood corner spot that Stone says caters to Manhattan Republicans, "including Rudy."

When the owner greets him by name, Stone advises to look for a mention of his place in an upcoming tabloid column as the scene of a clandestine political meeting. (My hunch is that when it is published, he will be named as one of the attendees.) The owner offers a round. Stone demurs.

Walking to dinner, Stone tells me we are headed to an Italian restaurant favored by another GOP strategist, Ed Rollins. "I might stick a fork in his neck if we see him," he tells me, not laughing. I still think he's kidding until he reveals that he's been dealing with a painful detached retina brought on by a boxing match with "some young guy."

Rollins is not his only nemesis. He has famously tangled with former New York governor Eliot Spitzer, making certain that Spitzer's penchant for black socks made the tabloids. (I make a mental note to pick up the tab.)

Stone tells me about his current workload. He's enjoying success as an author. His book *The Man Who Killed Kennedy: The Case against LBJ* is a *Times* best seller, and he will soon publish *The Clintons' War on Women*.

"She didn't kill Vince Foster but she helped move the body," he tells me, before commencing a dissertation on carpet fibers and an explanation of how Foster's body was found on a muddy trail with no dirt on his shoes.

He says all the recent notoriety with Trump has been good for his business. "I get calls from potential clients who need a ballbuster," he says.

Hearing this, I immediately think of a scene in the 2008 HBO documentary *Recount*, directed by Jay Roach (*Meet the Fockers* and the Austin Powers movies), which tells the story of the Florida vote in the 2000 election.

When the Republican tally is in trouble, Bush family confidant James Baker barks, "Get me Roger Stone." Stone then orchestrates what was described as "the Brooks Brothers riot," in which congressional staffers protested the counting of ballots in Miami-Dade.

"That's not a dirty trick," he tells me over pasta, at the finish of another story, this one concerning his success, at the request of a client, in having a candidate removed from a ballot due to phony signatures.

To hear him tell it, politicians at all levels have sought his counsel over the years, including some who have kept their distance. "I never met the man," Stone says about a big city mayor who he claims engaged his services to research the contributions of an elected political critic, in the process uncovering widespread fraud in the form of straw donors. Stone is a real life Ray Donovan—only his clients toil in state capitals and Washington, D.C., not Hollywood.

My glass of Montepulciano is long empty, so when a busboy approaches to offer water, I ask for another round of wine.

"Stone's rules: Never ask a busboy for wine," Stone snaps. "They barely speak English."

There's that, too. Stone has rules for politics and rules for life that he promises to assemble in book form someday, including:

White shirt only after six.

Admit nothing, deny everything, launch counterattack.

If you're explaining, you're losing.

Until recently, Trump seemed to be following Stone's rules. An internal Trump campaign memo leaked to the media last week was presumably written by Stone (he won't publicly say) and includes a blueprint the candidate has been following. The memo reminds Trump of what Roger Ailes once told Ronald Reagan: "You didn't get elected on details, you got elected on themes."

While Stone won't say that the memo is his handiwork, he's awfully knowledgeable about the contents. And there is something else he will not say—bad things about Trump, in stark contrast to his willingness to trash talk the rest of the field. Instead, he has emerged on television as Trump's biggest cheerleader.

I later hail a cab wondering whether his departure from Trump is all just part of the plan.

AFTERWORD

Roger Stone publicly parted company with Donald Trump early on in the 2016 campaign while the calendar still said 2015. Stone claimed he quit Trump after the candidate went after Megyn Kelly from Fox News. Trump said he'd fired Stone. Trying to figure out what really happened between them is harder than deciphering the meaning of Stonehenge. My hunch is that they mutually agreed to separate because it suited both of their interests.

All I know for sure is that, at my invitation, Stone soon became a regular guest of mine on CNN talking about the campaign. He was a great guest. Insightful. Colorful. Always well dressed. But then he crossed some folks with his active Twitter fingers and became persona non grata at the network. Some time passed before I could have him back, and no sooner did I, than he was again on the outs, for reasons that had nothing to do with anything he said on my show. Nevertheless, he seemed to blame me for his exile, though I was the one responsible for his initial invitations.

As the campaign progressed, his e-mails to me became increasingly antagonistic, and finally, he wrote to say that he would soon refer to me with the "C-word" on the Internet television program of Alex Jones (a conspiratorial broadcaster with some twisted ideas about what happened at Sandy Hook, among other things), whom Stone told me had "4xs" the viewership of my own network. I downloaded an app and tuned in to Jones's show, only to hear Stone say that I'd once been fired by HUD Secretary Jack Kemp.

I quickly informed him by e-mail that, to the contrary, I was actually the only HUD political appointee who was held over from the Bush/Kemp to the Clinton/Cisneros administration, after Philadelphia mayor Ed Rendell (among others) told the Clinton administration that I was doing a valuable job and that they should keep me—which they did. I also noted that I could have stayed much longer, but after staying for the agreed-upon short term, I then went to practice law—trial law—including defamation law, an area in which I am an expert. He got the picture.

Stone then went back on Alex Jones's show and corrected the record, being careful to make sure I was aware of the retraction.

At the end of 2016, he apologized for the way he'd treated me, which he attributed to "getting caught up in electing a president." I can't imagine that there are too many of us to whom Roger has apologized. I doubt Roy Cohn or Mr. Trump would approve, but I appreciate it. And, where he has picked up the mantle from the deceased Mr. Blackwell, I again made Stone's 2016 Best and Worst Dressed List. The former, not the latter.

FAMILY FARMER WHOSE
LABORS NEVER END

Philadelphia Inquirer, Sunday, September 6, 2015

THE 9 O'CLOCK BELLS from nearby Forest Grove Presbyterian are chiming as I climb into Fred Slack Jr.'s Chevy Trailblazer. He's wearing boots, jeans, an orange T-shirt, and a baseball cap. Already the sun feels hot, and the forecast calls for a week of 90-degree days. He's been up and working since 5 A.M. despite watching an Eagles game on TV with a friend the night before.

"That was only the second night I've been out all summer," he tells me.

I'm not surprised. Fred's days run 14 to 16 hours this time of year. I know because every time I drive by his farm I see him working.

As an aficionado of his legendary Bucks County–grown tomatoes, I've long wanted to see the patch where he grows what the locals call "Freddie's." Slowly we wind down his gravel drive, past a farmhouse that is the centerpiece of a property that has grown crops for three generations of Slacks. In the rearview mirror is the open garage with a picnic table full of freshly picked tomatoes and a sign reading "$2.50 per pound." The honor box will have to cover until we return.

The tomatoes are named for Fred Sr., who passed almost two years ago at age 90 (mother Evelyn passed in 2012). Continuation of the family farming tradition is now solely in Fred Jr.'s 53-year-old hands, although in the backseat is 23-year-old Fred III, a student at Delaware Valley University. (Daughter Deanna is a student at West Chester University.) Today, Fred maintains 250 acres, approximately 60 of which are his. In the mid-1990s, Buckingham Township bought its first farmland conservation easement, protecting the Slack farm from development.

"I grew up grain farming," he says as he begins my tutorial. "Corn, soybean, wheat, and hay were the basics." He tells me he almost went under years ago. "I'm getting the same $5 for a bundle of hay that I was getting 30 years ago," he says. Pumpkins saved him.

"I was always infatuated with pumpkins," he tells me. "One year I grew 12 plants and got about 20 giants, for which people paid $100 to $200 apiece. Some of them ended up in New York City restaurants. The next year, I planted 40 acres of pumpkins. They took me out of debt."

While Fred has had a good run with sweet corn and strawberries, and is always experimenting with different crops, tomatoes are his constant: four types

Fred Slack Jr. in his tomato patch in Forrest Grove, Pennsylvania, summer 2015.

and certain experimental hybrids. It's been that way since his father and uncle grew them for Campbell Soup for two decades until Campbell's stopped canning in Camden.

We drive through a property dotted with farm equipment, some operational, some otherwise. He explains that he staggers his tomatoes into three plantings to maximize the selling season. Currently he has three two-acre tomato patches, each with about 4,000 plants.

Perhaps the best barometer of just how special they taste can be found 2.8 miles down the road at the Pineville Tavern, where they are dressed up with blue cheese and onions, doused with oil and vinegar, and sold as an $8 appetizer ($9 with mozzarella, $12 with chicken). This time of year, the sign in front of the tavern, established in 1742, touts the sale of "Freddie's."

"They're a tough crop to grow," he tells me as we drive into the first patch. Fred's process begins in February, when his "special" seeds are planted in greenhouses. In early May they are transferred to his soil. His first pick usually falls on his birthday, July 28. This year, depending on the frost, he thinks he'll have tomatoes into early October. When I tell him I see no irrigation, he says he's "relying entirely on Mother Nature. And right now, we're in a drought." Earlier in the summer he wanted water—now he worries that a heavy rain could damage his crop.

"All summer I've watched thunderstorms pass me by," he says. "This is the driest part of Bucks County."

The Chevy stops after a short distance, and there they are—giant, red, ripe tomatoes, many with diameters in the five- to six-inch range. One of Fred's long, lean arms reaches under the green leaves. "That's a box filler; there's some real meat on that," he proudly tells Fred III and me. Fred shares that these are a new variety with which he's been experimenting. They'll next be picked and hand wiped before being sold fresh to wholesale and retail customers who come from miles. Clutching his produce, he scoffs at grocery store competitors that "sell the fakes from California," which, he says, get pumped with gas to look red when they aren't really ripe.

"Picking a tomato, red, right off the vine, and presenting it to the public, that's what I do," he says. "But before that happens, there are 1,001 things that can go wrong. Labor. Fungus. Splitting from a heavy rain. Weasels. Mice. I have to watch the plants every single day. Knowing your soil, that's the secret."

Fred feels the encroachment of major developers who are building nearby. Development has driven the deer to his land, where they eat his blossoms. ("They can devastate a pumpkin patch in minutes," he says.) He can't afford the fencing that would be required to keep them out. Nor does he have crop insurance. ("The book work is phenomenal," he says. "The businessman has all that done for him. Not me.") His reflections don't sound remorseful. Fred's a hard worker with no regrets.

"I love what I do. I can't see doing anything else," he tells me. "I'm my own boss. I'm outside in the elements. I love the dirt. I see beautiful moons. And even when I come home dead-ass tired, I like it."

We circle back to his garage just in the nick of time. "You can tell church has let out," he says. I see four cars pull off Forest Grove Road and fill his driveway. It's time for Fred to take over for the honor box.

AFTERWORD

Several months after I wrote this column, I dropped by Fred's farm in the spring just as he'd taken possession of his season's tomato plants, which had been grown off-site from seed. I cajoled him into giving me a few of them for my modest backyard garden. Then I went to Home Depot and bought a few of their tomato plants and put them in a bed next to Freddie's. Late that summer, we had a family taste test. There was no doubt. The plants he'd given me produced better-tasting tomatoes than the yield from the Home Depot plants. But as I continued to buy tomatoes from the man himself, I had to admit that the best of mine were no match for any of his. My conclusion is that what Fred Slack Jr. has going in Forest Grove can be imitated but not replicated. And while I'll continue to try to match his bounty in my own backyard, I don't intend to stop driving to his farm to buy the best.

A SUBJECT'S PORTRAIT
OF THE ARTIST

Philadelphia Inquirer, Sunday, September 13, 2015

NELSON SHANKS treated me like royalty. For nearly three hours in front of a rapt crowd of several hundred people, the man who painted Ronald Reagan, Bill Clinton, Pope John Paul II, Luciano Pavarotti, Antonin Scalia, and arguably his favorite subject, Diana, Princess of Wales, made me the focus of his canvas. We were both miked so I could interview him for the benefit of a paid crowd while he painted me.

As soon as he began, I said I wondered if he ever granted himself a mulligan and started over?

"Sure, a lot," he said. "Or sometimes I just throw things and the sitter gets the idea. I'm just joking. I'm only looking for the best that I can get."

The event was a fund-raiser for Studio Incamminati, the Philadelphia art school he founded in 2002 with wife, Leona. A camera trained on his easel enabled the audience to chart his progress. (In the last five years, a time-lapsed version of his night's work has been viewed nearly 60,000 times on YouTube.) Shanks began by sketching on canvas with a neutral color, but, within minutes, it was completely gone, covered with other paint. He told me he was careful not to draw with too much detail. ("That would be a disaster because then I'd try to fill in the drawing; I would rather build up to that drawing at a later stage.")

Shanks, who passed recently from prostate cancer at age 77, stood while he painted, wearing a purple shirt and tie with dark slacks. His concentration was not mitigated by the presence of the audience in the ballroom at the Union League, or my questions. Was painting work or fun? I asked.

He replied:

It's obligatory, it's habit, it's endless curiosity to try to get it right. It's, I guess it's a kind of plague that gives me a lot of pleasure. I'm not sure what it is, but it's very difficult for me to not paint or not get out to the studio even before it's light and get to work. So there's just so much to do and so much time, so I don't want to waste it.

For his commissioned portraits, he told me his job began long before he lifted a brush.

I've been through some pretty intriguing closets, including Diana's, which was about the size of a small football field, but I was a little disappointed because most of the clothes looked like prototypes for the Des Moines, Iowa, senior prom.

I called her one day and asked her if she had any white blouses and she said, "No, but come tomorrow at 1." And I came tomorrow at 1 and there was a rack of 18 of them that she had gotten from London designers. They had run them over, panting, I'm sure.

Shanks was good company and possessed a quick wit. He told me that when he asked Diana whether she had anything green—"maybe a choker?"— the princess replied, "Well, would Queen Mary's emeralds do?" His reply: "Oh, everyone asks me that." No wonder the painter from Andalusia, Bucks County, quickly became a confidant of the Princess of Wales, who was then in the depth of her despair. He said:

As far as I know, I became one of her best friends for a long time, so that was, for me, a great privilege, obviously, and I just got lucky. But,

Being painted by Nelson Shanks in front of a live audience at the Union League of Philadelphia while raising funds for Studio Incamminati on March 24, 2010.
Photo courtesy of Walter Kosch. Photographed by Mark Garvin.

of course, it was a very sad time for her in many ways. But we had a lot of good laughs; we had a lot of good times.

Shanks painted Diana at his flat in London, a "beautiful studio." He said Diana sought refuge there from her existence at Kensington Palace. In his portrait of her, there is a doorway visible. Shanks said he put it there deliberately, adding:

I didn't have to, and it's slightly open, and the idea was that metaphorically she's going to a different place. She went a little further than I had in mind eventually, but at any rate it was slightly prophetic, I suppose.

At the same time he painted Diana, he was also painting Prime Minister Margaret Thatcher. ("We had a great time. I spent a lot of time with her and [her husband,] Denis, dinners and things, so that was pretty special. It was an amazing time in my life to be around two of the most famous women in the world.")

Shanks told the story of how, one day, Thatcher brought to his studio a beautiful silver-framed portrait photograph of herself, signed with "Great respect to Nelson and Leona." Then Diana saw it. Shanks recalls:

Well, the following day, Diana comes in with a royal framed photograph of herself, signed, "With much love from your dear friend, blah, blah." So there was a certain competition there. It was pretty funny.

I wondered if he had good days and bad days. He said:

I have good days and better days. Usually I don't blow it, unless I don't like the light. If it's a hideous light and it gets really dark for a half an hour, and then the light comes out and bounces all over the place and one thing and another, I go look for the vodka.

The hour drew late. Before the crowd in Center City dispersed, I'm glad I said this to him:

I want you to know that for me to sit here for a couple of hours and ask you questions and watch you work is a tremendous honor, and I appreciate you having invited me to do it, and I'm grateful to the audience as well. What makes me feel wonderful is to see how many people wanted to be here and watch you work, which I think speaks so well of you and of Studio Incamminati, so allow me to thank you on behalf of the audience to watch as you work. It's really great.

The audience five years ago stood and applauded Nelson Shanks.

Last week, the Shanks family issued a statement saying it is "dedicated to keeping the flame of Nelson's vision alive by continuing to share his knowledge with future generations through Studio Incamminati."

AFTERWORD

To fully appreciate Nelson Shanks's gift, please take 56 seconds to watch a time-lapsed video of Shanks painting me. As of this writing, it has been viewed more than 64,000 times: https://www.youtube.com/watch?v=xBBZ8ZlPzHo.

I'd written about Shanks once before, about a year and a half earlier, when I consulted with him to critique the work of an aspiring artist: former president George W. Bush. President Bush had taken up painting as a pastime, and I thought Shanks would have an opinion. True to form, he obliged:

> *I'd give him an A for effort. He certainly could use some training because his things, at this point, are what I would call kind of thin and quite cartoonish, and certainly lacking sophistication in many senses. But, on the other hand, they are interesting. I would say, remarkably, they have a certain similarity to David Hockney. . . . Hockney has very little more ability to produce realism in a classic way than Mr. Bush. So I'd say that the ex-president is doing beautifully.*

Shanks told me that portraits, the area for which he was best known, are the most challenging for a painter. He said:

> *It's very interesting that a painter can paint a hundred still lifes, 10,000 landscapes, and various other things, and 10 portraits and he'd be known as a portrait painter. So calling me a portrait painter is both flattering and demeaning. . . . I'm very sensitive to being called a portrait painter, because there are so many bad ones that it kind of has a bad connotation.*

Which is why Shanks refers to himself simply as a "painter," adding, "But, of course, people then ask, 'Do you do interior or exterior?'"

That wit reminds me of a lingering regret. I wish that Shanks had taken my advice and written a book about his interactions with subjects to append to a coffee-table version of his famous works of art. As I relate in this column, he had so many stories about the remarkable people he painted. Imagine him painting Princess Diana and Baroness Thatcher at the same time! The walls couldn't talk, but maybe Shanks could have. I can't help wondering whether his failure to publish such a book was attributable to the fact that he regarded his relationship with his subjects as akin to penitent and preacher, doctor and patient, or lawyer and client. Having had the experience of his painting me—although in front of a large crowd—I quickly came to realize how one could grow comfortable in his company and reveal things one would do to no stranger. Perhaps that also explains the ease with which he seems to have separated so many female subjects from their clothing!

TAKE NOTE, CANDIDATES,
OF REAGAN'S WORDS

Philadelphia Inquirer, Sunday, September 20, 2015

DONALD TRUMP should have toured the Ronald Reagan Presidential Library before he debated at the Simi Valley venue Wednesday. Perhaps he'd have seen the permanent exhibit showcasing index cards on which the Great Communicator handwrote his favorite one-liners.

According to the library display, Reagan began making such notations in the 1950s, drawing on the wisdom of diverse figures like Greek playwright Aristophanes, Roman philosopher Cicero, and President John Adams. For 40 years, it was his practice to keep them in a makeshift photo album. The 3-by-5 cards holding his favorite one-liners for dinner speeches and campaign rallies were wrapped with a rubber band and kept in his briefcase.

Reagan Library executive director John Heubusch told me that the note cards were almost lost to history.

Back during the Reagan centennial, the 100th anniversary of his birth, I asked our staff here to go in search of material that was not on display here at the library but perhaps find something new and interesting.

After months of searching they found a box which was not marked in any way, just a brown cardboard box high up on a shelf. In this box was the contents of President Reagan's last working desk, so it had in it rubber bands and paper clips and things like that you'd find in a desk.

That box also contained the index cards. Heubusch said:

What's very fascinating is that we found the quotations and things he wrote in his own hand later on in many of the most famous Reagan speeches. It was like his treasure trove of ideas and expressions that he wanted to remember his whole life.

Touring the Reagan Library last week on the eve of the GOP presidential debate, I spied a note card with a line that reminds me of Trump: "Never start an argument with a woman when she's tired . . . or when she's rested."

Trump violated that sage advice when, in the presence of a *Rolling Stone* reporter, he spied Carly Fiorina on television and said: "Look at that face.

Would anyone vote for that? Can you imagine that, the face of our next president?"

His record of misogyny is well documented. This time, there was a swift response. Fiorina cleverly released a campaign video: "Ladies, look at this face, and look at all of your faces—the face of leadership."

And then came the debate. When given the opportunity to respond to Trump's offensive statement, Fiorina took the high road, saying:

> It's interesting to me. Mr. Trump said that he heard Mr. Bush very clearly and what Mr. Bush said. I think women all over this country heard very clearly what Mr. Trump said.

Arguably, Trump's critique of Fiorina's appearance elevated her profile, which contributed to the number of questions that came her way. Trump ensured she received more than her share of face time.

And Trump's comments about Fiorina are just the type of behavior that causes Reagan's elder son, Michael, to believe Trump is the least Reaganesque of the lot. Last week he told me:

> Ronald Reagan didn't attack the people around him. He didn't demean the people around him. He brought everybody together at the end. If Republicans don't bring everybody together at the end of the day, we do not win elections.
>
> We are the smallest bus in the building. We don't have the ability to throw people off the bus and demean them. We have to figure a way to put people on that bus, and move it forward to Washington, D.C., and I don't think that Donald Trump is the guy who, in fact, fills the bus.

Many expected Trump to go after Ben Carson in the debate, but The Donald played nice. Perhaps Carson should also take the tour, and pay attention to another note card in Reagan's handwriting: "Beware of those who fall at your feet. They may be reaching for the corner of the rug."

AFTERWORD

After reading this column, the famed literary agent/attorney Robert Barnett sent me a book published in 2011, edited by the historian Douglas Brinkley, entitled The Notes: Ronald Reagan's Private Collection of Stories and Wisdom. *I had no idea there'd been an entire book devoted to this subject, but I'm not surprised.*

In the introduction, Brinkley writes: "The reason the Reagan Library calls The Notes *a Rosetta stone is that the general public can easily deconstruct from this collection Reagan's own philosophy." Brinkley assorts the cards by subject area, including a section titled "Humor," a series of one-liners that were collected by the Gipper in a fat stack of cards with a rubber band around them. Things like: "Simple diet—if it tastes good, spit it out."*

The book is a must for any student of Reagan, and for those who take seriously the role of public speaking.

IN PHILLY, SINATRA AND
SID MARK PLAY ON

Philadelphia Inquirer, Sunday, November 29, 2015

THE MANY PLANNED COMMEMORATIONS for the centennial of Frank Sinatra's birth on December 12 have already begun. James Kaplan just published the second and final installment of his biography, *Sinatra: The Chairman.* Tina Sinatra's book from 2000, *My Father's Daughter: A Memoir,* has been reissued. *Sinatra 100—An All-Star Grammy Concert* will be taped this week in Las Vegas and air December 6. It features Tony Bennett, Garth Brooks, John Legend, and Alicia Keys. And at noon on Sinatra's birthday, HBO will re-air Alex Gibney's two-part documentary *Sinatra: All or Nothing at All.*

But at the Philadelphia studios of WPHT-AM, Sid Mark doesn't need a milestone to celebrate Sinatra. It's something he has been doing since a listener suggested he play a solid hour of Sinatra 59 years ago. Sid never stopped. And in 1979, a syndicated version of his *The Sounds of Sinatra* was rolled out across the country, airing on 100 stations from coast to coast.

Sinatra passed in 1998 at age 82. While Sid might be in the autumn of his years, he told me recently that Frank Sinatra Jr. reminded him that his father was in the business 60 years, which Sid took to mean he's not finished yet.

"I admire him like an older brother," Frank Jr. told me last week. "I respect his dedication to doing things in a way he has always done them," he added, noting that his father was eternally grateful that Sid kept the music going for his radio audience all these years.

That gratitude was on full display in front of 17,500 people at a sold-out Sinatra show at the Spectrum on November 9, 1991. Old Blue Eyes interrupted the performance to raise his glass to Sid Mark, who looked on with his family. The two had first met at the Sands in Las Vegas in 1966 after Sinatra invited him to be his guest. In Philadelphia, the tuxedo-clad Sinatra first offered a toast in Italian, and then explained:

> That means "I wish for you to live to more than 102 years or 204 years. And I'll be around looking at you all the time." I should like to take a moment to introduce to you a friend who has been a friend for as long as I've been in this business. That's been a long time. This guy is some kind of a man. You all know him so well, because he lives among you here, and I should like to have him stand to take a bow.

And I speak of the wonderful Sid Mark and his family, who are here this evening. There he is right there. I drink to you, Sidney.

It's wonderful to have a friend like Sidney. And I've had maybe four or five in my career of people who have stayed with me when things were dark and didn't change at all whenever anything else changed. And that's the kind of man he is. And I love him, and I say that publicly. I love him. He's one of the best friends I've ever had in my life. I had a lot of friends, but about three days later they were all gone. I ran out of money. But Sidney is a great man, and he's absolutely wonderful.

Jerry Blavat, who was tight with Sinatra and has known Sid since the 1960s, wasn't at the Spectrum that night. But he did see Sinatra, still clad in his tux, later that evening at Jilly's Saloon in Manhattan. "I was at the bar with Frankie Valli, and the place was empty," Blavat said with a laugh. "Fabian was there, too. Well, Frank walked in around midnight and suddenly it was packed."

"Sid's never followed a research chart," Blavat said of his friend and colleague. "Sid knows all there is to know about Sinatra because he loves Sinatra. He eats, breathes, and lives Sinatra."

Joe Piscopo, perhaps best known for his Sinatra impressions on *Saturday Night Live* between 1980 and 1984, is another fan of both men. Piscopo noted that most who know Sid are listeners who've never had the pleasure of meeting him. But for the lucky ones who do, the best is yet to come. "Often you hear a person on radio and then meet them and it's a letdown. But with Sid, knowing him is the icing on the cake," Piscopo said.

Today, the former *SNL* star often headlines casino showrooms doing Sinatra. On the birthday, he'll be singing Sinatra with a full orchestra at the Sands in Bethlehem. But for Sid, he was once willing to play a restaurant in South Philly.

Backstage at Harrah's Casino in Atlantic City in November 2006 with Frank Sinatra Jr. (center) and Sid Mark (right) on the occasion of the 50th anniversary of Sid's Sinatra-centric radio program.
Photo courtesy of Sid Mark.

Four years ago, on Sid's 55th anniversary, he asked Piscopo to sing Sinatra at Galdo's, a catering hall on West Moyamensing Avenue. Piscopo had a scheduling conflict with a family wedding. He said:

> My cousin Pauly from Jersey said, "You have to be at my daughter's wedding." Then Sid invited me to sing Sinatra. The only way I could make it work was to take a helicopter from one to the other. Only for Sid would I sing Sinatra in a restaurant and then take a helicopter to a wedding. And Sid got the City Rhythm Orchestra to play with me and the night was magical.

Frank Jr. has often sat in Sid's studio, marveling as he applied his trade. He said:

> Sid as a broadcaster is old-fashioned, old-school. He's . . . incensed at the thought of making music on a computer. He now uses CDs, but he's still "jockeying discs"—most in radio never even heard the expression.

Junior credits Sid's wife, Judy, as Sid's inspiration—she has been the lady who never left her escort.

That night at the Spectrum, after Sinatra toasted Sid Mark, Old Blue Eyes introduced a song by Rodgers and Hart telling the crowd, "We all know of these songs, because I don't do anything that's new, because there's nothing new."

It's the same with Sid.

AFTERWORD

As I write this, Sid Mark has recently celebrated his 60th anniversary and is still going strong on the radio. My friend Mike Baldini, who emceed the latest anniversary show, told me that Joe Piscopo again performed for Sid and was great, but that Bobby Rydell stole the show. I called Sid to congratulate him on his continued success, and after our long chat, he sent me an e-mail: "Just googled LOYAL FRIEND and your photo came up. . . . Thanks for always being there." That's the highest praise!

In this column, I reference my own participation at Sid's 55th anniversary, but I do not detail the speech I wrote and delivered, of which I am quite proud. I worked hard to incorporate Sinatra lyrics into my tribute. I worry that my delivery was off that night, and I welcome the opportunity to present my words here:

It seems we've stood and talked like this before. We looked at each other in the same way then, but I can't remember where or when.

Good evening, ladies and gentlemen. Proposing a toast to Sid Mark is no easy task. I've struggled with how to sum up 55 years. And my solution is to get a little help from Mr. S.

Not that I don't have original thoughts of my own.

You'd never know it, but, buddy, I'm a kinda poet and I got a lot of things I want to say.

Truth be told, I have known Sid Mark all my life.

Like you, I knew Sid Mark before I met him. He was a constant presence, a fifth member of our family at 24 Mercer Avenue in Doylestown.

I don't know if the first time we were introduced was in the living room. Dining room. Kitchen. It might even have been the bathroom. Because Sid was everywhere.

And he was always with us. He was with us on Fridays. He was with us on Sundays. He was there on birthdays. Happy occasions. Sad events. And all the holidays. Thanksgiving. Christmas.

I remember when Sid introduced us to Sinatra: The Main Event, in 1974. We bought the album. It played so often that at age 12, I memorized Howard Cosell's remarkable introduction of Mr. S.:

> *Live from New York, a city whose landmarks are*
> *familiar all over the world. . . .*

Sid made me a Sinatra fan in my teens.

In fact, when I was 17, it was a very good year.

Sinatra came to the Valley Forge Music Fair and my parents sent my brother and me to the concert as birthday gifts.

Over the years, Sid inspired me to see Frank in concert several times. Including at an outdoor amphitheater at the old Golden Nugget. I will always remember that August night.

The summer wind came blowin' in from across the sea.

My appreciation for Sid and Sinatra continued through college.

Their relationship became a backdrop for some of my relationships. I finally figured out what Frank was singing about.

When I was 21, it was a very good year. It was a very good year for city girls.

But I'm not going to get into that here.

Ultimately I was introduced to Sid Mark when we worked together at the old 96.5FM, WWDB, The Talk Station.

I guess when you met me, it was just one of those things.

Am I right?

You came along and then everything started to hum.

We've been friends ever since. Over the years we've seen many changes in our biz, Sidney. We share one another's perspective on much of what we've witnessed.

Some of it . . . it's witchcraft, wicked witchcraft. And although I know it's strictly taboo. . . .

Enough said.

Sid's voice and all of our memories are inseparable. He has no equal in broadcasting. I can't remember a time in my life when he wasn't present. Radio without Sid Mark?

Then I'd rather, rather have nothing at all.

I'd like to hear more of him. To see more of him.

I get a kick every time I see you standing there before me.

And I know this audience feels the same. Look at us here at Galdo's.

Strangers in the night, exchanging glances.

This is a special crowd. All fans of Sid Mark.

My kind of people, too. People who smile at you.

Speaking of which, there is one other person in this room who deserves acknowledgment.

Sid's wife, Judy.

A lady never leaves her escort.

She's been at his side all these years—sharing Sid with Angie. Maybe Ava, too.

So let us toast our friend. Even though I know what he will say.

Mere alcohol doesn't thrill me at all.

Sidney—3 things:

It had to be you, wonderful you, it had to be you.

The best is yet to come.

King of the hill. Top of the list. Head of the heap. King of the hill.

And finally,

Drink up all you people. Order anything you see. And have fun, you happy people. The laughs and the drinks are on Sidney.

To Sid Mark.

TRUMP'S CANDIDACY
IS RIGHT OUT OF *SEINFELD*

Philadelphia Inquirer, Sunday, March 13, 2016

DONALD TRUMP'S SUCCESS as a presidential candidate is both surprising and easily explained.

He's questioned the heroism of a former POW and standard bearer of his own party. Fought Fox News and its most ascendant star, including questioning her menstrual cycle. Picked a fight with the pope over immigration. Mocked a disabled reporter. Incorrectly cited a Bible verse while courting evangelical Christians. Promised to be an honest broker in the Middle East instead of reflexively siding with Israel. Refused to release his tax returns. Conducted news conferences while accepting victory on primary election nights. And assured us of the size of his manhood.

In every instance imaginable, Trump has done the opposite of what is expected of a presidential candidate, making him the George Costanza of the 2016 cycle!

Seinfeld fans will surely recall what happened in Season Five after an exasperated George walked into Monk's Cafe and told Jerry: "It's not working, Jerry, it's just not working. Every decision I've made has been wrong. My life is the complete opposite of everything I wanted to be."

Replied Jerry: "If every instinct you have is wrong, then the opposite would have to be right."

Immediately thereafter, after spying an attractive blonde seated at the lunch counter, George approached and delivered a line that is now part of *Seinfeld* lore: "My name is George. I'm unemployed and I live with my parents."

"The Opposite" episode was the brainchild of Abington native Andy Cowan, who shares writing credit on the script with Larry David and Jerry Seinfeld. He too sees the parallels between George's willingness to criticize George Steinbrenner while applying for a job with the Yankees and Trump's temerity to confront Roger Ailes's oracle of the GOP, Fox News. Cowan said:

> What's interesting is that instead of focusing on the electorate, the people, the country, Trump decided to do the opposite, focus on himself, his amazing ego, his amazing polls, the amazing size of his no longer private parts, and who wasn't very nice to him. He'll come out during a debate and say, "Thank you, Thank you!" as if it's a per-

sonal appearance, all about him. They called the '70s the me decade. If Trump gets in, it'll be the I-I, me-me decade.

Cowan is quick to cite additional instances where Trump's campaign style has been replete with Costanza-like opposites: a lack of policy specifics, no TelePrompTer, the spouting of the same stream of lazy catchphrases. And he notes that it has also induced the media to do the opposite of what would have been heretofore unlikely: cover him wall to wall as if it were news.

"Two other walls Mexico won't pay for," he quipped.

The man who has written for *Cheers*, *Seinfeld*, and *3rd Rock from the Sun*, and has authored the late 2016 scheduled release, *Banging My Head against the Wall: A Comedy Writer's Guide to Seeing Stars*, began his Hollywood career in the '80s as talent coordinator, writer, and performer on *The Merv Griffin Show*. He remembers well the origin of the legendary *Seinfeld* script.

> I was pitching stories to Larry David left and right, and there was a bra story that he liked, and I still love to this day, about George finding a lost bra in a dryer, a huge lost bra, and then trying to find the woman who owned it, almost like a glass slipper. Until Kramer convinces him it looks more like a grandmother's bra.
>
> We were getting close to his saying yes. And then just as a lark I threw him—because I've always thought about it in my own life—what if I'd done the complete opposite? Would I have been better off? I could tell he took a shine to it right away. He said, "All right, start working on that."

Jeff Greenfield, the author, Emmy-winning journalist, and political observer who once worked for Robert F. Kennedy, also sees the connection.

Greenfield notes that while Trump is "boorish, vulgar, crude, seriously misogynist, [and] nativist," his supporters say, "'that proves he's not politically correct and tells it like it is.'" He adds:

> And when he's revealed to be profoundly ignorant of the most basic public policy facts, his defenders respond, "Well, look what the experts have given us."
>
> Or when presented with facts . . . about his business failures, or his hypocrisies on sourcing, etc., etc., it engenders the response of: "Anything bad the media say about Trump is a lie, because the media always lies."

Of course, in the world of television, Costanza's strategy resulted in a happy ending. He got the girl and the job. So will Trump get his happy ending? "I have my doubts," Cowan said.

> The big opposite this year is the opposite sex who could finally be represented in the Oval Office. Three years ago, Trump said, "I think Hillary's doing a good job." Now it's, "She's the worst secretary of state in history," the opposite. He donated money to her in the past. Maybe he decided this time that acting like the opposite of sane will give her even more than money—the White House.
>
> Which begs the question: When Hillary and Bill dance at the Inaugural Ball, who leads?

Not that there's anything wrong with that.

AFTERWORD

On election night 2016, I sat down at 7 P.M. as a CNN panelist in a group to be moderated by Anderson Cooper. I was scheduled to get out of the chair at 1 A.M. but when they came to replace me, I said I didn't want to leave until it was over. I ended up staying until 4 A.M. because the night's proceedings were so topsy-turvy. That night, CNN had the largest cable audience of any cable program in history—13 million were watching us.

Corey Lewandowski, Trump's first campaign manager, arrived on the CNN set at about 3 A.M., which was at a point where we knew his candidate had won. When asked on camera how he felt now that his candidate was victorious, Lewandowski was more dour than you'd expect. He looked at me and noted that many had ridiculed his candidate, one going so far as to compare him to George Costanza, a reference to this column and a similar commentary I'd delivered on CNN. Then, the following week, he gave a speech in England at the Oxford Union. Early in his remarks, he repeated the Costanza affront, this time citing me by name as its originator. There's no way he could have known, but one of my sons was then an Oxford student. So, the world being flat, word reached me before Lewandowsky even got to his Q and A. Maybe the reason he's so sensitive is that my Seinfeld analogy was so prescient. What he mistook was the tone and intent with which I wrote this column. Connecting Trump's campaign with the personality of George Costanza was my observation of Trump's never-before-seen strategy in American politics. But clearly the joke was missed by Lewandowski, who used what I'd written as ammo in his continuing attack on the media.

A MUST IN LIFE:
TRY, TRY AGAIN

Philadelphia Inquirer, Sunday, May 22, 2016

WHEN WIDENER UNIVERSITY honors me this weekend by allowing me to be its commencement speaker, I will share with the students the reaction at our dinner table several months ago when the invitation arrived.

"Dad, the students must be bummed," was the response from our eldest son, himself in college.

His dismissal became a source of motivation. How to achieve my objective, I wasn't so sure. My thought process included reviewing well-received commencement addresses. Only I'm not Bono, Bill Gates, or Ali G. I'm not particularly funny. I try not to be verbose. And I don't live life by any particular quote.

I can report that being invited to deliver a commencement address demands introspection, an evaluation of one's life. In my case, there's more to be learned from the journey than the destinations I have reached. I know that sounds like a slogan plucked from one of those posters you order in the back of an airline magazine, but it's been the pattern of my entire life. Perseverance has been the hallmark of "My Climb," which became the working title of my speech.

I will begin by explaining that I'd attended the law school of my dreams (Penn) only because, after being wait-listed, I disregarded the application brochure admonition that interviews were not given and parked myself in the admissions office until I attracted the interest of the dean. And that, while if you looked at my progression as a radio host on a graph it makes perfect sense (guest, then guest-host, Sunday night host, Saturday and Sunday morning host, afternoon host, morning-drive host, syndicated host, SiriusXM radio host), that doesn't tell the story of rejection and opportunities lost.

Like how for five years I was not only hosting a successful morning-drive program in Philadelphia, but also guest-hosting for Bill O'Reilly on 500 stations across the nation. I thought I was paying my dues.

But when O'Reilly decided to give up radio, his syndicator, Westwood One, didn't hire me. It said it wanted a "name" so instead hired a former actor (think *Hunt for Red October*) and U.S. senator named Fred Thompson.

I will share that MSNBC had me fill in for Joe Scarborough when he had a 10 P.M. program. Many nights I'd guest-host his show until 11 P.M. in Secau-

Delivering the commencement address in a downpour at Widener University on May 21, 2016. Photo courtesy of Widener University.

cus, New Jersey, then sleep in the back of a Town Car back to Philadelphia, only to get up at 4 A.M. to host my own morning radio show. Suddenly, Don Imus, the MSNBC morning man, was fired for an inappropriate comment. Quickly, they put me in his seat. I was given a weeklong tryout on live television. Funny thing, they ultimately gave the Imus show to Scarborough. Worse, I wasn't offered the Scarborough time slot either!

Soon came the 2008 presidential campaign. MSNBC launched a daily program called *Race for the White House.* It named David Gregory the host. I became a regular guest. So, too, did an Air America radio host named Rachel Maddow and Jay Carney, the Washington bureau chief for *Time* magazine. We appeared together daily.

When the campaign ended with President Barack Obama's election, Gregory was asked to host *Meet the Press.* Maddow was given her own show in prime time. Carney was named director of communications for Vice President Biden and later became press secretary for Obama.

Me? I was the only one not to get a new job. Instead I received more fill-in work. This time for Chris Matthews on MSNBC's *Hardball.* Whenever Matthews vacationed, I was in his chair. Just as I had done for O'Reilly and Scarborough, and by now for Glenn Beck too, on HLN. My ratings were strong.

For five years, I was Matthews's go-to person. And, of course, I really wanted a show of my own.

The president of MSNBC, Phil Griffin, used candor that I appreciated even though his words stung. He said that while my fill-in work was appreciated by the network, I would never have a show of my own there.

"Smerc," he said, "we are young, liberal, and nerdy, and you are none of the above."

By now, my wife and I had four children. The older you get, the more difficult it becomes to take risks. I second-guessed the choices I'd been making and wondered: Had I sacrificed a stable and secure career path in the law to stroke my ego in the media?

I have Jeff Zucker, the president of CNN, to thank for a big break. In the middle of an ice storm 2½ years ago, he invited me to meet with him on short notice. How to get there was an issue.

Our eldest son was then a senior in high school and he drove a Jeep. The only way I could get to New York City was to drive his vehicle. But while that son is a bona fide rocket scientist, he hadn't screwed the roof on properly, so it leaked, and the interior was filled with ice. I nervously drove up the New Jersey Turnpike sliding in my seat. Luckily, Zucker and I immediately bonded. In a conversation that didn't last 15 minutes, he offered me a show of my own on CNN. I celebrated, slipping all the way back to Philadelphia.

Today I'm pleased to host both a radio program heard nationwide on SiriusXM and a television show on CNN that bears my name, in addition to writing this column, which is routinely reprinted in newspapers across the country. But better than the wins has been the navigation of the path—steering around roadblocks and overcoming rejection.

I will tell the Widener graduates that while we all know people to whom things have come effortlessly, that hasn't been my experience nor can they assume it will be theirs.

> My climb has taught me that in order to succeed, you must first ask
> for the order.
> You'll need to request the meeting.
> So be prepared to introduce yourself.
> To write the e-mail.
> Better yet—sign the letter.
> Make the phone call.
> Show up where not invited.
> And find a mentor. People like to be asked for assistance.

Your level of success in life will be determined by your unwillingness
   to accept rejection and failure.
Then I will thank them, and say I hope they weren't bummed.

AFTERWORD

When Widener University's 2016 Commencement exercises began, I was stand-
ing alongside the university's president, Dr. Julie E. Wollman, as we processed
under threatening skies. The more than 800 undergraduates receiving diplomas
and their families all sat exposed to the elements, while the school leadership,
including me, were shielded under a temporary stage. Just before my speech, the
skies opened and the rain began to pour. I asked Dr. Wollman whether I should
deliver my remarks as intended or give a significantly abbreviated version. We
agreed that I would deliver the full speech. And the only time I remember receiv-
ing any applause from the students is the moment I waved off a school em-
ployee who approached me with an umbrella. It was a great honor to speak, but
I wonder whether I should have used the CliffsNotes version because of the
weather.

   For space reasons, this column does not contain my complete address. There
were other stories of rejection that I included in the full version, including this:

   Fresh out of law school, my brother and I formed a title insurance
   agency, and we initially floundered. Business was slow, and our debts
   quickly accumulated.

      One day I read in the Philadelphia Business Journal *that a large*
   Center City apartment building called the Wanamaker House was to
   sell its units as condominiums. That represented an enormous piece of
   potential business—333 separate real estate transactions on which we
   could collect a fee—if only I could win over the project's developers.

      Trouble was, I didn't know the name of any of these New York–
   based partners. Their identities were not in the story—only their com-
   pany was referenced.

      Now, keep in mind, this was pre-Internet. No Google. The only tool
   at my disposal was a phone book and landline telephone, and this was
   the age of secretaries acting as gatekeepers. When I called the business
   office, the receptionist refused to release the identity of the principals.
   You'd be right to question the ethics of what I did next.

      I waited, and called again. This time I said that I was with Federal
   Express, had a package that needed to be delivered to the president of

the company, but that the name and address were smudged on the envelope.

"Oh," she said, "that must be for Allen Weinstein. He's our president." And she gave me his address. I now had a name. I wrote to him. Met him. Told him how I got to him—which he appreciated! Won his business. Saved ours.

I delivered the full speech on radio the Monday after the Saturday commencement, and the Allen Weinstein story caused a listener to call in and tell me he thought that I had given the graduates bad ethical advice. It made me wonder what had happened to Allen Weinstein, and the more I thought about it, the more I also wondered what he would think of the fact that I told that story to a group of college graduates at their commencement. So, after 25 years of no contact, I tracked him down and was pleasantly surprised to learn that Allen has himself written a book called Memoirs of a Learning Disabled, Dyslexic Multi-millionaire (2015). Anyone who reads his book, which I highly recommend, will understand why Allen appreciated the initiative I used to meet him, and why he thought it was an appropriate story for a commencement speech. After all, it was almost straight out of his book, which contains his tips for life, and we are kindred spirits in many respects.

MY HEIMLICH MANEUVERING

Philadelphia Inquirer, Sunday, June 5, 2016

HENRY HEIMLICH used the lifesaving technique that bears his name to rescue a fellow senior last month. Depending upon whether you believe some of the current press accounts or his Wikipedia page, it was either the first or second time the 96-year-old surgeon was thus called to action. The event occurred in a Cincinnati assisted-living home, where Dr. Heimlich saved 87-year-old Patty Ris. "God put me in this seat next to you," she wrote him in a thank-you note.

That's quite a storybook ending, but the saga reminded me of my own close encounter with the good doctor.

In 1993, I left a federal position to which I'd been appointed by the administration of George H. W. Bush to join the legendary James E. Beasley in the practice of trial law. Our introduction came when I sought his legal advice after *Inquirer* columnist Steve Lopez wrote about me, questioning whether I'd ever "find honest work." I thought he was calling me dishonest, and contacted Beasley, who'd earned quite a reputation handling defamation actions. Beasley said he'd take the case—and he also hired me. (No lawsuit was ever filed, though. Months after I'd joined him in practice, Beasley said to me: "You walk down the street thinking about that column. Nobody else does.")

One day soon after my arrival at the firm, he handed me a case.

The matter concerned a Philadelphia man who'd choked to death at an all-you-can-eat buffet in the city. Beasley had accepted the case more to create case law than to earn any fee. His success had enabled him that type of case selection.

Beasley was angered that a restaurant employee who witnessed the death was reportedly not permitted by a manager to perform the Heimlich maneuver. Beasley wanted to establish a duty on Pennsylvania restaurants—similar to one in New York—to perform the maneuver. But when the restaurant owner turned out to be a Florida corporation and the case was moved to federal court (where no state law could be created), Beasley lost his appetite for the file and handed it to the new guy.

This case about a man's tragic passing in a public place had more than its share of characters and drama and was my initiation into the practice of law. I struggled to find the critical witness—the cashier—but local celebrity sleuth Russell Kolins did—in prison. My concerns about her credibility were offset by the discovery that she was CPR-trained and carried a certification (including Heimlich) in her wallet.

There was also the fact that the decedent had been eating corned beef in the men's room, apparently so as not to be seen by his dining partner, a girl-friend who was vigilant about his weight. The mention of her presence didn't sit well with his adult children. Neither did my reluctance to assert a lost earn-ings claim for their father's estate, as his business had been under federal in-vestigation at the time of his demise.

To top things off, the District Court was involved in a pilot program ex-perimenting with cameras in the courtroom.

Rookie lawyer or not, I knew that at trial I'd need to introduce one of the ubiquitous posters showing how the Heimlich maneuver is performed. Having tracked one down, I noted that its disclaimer included a reference to the Heimlich Institute and an Ohio telephone number. I called in the hope of obtaining additional materials to explain the method to a jury. I'll never forget when, after explaining my purpose to the female voice at the end of the line, she replied: "Oh, Dr. Heimlich would be most interested in this."

Dr. Heimlich? I was a complete knucklehead. It never occurred to me that the procedure was named for an American physician, much less that he was alive.

Up until this point, the very able Philadelphia defense attorney represent-ing the buffet, James Bodell, had been a gentleman but outwardly dismissive of my case. Now, after the resources of the Beasley firm enabled me to retain Heimlich as a plaintiff's expert who would explain his method to the jury, his guffaws abated. Heimlich's expert report was attached to the pretrial memo I filed with Judge Jan E. "Bud" DuBois. When we met in chambers, DuBois informed Bodell and me that Court TV had requested to televise Heimlich's testimony.

Soon thereafter, the matter resolved. And where Heimlich's witness fee had been paid but his Philadelphia appearance was not necessary, I was able to cajole him to appear on my radio show, where he explained his discovery of the method in 1974. The audience seemed appreciative of his good work, except for one man who wrote to me challenging the authenticity of Heim-lich's discovery. Strangely, the "skeptic" was his son.

Not long thereafter, I became engaged to my wife. Bodell was kind to write, in jest, and offer a discount on the use of the buffet for our reception. We passed.

AFTERWORD

Soon after this column was published, I was contacted by the aforementioned "skeptic," Peter Heimlich. I was taken aback when he told me that much of his father's work was a fraud. Peter (along with his wife, Karen) runs a website called medfraud.info, where lists of hyperlinks to outside sources backing his claims appear under such headings as "Medical experts speak out against my father's history of misconduct" and "My father's history of abusing colleagues."

Online, Peter says his interest in outing his father began in 2001, when, after learning of serious health problems in his family, he was appalled to find that his father was not addressing them. That discovery led to his heightened curiosity and further investigation. As he asserts on his website:

> *In spring 2002, my wife Karen and I began researching the career of my father, Dr. Henry J. Heimlich of Cincinnati, famous for the "Heimlich maneuver" choking rescue method. To our astonishment, we inadvertently uncovered a wide-ranging, unseen 50-year history of fraud.*

Peter Heimlich expresses serious doubt about whether his father invented the life-saving technique that bears his name and similarly questions the veracity of the doctor's other supposed accomplishments, including the invention of the Heimlich chest drain valve. Where Dr. Heimlich claimed to have performed the world's first total organ replacement (on a dog) in 1955, Peter points out that the surgery had already been done dozens of times on humans by a Romanian surgeon. But Peter believes his father's "most bizarre" medical claim is "malariotherapy," which Peter's website describes as "a quack cure for AIDS, cancer, and Lyme disease that consists of infecting patients with malaria." He also notes that though the American Red Cross once adopted the Heimlich maneuver as a lifesaving technique for a choking victim in place of back slaps, the organization has since, quietly, returned to favoring the latter. And while the American Heart Association continues to recommend the Heimlich maneuver, they now do so without using his name, referring to it instead as "abdominal thrusts."

Perhaps unsurprisingly, referring to the focus of my column—the story of Dr. Heimlich's performing the maneuver for the first time at age 96 and saving the life of a neighbor in a retirement home—Peter notes that his father claimed to have done so in 2001 at Cincinnati's Banker's Club restaurant. Indeed, research verifies that Dr. Heimlich told the BBC in 2003 that he had used the maneuver on an 80-year-old man who was choking in a restaurant.

Peter Heimlich is far from being his father's only critic, but it astounds me how much effort Peter has put into disparaging his dad. After all, regardless of whether the doctor invented the Heimlich maneuver, he certainly popularized it. And by Dr. Heimlich's estimates, it has saved tens of thousands of lives.

Dr. Heimlich passed away on December 17, 2016, at age 96. I was interested to see how major newspapers like the New York Times and Cincinnati Enquirer (Dr. Heimlich's hometown newspaper) would treat the controversies raised by Peter in Dr. Heimlich's obituary. Both gave ample coverage.

THE RIGHT SPOT FOR THE RIZZO STATUE?
RIGHT WHERE IT IS

Philadelphia Inquirer, Sunday, August 21, 2016

A WINTER SNOWSTORM hammered Philadelphia on February 23, 1987. I'm not normally a horoscope person, but for some reason I saved my Pisces directive that day: "You'll have reason to celebrate. . . . The boss recognizes your value." I'd like to think that was true. It was my first day working for Frank L. Rizzo.

Due to the weather, I was the only staffer who made it to work. For me it was easy. I lived in a small studio on Rittenhouse Square and needed only to walk three blocks to 1528 Walnut Street. Either Anthony or Joe who managed the building let me into Suite 2020, where I sat in the outer area reserved for visitors to the former mayor. Despite the snow, the telephone that ended in "1987" started ringing. And I remember the first call that I answered.

It was a woman from the Northeast whose block was debilitated by the weather. She wanted her street plowed and she was calling Rizzo. It mattered not that he hadn't been in City Hall for seven years.

That first day was typical at the campaign office. For the next nine months, I was constantly at his side. My business card said "Political Director," but my role was often that of body man, especially when he crisscrossed the city at night making campaign appearances in his run for mayor. That meant attending to the candidate's personal needs and also serving as a buffer in his public encounters.

If there was one constant every night, it was that people would seek his assistance. Potholes, broken streetlights, trash-strewn lots. Jobs—always people asked for work. Abandoned automobiles, lack of police patrol, missing dogs. Yes, lost pets.

You name it, people asked for his help. They'd make verbal requests that I'd notate or they would stick handwritten notes in one of his enormous hands that spelled out their problem and included a telephone number. Rizzo would pass the notes to me for safekeeping, and I'd return them to him the following day in the office. He would seek to match the need with friends he still had at all levels of city government. No matter the nature of the problem, he always tried to help.

Here's something else that might surprise: If someone called the City Hall switchboard after he left office and asked for Rizzo, the operators would connect the caller to his house in Chestnut Hill. I know. I not only reached him that way; I also sat at his kitchen table on Crefeld Street and watched him accept those redirected calls.

Which is why I've always seen the Municipal Services Building as the ideal home for his statue. It's the building that houses so many who are responsible for the delivery of city services. The added attraction for the location was that Rizzo's first mayoral office was in the MSB, and that vantage provides a vista for his likeness to look fondly across the street toward City Hall. Some originally believed the police Roundhouse to be a natural, but I disagreed. While for some his public persona will always be that of the patrolman who rose through the police ranks and became mayor, the Frank Rizzo I knew was 16 years removed from the department, and with the city's turbulent past behind it, his primary focus was on the unglamorous task of meeting basic needs.

A few months ago, I heaped praise upon *Rizzo*, a play by Bruce Graham then running at Theatre Exile in Old City. It was based on the book *Frank Rizzo: The Last Big Man in Big City America* by Sal Paolantonio. I noted just one criticism: "Missing, for me, in the play were sufficient illustrations of what made him tick, what gave the man big enough to wear a size 52 'long' suit his greatest personal satisfaction—helping people and improving the city he loved."

The effort to remove the Rizzo statue from its current home is part of a national attempt to rewrite history, especially on matters of race. This has been particularly true on college campuses. When some sought the removal of Harvard Law School's seal because it was tied to a slaveholding family that endowed the school's first professor, the university president, a Civil War scholar, said something that applies to many of these debates.

"I feel quite strongly that we should not be trying to erase our history of names," Drew G. Faust told the *Crimson*. "I think we're all going to be facing these questions, and the case that I would make is . . . about the importance of sustaining our history, not erasing it."

She's right to argue that it's better to understand this type of symbolism in context, rather than change memorials in a manner that seeks to alter historical legacy.

There's been no new revelation, no new finding regarding the Rizzo record since the statue was erected in 1998. If new information had come to light about the man or his actions, this might be a reasonable debate. At least when they removed the Joe Paterno statue outside of Beaver Stadium in Happy Valley, it was as a result of former FBI Director Louis Freeh's concluding that the longtime coach probably knew about Jerry Sandusky's sexual abuse of children.

In contrast, rather than argue new facts, the petition that promotes the removal of the Rizzo statue offers a diatribe of specious generalizations about a man not here to defend himself. ("Rizzo was an unrepentant racist who stopped at nothing to torture and hold Philadelphia's African American community as his personal hostages.") Plus, this contrived dispute is much larger than the biggest man on Philadelphia's political scene in the 20th century and could set a dangerous precedent. Consider that the petition makes clear that removing Rizzo's statue is but a first step, and that even war heroes must be replaced:

> The black community would rather see representations of the great contributions made by African Americans and other people of color to this city's development. These statues should be erected in place of the constant representations of Christopher Columbus, war heroes, Frank Rizzo, and others who have held communities of color in subjugation.

Moving Frank Rizzo isn't appropriate. Better that he continue to stand where he is, and that his legacy be subject to civil debate rather than an erasure of history.

AFTERWORD

The statue controversy evidenced the never-ending debate over Rizzo's legacy. Another reminder came in the play I mention in this column. At Sal Paolantonio's invitation, I attended a performance one night at Theatre Exile in Old City. I wrote about the evening—28 years to the day after Rizzo lost his rematch with W. Wilson Goode (a campaign for which I worked)—in another Sunday Inquirer *column published November 8, 2015. I noted that the night had a reunion feel. People were gathered to watch the play and to engage in a postshow debate about Rizzo. The Pulitzer Prize winner Buzz Bissinger was there (Rizzo had attributed his 1987 loss to Bissinger's hard-hitting coverage of his record with regard to policing). I sat with my friend Larry Ceisler, now a public affairs executive, who had a role in Mayor Goode's '87 campaign similar to the one I had played for Rizzo.*

The play featured a scene in which a 1987 Rizzo campaign ad was filmed. In the ad, Rizzo stood in a trash-strewn Kensington lot and attempted a rebrand with a self-deprecating quip, followed by a gesture toward the debris and the concluding line: "How long do you think I'd put up with this?" What the play didn't portray about the ad is something I witnessed live during its actual filming. Rizzo's campaign manager, Martin Weinberg, had decided not to show Rizzo the script until he was on the set, knowing he'd have difficulty getting Rizzo to say the self-deprecating line, "When I was mayor, . . . I said some things I shouldn't have said." And Weinberg was right: Rizzo refused. So the two negotiated while an expensive film crew waited. Finally, Weinberg prevailed, but only after Rizzo told him, "So you'll know, Weinberg, I meant every fucking thing I ever said." Then he looked into the camera and nailed the line.

It's one of my favorite stories, among many, from my time spent with the man. At Theatre Exile, many audience members had their own Rizzo stories, and some were eager to share. And while all were complimentary toward the play we'd just witnessed, the debate about Rizzo's influence on the city divided the audience as much as it separated Philadelphia when he was alive.

The Rizzo debate usually boils down to one question: Did Rizzo maintain the city's stability as police commissioner and mayor amid a turbulent time, keeping order while other large towns devolved, or did his brute force and bombast hinder its forward progress? But the real question may be whether that question can even be answered. There has always been a temptation for many to see Rizzo as an all-or-nothing proposition. Supporter or opponent? Friend or foe? Guardian or antagonist? His approach did not elicit common ground. Maybe that's a reflection of the way the black wards and white wards so cleanly divided when Rizzo's name led the ballot. But neither version of the man is the one I remember.

To ride with him in the campaign car for a full year as a 25-year-old law student and campaign aide was to be provided a backseat view of the real Frank Rizzo. As we crisscrossed the city nightly, no subject was off limits. He had a story for every intersection. A bust made. A pothole filled or a streetlight repaired. Or often a joke that came to mind. Up close, he was nuanced, complicated, and sometimes contradictory—but never dull. Rizzo's gone, but the stories will last forever.

CIVILITY WINS IF
"COMMENTS" UNPLUGGED

Philadelphia Inquirer, Sunday, August 28, 2016

TUESDAY WAS the final day that comments could be posted on news stories at NPR.org. The decision was announced one week prior by ombudsman and public editor Elizabeth Jensen, who quoted NPR's managing editor for digital news, Scott Montgomery: "We've reached the point where we've realized that there are other, better ways to achieve the same kind of community discussion around the issues we raise in our journalism."

Not surprisingly, the decision didn't sit well with many of those who posted 3,375 comments to the announcement. Among them was someone who self-identified as "Abbi Baily": "This is the only place I've found where it is (was) possible to have an intelligent, fun conversation about politics, science, history or philosophy, where a professor of said subject is at your virtual elbow to recommend further reading or correct bad grammar."

That was just one of 32,200 comments Abbi Baily had posted at NPR.org. And it drew a response from The Original DB, whose image is that of a chimp. The reply represented the 4,530th time The Original DB posted a comment. And it drew a reaction from Running Dog, who had 9,987 comments to his credit.

The three evidenced something else reported by NPR's Jensen. She wrote that in July, NPR.org recorded nearly 33 million unique users, and 491,000 comments, but that those comments came from just 19,400 commenters, which translates to just 0.06 percent of all users. Moreover, NPR determined that for the months of June and July, just 4,300 users posted about 145 comments apiece—or 67 percent of all comments for those two months!

At least many of the NPR comments were civil compared with what I've seen elsewhere. Take, for example, those who posted comments to Chris Cillizza's The Fix blog at the *Washington Post*, which is where I first read the news about NPR. Cillizza opined: "This is terrific news. And, all other major media organizations should follow NPR's lead." His view drew a caustic response.

"Petronius_Jones" said: "It's hard to blame Cillizza for hating comments sections. As a lazy facile writer, all of his pieces attract negative and personal comments."

"Dr_Cheese_Souffle" offered: "Chris Cillizza is a tool for suppressing free speech everywhere."

And "Nickotime" said: "If I wrote Cillizza's garbage I'd want comments gone, too."

These comments proved something Cillizza told me when we discussed NPR's move: "It's the loudest, often most obnoxious person in the room with the most time to dedicate so they will always outlast you unless you are willing to stay online and fight with them 22 hours a day."

Cillizza bristled at the argument that he is advocating the stifling of free speech, and said that role is actually played by those who take over news sites and don't allow room for a casual observer, who would be afraid to jump in during the level of routine vitriol.

He's right.

It's been years since I read any of the comments appended to my own column. When I did so long ago, I found them to be largely angry, uncivil, and unresponsive to the merits of whatever I was arguing, and not worthy of a response, especially when commenters hide behind pseudonyms. I've always suspected what NPR confirmed—that comment boards are dominated by a tiny sample of the readers at large who don't represent anyone but themselves.

Please don't misunderstand. I welcome debate, which I prove for 15 hours every week while hosting a nationwide radio program. My studio's nine toll-free telephone lines are usually full with callers of every political stripe from all across the country who are interested in discussing issues of the day.

Here's a secret: If you want to butt the line, just tell my screener you disagree with my position. She will alert me, increasing the odds that I will speak to you sooner than later. She knows I look for disagreement, but with a caveat: It has to be civil discourse. Not sanitized, just reasonable. I don't name-call, and I expect my audience to behave likewise. Thankfully, my SiriusXM callers comply. I have no recollection of when I last needed to hang up on a caller who was abusive. I know it hasn't happened during this contentious campaign, which says a lot.

While the Internet has made our lives exponentially easier, the use of technology is not without its drawbacks. One liability is the beer muscles some grow when given the opportunity to express themselves anonymously. Just like the drunk who has an inflated measure of his power at closing time, many bloggers adopt a tone and say things online that they would never offer if their faces were seen and identities known.

I know, because when not typing out a column on a computer, or sitting in front of a radio microphone or television camera, my day-to-day life is filled with plenty of encounters with newspaper readers, radio listeners, and television viewers who seek to engage me on news headlines or opinions I have expressed. To a person, those with whom I have spoken while pumping gas, grocery shopping, or at a back-to-school night are courteous and engaging. Do they always agree with me? Of course not. Nor do those with whom I share a Thanksgiving table.

Our political dialogue is far too coarse. Nasty, anonymous comments are a significant part of a much bigger problem, but one aspect we can easily control. Let's unplug them.

AFTERWORD

Within 24 hours, there were 332 comments appended to this column. I read none of them.

YEAH, YEAH, YEAH:
LARRY KANE, FAB HISTORIAN

Philadelphia Inquirer, Sunday, September 4, 2016

R ON HOWARD'S new Beatles movie, *Eight Days a Week—The Touring Years*, is being advertised with a trailer that begins with a familiar voice saying: "This is the greatest phenomenon in the century thus far."

That 1964 assessment came from a 21-year-old radio reporter at Miami's top-40 WFUN. Fifty-two years later, Philadelphians will instantly recognize the unmistakable voice of a young Larry Kane. The legendary local newsman has a significant on-screen presence in the movie due to his unique, front-row seat to the Beatles' invasion of America.

"The reason this film is so unprecedented, and so unique, is that it takes you there," Kane told me last week. "Ron Howard assembled never-before-seen footage. I got chills feeling like I was back in '64."

That year, Kane was a cub reporter with a business card that said "news director." When it was announced that the Beatles would play an unprecedented 35 concerts in 25 American cities during their maiden U.S. tour, Kane sent a letter to band manager Brian Epstein on a letterhead that listed his own top-40 station, and six others that catered to African American audiences.

"I think he thought I was a big shot," Kane recalled with a laugh. "Truth is, I was only looking for one interview."

Instead, Epstein invited Kane to accompany the Beatles at every stop. Believe it or not, he was slow to accept. Kane explained to me:

> Muhammad Ali was training just around the corner from me in Miami. Vietnam was escalating. There was an enormous Cuban influx into Florida. We were living post–JFK assassination amid escalating racial tensions. And the Ford Mustang was all the rage. I didn't want to miss any of it.
>
> As I say in the movie, "Why would I want to travel with a band that will be here in October and gone in December?"

There was added reason for Kane's reluctance. Just before the tour began, his mother, Mildred, passed at age 40 from multiple sclerosis.

"She was my inspiration," he said. "When I was going into a radio station till midnight during high school, she would leave notes on my pillow telling me how my newscasts sounded."

Meanwhile his father, a World War II veteran, expressed misgivings: "Larry, watch your back. These guys are a menace to society."

In the end, his radio station forced him to tour with the Beatles, an edict he appreciated.

"I quickly sensed that the band represented the biggest cultural shift in generations, and maybe ever," Kane told me.

He attended every Beatles concert in America in 1964 and 1965, and a few in 1966—46 in all. And he watched three performances on *The Ed Sullivan Show* in person. Which is why *Eight Days a Week* relies so heavily on his narration.

"This is Larry Kane with the Beatles flying over America," he intones in archival audio used in the movie.

The special rapport he enjoyed with the Fab Four is plainly evident in the film. Kane attributes a certain level of bonding with Paul McCartney and John Lennon to the fact that both had also lost their mothers at an early age, a point underscored by Howard's inclusion of a home movie showing Mildred Kane blowing a kiss. And, Kane says, the Beatles shared his nose for news.

> We got along well. They were very intellectually curious. I didn't ask them the questions most asked, like what they had for breakfast, how

Larry Kane aboard the Beatles' chartered airliner with Paul and John on the 1964 tour of North America. Photo courtesy of Larry Kane.

they styled their hair, or what they liked in women's hemlines. I asked about war in Vietnam, racial division, immigration in Europe, the royal family, Cuban refugees to Miami, and life after President Kennedy.

As detailed in the movie, it was Kane who, inside a Las Vegas hotel room, told the band that a concert at the Gator Bowl in Jacksonville, Florida, would be before a segregated audience, which McCartney immediately derided as "stupid." When the Beatles refused to play, jeopardizing $50,000, the seating was changed.

But the interplay between the burgeoning newsman and international sensations was not all serious.

"They goofed on me," Kane told me.

"Only kidding, Larry," Lennon says jovially in the movie.

In 1965, while filming *Help!* in the Bahamas, Kane discovered the Fab Four were high from smoking marijuana. "I'd never seen that before," he says in the movie.

Kane's work on the Beatles caught the ear of Philly's WFIL-AM (560), his first stop in a rapid rise through the local media market. In 1970, at age 27, he became the first *Action News* anchor, and one year later, the station was No. 1.

Kane kept in touch with the band, even calling in a favor from Lennon. In 1975, Kane was raising money for MS, a passion that began with his mother's passing and that continues today. Lennon agreed to come to Philadelphia to help.

"The station management never believed he'd show up," Kane told me. "But he got on a train alone in New York City and got off at 30th Street."

During a weekend spent in town, Lennon delivered a now-legendary, impromptu weathercast, live on Channel 6, while thousands of fans waited outside in a parking lot on City Avenue.

"Frank Rizzo sent a stakeout squad," Kane remembered. "And when I asked him why, he was prescient. He said, 'A man like Lennon could get shot.'"

Kane's involvement with *Eight Days a Week* began several years ago when he was contacted by Jonathan Clyde, the director of production and marketing for Apple. He said:

When I first went to Los Angeles to meet with the crew, I took with me a list I'd prepared of the seminal moments of the Beatles' tours of America. So began many interviews, but my more recent contributions were recorded here in Philadelphia, with engineer Matt Teacher at Sine Studios.

Kane said that working with Ron Howard was a wonderful experience and that he was "as approachable and nice as you would expect."
Howard responded in kind:

Larry is such a valuable eyewitness to an aspect of the Beatles' story I wanted to focus on, which was the brief intense period when Beatlemania morphed from "novel and fun" to "seismic, political, and polarizing."
Larry's brilliant coverage then, and his ability to articulately analyze it all over again from his perspective today, meant so much to our documentary. He was and remains a very impressive guy.

Eight Days a Week will premiere in London on September 15, and Kane will be in attendance. That day is also the 50th anniversary of his arrival in Philadelphia. The veteran of 23 political conventions enjoyed an anchoring career that spanned 39 years, and included stints at all three Philadelphia network affiliates. He's not finished. He can still be heard offering political analysis for KYW Newsradio. And now his role as the only broadcast journalist to travel to every stop on the Beatles' 1964 and 1965 tours is the stuff of celluloid fame.

Stick around for the rolling of the credits at the end of this spellbinding concert movie. In a list acknowledging on-screen performances that include Whoopi Goldberg, Elvis Costello, Malcolm Gladwell, and Sigourney Weaver, you will see the name of the onetime 21-year-old who had to be ordered to travel with the Beatles.

AFTERWORD

It gave me great pleasure to write this tribute to Larry Kane for several reasons, mainly because he deserves the recognition. That he accompanied the Beatles on their initial tours of the United States—and didn't want to go!—is an amazing story. But also because Larry has been a broadcast mentor to me, and I always love telling the story of how we first met.

I grew up at 24 Mercer Avenue in Doylestown. Solidly middle class. Son of a public school guidance counselor and stay-at-home mom turned secretary turned Realtor. A few doors down, at 42 Mercer Avenue, lived the Stachel family: Arlene and Mike and their two children, Kelly and Mike Jr. The Stachels are wonderful

people. Hard working. Good neighbors. Generous to a fault. Mike Sr. once sold my brother and me two go-karts for $25—$12.50 each because he thought it was important we believed we were paying for them rather than being given them (which he was doing). They had the only in-ground pool on Mercer Avenue, hence our nickname for their house: Stachel Valley Country Club. Mike Stachel built pools for Sylvan and then started building them on his own. With Arlene he opened a family business that not only built and serviced pools but also furnished their surroundings. Mt. Lake Pool and Patio was initially located at the end of Mercer Avenue, and the Stachels quickly became an employment center for any kid in the neighborhood who wanted to work. That certainly included me.

When I turned 16, Mike Sr. had me delivering patio furniture and pool supplies to customers in a panel truck, often accompanied by Mike Jr., who was a contemporary and friend of mine. One day, Mike Sr. asked us to take a bucket of chlorine to Larry Kane's house in Rydal, Pennsylvania. This was a big deal. Larry was an A-list celebrity in the Philadelphia area, although as I recall, he was then doing the late news for WABC in New York City. With a 3x5 card bearing Larry's address, we ventured out from Doylestown for the 40-minute drive. Upon arrival at the Kane residence mid-morning, we were disappointed when a woman working in a domestic capacity answered the door. This would not stand. After all, we'd left Doylestown with a Polaroid Instamatic, one of those cameras that you'd take a picture with and then you'd shake the image for 10 to15 seconds while it came into focus. We wanted our pictures with Larry Kane! So we told the woman that Mr. Kane needed to sign the "bill of lading." We had no idea what that meant. All we had was the 3x5 card. But she bought it. After a few minutes, a disheveled Larry Kane, no doubt having been up late after delivering the news, approached the door. He was wearing a pair of shorts with the fly down, no shirt, hair disheveled. Before he knew what hit him, the two punks from Doylestown had swapped positions and each taken a picture with him. It's a photograph I treasure.

BIRTHS TO ILLNESSES,
OUR LIFE WITH GRACE

Philadelphia Inquirer, Sunday, October 9, 2016

"HOW DID I get so lucky?"
Those words from anyone else in Grace Snaggs's situation would probably be offered with sarcasm. But she means it.

She's sitting opposite me in a dimly lit living room in West Philadelphia on a Sunday afternoon. Oprah is saying something on a nearly muted television in the background. Bespeckled and with shoulder-length gray hair, Grace is outfitted in a navy print dress with a sweater draped over her shoulders. She has yellow hospital socks on her feet and a cane nearby.

I'm visiting to deliver lentil soup made by my wife and am struck by the incredibly appreciative attitude of a 72-year-old woman who is scheduled for chemotherapy the following morning, "one bus stop away" as she puts it, at Penn. Unprompted, she continues to voice her thanks.

> I'm so grateful.
> I'm so blessed.
> So many good things have happened to me.

As we talk, it occurs to me that Grace knows me better than I know her. That's my fault. She's been in our employ for a quarter-century, but she's family. She likes to joke that she "came with the house," a reference to having worked for Kenny Gamble 28 years ago when my wife acquired his home.

Grace is the mother of three, two daughters plus Rudyard, the apple of her eye, whom she raised in a second-floor walk-up on the Main Line. She was born in Tobago and went to school in Castara, a fishing village. She's the oldest of nine siblings. A brother died at age 36, but all others are living and still on the island. She came to the States at age 29, attracted by the presence of her cousins, and has worked in various domestic capacities ever since.

Our dear family friend Grace Snaggs, 2016.

She first worked for a family in New Jersey, then for Flossie and Richard; Jolly; Diane; Kenny; Frank and Jane; and us. Many of them, and her large circle of family and friends, came to our house when we celebrated her 65th birthday with steel drums in the backyard

We haven't celebrated many family milestones without her. She was one of my wife's bridesmaids—the only one not related, and the first asked by my wife. There for the boys' births. And all of the kids' confirmations. Several holidays. She was there for my father-in-law's battle with cancer (the only one he would let in his room when he was really sick), and bedside for the passing of my mother-in-law: "I called [your brother-in-law], but I knew better than to say she'd passed. Instead I told him, 'I can't wake up your mother.'"

That sense of decorum and discretion has always been her hallmark. I've seen Grace get overwhelmed, but never angry, which is more than she can say—but never would—about me. Helping a family that once consisted of two parents, four kids, and four dogs can cause the former.

When she thinks I'm too involved in affairs on the home front, which is often, she'll call me an "auntie man," but as pronounced by Grace, it's "a-h-n-t-i mon." Grace also has a head full of island sayings, like, "You don't know if the roof leaks until you live inside."

Our daughter remembers once locking her in a closet while Grace was babysitting for her at age 4. And Grace teaching her to dance in the laundry room.

"But mostly I think about how, on her way home from finding out she became a citizen, she told me it was the proudest day of her life," my daughter said, "and then proceeded to chastise me on my lack of immediate knowledge of American history."

The three boys have sometimes been less hospitable. After tiring of her talking to herself or hearing one too many versions of her singing "Red Red Wine," they've called her under the laundry chute with the ruse of "needing to tell her something," only to pelt her with socks—which she knew were coming, but would still oblige their high jinks.

"Don't you remember when you brought home Michael Jr. from the hospital and Winston [our cocker spaniel] came out of the house to sniff the car seat with him still in it? I took that picture," she reminds me, about a snapshot that I prize in a family photo album. I didn't recall that she was the one who captured the image, but I'm not surprised.

I ask which of our four dogs has been her favorite. Grace doesn't take the bait, but does make a point of telling me that she was never able to get mad at Checkers, our white Lab.

"She had that habit of putting her head on my lap," she remembers with a smile. "Winston never liked to be alone. So I'd make him a bed while I did laundry and he'd lay nearby."

Thankfully she's supported in her current fight by many cousins: Audrey, Angela, Peola, Lennox, and Ancil, in whose house we are seated.

"Ancil told me, 'Grace, you've cared for everyone, so now we are caring for you,'" she says, beaming.

Another of her sayings pops into my head: "Thank God for nothin'; there ain't no trouble with it."

That outlook from a septuagenarian who has worked her entire life in service to others reminds me of a story I once read recounted by Jack Bogle, the legendary founder and former CEO of the Vanguard Group Inc. In a book called *Enough: True Measures of Money, Business, and Life,* Bogle shares a conversation between writers Kurt Vonnegut and Joseph Heller during a billionaire's party on Shelter Island.

At one point, Vonnegut pointed to the host and asked Heller: "Joe, how does it make you feel to know that our host only yesterday may have made more money than your novel *Catch-22* has earned in its entire history?"

"Yes," Heller responded, "but I have something he will never have: Enough."

Grace has enough. I'm hoping she can teach me.

AFTERWORD

I called Grace on the afternoon that this column was published. She was back in the hospital for a chemo treatment, but she was pleased to hear from friends locally and as far away as Tobago who had read what I'd written. Grace was her usual humble self and very appreciative of the attention. We spoke for a few minutes, which was long enough for her to offer me more island wisdom. "Prophet doesn't have honor in the old country," she said. I asked what she meant and she told me:

> *Sometimes those who know you so well don't take you seriously. You can be around people and they don't notice your good points, but in another place, among those who don't know you so well, they recognize what you do.*

Sadly, Grace left us on October 8, 2017, but I was pleased to read this column at her funeral service.

TRUMP NOT MY FAN, BUT
QUITE A LOYAL FOLLOWER

Philadelphia Inquirer, Sunday, November 27, 2016

I LIKE TO JOKE that during the campaign, Donald Trump single-handedly boosted my television program ratings among billionaires. He seems to have never missed my Saturday CNN show, even though he never accepted one of my many invitations to personally appear.

As best I can reconstruct, I must have got his goat by interviewing McKay Coppins from BuzzFeed on my SiriusXM radio program after Coppins wrote "36 Hours on the Fake Campaign Trail with Donald Trump." The 2014 story recapped 25 years of Trump engaging in charade by threatening to run for president. The story was well written and very funny.

Thereafter, I too continued to poke fun at the idea of Trump running for president, both on radio and on television. And he took notice.

One month after the launch of my CNN program, Trump weighed in with his review: "I can't believe that @CNN would waste time and money with @smerconish—he has got nothing going. Jeff Zucker must be losing his touch!"

Then again, on May 5, 2014, Trump took a shot at me while doing a telephone interview on *Fox and Friends*: "You have some guy named Smerconish, who I've never even heard of. . . . [H]e goes on the air and says, 'Trump is defending [LA Clippers owner Donald] Sterling.' Reporters are really dishonest, especially political reporters," he said, before commenting on the need to reinstitute libel laws.

But here's the funny thing. Despite his view that CNN was wasting time and money on me, or that I am dishonest (all the while pronouncing my name impeccably), Trump proved himself to be a very loyal viewer of my program. On several occasions he tweeted about my segments, although he was usually careful not to specifically reference that it was my program. Here are a few:

January 19: "Pat Buchanan gave a fantastic interview this morning on @ CNN—way to go Pat, way ahead of your time!"

February 13: "A very big thank you to Bill Donohue, head of The Catholic League, for the wonderful interview on @CNN and article in Newsmax! Great insight."

The only time I had any direct interaction with him came on February 25, at a CNN debate at the University of Houston. My plane was late and I arrived in the hall just as the debate was to begin. Serendipitously, my path backstage crossed with the gaggle of candidates as they were getting ready to walk on-stage. Just a few feet from me were Ben Carson, Ted Cruz, John Kasich, Marco Rubio—and Donald Trump. When our eyes met, he waved—but with his fingers not a full hand. Then he motioned for me to come nearer. We shook hands. And he said, dripping with sarcasm, "L-O-O-O-O-V-E your show."

On April 2, Kasich was a guest of mine. Later that day, Trump addressed a rally in Racine, Wisconsin, and told the crowd: "I watched Kasich today on CNN on an abortion question. I said what a terrible answer that was. That was a terrible answer. He didn't want to talk about it."

Again, my show.

Plus there were several instances where he reacted to specific things I said as a CNN primary/caucus election night commentator. But as he would reference specific things I had said, there was no doubt as to what provoked him.

On April 23, I did a segment on the convoluted nature of Pennsylvania's Republican nomination process, in which delegates are not bound to follow the electorate. Trump took note, tweeting: "Pennsylvania: Cast your vote for Trump for POTUS & ALSO vote for the TRUMP DELEGATES in your congressional district!"

Then finally, he admitted he watches.

It happened on April 23 during a rally in Waterbury, Connecticut, when he said: "I watched on television today . . . on *Smerconish* . . . who doesn't necessarily treat me good."

There were several more instances. Such as when he reacted to specific comments from a focus group I assembled on May 3, or how he called a Pennsylvania congressman because of something the man said on my program, or how he quoted something Libertarian candidate Gary Johnson told me, or when he tweeted a reaction to my interview with *New York Times* columnist Maureen Dowd: "Wacky @NYTimesDowd, who hardly knows me, makes up things that I never said for her boring interviews and column. A neurotic dope!"

And then a minute later: "Crazy Maureen Dowd, the wacky columnist for the failing @nytimes, pretends she knows me well—wrong!"

It's amazing to me that, while running for president, he had so much time to watch TV. I'm pleased he was such a fan of my program and I'm counting on him to boost my demographics from 1600 Pennsylvania Avenue.

AFTERWORD

Trump continued to watch my program after becoming president, even while at war with CNN. I know because one month after his surprise victory, on December 10, I had a particularly contentious interview with Sean Spicer, then the chief strategist and communications director for the RNC. The subject was the presumed Russian hack of the election and a tweet Trump had sent the night before in which he downplayed the intelligence community assessment. I pressed Spicer on Trump's unwillingness to acknowledge the Russian role and things got heated. The clip of our confrontation got lots of traction. Seth Meyers was among those who used it, in his late-night comedy montage. I knew that Spicer was pleased with his performance because the RNC released a full transcript of the exchange about an hour after it ended, including this:

SMERCONISH: *Regardless of whether . . . the RNC was hacked, and that would be a big and new development—I think we know to a certainty, given Podesta and Debbie Wasserman Schultz, that the DNC was hacked—why aren't we, as Americans, upset about the fact that a foreign hostile actor apparently put its thumb on the scale in our election, and why doesn't Donald Trump want to get to the bottom of that as he takes office? That's the e . . .*

SPICER: *Well, first of all, okay, there's a couple things. One, is I am outraged. I don't think any foreign entity, any individual . . .*

SMERCONISH: *Why don't you say that? Why didn't Trump say that? That's what I haven't heard.*

SPICER: *Stop and let me—okay; I just said it. Let me actually take yes for an answer. I said it. I don't think Donald Trump doesn't think no one thinks that a foreign entity should be interfering with the U.S. elections. Now let's get to the next thing: What proof does anyone have that they affected the outcome? Zero. Show me what facts have actually shown that anything undermined that election. Donald Trump [got] 306 electoral votes, 62 million Americans voted for him, so what proof do you have or anyone has that any of this affected the outcome of the election?*

SMERCONISH: *I'm just an American who is trying to discern all that I'm reporting on and reading.*

SPICER: *Answer the question, Michael.*

We were each satisfied with how the debate had played out, and when it ended, we quickly exchanged texts saying so and reiterating that there were no hard feelings. Later that day, David Urban, who ran the Trump campaign in Pennsylvania and is a West Point graduate, hosted the president-elect for one half of the Army-Navy football game. He told me that when Spicer entered the box, he was given a hero's welcome by Trump for the way he had handled me. Trump had again been watching in real time. Then, two weeks later, Trump announced that Spicer was going to be his press secretary. I texted Sean: "Happy for you—you earned it (and I think I helped!). Merry Christmas."

Spicer quickly replied: "You did! Thank you. Merry Christmas."

Spicer, however, did not return as my guest while serving as press secretary, a casualty, I am sure, of the poor relationship between his boss and my television network. Occasionally we'd share a text, and on Friday, July 21, 2017, I finally had the opportunity to take him up on his offer to visit him in the White House. Our appointment in his West Wing office began at 9 a.m., and we spent forty-five minutes with one another in an off-the-record and wide-ranging chat. The only interruption came when Sarah Huckabee Sanders dropped by to tell Spicer something. He'd made it clear that he had a 10 o'clock meeting with the president and from time to time I saw him glance at his watch. I departed at about 9:45. By the time I returned to my hotel and turned on the news, word was breaking that Spicer had just quit his job as press secretary in a disagreement with the president over the appointment of Anthony Scaramucci as White House communications director. (Scaramucci was famously fired after just 10 days on the job; Sanders was soon named as Spicer's replacement.) So I was Spicer's final appointment as press secretary. How appropriate, given that it clearly was our campaign exchanges that helped him get the gig. As I detailed in a Sunday Inquirer *column at the time, I didn't know his departure was imminent when we met. The timing took me by surprise, though not necessarily the outcome. And in retrospect, he did take a keen interest in how I juggle my platforms—radio, TV, print—and especially my paid speaking engagements. Soon after his departure, it was announced that he would be hitting the speaker's circuit.*

A CHANGING OF THE GUARD
IN GLADWYNE

Philadelphia Inquirer, Sunday, December 18, 2016

THE GUARD HOUSE was never just a restaurant. Sure there's fine dining: Fresh Dover sole, "the best" fried oysters, and homemade meat loaf. There's a friendly bar, where Joe didn't need a tutorial from *Mad Men* to know how to pour an Old Fashioned the right way. And a wait staff of professionals who viewed their work as a career. Not to mention a rustic, unique decor born of real, 200-plus-year history, not re-creation.

But it's been the combination of all that, plus the attention to detail of proprietor Albert Breuers, that made it a Main Line institution. A destination, not a rest stop. The kind of place where life's milestones get celebrated. A first holy communion. Fortieth birthday. College acceptance. When good things happened, it was the only place my family wanted to be.

Now, after nearly four decades under Albert's stewardship, the Guard House is closing on New Year's Eve and will reopen in early 2017 only to members of the Union League. "The Guard House, located within five miles of approximately 800 of our members, has institutional integrity, is a part of American history, and is the appropriate scale to be a wonderful member amenity," said a club bulletin.

I'm one of the lucky ones who'll continue to take a meal in the heart of Gladwyne, and I'm sure the Union League will run a fine establishment. But it will never be the same. And I'm not thinking of Michele never complaining about my penchant for showing up without a reservation. Or the summer plate of roast beef and fresh seafood, the homemade hooch that would sometimes show up at the table after dinner, or Inge's famous bread pudding. The missing ingredient for this famed restaurant will be its owner.

Albert is one of those pillars who gives a community strength. The type who recognizes that, while his personal goal might be to make a spectacular Wiener schnitzel, his greater responsibility is to be a good neighbor. Watching him operate at a distance for so many years, I know he has succeeded by taking it all so personally.

Albert's commitment has extended from the kitchen to the curb of Youngsford Road. It's there, in the midmornings, when I'd see him alone, cleaning up, planting and watering geraniums in the summer and mums in the fall, attired in his black-and-white checked pants and white chef's toque.

He's old school, a man who knows his customers better than they know him. And he has probably been brought into people's confidences as often as Monsignor Leighton holding confession down the block at St. John Vianney. As a result of Albert's stewardship, people mixed well at the Guard House. Green sport coats didn't stand out, but neither did the hip millennials starting families.

We charted our kids' growth at the Guard House, and I remember fondly that when they were younger, the building, built as an inn circa 1790, was the stuff of endless fascination. "How did that bunny hanging over the bar grow antlers?" they'd want to know about the jackalope. And they'd ask about the effigy—even if they couldn't understand the word—of local TV host Captain Noah (Carter Merbreier and his wife, Patricia, were regulars) they once saw stashed in a closet.

But the biggest mystery—the source of countless dinner discussions— was: What lies upstairs? (One night, Albert showed them, but he must have sworn them to secrecy.) Every night ended the same way—with one of the boys ringing a brass bell, which hung outside on the front porch, before making a run for our car.

The Guard House, Gladwyne, Pennsylvania, December 2016.

There are plenty of restaurants, but only a few that take on the stature of a Guard House. I knew one other: Conti's Cross Keys Inn in Doylestown. Walter Conti was the family patriarch and a proud member of the Penn State board of trustees, ably assisted by sons Joe and Michael. Leroy Neiman's famed sports paintings hung on the walls and any celebrity who had reason to be in Bucks County would always stop by for the prime rib. But with Walter gone and his sons pursuing successful careers (Joe was a longtime state senator), the business closed and the site now houses a gas station. Thankfully that won't happen to the Guard House.

Two weeks ago, at my wife's holiday party in the back room, Albert's son Marc reminded me that it could've been worse—the building could have been razed for a chain drugstore. He's right, of course. And I was happy to hear that the telephone hasn't stopped ringing with well-wishers and those who also wanted to book a final meal, which is now the area's most prized reservation. Marc also noted that the staff will be invited to stay under generous terms.

When the Guard House reopens, I'll go back. I'm going to invite Albert and Marc to dinner.

AFTERWORD

Funny that two of my favorite columns were written about places where I eat and that could not be more different, despite being located on the same block. I wrote about Gladwyne Village Lunch for the Daily News *in July 2005 (included in this compilation), which, as the name implies, was a lunch counter, and then this piece about the Guard House, which is fine dining.*

How appropriate, then, that when I ate my last meal at the Guard House one week before its closing, at the next table were Laura and Bill, who used to own the former. Also present that day was Monsignor Leighton, who in a light-hearted way took issue with my having written that Albert had heard as many confessions as he. He said that if it was so, it was only because Albert had been in the neighborhood longer!

2017

IN 2017, GETTING TO KNOW
THE OTHER HALF

Philadelphia Inquirer, Sunday, January 8, 2017

I MADE TWO NEW YEAR'S RESOLUTIONS: one personal, one professional. The personal is patience. I'm forever trying to lengthen my fuse. Hopefully this will be the year. Professionally, my goal is to be better grounded.

I'm feeling a disconnect to just under half the nation. My failure to see Donald Trump's ascension was compelling evidence of my being out of touch with 46 percent of the country.

I attribute that to my living in a virtual gated community defined by a number of factors, including: my zip code (No. 189 in the nation for home value, according to *Forbes*); my Penn Law graduate degree; my political registration as nonaffiliated; where our kids go to school; the car I drive; my weight consciousness; and even the TV I watch (loved *The Crown*; *Duck Dynasty* not so much). Even my Christmas lights—white LEDs—not the fat, colored bulbs of my youth.

And while I'm well-read from sources across the spectrum, I admit that I'm quick to discount many stories due to their origin.

My bubble is a world much different from my grandparents' roots or the environment in which my parents raised my brother and me. Our family are Pennsylvania coal crackers who came from Eastern Europe with nothing. I grew up on a quarter-acre lot, in a three-bedroom house, which had no shower until I was in the eighth grade. That bathroom renovation was performed by an inmate on work release from the Bucks County Prison, where my father, a guidance counselor by day, ran the adult-education program. My mom stayed at home, then worked as a secretary, and, when I was in high school, hit pay dirt as a hardworking Realtor. I won't tell you her age, but she still works, long past the point where she needs to.

I attended the Central Bucks public schools K-12, worked at McDonald's when I turned 16, played sports with a cross section of the community, and vacationed on the Ocean City boardwalk. (I vividly remember sleeping on the floor of Mrs. A's Boardinghouse.)

Charles Murray was prescient five years ago when he wrote of the isolation of the new upper class and the negative consequences that flow when they are segregated from the working class. In his book *Coming Apart: The State of White America, 1960–2010*, Murray included a quiz that was designed to show people like me just how isolated they'd become. His questions were no-brainers, he argued, for ordinary Americans: Have you ever walked on a factory floor? Who is Jimmie Johnson? Have you or your spouse ever bought a pickup truck? Since leaving school, have you ever worn a uniform? Have you ever watched an episode of *Oprah, Dr. Phil,* or *Judge Judy* all the way through?

I scored a 42, where 77 is a typical mark for a lifelong resident of a working-class neighborhood. Still, I didn't appreciate the political significance of Murray's work until this election, a point driven home during Christmas break, when I shared breakfast with a near-nonagenarian in southwest Florida. The meal became an exercise in field research. We were at a diner on Route 41, the Tamiami Trail in Collier County. Collier had the highest percentage of registered voters (87) who cast ballots in the state. Trump won Collier by about 45,000 votes en route to a critical Florida victory. The diner was as red as the county. I'd stepped out of my bubble and into another.

There were about 40 of us having breakfast, mostly male, all white, save an African American father and son, the former of which sported a county EMT uniform. The decor was accentuated by the grille of a 1957 Chevy coming out of the wall. Marilyn Monroe's portrait hangs on the wall. So too, numerous recognitions from the local newspaper praising the food. In the background, the Fleetwoods were singing their 1959 hit "Come Softly to Me" (*dahm dahm, dahm do dahm, ooby do*).

Not surprisingly, Fox News was playing on the largest of several TVs. This was what President Barack Obama was talking about in a November *Rolling Stone* interview when he partly attributed Democratic losses to "Fox News in every bar and restaurant in big chunks of the country." My dining companion had sausage and biscuits; for me, scrambled eggs.

"Trump is the only shot we have of turning this around," he told me, never quite defining what "this" is.

That day's main headline concerned President Barack Obama's evicting 35 Russian diplomats from the United States as a result of the presumed hack of our recent election. "Isn't that a serious issue?" I asked.

"Who knows if it was the Russians? How can we be sure that's true?" said my guest.

"Besides, we shouldn't alienate the Russians," he added. "They're the only ones we can rely on to straighten out this situation with the Arabs. Maybe Trump can get the Chinese to help. It's time to get this over with."

I sought counsel last week from J. D. Vance, author of the best-seller *Hillbilly Elegy: A Memoir of a Family and Culture in Crisis.* He told me he sees the nation's divide as follows:

These two separate communities: They go to different schools, they eat at different restaurants, they watch different TV shows, they send their kids to play at different sports even. And eventually I think that separation is starting to infect our culture and our politics. It really worries me that so few people even understand why someone would vote for Donald Trump.

Vance advises that people seeking a better understanding make it a point to interact with folks of a different social class, which can be a challenge today in comparison with 50 years ago, when there was more mixing in the military, workplace, home, and at church.

So look for me taking more meals at Cracker Barrel, shopping at Walmart, or even lingering in the parking lot at Lincoln Financial Field instead of sidestepping tailgaters. In 2017, I'm out to burst my bubble.

AFTERWORD

I wrote this column while still licking my wounds at having missed the political rise of Donald Trump, which I attributed in large part to my geographic and socioeconomic bubble. I was, and remain, especially embarrassed at not having seen the signs where I had a front-row seat to the factors that allowed for his ascension. It was a subject I returned to in my paid speeches to private groups in early 2017, wherein I sought to explain his trajectory against the same three-decade backdrop in which my own media career was on the rise. Viewed in this context, I think I offer a pretty cogent, post-hoc analysis of how it all happened.

The short version is that I graduated from law school in 1987, by which time I'd already enjoyed a number of unique, Republican, political experiences. I'd met Ronald Reagan and George H. W. Bush while still in high school. Formed a campus club for Reagan/Bush at Lehigh University. Became an advanceman for Vice President Bush while still in college. And even ran unsuccessfully for the Pennsylvania state legislature while a full-time law student. My final year of law school, in 1987, I worked to get Arlen Specter reelected to the U.S. Senate and helped Frank Rizzo win a Philadelphia Republican mayoral primary. Meanwhile in Manhattan, Trump was becoming successful and ubiquitous. Having taken over the family business in the early 1970s, he obtained an option on the West Side railroad yards and enticed New York City to make the site a convention center. He obtained an option for the Penn Central Hotel near Grand Central Station and lured Hyatt to town. He leased a site next to Tiffany and Co. and built the Trump Tower. And then he entered Atlantic City, where he acquired the largest hotel casino in the world, the Trump Taj Mahal. In 1985, he bought Mar-a-Lago. Then, the year I graduated from law school, he published The Art of the Deal, *a "yuge" best seller. And that's when he made his first visit to New Hampshire. Invited by a GOP activist named Mike Dunbar, Trump spoke to the Portsmouth Rotary Club at the legendary Yoken's Restaurant ("Thar She Blows") on October 22 and stoked speculation that he would run for president. Over the next three decades, he came back to New Hampshire six times, usually in election season, and continued to fuel interest.*

The nation wasn't ready for Trump in the late 1980s, but it was by 2016. What changed in the interim? While he made his fortune, I was earning my stripes in the media world, particularly talk radio, which gave me a unique perch from which to see the transformation of the political environment. There was partisanship when I graduated from law school on Ronald Reagan's watch, but not polarization. The media world was a rather liberal place. There was no Internet, no cable TV, no satellite radio. The major media outlets were the New York Times *and the* Washington Post, *plus the big three television networks, with anchors named Brokaw, Jennings, and Rather. Conservatives lacked a clubhouse. Things changed at the time of the first Gulf War, when Rush Limbaugh had success as a Sacramento talker and was placed into syndication. Limbaugh filled a vacuum and had great success. Soon, talk stations across the country wanted Limbaugh and a stable of his imitators. Now, ideology was important, not personality. When Fox News came on the air in 1996, it took a page from that playbook. Online, the right-leaning DrudgeReport reached a zenith in 1998 with revelations about Bill Clinton's intern scandal. The Huffington Post and MSNBC duplicated the strategy on the left. We suddenly had a polarized media landscape, and the politicians adapted by taking many of their cues from the talking heads. And ultimately, Donald Trump would be the primary beneficiary.*

*In the three decades since he dipped his toe into the political water in Portsmouth, the political scene underwent systemic change. By the time he rode the escalator at Trump Tower to his campaign announcement in July 2015, an audience had been preconditioned for the Howard Beale/*Network *candidate of the 2016 cycle: "I'm mad as hell and not going to take it anymore!" Sure, there were other contributing factors to polarization—money, social media, geography/gerrymandering, and self-sorting—but Trump would never have made it this far without a media climate 30 years in the making. It was right in front of me, but still I didn't see how he would be the beneficiary. He was the nation's first nominee to mirror the talk radio, Fox News, DrudgeReport,* Breitbart *view of the world, even though some of those media mouthpieces ultimately turned* *against him. When, after winning the nomination, he hired Breitbart's executive chairman, Steve Bannon, to be his second campaign manager, the transformation of our political leadership was complete. The road was also paved for his general election victory, where among the factors that led to his upset win was certainly a distrust in the Clintons and the mainstream media, which had been made easier by years of talk radio's assault on both.*

ACKNOWLEDGMENTS

I OWE A DEBT OF GRATITUDE to the Lehigh University Department of Journalism (in my era called the Division of Journalism). I graduated with a double major in government and journalism—the former was planned; the latter evolved after an upperclassman advised me during my freshman year that the journalism department had some interesting courses and entertaining lecturers. The best known was Journalism 122, Law of the Press, taught by Joseph B. McFadden (I still have that course number in my head). I similarly enjoyed the offerings of Professors Robert J. Sullivan and Wally Trimble, whose courses I took repeatedly, and before I knew it, I'd amassed enough credits for the major. I thank them all for furthering my interest in writing.

Zack Stalberg was the editor of the *Daily News* who facilitated my writing a weekly column for a big-city newspaper. I have immense respect for Zack and personal fondness for both him and his wife, Deb, and I will never forget the opportunity he provided. I also appreciate support I received from others at the *Daily News*, including Frank Burgos, Sandra Shea, Michael Days, and the man who edited my *DN* column, Michael Schefer.

This book literally would not exist without the assistance of Bill Marimow, the two-time Pulitzer Prize–winning former editor at the *Inquirer*. He was supportive from the moment of inception, just as he has been encouraging of my work as a Sunday *Inquirer* columnist. Thanks go, as well, to Suzanne Mitchell Parillo for working with me to secure the permissions that were necessary to republish the columns, Stan Wischnowski, executive editor and senior vice president of Philadelphia Media Network, and Terrance C. Z. Egger, publisher and CEO of the PMN, for graciously agreeing. I also extend gratitude to those who have assisted me over the years with my work as an *Inquirer* columnist, including Harold Jackson and the man who edits my Sunday *Inquirer* column, Kevin Ferris, as well as John Timpane, who used to fill that role. Kevin has edited more of my columns than anyone else, always with an eye toward making the words stronger and never in a manner intended to alter my meaning, for which I am most grateful. I am also mindful of the fact that I'd never have become associated with the *Inquirer* without the invitation that was extended by Brian Tierney, the former publisher.

Whitney Cookman, a gifted designer, crafted the cover design for this book, and I appreciate his willingness to donate his services in recognition of the value of the Children's Crisis Treatment Center (CCTC). Greg Jones edited this manuscript with similar selflessness. Greg did an excellent job with my novel, *Talk*, and it was nice to reconnect with him. Buz Teacher never wants public recognition, but I'd be remiss if I did not mention my friend, who is always willing to lend me an ear me and, coincidentally, has been extremely generous to CCTC. More than anyone else, Buz was the person I turned to in search of advice about how best to bring this project to fruition. I thank Gary and Deirdre Smerillo for their competent contract review. And I thank Gail Fogel for so ably cataloguing my columns over the years, which enabled me to reread them in hard copy to decide which to republish here.

It was very important to me to be able to title this book *Clowns to the Left of Me, Jokers to the Right*. I love the song by Stealer's Wheel, and the lyrics sum up my political view of the world. My SiriusXM radio program listeners know how frequently I play the music, and I have many to thank for being granted permission to use the great lyrics in the timeless hit "Stuck in Middle with You." First and foremost, I am grateful to Joe Egan and Baby Bun Music, Ltd., as well as the Estate of Gerald Rafferty, the Music of Stage Three, with particular thanks to Tracie Butler at BMG Rights Management for securing the rights to use the lyrics as the book title. It was a bit of a struggle tracing the rights, for which I thank Lisa Thomas from Lisa Thomas Music Service LLC for her sleuthing efforts and Del Bryant, the former CEO of BMI.

David Axelrod is both a CNN colleague and a friend who did not hesitate to provide the Foreword, especially when hearing about my interest in boosting the work of CCTC.

I think this project has found an appropriate home at Temple University Press, which would not have come about without Aaron Javsicas, the editor-in-chief, and Marinanicole "Nikki" Dohrman Miller, editorial assistant and rights and contracts coordinator. Joan Vidal and Debby Smith provided me with an important and thorough prepublication review of the columns and the Afterwords. I am also grateful to Kate Nichols for the interior design and to Ann-Marie Anderson, Irene Imperio Kull, and Gary Kramer for their marketing expertise. Way back in 1980, I had a difficult choice between whether to study government at Lehigh or radio, television, and film at Temple. Having opted for the former, I feel as though I've now brought the process full circle!

Finally, I thank the interns Marian Lurio and Lillian Crager for all their research in support of both the book and its audio offering and TC Scornavacchi, my friend and radio producer, who—in recognition of the charitable intent of sales, and without a single complaint—undertook the most difficult task of all: editing the audio recording of my reading of each of these columns and their corresponding Afterwords. I'd like to tell you I nailed them all on the first take, but the truth is I nailed none of them at first—as Marian and Lillian would point out after carefully listening and TC would then have me correct so that she could edit accordingly. This was a long and laborious part of the project, which TC undertook with utmost patience. Just how frustrating was the recording process? That will be revealed if TC's outtake reel ever sees the light of day! (I can only hope not.)

Thank you all.

MICHAEL A. SMERCONISH is a SiriusXM radio host, CNN television host, and Sunday *Philadelphia Inquirer* newspaper columnist. A Phi Beta Kappa graduate of Lehigh University and the University of Pennsylvania Law School, he is of counsel to the law firm of Kline & Specter. He resides in the Philadelphia suburbs, where he and his wife have raised four children.